Studies in Musicology
1935–1975

STUDIES IN MUSICOLOGY 1935–1975

Charles Seeger

UNIVERSITY OF CALIFORNIA PRESS

BERKELEY • LOS ANGELES • LONDON

University of California Press
Berkeley and Los Angeles, California

University of California Press, Ltd.
London, England

ISBN: 0-520-02000-6
Library of Congress Catalog Card Number: 76-19668
Copyright © 1977 by The Regents of the University of California

Printed in the United States of America

1 2 3 4 5 6 7 8 9 0

Contents

Preface

The eighteen essays selected for inclusion in this book are allotted almost equally to the orientations systematic, historical, and a mixture of the two. Published, as they were, over a period of forty years, some have been lightly, others heavily edited and some rewritten. The Introduction and essay three are condensations of two pair of separate papers. Superscript numbers after each title identify the original texts listed and numbered in order of publication in the Bibliography. I am indebted to their editors and publishers for permission to republish.

My intention had long been to devote a first half of a larger volume to a section of pure theory, *Principia Musicologica,* including a revised and extended version of my *Tractatus Esthetico-Semioticus*[80] and the three Prefaces to the Description of Music, to the Critique of Music, and to the Compositional Process of Music. These nine essays have been drafted and redrafted, and some, in preliminary forms, published, but they are still in work. The Press has kindly offered to publish them separately when ready.

It is with special pleasure that I take this occasion to express my appreciation of the generous support of my work by the University of California, Los Angeles, in whose Institute of Ethnomusicology I served as research musicologist from 1961 to 1971 and of participation in the memorable Wednesday afternoon general seminar together with Leon Knopoff, William Hutchinson, and William Bright, which was led by Mantle Hood and Klaus Wachsmann for a roster of capable students too numerous to list personally.

C. S.

Bridgewater, Connecticut
March 31, 1976

Introduction

SYSTEMATIC (SYNCHRONIC) AND HISTORICAL (DIACHRONIC) ORIENTATIONS IN MUSICOLOGY

The word *orientation* is to be understood here to name the direction in time in which a speaker turns his attention toward what he is speaking about.

To best of present knowledge, Guido Adler first divided the field of the then newly named study *Musikwissenschaft* as a whole into the two separate branches: *Historisch* and *Systematisch* (Adler, 1885). About the same time or shortly afterward, Ferdinand de Saussure broadened and defined more precisely both orientations and their independence of each other in the then newly named *linguistique* by introduction of the terms *synchrony*, "at any one time" (internal, static, structural) for system, and *diachrony*, "through" or "over the course of time" (external, evolutionary, functional) for history (de Saussure, 1972). He illustrated the case by the diagram shown in figure 1*a*, below (ibid., p. 115), where simultaneity (the systematic orientation) is represented by line AB and succession in time, by the line CD. Musicologists, of course, would turn the figure 90 degrees anticlockwise in accord with the coordinates *x* and *y* of the conventional graph as at *b*, but the point would remain the same.

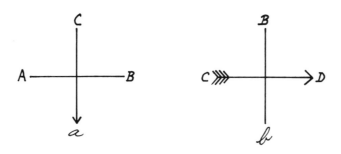

FIGURE 1

1

De Saussure noted that the natural sciences have been unaffected by this duality, that is, they have not confused the history of the study of a science with the history of the data of the science, but that the studies of man introduced the factor *value*, which opened the two orientations to two completely divergent approaches—"deux routes absolument divergentes" (III.i). My earliest and very juvenile papers (1923-1930) were written under the aegis of Adler's path-breaking paper, but I interpreted it in accord with de Saussure's broader and more precise statement of the case, although I did not know of his existence or theories until I read about them in Bloomfield (1933) some time in the 1940s. Unfortunately, I did not hit upon the felicitous terms *synchronic* and *diachronic*.

Musicology has a lot to learn from linguistics. On the one hand, the former has lagged nearly a century behind the latter in sheer intellection of its potentialities. Linguistics escaped from the excessive historicism of comparative philology during the latter half of the nineteenth century, whereas musicology is only now in the 1970s beginning to show signs of escaping from its own brand of excessive historicism. True, its solipsistic view of itself has been tempered by the valiant attempts first by comparative musicology and later by its bastard offspring the so-called ethnomusicology, but at the expense of setting up a subspecies and thereby losing the integrity of its own wholeness or unity. There still is not, in the study of music, the broad and deep understanding between synchrony and diachrony, historiography and history, historiography and system-building achieved by linguistics. On the other hand, linguistics has prospered on account of the very wide general acceptance of the study of language as over against the reluctance to organize the study of music as a discipline on the level of scholarship of the longer established academic studies.

But de Saussure and his followers made one mistake and his followers, an omission—both serious. The mistake was that the "absolute divergence" of history and system holds only for the systematic orientation—and even then, only in the early stage of its development. In the historical orientation, it holds only in the elementary stage of historical writing: the "catalog of ships." With each succeeding stage of the development of its potentialities, systematization becomes more necessary, hence the setting up of style periods, classification of idioms, critiques of *opera omnia,* all synchronically oriented system-building. Consider, first, the synecdoche inherent in the use of such words as *history.* It names both the act of speaking and writing about something and that something itself. But historiography is not history. Second, consider the development of historiographical method during the last two or three centuries. Until then, historians viewed their job as the account of "what was" diachronically as successions of events in time.

There were philosophies that governed the selection of what was considered worthwhile writing about, and these often, as in the case of Herodotus and many another, seemed to illuminate a past and made readers think they comprehended "what was." Actually, "what was" was a succession of synchronic glimpses into states of affairs linked together by the imagination of the historiographer, who was often something of a poet and presented his readers with speech constructs that by synecdoche they took to be "knowledge of history." And we must admit that wide of the mark as they may have been as documentarians, as interpreters of the potentials of man they may have given us the only notion of "what was" possible with the facts they had at hand.

With the growing conviction that the theory of evolution had some bearing upon the history of man, historiographers began to ask "how did what was come to be what was?" At the same time, the successes of the natural sciences in synchronic accounts of "what is" led historiographers to perceive that "what was" could no longer profitably be solely of a chain of events but a succession of states of affairs—structures, if you will—whose linkage was so multifarious and so subject to continual change that the processes of linkage and change must be conceded to have continued to the present and be continuing into the future. In short, synchronically described structures, events, and states of affairs moved. We could regard them as static, as points, but we could plot them upon a line representing the unfoldment of a diachronic process. Structures were seen to be bundles of functions: functions, properties, attributes, characterics, or whatever of structures. The various dichotomies of the speech compositional process became seen not only synchronically as opposites and divergencies but also diachronically as complements and convergencies.

From the first two steps "How things were" and "how things came to be as they were," the inevitable third step was to ask "how things are." The nemesis of "scientific" historiography faced us: subjectivity. When one reads, even in contemporary musicological writings, that music "history" (meaning historiography) is a science, one wonders if in any other field of learning one could find today so preposterous a statement. Surely, the historiography of music has its aspects that can be approached by rigorously scientific methods; but there are as many more that are matters of value judgment and still as many, or more, about which we can speak or write little and, eventually nothing in terms of scientific method.

If, however, we face frankly the question "how things are," we are finally in the lap of synchrony. But diachrony is in turn the child of synchrony. The very nature of the systematist's viewpoint impels him to find out more of nature, of what he views, that is, to give a better account of it than did his predecessors. To do this, he falls into the lap of diachrony. "What," he virtually asks, "is there in the account of my predecessors that was not contemplated, ignored, falsifiable, unverifiable, incomplete, given wrong emphasis, and so forth. He becomes as involved in the problem of "how things may come"—or, to be frank, are coming or must come—"to be . . ." For here we are caught in another case of synechdoche: using the same word "to be" both for what is said "to be" and for the saying of it. We have to revise the whole set of questions to read:

1. How can we say what the things were that were said to have been?

2. How can we say how they came to be what they were said to have been?

3. How can we say what things are?

4. How can we say how the things that we say are came to be as we say they are?

5. How can we say how the things that we say are must or will become what they will be?

It is futile to protest that prediction has no place in musicology. Whether or not the theory of evolution holds for or can be adapted to culture, music, or language, every composer and every musicologist who is worth his salt, when he sits down to construct a new piece of music or speech, virtually says to himself (if not to the world) "this is what will be." The implication is clear: "in the future, things in music will be this way or will take account of this way."

The omission made by most of the followers of de Saussure which I have been able to check have not referred to the concepts *synchrony* and *diachrony* to the dual temporality and spaciousness of the speech event itself, which exits in general time and space but also creates its own unique time and space, that is, the time and place in which it is spoken and the area in which it is heard.

General time is a given quantity over which we have no control but to act in it; speech time and space—as is music time and space—is a creation of man over which he has almost unlimited control.

Theoretically peers, then, where precision is the aim they may be seen as "absolutely divergent," but where comprehensiveness and balanced judgment are the aim they are to be seen as absolutely convergent. It is only the brevity of the individual student's life and the decay, loss, or unintelligibility of evidence which give a primacy to synchrony and system, and falsifies the old saying that "the present can only be understood in terms of the past," whereas, it is only too plain that the past can be understood only in terms of the present. The student may—indeed, must—choose which of the two he will employ, or the connection and sequence in which he will employ both. Broadly speaking, the aggregate of historical studies presents the history of systems; that of systematic studies, the system of history. For system, like history, is ultimately concerned with the relationship of structure and function, event and process, products and the traditions in accordance with which production is achieved. Yet the individual musicological work will inevitably be predominantly either a historical or a systematic presentation. It is itself a product in a tradition, a structure, that as soon as publicized takes a place in the stream of that tradition and bears a functional relationship to other products or structures of its kind and, so, to the cultural processes in which all have their being. Thus, it would appear that while the two orientations cannot in fact be totally joined, neither can they for long be held entirely separate. And students will inevitably fall into one or the other of two classifications—of historians or of systematists—according to the emphasis predominating in their work.

Instances are not rare, of course, in which our knowledge of music is mostly or wholly of one sort. There is history but no music (as in Ancient Mexico) or there is music but no history (as in some tribal cultures at the present day). In such cases, the preliminary work must be entirely of the character of one or the other orientation. But the musicological task cannot be considered much more than begun until, by use of frames of reference, of techniques of comparison, of hypotheses of construction or reconstruction, and of other devices of speech presentation, the purely reportorial phase is followed by that of interpretation, and, finally, by that of integration with the main body of musicological and general thought, at which point the other orientation is inescapable and the theoretical complementarity and interdependence of the two orientations again appear. A balance between them can be then striven for in a speech presentation.

The problem is not, we well know, peculiar to musicology but is encountered to varying extents in other scholarly disciplines. All of them, including musicology, conducted as they are in the art of speech, make use of the power but suffer the limitations of the semiotics of that medium of communication. Musicology, be it said, is in an especially delicate position in this respect. For music has, in addition, its own peculiar semiotics, study of which, with modern methods of investigation, can hardly be said to have begun.

The consideration of pure theory involved here constitutes, then, a perennial challenge to the serious student. And the concrete situation in which we find ourselves is no less compelling. The aim of the present undertaking, therefore, is to propose a theoretical basis for systematic musicology in terms of which improved relationships may be established

(1) between musical and nonmusical or extramusical viewpoints, (2) between historical and systematic orientations, and (3) between scientific and critical methods. It is hoped that this apparatus will serve as the base for the description of any music with maximum objectivity. But until it can be tested in many particular cases, claims for its universal validity should not be made. The present proposal, then, is advanced as valid for the Occidental art of music as of the mid-twentieth century alone.

My first proposition will be that distinction between historical and systematic orientations in musicology may best be made upon the basis of two separate but related concepts: a general physical spacetime; a specialized, cultural, musical timespace; the historical orientation viewing music diachronically as occurring in general spacetime, the systematic, synchronically in music timespace.

Although the concept of music timespace is a novel one and has not yet been given formal statement, it has already been adumbrated in a manner similar to that which led to the formation of its parent, general spacetime. Particular experiences of particular persons, observed to be like or unlike, related or unrelated, have been designated by words through group agreement over centuries of time. Ultimately, words of the nature of concepts, that is, symbolizing classes of things talked about, have led to the formation of higher generalizations and abstractions until a formidable structure of speech reference to music has been built, the more deliberately methodical segment of which we call musicology.

The concept of music time comprehends three dimensions: frequency of event (tempo); amplitude of event (relative duration); density of event (a concept comprehending the number and relative regularity and irregularity of divisions of beats, motifs, phrases, and so forth). In the compositional process all three are highly elaborated and have customarily been correlated easily with the concept of general time. By comparing a clock or a metronome with the beat or pulse of music, musicians and laymen alike easily distinguish roughly wherein music time differs from general time. The conception of music sound also comprehends three dimensions: frequency of event (pitch); amplitude of event (loudness); density of event (tone-quality, timbre), though even more highly elaborated, has been slow in development into a concept of music space. Derivation and distinction from a concept of general space has been common only recently.

A single concept of timespace is, of course, quite different from two separate concepts of space and of time. It would seem to conform, however, more closely to the facts of direct music experience, in which tonal and temporal factors can be appehended by us in an intimate fusion or integration that is quite different from the perception of the two as separate objects of attention. A concept of music timespace is therefore advanced here as one quite as necessary to study as the two conventionally accepted separate concepts of space and of time.

It is important at this juncture to point to the relatively opposite situation in which we find ourselves, as students of music, with respect to the instrument of communication we use in our study, namely, the art of speech. We are so attentive to what we say about space and time that there is a constant temptation to forget the fact that what we say itself occupies both space and time. The careful student will keep ever in mind that fact that he is employing one art utilizing a highly selective set of sonal and temporal materials (speech) to deal with another utilizing a somewhat different but no less highly selective set (music). Consideration of the complications of speech alone involved here could easily be so protracted as indefinitely to postpone arriving at a consideration of music. Perhaps it would suffice to suggest that concepts of speech timespace function as a kind of lens through which we observe and report upon music. We cannot pretend to measure the distortion. But neither can we assume there is no distortion.

With this warning (which I beg be taken with utmost seriousness) that the operational idiosyncrasies of our instrument of study, speech, must of necessity color the subject studied, music, in certain predictable ways, I may proceed to more detailed consideration of the nature of music timespace (1) as a phenomenon in general spacetime, (2) as a concept derived from objective analysis of musical processes, and (3) as basic in the definition of the scope, methods, and aims of systematic musicology. Concepts of speech space are highly developed and are customarily well integrated with concepts of general space. Such parallelisms and apparent contradictions as those between acoustic phenomena and music practice seem not to embarrass the student of linguistics. A concept of speech time, however, is practically nonexistent, the only elaboration given to it being in versification. I do not mean to imply that temporal organization is unimportant as a factor in speech technique. I might even go so far as to suggest that perhaps some of the many problems posed by the study of the semantics of speech may rest in part upon the lack of a refined concept of speech time and the consequent tardiness in exploration of a concept of speech timespace. Among the predictable distortions of music that may be expected in speech handlings of music might be mentioned: (1) the overemphasis upon music space in the disciplines of composition (harmony, counterpoint, form, etc.) all of which are heavily implemented by the art of speech; (2) underemphasis upon music time in these same disciplines—both, it would seem, owing to the greater ease with which discoursive speech handles spatial concepts as over against temporal; (3) preponderance of analysis as over against synthesis, of the event as over against the process, of the product as over against the tradition, of the structure as over against the function, of the static as over against the dynamic, and, consequently, of the preference for dealing with spatial and temporal concepts of music separately rather than together.

Concepts of both music and speech timespace should be viewed as specialized examples of the more general class of (human) product timespace. A conception of product timespace refers to the integrated temporal and spatial factors involved in the creation and consumption of products of human ingenuity. (See "Music as a Factor in Cultural Strategy," Abstract in *Bulletin of the American Musicological Society*, no. 3 [April 1939; as of June 1938], p. 18.)

My second proposition is that elaboration of a concept of music time-space rests upon its distinction from a concept of general spacetime. I shall review this distinction briefly under seven headings, passing from use of the term *music timespace* as a concept to its use as denoting what is conceived. "What is conceived" is, in the present instance, an infinite number of particular music timespaces, or "area-periods" of music timespace in general. By definition, all exhibit the common characteristics that constitute the class to which the term *concept* is given. It is comparatively easy to speak of the music timespace (area period) occupied or constituted by a composition of which a single authoritative written version exists. The problem arising from the existence of two or more (written) versions, however, is simple in comparison with that arising in the study of products in idioms that are inherited and cultivated mainly or solely by oral transmission, which, by definition, have no one authoritative version and are known only in variants of one or more versions.

1. *Occurrence.*   General spacetime is, to present knowledge, universal. Music timespace occurs within it.

2. *Provenience.*   General spacetime is, for us, a given thing. Music timespace is manmade.

3. *Identity.*   General spacetime is unique: whether there is more than one, either in concurrence or in sequence, or whether it is repetitive, duplicative, curved, or runs also backward (antitime matches antimatter) is not known to us. Music timespace, on the contrary, is multiplex: there are as many particular music timespaces as there are distinct structures (compositions). It may be repetitive and duplicative in general space-time, occurring in many places simultaneously, as also successively in one and the same place. But it is not repetitive or duplicative with respect to itself, that is, a particular music timespace is not repetitive or duplicative

qua music timespace. It is always itself. Each structure defines its own music timespace. Any one can be run backward (*cancrizans*) in time, upside down in space, or both. Two or more can be combined in one particular instance of general spacetime. As, for example, when two tunes, ordinarily recognized as separate, are performed together, thus creating a separate event in music timespace and constituting a new instance of it.

4. *Continuity.* General spacetime is, as far as musicology is concerned, a completely uniform continuum without known beginning or end. Music timespace is a continuum that varies infinitely among various structures, and has as many beginnings and endings as there are instances of it.

5. *Control.* General spacetime is entirely outside our control. Music timespace is entirely within it.

6. *Measurability.* General spacetime is measurable by norms of the art of speech, in speech timespace, but is not itself constituted by any known norms of its own. Music timespace, in contrast, while measurable as a phenomenon in general spacetime by these same speech norms (as is speech timespace also), is itself constituted by norms of the art of music known by the carriers of the music tradition or traditions in which any structure is cast. Thus, the tenth measure of the *Eroica* is its tenth measure—a very different thing from the number of seconds any particular performance took to reach it—in music timespace. Separate speech norms are conventionally used to designate these music norms as events in music timespace.

7. *Variability.* The norms of speech used in measurement of music timespace viewed as an occurrence in general spacetime, that is, as performance, refer, as far as musicology is concerned, to invariables (cycles, seconds, etc.). Those used with respect to music timespace itself refer to variables (tones, beats, motifs, chords, phrases, forms, etc.). These are variables not only in music timespace but in general spacetime as well.

The kind of relationship that obtains among our three integrations of space and time should need, perhaps, no further elaboration here. It is plainly that of a fixed system (general) and a variable system (music), both reported in a second variable system (speech). Its recognition, though this be scarcely more than superficial understanding of the operational details, should at least clarify some of our most vexing problems. Two examples may suffice. One is the relationship of the invariable system of the harmonic series to the variable one of diatonic harmony. Some parallelism must, it seems, be admitted; but complete causality is questionable. Another is the relationship of a music to the culture in which it flourishes. Some causality, it seems, must be admitted; but complete parallelism is questionable.

Between general spacetime and music timespace, then, there should be no postulation of a one-to-one correspondence, least of all when one bears in mind that between neither of them should there be such postulation with respect to the instrumentality of the situation—the art of speech.

My third proposition, and one of an importance to musicology equal to that of the preceding two, is a concept of the music event as occurring in both general spacetime and music timespace. In the former, the music event may be regarded as a phenomenon: in the latter, let us say tentatively, as a "normenon." There is, unfortunately, no word to denote, upon the level of abstraction required here, the class of man-made product that serves primarily a function of communication. The term *art work,* or *work of art,* is too subjectively loaded. And it is clumsy. In coining a word I have wanted first of all to emphasize the patterns or norms of tradition whose linking together in small and large units constitutes the essential process of production of the communicative product. At the same time, it has seemed desirable that the word denoting the product as an event in production timespace have a form resembling that denoting it as an event in general spacetime, even if the artifice seems a bit more pat than I would like it to be. I am aware that combination of the Latin noun *norma* ("carpenter's square or pattern") with the Greek participle ending results in an etymological mongrel and I had thought of the slightly more proper spelling "nomenon," from νομίζω, future νομίσω ("use customarily") and related to νόμισμα ("that which is in continual practice, use or possession"; see H. G. Liddell and R. Scott, eds., *A Greek-English Lexicon,* rev. by Henry Jones [Oxford: Clarendon Press, 1925]). But the fact that νόμος was commonly used in a different musical sense would be confusing to the generalized use of this spelling. I do not wish, however, to become involved with the Greek γνώμων ("carpenter's square," from γίγνω "to know"; see James H. Murray, *A New English Dictionary* [Oxford: Clarendon Press, 1901]) for that would suggest an epistomological rather than a semiotic function. Furthermore, γνώμων would suggest a critical function.

Perhaps I should state specifically that the normenon, as here conceived, is not to be confused with Kant's noumenon. If the phenomenon is defined in general spacetime and the noumenon (as the class of non-empirical concepts) out of space and time, the normenon will be found in a median position, both a phenomenon and a noumenon, depending upon the viewpoint from which it is regarded. For example, *The Critique of Pure Reason, qua* normenon, has not only its phenomenological aspect (its printed page, the sound of its reading, and its frequent reference to physical reality) but also its noumenological aspect (particularly the nonempirical concepts themselves and the ultimate structure of the content of the work). Bach's *Art of Fugue,* also qua normenon, has its phenomenlogical aspect (its printed page, the sound of its performance, and its aesthetic or other "affect") and as well its musical "idea" from which, though we cannot circumscribe it in a speech normenon, we cannot reasonably withhold attribution of a homologue of the (speech) noumenon. Take, for example, any musical unit—a primitive ritual chant, a popular dance, a folk song, a symphony, or any part of one of these—for brevity's sake, the seventh to tenth measures of the first violin part of the *Eroica.* Each of the many performances this has been given can be regarded as a separate event in general spacetime. But in music timespace, all these performances have been of one single event, one and the same normenon, that is to say, the passage from the *Eroica,* unless its identity as such as been conceded to have been lost through excessive variation, in which case the music timespace must be conceded still to have existed in general spacetime but occupied, or constituted by, another normenon and peculiar to it, not to the *Eroica.* The question, "to what extent may performances very yet still present one and the same normenon?" is an interesting one. The *Eroica* has probably been played with variations of the "standard" *A* from at least 360 to 500 cps and still been accepted by competent judges as "*the Eroica.*" Similarly, the tempo of the first movement has probably strayed equally widely from $\mathbf{\downarrow \cdot} = 60$ with the same result. Which technical factors can be greatly varied without loss of identity and which cannot, and the conditions under which variation can take place almost unnoticed or can effect change of identity, remain to be thoroughly investigated. Findings would bear upon such diverse critical problems as the artistic validity of the twelve-tone row, the legal claim to copyright, and the definition of what is a version and what a variant in the study of folk music.

As long as we confine our interest to the Occidental fine art of music, the plotting of norms of variation may not seem very pressing. Standards of notation and of performance are increasingly uniform and high. But as soon as we extend our view to comprise other musics of the world, or even European folksong, we cannot get our study under way for sheer lack of understanding of the nature of these norms and the limits beyond which variation changes identity—limits that vary even in various idioms of our own culture.

Pursuit of this understanding brings us very quickly to the problem of a universally valid foundation for the study of music. It is time we cease analyzing and evaluating other musics, or even other idioms of our own

TABLE 1

Conspectus of the Organization of Musicological Study upon
a Basis of the Systematic Orientation

I. Music Viewpoint (Viewpoint of the knower and valuer primarily of
    music)

A. Systematic Orientation

1. *Scientific Method.* Music normena as structures and/or functions of
   a tradition contemporary with the student and of which he is a
   direct knower. The science of music in its aspect as what students
   know qua handlers of the forms of music-making in a tradition (or
   traditions) of which they are carriers.

2. *Critical Method.* Music normena as resources of a tradition contemporary with the student and of which he is a direct valuer.
   The critique of music in its aspect as what students value qua
   handlers of the values of music-making in traditions of which
   they are carriers.

Note. Integration of operations I,A,1 and I,A,2 constitutes the systematic
study of style as a thing in itself, in time present to the student.

B. Historical Orientation

1. *Scientific Method.* Music normena as structures and/or functions of
   traditions not contemporary with the student and of which he is
   an indirect knower, viz., through notations. The science of music
   in its aspect of what students know qua students of the forms of
   music-making in a tradition of which they are not carriers.

2. *Critical Method.* Music normena as resouces of a tradition not contemporary with the student and of which he is an indirect valuer.
   The critique of music in its aspect of what students value qua
   students of the values of music-making in a tradition of which
   they are not carriers.

Note. Integration of operations I,B,1 and I,B,2 constitutes the historical
study of style as a thing in itself in time past to the student. The data and
evidence are secondary sources of study (1) because notations are not music
but rather blueprints of it, and (2) because these must be rendered into music
by performance using primarily norms of a tradition present to the student
and of which he is a carrier. Integration of I,A,1 and 2 and I,B,1 and 2
constitutes the comprehensive study of style in a tradition. Comparative
studies of style between two closely related traditions, as, for example,
between the idioms of fine and folk art in certain Occidental regions, could
probably be initiated today. But whether comparative study of style upon a
world basis could be initiated in the foreseeable future is a question
respecting whose answer we can formulate only a few tentative conditions.

DATA PRIMARY FOR STUDY

DATA SECONDARY FOR STUDY

DIRECT EXPERIENCE

INDIRECT EXPERIENCE

DATA SECONDARY FOR STUDY

DIRECT EXPERIENCE

II. General Viewpoint (viewpoint of the knower and valuer primarily of things other than music)

A. Systematic Orientation

1. *Scientific Method.* Music phenomena in their aspect as data, present to the student, of physics, physiology, psychology, sociology, etc., viewed in or out of their music context by relatively noncarriers of a music tradition.

2. *Critical Method.* Music phenomena in their aspect as evidence, present to the student, of other or general values, viewed in or out of their music context by relatively noncarriers of a music tradition.

Note. Integration of operations I,A,1 and 2 and II,A,1 and 2 constitutes the comprehensive study of systematic musicology.

DATA TERTIARY FOR STUDY

INDIRECT EXPERIENCE

B. Historical Orientation

1. *Scientific Method.* Music phenomena as data for general history—chronology, geography, biography, bibliography, etc., of which the student is an indirect knower, viz., through (speech) writing or other non- or extramusical media of times past to him.

2. *Critical Method.* Music phenomena as evidence for general or other history—literary or art criticism, critical philosophy, etc., of which the student is an indirect valuer, viz., through (speech) writing and other non- or extramusical media of times past to him.

Note. Integration of operations I,B,1 and 2 and II,B,1 and 2 constitutes the comprehensive study of historico-musicology. The term *comprehensive* as used in this and the three preceeding Notes is definitive only in actual practice. Science and criticism, history and system, and, indeed, musical and nonmusical viewpoints, can never be wholly separated nor wholly joined.

music, in terms of the Occidental fine art alone. The last attempt to account for the non-European languages in terms of Latin grammar, Leonard Bloomfield tells us, was before 1800. This is a thoroughly systematic viewpoint and should be taken as encouragement to equally thorough systematic studies in music. Lest it be taken for a recommendation of artificial contemplation in *vacuo,* let it be said that absence of historical considerations in purely descriptive analysis of primary data does not constitute a vacuum. Rather, it means a clearing away of underbrush and overlying preconceptions. After the ground is accurately mapped and described, there will always be plenty of time for integration with history. The apparatus proposed here is mainly for use in this clearing function.

Organization of such an apparatus is preeminently the task of systematic musicology. It would appear to be predicated upon the criterion of the equal importance to study: of both musical (intrinsic) and nonmusical or extramusical (extrinsic) viewpoints—I and II in the table; of both systematic and historical orientations—A and B in the table; and of both scientific and critical methods—1 and 2 in the table.

Table 1 outlines briefly the function of eight possible operations, each engaging one term of each of these three dichotomies. Competence in handling this apparatus will require, in every one of the eight operations, knowledge and judgment in the handling of the requisite speech norms of both general spacetime and music timespace. The four operations under heading I require, in addition, knowledge and judgment in the handling of the requisite music norms. The two operations under I, A refer particularly to traditions of idioms contemporary with the student; the two under I, B in addition to these, to knowledge and judgment in the handling of one or more notated traditions not contemporary (or not wholly contemporary) with the student. Competence in the four operations under II can be plotted on this pattern, adding or substituting, for the norms of music, the special norms of speech required by one or more of the specialized studies employed.

The order in which the eight operations are presented produces an organization of musicological work in which the core is the systematic study of the particular tradition (or traditions) of which the student is a carrier (or has the equivalence in knowledge) around which a succession of layers may be wrapped, each more remote from that tradition until the universe of speech discourse is completely comprehended in its relation to the universe of music discourse. Or, perhaps we should say in both cases "universe of communication." For the philosopher might withhold the word *discourse* from use in connection with music, as peculiar to the art of speech alone.

In conclusion let me say that the apparatus as a whole may hardly be expected to be employed in its full development by any one man. Actually, we each of us carve out, according to our individual interest or competency, a section that we use. It is to be hoped that some day, among the lot of us, all eight operations will be fairly equally deployed.

I hope it is clear that the music event is not to be confused with the verbal report of it. We cannot remind ourselves too often that the sound patterns of speech normena and their meanings cannot represent the sound patterns of music normena and their semiotic homologs of speech semantics without distortion. The task is to find a terminology and a method of handling it most suitable to the particular idiom under investigation. Since in this mid-twentieth century we do not start with *tabula rasa,* we must, of course, make use of the terms of current acceptance found more nearly universal in application. But we must carefully criticize each one, that it bring not with it preconceptions at variance with the primary data before us. There can be no substitute for the accurate description of a music idiom known firsthand by the student, whether or not it has a history, and whether or not it fits into the history of our study. It is only upon such a base that sound comparative studies of separate musics and music idioms can be made and, so, a world view of music envisaged.

I
Speech, Music, and
Speech about Music

When we talk about music, we produce in the compositional process of one system of human communication, speech, a communication "about" another system of human communication, music, and its compositional process. The core of the undertaking is the integration of speech knowledge in general and the speech knowledge of music in particular (which are extrinsic to music and its compositional process) with the music knowledge of music (which is intrinsic to music and its compositional process).

In speaking of another system of communication we are speaking of an item of attention radically different from other items of attention. Whether we like it or not, we are speaking comparatively. In this manner of speaking, the compositional process of speech requires dependence upon the peculiar devices of its technique known as homology (identity), analogy (similar but different), and heterology (difference only).

There are no grounds for assuming that the two kinds of knowledge and compositional processes are either wholly identical or mutually exclusive. The undertaking must, then, be conducted mainly in terms of speech-music analogy, allowing for indeterminate amounts of homology and heterology. The aspects of an undertaking upon which these three devices bear and the relative emphasis given them are, however, matters of wide disagreement. The subject of this paper concerns the principles or criteria for judgment in the formation of a comprehensive theory in whose terms orderly discussion of the case may be conducted.

I

In speaking of music it is of prime importance to know in advance in what mode of speech usage one proposes to speak and to be aware of lapses into other modes; for their boundaries are often hidden from speaker and listener alike and the crossing of them is common practice—and sometimes confusing.

It is generally recognized, I believe, and unfortunately considered too obvious for special notice, that three distinct modes of speech usage are traditional in the Western world. Two of them are specialized in the sense that each distinguishes itself from the other and from the third, both endosemantically (intrinsic reference) and ectosemantically (extrinsic reference). The names of the specialized modes vary. I shall call one the affective mode (the mode of feeling); the other, the reasoned (the mode of deliberately methodical speaking).

It is in the affective mode that men have produced the great religious and mystical writings from ancient Greece to the present day. Its main concern is the recognition and assertion of value. Value is understood, here, to be of two kinds: inner, biological experience (the appetite to live and procreate); outer, sociocultural experience (accommodation with inner experience). The mode is end-motivated, teleological. The highest value, reality, tends to be beyond verbal expression, ineffable. Sometimes its name is sacred, as in Judaism, Christianity, and Islam. Sometimes, it cannot even be named, as in Taoism: "The name of Tao is not the name of Tao" (*Tao te Ching*, line 1). Sometimes it can be named but is said neither to exist nor not to exist, as is "Tat" in *Rgveda*, X, 129, stanza 2.

The reasoned mode has produced the great sciences. Its special concern is to discover and report upon what men can conceive and perceive to be reality in the physical universe and to create accounts and models of it in the compositional process of speech. The mode is origin-motivated, from cause to effect. At present writing it seems in accord with Heisenberg's principle of uncertainty (and even its uncertainty) to say that scientific reality is also ineffable but that it is worthwhile, that is, valuable, to try to make it effable as fact—the opposite of the affective mode whose ultimate position is that trying to make it effable is not worthwhile.

The third mode is generalized rather than specialized. It is the mode of daily life, of common sense, the discoursive. In its elaboration as "uncommon sense," and mixed variably with one or the other of the specialized modes, it has produced the bulk of literary work, poetry, philosophy, and humanistic study. It overlaps the specialized modes that may have been developed from it. There is no question of the effability or ineffability of reality, its factuality or valuality. Reality is what the user is, thinks, feels and does. The strength of the discoursive mode is that if this is not the case, then neither affective nor reasoned modes can make sense.

All three modes are cultivated with varying degrees of skill and with varying degrees of rigor in the maintenance of their own peculiar characters. Figure 1 shows a two-dimensional visual model of the case. The large square represents the total potentialities of speech communication; the dotted line, the division between the affective (A) and reasoned (R) modes. The positions of the traditional speech disciplines, from physics through the social sciences to philosophy may be ranged from left to right under the top line; the traditional literary genres, above the bottom line. The inner square represents the discursive mode (D); the central dot, the ultimate goal of the critique, the perfectly balanced judgment of fact, of value and of the relationship of fact and value. The perfectly balanced judgment is assumed to be unattainable. In its more deliberately cultivated variant of "uncommon sense" the discursive mode is the prime vehicle of the critique. The present essay pretends to be written in that variant of the discursive mode and to be an example of the scientistic criticism, that is, with the ineluctable imbalance in the presentation of its judgment on the side of the facts of the case so as to be locatable, optimally, a little to the left and above the central dot, at *x*, on figure 1. If it were an example of the affective criticism the essay would be locatable, optimally, to the right of the central dot, as at *y* in figure 1.

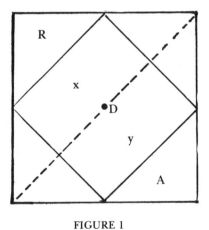

FIGURE 1

II

The more rigorously the specialized modes develop their peculiar characters, the more extreme become their stance vis-à-vis one another. The affective mode pits a belief in nonspeech and the knowledge of inner experience against speech knowledge and social values; the reasoned mode, speech knowledge and social values against belief in non-speech inner experience. Unlimited pursuit of nonspeech experience of value makes an illusion of speech, speakers, and what speakers say. One winds up with paradox: any speech statement about reality, too, must be illusory if it is a product of so much illusoriness (see Chung Tzu). Un-limited social pursuit of speech knowledge of fact is based upon the assumption that the pursuit is worthwhile—an assumption for which there is no scientific support whatever. It is a pure, subjective value judgment, incidentally falsified, at least for the present, by the deteriora-tion of man's ecosphere, which is directly traceable to the purest of pure science.

In this dilemma, to which I refer as "the musicological juncture," our best recourse would seem to be: to set about readjusting the potential (enabling) and the limiting (constraining) resources of the compositional process of speech to match more closely the enabling and limiting resources of life in the two universes of physical fact and human value; then, to use our best judgment in fitting them together.

In proposing to achieve such a fitting together of the affective and reasoned modes of speech communication in a single unified model of their relationship to music and its communicatory process, it is necessary first to distinguish what it is that the words *music* and *communication* name. This is preeminently the task of the discursive mode. The words are ambiguous. They name not only concepts but also percepts, not only abstract universals but also concrete particulars.

As concepts, the words *music* and *communication* are both endosemantic speech constructs upon a relatively high level of ratiocination; as percepts, they are both ectosemantic speech constructs upon a relatively high level of sensory experience. The rhetorical figure synecdoche, by which a more comprehensive term is used for a less comprehensive, or vice versa, not only permits but encourages the ambiguities and leads to the pitfalls that trap us into many of our most enduring controversies. I shall consider communication first, as the more comprehensive term.

III

The word *communication* will be understood here to name transmission of energy in a form.

In the reasoned mode of speech usage, this concept can be spoken of with utmost conciseness and comprehension with the symbols of mathe-matics and symbolic logic. The symbols, which are of infinite generality, can be communicated only as percepts—that is, by audible sounds or visual symbols for them which are perceived—and can be used to deal exhaustively with the universe of physical fact. The extent to which they can be used to deal with the universe of human behavior in its finite particularity and what is known in the discoursive and affective modes of speech usage as "value" is debatable (see however, Hartman, 1967). In the affective mode, energy and the physical forms in which we perceive it are likely to be merged in one Gestalt—one's own disposition and/or will to feel and assert it.

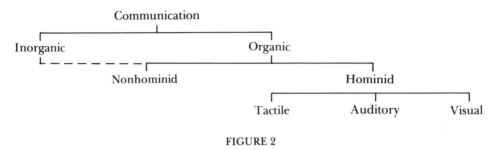

FIGURE 2

Figure 2 represents visually a taxonomy of the genus or class "communication," gustation, and olfaction being considered tactile. The dotted line indicates the fact that man can communicate only through the forms of energy more or less uniform throughout the physical universe, but that the raw physical forms have been manipulated—"cooked"—(Levi-Strauss, 1966) by men in their communication among themselves and gathered together in repertories by evolutionary-historical processes of sociocultural tradition-making. It is from these repertories that choices are made by individuals in the use of the compositional processes of their various systems of human communication.

IV

One of the first questions we meet at this point in the making of our model is: what is the relative extent of the independence and interdependence of tactile, auditory, and visual communication? The percepts of concrete experience must lead us to dispense equally with the possibility that these three media of human communication are identical or mutually exclusive. Because there is no unit of measure for the case, figure 3 presents three entirely arbitrary diagrams of possible minimal, medial, and maximal interdependence among the three media. I suggest that the range of variance between maximal and minimal interdepen-

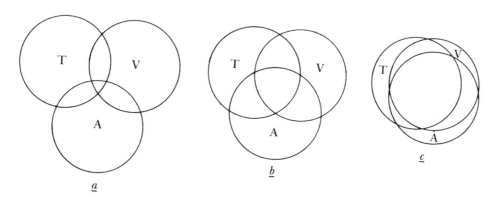

FIGURE 3

dence be regarded as exemplary only—a gamut or range of speech semantic variance upon which each particular instance of human communication may be located, depending upon the mode of speech usage employed, the context in which and the purpose for which it is employed. In view of our abysmal ignorance concerning the case, I feel most comfortable with diagram *b*. I suggest that the central, curve-sided triangle formed by the overlapping of the three circles represents the primordial biological function of the brain, upon which the mystical conception of the human "mind" has ultimately been erected.

As a concept, the word *music* names a large class of subspecies of communication which are manmade systems that we call by the new name *musics*, very like the way in which we say the word *language* names another class of subspecies of communication which are manmade systems that we call by the ancient name *languages*. I would say that music and speech are the two principal systems of auditory communication among men. The possibility of distinguishing a third, song, a 50-50 association of speech and music, is to be taken seriously.

We customarily distinguish three systems of visual communication as traditional among men: graphics (drawing and painting), which are two-dimensional; sculpture and architecture, which are three-dimensional, as is also artifacture, understood here as comprising all materially produced objects from oil tankers to toothpicks.

While auditory and visual systems of communication have been extensively and elaborately studied in terms of speech, tactile systems of communication have been little thought of as such. Even its principal categories are not named *tactile*. Tactile communication is produced by bodily movement, which is perceived, primarily, as touching. I distinguish three principal systems of tactile communication: dance (by the single person and groups of single persons); corporeality (combat and procreation—the borderline is very indistinct); cybernetics (where one person directs, with much talking and little movement, the activity of many persons, with much movement and little talking on their parts, be it an army, a factory, a bank, or a government bureaucracy). Figure 4 elaborates diagram *b* in figure 2 reading anticlockwise: speech (Sp), graphics (G), sculpture and architecture (Sa), artifacture (A), cybernetics (Cy), corporeality (C), dance (D), music (M), song (S).

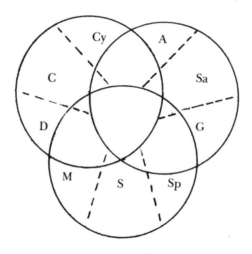

FIGURE 4

V

The system of communication in which most musicologists communicate is, roughly speaking, this same variant of the discoursive mode. Yet to speak of music or any other system of human communication we must use an extention of the rhetorical figure synecdoche. We must use the less comprehensive terms of speech to communicate about the more comprehensive term of communication and all the systems of communication other than speech which the term comprehends, including music. None of these other systems names communication or anything else. We know and use them independently of speech. And it is clear that they communicate much that speech does not. This is synecdoche gone wild. Even in its mildest forms, it is supposed to be abhorrent to the reasoned mode of speech usage where, at its most rigorous—logic and mathematics—no word or symbol stands for more than one definable item of attention. The following summary of principles or criteria for judgment in this linguocentric predicament every musicologist operates in, is offered for whatever consideration may be given to it.

The primacy of communication.   We take as biologically given (*to* us) the capacity to communicate without which man can neither come to be nor continue to be.

The act of distinction.   We take as partly biologically and partly culturally given (*by* us) the capacity to distinguish between one thing and another.

The principle of the prime acts of distinction.   There is no one prime act of distinction; but several acts of distinction should be listed here, namely: (1) distinctions are made via three principal media—tactility, audition, and vision—olfaction and gustation being considered, for hominids, tactile. The media are biologically defined; (2) the eight or nine traditional systems of human communication are culturally defined and serve, variably, use (esthetic) and communicatory (semiotic) purposes; (3) to the extent they are semiotic, systems are variably direct (asymbolic) and indirect (symbolic): speech and the visual systems, more indirect and symbolic; music and the tactile systems, more direct and asymbolic.

The principle of the interdependence and the independence of the systems of human communication.   In the reasoned speech usage the tendency will probably be found to judge interdependence as minimal; in the affective mode, as maximal; in the discursive mode—at the level of uncommon sense—toward minimal or maximal in accord with the imbalance resulting from the impossibility of achieving the 50-50 judgment (see fig. 3).

The communicatory act as an act of model making.   All human communicatory systems produce concrete visual, auditory and/or tactile products that in their own respective forms of transmitting the energy used in their production are models of the act of production on the parts of their producers. To the extent the receiver is a participant in the same sets of physical, biological, and cultural contexts he may wish or be impelled to approximate the act in accord with his competence in use of the system, or to ignore it. To the extent the compositional process of the system is direct and asymbolic the transmission of energy transmitted in the forms of the system will parallel or run a course paradromic to the act of its production by its producer and may, under the circumstances cited, elicit in a receiver a similar act. This concert of acts tends to be similar with respect to the course of the transmission: to tense with tension (high, loud, bright, active, strong, fast, hard, sharp, and so forth); to relax with detension (low, quiet, dark, passive, weak, slow, soft, dull, and so forth); to revolve around or revert incessantly to a medial axis analogous to the firm vigor of a living organism that is competent in the context of his life—a tonicity like the tonicity of the living, not the dead or fevered muscle at rest.

To the extent the compositional process of the system is indirect and symbolic, the transmission of energy that is apprehended by us in the forms of the system of its production will be converted—translated, as it were—from the particular and concrete to the general and abstract in the symbolism of the speech compositional process. For most of the words of a language are abstract, universal concepts, empirical concepts and generic terms—names of classes of things. There are very few proper names that designate just one thing and no other. To achieve this the compositional process of speech has developed grammars, syntaxes, and a large and still controversial semantics unlike the compositional process of any other system. This tends to cast whatever it deals with into similitudes of speech to an extent difficult to estimate and to compensate for.

The principle of parity among human communicatory systems.   There is no reason to rate the potentialities of the eight or nine principal communicatory systems among men as other than equal. Why they have not so developed is still a matter for inquiry.

The relative interdependence-independence of the systems of human communication.   The full extent and nature of the interdependence is, at present, difficult to trace beyond superficial or surface factors. Total independence is probably illusory.

The total communicatory potentiality of the speech compositional process and its limitations.   The total potentiality may be described in terms of mentionability. Mentionability is of several different kinds: nameability (from strict, one name for each named, through unclassifiable degrees of looseness and ambiguity) to simile, metaphor, metonymy and synecdoche, paradox, imagery, and suggestion; negative naming (the saying something cannot be named or what it is not) comes close to unmentionability. The class of unmentionability is being continually invaded; new distinctions are named or made mentionable in one way or another; but the bank of distinctions already made is indeterminably large and what lies outside our capacity for making distinctions is indeterminately large.

Importance of the principle of the inevitability of bias in the use of the speech compositional process.   It is wise always to allow the benefit of the doubt to what is talked about: there may be more to it than can be said about it.

The principle of the complementarity and interdependence in the speech compositional process of reason and affection, fact and value.   The reasoned mode of speech usage will be found to tend to keep them separate; the affective mode, to disregard the distinction and the discoursive mode to adhere to the principle. In all modes, where one fails, resort tends to be to the other.

The complementarity of the terms of the dichotomies of the speech compositional process. The time-honored way of handling the terms of the sixty or more most used dichotomies (opposites, polarities) has been and still is: to favor one, deplore the other, make isms out of both and continue an old or launch a new controversy. The vogue of any one ism, if not accompanied by a budding vogue for the other, tends to be followed by one. Thus, nominalism and realism, idealism and pragmatism, phenomenologies of the sense stimulus and phenomenologies of the sense datum, structuralism and functionalism, and so forth. Attempts to reconcile the opposites by positing third terms between or comprehending them have crowded upon one another and made the history of philosophy the exciting but exasperating thing it has always been. The present device is to regard the opposite terms as possible limits of ranges, gamuts, or parameters of speech semantic (semiotic) variance upon which the isms can be located as well as much of the reference to economic, social, political behavior of man.

Relevance to musicology of the linguistic distinctions "langage / langue / parole" (de Saussure, 1974). Owing to the fortunate idiosyncrasy of its lexicon, the French language affords three nouns for these useful distinctions for which the lexicon of the English language affords only two: *speech* and *language*. As I use them here:

> *langage* = speech, the universal cultural system of predominantly symbolic auditory communication.

> *langue* = language, the particular spoken subsystem that is one of the many languages of man.

> *parole* = the speaking of a language by the individual speaker(s) of it.

Musicological analogs of these linguistic distinctions are all in current use, but the vocabulary affords only one noun—*music*. The analogs must be named by qualifiers of that word:

> speech = *the concept music,* as the universal cultural system of predominantly asymbolic auditory communication;

> language = *the percept music,* as the particular sung and played subsystem that is one of the many musics of man;

> the speaking of a language by individual speakers = *the singing and playing of a music* by individual musicians.

Relevance to musicology of the interdependence and parity of fact and value. The production of every product of the compositional process of speech is both an event in the physical universe and a value, variably positive or negative, in the culture it serves. Each principal mode of speech usage accepts this consideration in accord with its peculiar objective. In the monophonic, single string, speech compositional process, the potentials of the process traditionally are divided in the following way: (1) the reasoned mode deals mainly with fact upon the (unspoken) assumption that this is worth while, that is, valuable; (2) the affective mode deals mainly with value with the (unspoken) implication that the dealing is a fact and is therefore, true; (3) the discursive mode mixes the two extremes together; at the lower levels, indiscriminately; at the higher, optimally dealing equally with the factuality of value and the valuality of fact. It may challenge the reasonable mode to face and examine its unreasonable assumption of worthwhileness.

The principle of the variance of concurrence and divergence of the extrinsic, speech valuation of music and the intrinsic music valuation of value in music. The dual system of values—the biological (personal) and cultural (social)—has often been cited as the criterion of judgment of music in extrinsic (speech) terms; but I find no trace of a dual system of values in the music compositional process, nor of any analog of the codes of morality in whose terms speech control of music is justified. Music is not immoral unless it is put to immoral uses; it is simply amoral.

Relevance to musicology of the distinction particularity/singularity. There remains, however, a fourth distinction that is valid for the compositional processes of both speech (Saussure might have made use of it) and music: (1) the *concept* of the "piece" of speech or music as a particular—particular, because it is similar in some respect to the members of a class of particular poems, dramas, rituals, songs, operas, or symphonies—and (2) the *percept* of it as a singularity—singular, because it is different in some or many respects from the members of any class of particulars and from all other members of the class of singularities. The reasoned mode of speech usage is suspicious of all singularity except that of the concept of the ultimate building block (reality) of the factual universe, which it seeks unremittingly. The affective mode is suspicious of all particularity as obstacles to the percept of the ultimate experience (reality) of the valual universe, which it seeks equally unremittingly. It is in terms of particularities that anthropologists, sociologists, psychologists, physicists, and others will tell you "all about music," in terms of the aspects of music which are data for their respective sciences. Critics will tell you all about what is better, best, worse, and worser in terms of the singularities of the pieces of music or their performance which they are reviewing. The agreement among the specialists in science is as noteworthy as is the disagreement among the critics. Integration of the general order of the facts of musicology and the general disorder of its values remains the principal focus of attention in the building of a comprehensive theory of musicology.

The total mentionables of the speech compositional process are both particularities and singularities. Mentionables are particulars with respect to their extrinsicality—the ectosemiosis of mentionability. Their classification in an indeterminate number of taxonomies by an impressive roster of specialized nonmusical disciplines from physics to aesthetics affords a multiplicity of particularized views of music *from the outside*—sound waves or the impaction of molecular particles, behavior of human neurons, a tradition of human cultures, an aesthetic experience. Mentionables are singularities with respect to the intrinsicality—the endosemiosis of mentionability. Their ranking in an indeterminate number of singular hierarchies by singular cultures, by the social classes within them and by the singular individual members of those classes in terms of any one or more modes of speech usage affords a multiplicity of singularized views of the potentialities of the speech process *from the inside*.

In speaking of a system of human communication other than speech, the speaker is prone to view the compositional process of that system in terms of the singularity of the compositional process of speech itself. But the view of the compositional process of the other system by the user of it is also a singularity and not necessarily the same as the view of the speech compositional process by its user. In case of musicology, where both the compositional process of the system of study and the compositional process of the system studied by the tool are auditory, the study is throughout a comparison of the two compositional processes. It would seem, therefore, that all musicologists should have a solid grounding in linguistics and all linguists, a solid grounding in musicology; for without either, the student cannot justly comprehend the sharing of the total potentiality of auditory communication by either or the overall sharing of the total potentiality of human communication, including vision and tactility.

The principle of the complementarity of speech and music in their use of the total resources of auditory communication.   The most readily available heuristic devices for weighing the two systems in this respect would seem to be the linguistic categories phonology, rhetoric, logic, syntax, grammar, and lexicon, all of which are currently used in musicology, though not, to best of present knowledge, as a set, as here.

1. One phonology serves currently in measurement of the timespace

of the auditory medium. The same instruments of the physical laboratory are used to measure the physical aspects of both systems. They are "more similar than different."

2. The rhetorics (performance practices) of both systems are so closely analogous that they may be intimately associated in song.

3. If one accepts a broad view of logic as two-pronged—a formal, syllogistic (structural) logic that uses words to name physical existentials (facts) and an informal, dynamic, dialectic that uses words to name inner and outer personal-cultural relations (value)—the analog for the two systems is of the type "as similar as different." The outstanding difference is that in speech logic the factor of contradiction is essential, whereas there is no trace of it in music. Complementarity seems to supplant it in a dialectic of relations.

4. The syntaxes of the compositional processes of the two systems coincide remarkably in the phrase, the period, and the paragraph or section; but these are surface aspects in the formal structures of the two systems and cannot be extended far without falling into pedantry. They are analogs of the type "more different than similar."

5. The grammars are so different as to be virtual heterologs.

6. The lexicons, or basic repertories of units of semiotic form, are totally heterologous.

On the whole, one may hazard the judgment that while speech is both endosemiotic and ectosemiotic, music is neither—or perhaps a very little of both—possibly by reason of its close association with speech in most sociocultural contexts and in song. The overlapping suggested by figure 3 may be most in the phonologies and progressively, in the order I have named them, to none in the lexicons.

The principles of certainty and uncertainty. There is no reason—and there should be no inclination on the part of the speaker in the discursive mode of speech usage—to question the *certainty* of the ultimate, ineffable reality as value in the affective mode any more than he would question the *uncertainty* governing, as of 1975, the ultimate, ineffable reality of fact of the reasoned mode.

The principle of bidirectionality in comparative speech-music semiotics. The distinction *in the compositional process of music* of homologs, analogs, and heterologs characteristic of the compositional process of *speech* and the distinction *in the compositional process of speech* of homologs, analogs, and heterologs characteristic of the compositional process of *music* must be checked against each other. Checking is still a speech process, but the bias may be tempered to the extents that we can bear in mind, while speaking, our direct knowledge of use of the music compositional process and may enlist the aid of other communicatory systems, especially graphics.

L'envoi. Had I felt competent, I would have added, here, a final principle or criterion in the synoptic manner of the foregoing eighteen to resume the status and role of mathematics in the formation of a comprehensive theory for musicology. As far as the arithmetic of the case is concerned I can hazard at least the following observations.

1. Auditory communication in human culture as a whole, as a singularity, is reported by speech structurally in six dimensions or resources, functionally as six functions. Four of the six are simple, numerically calibratable parameters of physical fact: pitch (frequency in space), loudness (amplitude in space), speed of event (frequency in time), proportion or meter (amplitude in time). Two of the six are compounds of two simple functions: a spacial (sonal density, timbre, or tone-quality); a temporal (rhythmic density or "thickness" of events in time). The compositional processes of both speech and music make use of all six resources or functions, but variably, to different extents and in different ways.

2. In the reasoned mode of speech usage reliance is solely upon tonal density; for it is in terms of this resource or function alone that the consonances and vowels produced by the human voice are formed into the words that enable us to name and write about, as here, not only this tonal density but about all the other things we name or speak. It makes no difference whether the law of gravity is enunciated in a high or low voice, softly or loudly, rapidly or slowly, in even or uneven metrical feet. In scientific writing or printing, there is no indication of such inflections of the voice. In the affective mode, however, reliance is upon all six functions, especially in verse. In written and printed verse, there is some indication and much traditional implication of inflection. In speaking, any one of the six functions may support, qualify, even contradict, the lexical semiosis and its extension by grammar and syntax. At the lower levels of the discursive mode, the case may be the same; but at the higher, a speaker may try to maintain a reasoned or affective stance to balance the two or to mix them variably. Although all the resources or functions of the physical materials of speech can be measured in the mathematical terms of its semiosis, the actual sounds used in the monophonic string of sound-in-time that is spoken sentence are most profitably described in terms of their deliberate enunciation of the controlled tensions, tonicities, and detensions of the human voice. Mathematics enters the deliberate organization of the speech compositional process only in the metrics of verse or verselike prose.

3. In the music compositional process, to the contrary, all four simple resources or functions of the auditory process are highly and deliberately organized by calibration in degrees of purely musical distinction so closely analogous to as to be homologous with the semiosis of mathematical speech. What the speech process communicates by sounds that symbolize mathematical quantities, the music process communicates by sounds that are themselves those quantities with respect to one another and to traditional scalings and gradings. We have here simply two different ways of numbering. In dealing with the tonal resources of Occidental music the only mathematical symbols required for musicological purposes are the first twelve integers and plus (+), equal (=), minus (−), and zero (0); for with reference to its minimal, medial, and maximal units of form, the compositional process of music is strictly additive and subtractive. Thus, the finding of scales, chords, children's songs, and such in the harmonic series is regarded with suspicion by users of the reasoned mode, with imaginative excursions into the cosmos by users of the affective mode and with some concern by users of the uncommon commonsense of the discoursive mode in which most musicology is written.

There are still too many gaps in the arithmetic of the speech report of the arithmetic of the music compositional process to warrant much dependence upon it in the formation of a comprehensive theory of musicology. But such a theory will remain incomplete until this "comparative" arithmetic is done.

II
Music as Concept and as Percept[76]

In the English language, the word *music,* as well as its equivalents in many other languages, has acquired many meanings over centuries of use. It names items of attention ranging from particular concrete percepts, through a number of different classes of them to fairly abstract universal concepts. Until we distinguish more carefully between these different meanings than we have in the past, we may find ourselves still producing histories of music that ignore 90 percent or more of the music of man and theories of it, ignoring nearly as large a percentage of its essential factors. We can begin the distinction of these meanings either with the names, which are words, or with the named, that is, what the names name; but since we have to talk about the latter in terms of the former, it would seem to be best to begin with the names.

There are three principal ways of clarifying the ambiguity of words such as *music*: identification (labeling or documentation), description, and definition. Suppose, for example, that someone says "I hear music." He is probably referring to and identifying a particular percept by the name of a class or species of item of attention long familiar to him which is only one of hundreds of such that are not familiar to him, some of which he might not even identify as music. For all he has told you, you cannot know, unless you are well acquainted with his personal idiosyncrasies, whether he heard a recently composed popular American song, a Tibetan Buddhist chant, or a motet of Guillaume de Machaut. If you should ask him "Can you tell me anything about it? What kind of music is it?" he might say, "No, it's just music," that is, something named by a generic term he could use thus. Or, if he were expert in the particular idiom, he might answer "What I heard was the repetition of the sixth line 'Al' si vila, al' si jutvornjica?' of the so-called women's song beginning 'Uranijo bego Omerbego' recorded by Milman Parry and Albert B. Lord at Gacko, Hercegovina, April 24, 1935, of the singing of Fata Krajisnik, their numbers R. 3137-3141; probably from a taped copy, for some of the sizzle of the old disc is missing." Note that the word *music* is also missing; for when documentation is extended to such comprehensive and detailed identification, it would be as unnecessary to mention an overarching universal music as it would be to mention the fact that Gacko, Hercegovina, was on the planet Earth at the time of the recording. If he were not expert in the discography of that particular item, however, but instead a serious student of the tradition of ballad singing in general, he might answer "No, I cannot identify it, but I can describe a number of factors that lead me to believe it is a recording of a traditional ballad singer"; after which he might launch into a description of the timbre, the singing style, its elaborate melismatic agogic, the mode, the meter, the cadential formula, the melodic curve, the steady dynamic level and beat, the rapid tempo, and so forth, and might hazard a guess of the area over which such a tradition flourished. Supposing a fourth person, well indoctrinated by school and college courses in music appreciation, should ask "But is it music?" you might find yourself embarked upon an inquiry into the defintion of the word *music* that could carry you—if he were as persistent as some of his kind are—into levels of abstract conceptualization involving universals that are not only world-wide but universewide in the universe of (speech) discourse.

Although neither of your learned friends found it any more necessary to mention these universals in their answers to your questions than it was for you to mention the location of Gacko, Hercegovina, on the planet Earth, sooner or later you always find yourself faced by the kind of argument imposed by the last of your four interlocutors. Then you realize that in all the preceding exchanges you had relied upon a funded aggregate—a bank, as it were—of ideation that you and your contemporaries carry as part of your beings and enabled you to find your way through the thicket of ambiguity surrounding the familiar term *music*. You may observe that you have formulated a strategy for the avoidance of explicit recognition of the kind of money this bank deals with and even of awareness of your responsibility in drawing unlimited checks upon it—a strategy without which you could not talk about anything else but the attempt to discover how to solve all the problems of talking in general and of talking about music in particular, a most difficult task because it has to be done with talking and in the silent talking called "thinking," that is, speech thinking.

There must be conceded to be other forms of thinking, as, for example, music thinking, but how do you handle them in talking?

The tactical devices with which you implement your strategy in your everyday talking and in all serious talk about music are many, but two are probably most widely depended upon. Both consist in some kind of an ordering of the names of the percepts and concepts funded in the bank of ideation of the culture that is carried by each of us, of which we form our own variant, limited variably by our genetic capabilities, by our education, by our individual life histories, and by our conscious effort. Both devices build and arrange classes of order (1) of the words of the language we use, (2) of what the words name. One kind of order is the hierarchy; the other, the taxonomy. A hierarchy tends to be mainly valual, to be focused upon the individual members of the class as it sets up, to be not averse to the formation of classes of one, as in some religious and political hierarchies and to be largely unconsciously and subjectively formed. A taxonomy, however, tends to be factual, to be focused upon classes as collectivities, irrespective of the singularities of their members and to be more consciously and objectively formed.

Hierarchies and taxonomies are constructed which are purely endosemantic, that is, which name solely items of attention within (intrinsic to) words, relations of words, and the compositional process of speech. They are rarely overtly stated, but exist as the repertory or bank of ideation. Our account in it consists in our ability to draw checks that are valid to the extent of our singular ways of understanding the potentials of the bank for development in the ongoing culture that we inherit, cultivate, and transmit. It comprises, as capital, at least four universes: (1) an ill-defined bundle of universes; (2) a universe of speech discourse, composed of other communicatory systems, tactile, auditory, and visual, variably interlocked with the universe of speech discourse; (3) a physical universe of fact which is purely ectosemantic, extrinsic to these two; (4) a universe of values, half biological and, so, components of the physical universe, half cultural.

The universe of discourse is ordered by man. We pick it up as we learn our own language and build our own variant out of our schooling and the subtraditions of the socioeconomic class we are born into or graduate into under the general conditions—political and ecological—we encounter.

The bundle of tactile, auditory, and visual universes is not yet ordered.

The physical universe is assumed to be in perfect order and one of our consuming urges is to make models of it in terms of the universe of speech discourse—unless, as is more often the case, we assume that we have a perfect one in the backs of our heads, which, of course, is not so.

The universe of value is a wholly manmade affair. It is in complete chaos. Each of us selects a roster of values from the biocultural bank and, to the extent of our competence in the use of speech, ranks them in a hierarchy of which we may think we are entirely conscious but rarely are.

In becoming more aware of these partly consciously and partly unconsciously made hierarchies and taxonomies in our singular, personal variants of the compositional process of speech, nomenclature becomes a matter of first consideration. The lexicon consists only of strings of sounds, words that name. Some words are proper names. They name one item of attention only. Most of them are concepts, abstract, empirical, generic—names of categories, classes of items of attention-namables or mentionables. When used without qualification, they function in the speech compositional process as abstract universal concepts or in the likeness of them. They can be used without reference to anything extrinsic to that process or to the universe of discourse, as are the names of the integers of the natural number series in arithmetic. To this extent, the universe of discourse is independent of and comprehends the physical universe external to it because it can name it and any namable in it. When used with qualification, as by the definite or indefinite article or by an adjective, both words name particular percepts, that is, items of attention in the physical universe that we have learned to regard by means other than speech as including speech and all the words it comprises. Thus, the percept is a concept and the concept is a percept, but in two different senses.

Thus each hierarchy is twinned to a taxonomy and vice versa. In terms of their inner orders, they are one another's contraries. In a hierarchy, of which the right-hand column on the following chart, is an example, the word *universe* names a manmade, teleologically order, half consciously, half unconsciously drawn toward the ultimate, most deeply felt aspiration of man of whose nature we are absolutely certain. There is no point in telling a lover that he may not be in love or one who says he has seen God that he may have been mistaken. A hierarchy tends to be a closed system. In a taxonomy, however, of which the left-hand column in the chart is an example, the word *universe* names a state of affairs that is assumed to be in perfect order, not manmade, with which we are totally integrated and which is driven by a rigorously causal momentum from origins of which we are totally ignorant toward ends of which we are equally ignorant, but of all of which we may make continually more and more refined speech models.

The order of a hierarchy is one of rank with respect to the highest value(s); the order of the taxonomy is plotted in terms of members of classes, each class becoming a member of the next more comprehensive class. The highest value tends to be regarded as a percept—one cannot reason about it. The highest, that is, ultimate fact cannot be felt; it is affectively neutral.

Both hierarchies and taxonomies tend to be pushed to the limits of the speech compositional process. The momentum of each tends to carry it beyond what is effable: the hierarchy, to intense feeling of reality; the taxonomy, to intense intellection of reality.

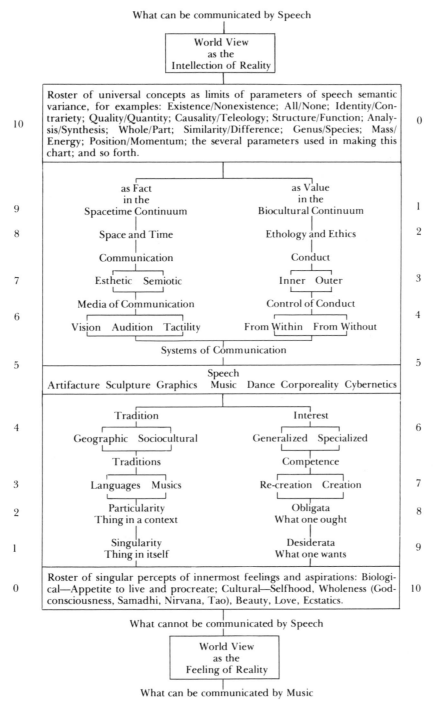

Inverse alignment of a taxonomy of conceptualization of fact and a hierarchy of perceptualization of value in musicology.

Associated with most elaborated and diversified musics of man there have been and are musicologies, variously embryonic and sophisticated, markedly different taxonomies and strongly biased hierarchies of music-making, musicianly competence, social status of musicians and music, ethical value, and so forth, which are as solipsistic and nonuniversal as our own. The well-organized musicology begins, however, not with these but with comparative study of them in their respective sociocultural contexts under the aegis of a comprehensive theory of music both in itself and in its world context as presented in terms of the speech compositional process chosen by the student.

The first step in the study of such a combined hierarchy-taxonomy would seem to be to place the term *music* in the optimal position for the development of the transformational process afforded by this dual gamut, range, or parameter of speech semantic variance. Upon the two-dimensional page this position would seem to be exactly midway between the two limits: the universal abstract concept and the singular concrete percept, as on the chart on page 35.

This chart pretends to be an outline that can accommodate all possible taxonomies and hierarchies expressed in terms of this parameter of speech semantic variance. The two columns of ten levels each are numbered inversely and are slightly staggered so that two zero levels may comprise the "pure" forms of the maximally comprehensive, universal concepts of speech thought that do not constitute classes because there is no higher genus of which they can become members, and the maximally intensive, singular percept that is not a class because it comprehends no members. The chart is to be read from the bottom up as well as from the top down, for one should try to compensate in as many ways as one can for the built-in speech biases that on the one hand rate the thinkable higher than the sensible or, on the other, the sensible higher than the thinkable.

The second step in this operation is to relate the generic term *music* of levels 5 to the levels 6 and 4 nearest above and below them. The basic relationship upward is by definition; downward, by description. This begins to submit the class to the transformational process characteristic of a taxonomy based upon this particular parameter of speech semantic variance: increasing universalization and abstraction of the concept with each upward move; increasing particularization and concretization of the percept with each downward move.

Before beginning to trace the transformation of the name *music* in either direction, however, the reader must be reminded that since both the concept and the percept *music* are named by a word, as are also the levels of conceptualization and perceptualization, by words, both the word as the name of an item of attention that it names, *music,* and the word itself and the kinds of concepts and percepts it names, are subjected to the same transformation. And since the words are all speech constructs, the name *speech* is inevitably implied by the name *music* every step of the way both upward and downward: the words *music* and *speech* are speech constructs. As far as the chart is concerned, the words and what they name are inseparable.

Definition, then, transforms both names of level 5 into two species of a single class "Auditory Communication" of level 6, which is, in turn, one of three classes that become species of the still higher class "Communication" of level 7 (see fig. 2, chap. I). The definition afforded by this transformation is classificatory and could read: "music is one of the two traditional systems of auditory communication among men, the other being speech."

Description, by contrast, transforms each class of levels 5 into a multitude of species by being parceled out among the (still increasing) number of specialized modes and methods of speech usage.

Transformation upward by definition in terms of increasing abstraction and universality is controlled by the factor similarity. The progress is toward unity and a macrocosm. Transformation downward by description is by the factor difference. The progress is toward plurality and a microcosm. Theoretically, the ultimate achievement, upon abstract level 10, would be a unified totality of speech reference that would produce one-to-one correspondence with the referents, the names with the named, the concept with the percept, reality with appearance, fact with value, identity with contrariety, causality with teleology, structure with function, music with talking about music. Persistently as philosophers have sought such correspondence—and only too often have thought or tried to persuade themselves and others that they have done so—they have never produced an exposition that has withstood the criticism of their successors and rarely that of their contemporaries. Nor have they convinced some of us that the feat is possible. Theoretically, also, the ultimate achievement on concrete level 10 could be a diversity of music value which would match the diversity of the concepts with which to talk about it and, so, facilitate the musicological attempt to find speech order in music. But here, the case is the reverse of abstract level 10. The speech knowledge of a music event is not the same as the music knowledge of it nor are the two mutually exclusive. The moot question is the extent of the overlapping and in what respect.

As a concept, the word *music* is definable. And the generic term *a music* is describable in great detail. If there is any one word that describes what it communicates, it might be oneness where the speech report is manyness. Somewhat similarly, the speech knowledge of the percept of highest values is not to be confused with the percept, which involves participation of tactile, visual, and nonsymbolic auditory media of communication. It is not definable. It is namable but describable in general, often vague, terms. It is ineluctably involved with the feeling of oneness, uniqueness, singularity. The biological values are, however, more closely describable than the cultural. These are purely critical judgments. There is no scientific evidence for them; nor can there be. One is talking in terms of affection, not of reason, though as reasonably as possible.

The chart presented here is not committed to any philosophy or to the possibility or impossibility of the search of philosophy for a solution of the impasse. It is designed solely to accommodate as many musicological possibilities as can be foreseen. It is not a philosophical system but a chart of the resources of speech communication viewed by one who is not a philosopher but a musician who has tried to find a way of using the art of speech to deal with the art of music and avoid as many errors of his predecessors as possible. To be remembered in this connection is that while during the last 150 years linguists have developed a superb discipline of speech about speech, musicologists have done nothing at all about a discipline of speech about music. And there is still no indication that there is any general concern about the necessity of such a discipline.

On the way to the greatest possible abstraction of the concept and the greatest possible concretization of the percept, the verbal transformation process to which we have submitted the word *music* and what it names has attracted to itself, and spread itself to, an increasing number of other classes and species of concepts and percepts, as would two magnetized steel balls rolling around in a field of iron filings. The attraction in this case, however, is more one of mutual absorption: music in other things and other things in music, so that by the time the twin transformational processes have reached their respective levels 10 the concepts are totally universalized and abstracted from the percepts, and the percepts totally particularized and concretized from the concepts, even though the concepts, to be understood must be perceived, that is, heard as words and the percepts conceived, that is, named as universals.

The accretional aspect of the process begins to show itself upon the two levels 6. Speech and music, as species of auditory communication, are linked inescapably with visual communication on the one hand and with tactile communication on the other. The facial expression, the body stance, the gestures, and the affective states and motor behaviors manifest in these, as well as in the making of the sounds of both speech and music, are invariable concomitants of both speech-making and music-making. Sometimes they communicate in their own ways as much as or more than does the auditory. The speaker or musician who is near—within touching distance—of another speaker or musician communicates also by fact of that nearness and all the more so if the two actually touch. One has seen this—and, perhaps, felt it oneself—in the kind of vocal quartet singing in the United States called "close harmony" or "barbershop quartet" singing, in which the shoulders of the singers are pressed as closely as possible against each other, so that the tensions, tonicities, and detensions of each tonal, rhythmic, and formative progression are felt as if it were, by precise "tuning" of touch as well as by that of pitch, loudness, and phrasal agogic. Often as not, the eyes are closed, as if one were seeing and feeling, as well as hearing, inwardly.

Upon the more abstract taxonomic level 9, for example, the space *and* time of level 8 become the spacetime of the physical continuum. The common sense sound (space) *and* rhythm (time) of music become the rhythm sound of the present musicological analysis and seen, as is spacetime by the physicist as single, not a dual, function: the music timespace continuum. Similarly, on the more abstract (and less perceptual) hierarchic level 1, the common sense distinction between the behaviors of nonhominids and hominids of level 8 is seen as a single biological-cultural continuum.

A large proportion of what is communicated by systems of human communication other than speech is not communicable by speech. There are no concepts in whose terms it can be verbalized. To the extent to which we may find in the compositional process of speech analogs of factors in the compositional processes of human communicatory systems other than speech, we may try to express in terms of the former what in itself is inexpressible in speech by direct observation. Perhaps the chart would be viewed as on a broad tape, so that its top and bottom could be joined to make a circular band, with the two levels 10 overlapping and, so, identifying themselves with, their respective levels 0.

Because no one has ever found a single order that can gain a substantial consensus, the main body of concept level 10 consists of an indiscriminate listing of some of the categories of Aristotle (substance, quantity, quality, relation, place, time, position or situation, state or condition, activity, passivity), the Five Predictables made famous by Prophyry (genus, species, difference, property, accident), Kant's two lists of twelve categories each under the four main headings of quantity, quality, difference, and modality, and Hegel's many dozens of dichotomies. I have grouped these concepts in pairs, trios, and quartets, separating them with a slanting line (/) to stand in a purely explanatory manner for the parameters of speech semantic variance which they define, in whose terms musicologists think, as well as in terms of the separate words, just as they can think of the individual degrees of a mode as well as of the intervals between them. I arrived at this way of building a dialectic about five years before I made my (still) rather distant acquaintance with Hegel; but I must give him credit for seeding his conception in the general cultural atmosphere in which I grew up. Although I appreciate his term "the interpenetration of thesis and antithesis," I cannot accept the necessity of imposing such a mystical notion, nor the even more mystical synthesis of the two, at this juncture. I am happier to regard them as simply associated side-by-side along the whole range or gamut of their respective parameters of speech semantic variance.

If it should appear to some reader that I have exceeded the limits of rational discourse by speculation too far into or beyond the fringes of the effable, I would admit the charge but claim that it is the very nature of the musicological juncture that this must be done. For the bulk of what can be said about music probably lies beyond the limits of (speech) rational discourse, and, thus, irrational qua reasoned speech; yet not musically irrational—this being valid upon the assumption, not to be dismissed out of hand, that there may be in music analogs but not necessarily homologs of both speech rationality and speech mysticism. If this is acceptable, one difference between the two arts would seem to be that in music the analogs may be compatible, whereas in speech they are not.

I can still accept the general agreement in the belief (for there seems no ground for disputing it) that order has been and can be found (1) in talking and writing which may be in one-to-one correspondence with an order in what is being talked and written about, and (2) that speculation into the fringes of rational discourse have frequently won portions of those fringes for inclusion within the limits of such discourse. These two kinds of deliberately methodical use of language, the scientific and scientistic, to which latter a substantial portion of all critiques belong, are the mainstay of musicological endeavor; but neither can penetrate very far into the other portion of the critique—namely, that which is unaccountably affective and subjective in value judgment and which is as essential in the conception of an axiological universe or universe of values as is its absence in the conception of a phenomenological universe or universe of fact. Still less can either, or speech as a whole, penetrate in the "content" of music communication if, indeed, there is any such thing. The test is in techniques of prediction. Upon the bases of historical reconstruction and of scientific and scientistic probability, limited prediction can be made of the act of music-making both as fact and as value. For example, the first two measures of Beethoven's Third Symphony might have been predicted by a computer sufficiently well programmed by one with knowledge of the symphonic tradition that Beethoven inherited and was trained in. The first movement would probably begin with the tonic in single octaves or with major or minor chords in root position, with full instrumentation, forte. By one knowing of Beethoven's penchant for iterated notes, the computer might have predicted possibility of the E-flats on the first beats of the first six measures. But the probability or even possibility of prediction of the seventh to tenth measures, with their six reiterated syncopated quarter-note values, seems indeterminately remote. And although the occurrence, somewhere later of six iterated half-note syncopations and of a subordinate theme in six slightly modified even quarters might have been predicted, just where and how, in the score, would seem to be utterly unpredictable by any theory of probability or possibility. No, the individual subjective factor in value judgment in music as in the other fine arts would seem to be beyond the speech rational. Yet the crux of the musicological juncture is precisely this: to talk about music we have to use the full armament of verbiage in the chart given here and much more, replete with universals and particulars, concepts and percepts, abstractness and concreteness, feeling and imagination, and so forth; yet to know that there is no evidence whatever that the music compositional process, whether precomposed or composed in the act of singing or of playing an instrument, operates in any such terms. It is almost obligatory to speak of music knowledge, music thought, music feeling, music imagination, and so forth, for there are no other words available unless we turn to mathematical expression, which some other speech disciplines in the humanities are already doing. This might be beneficial in more than one way. As I have pointed out elsewhere, discursive speech tends to overstructuralize whatever it deals with. With mathematics the case is the reverse: to overfunctionalize. Perhaps a symbolic logic integrating the two would produce the most believable results. We would have to wait and see.

For purely exemplary reasons, therefore, I have added to the chart two unnumbered boxes containing titles that enhance the relevance of the parameter concept/percept to our given topic. They define one of the several other such parameters that comprehend, are comprehended by, cross-cut, or otherwise affect one another variously with respect to the connection in which they are used—and make speech communication the very flexible and ambiguous thing it is. These two titles name facets or functions of human behavior: the concepts intellection and feeling. "Feeling" or affection, but not "emotion," for that term denotes the changes of affection without regard of the affective tone or tonicity from which the change emerges and with which it eventually remerges—

a tonic, a tonality, a ground continuum, which the wise keep as steady as possible between the pressures of collectivity and the urges of individuality.

By the nature of its defining terms, the chart pretends to be cast in a mode of the parameter reason/affection that is nearer to the first than to the second of the two terms. This does not imply that the second is to be ignored. The term *music percept* is, as already pointed out, an affective or mystical in terms of speech. But although affection and mysticism are not much more than mentionables in discourse that pretends to follow to some extent the demands of reason or logic, it is fully exploited by philosophy, aesthetics, belles lettres, poetry, and the varied aggregate of styles and manners roughly grouped in the chart under the title "ecstatics." By mention of such speech nonrationals as the music percept, however, the chart does pose the universe of rational (logical) discourse as comprehending it along with all other such mere mentionables.

The proposed name for this mutual comprehending—World View, *Weltbild, Weltanschauung*—is, by necessity, bipartite: on the one hand, a looking outward to a totality that may or may not be a unit; on the other, a looking inward to a totality that we deeply believe to be a unit.

By the individual who may with sincere conviction regard his view of himself and what is outside himself as a unit, the two World Views of the chart may be regarded as one and the same Gestalt or singularity. This is a commonplace of music, which does not even distinguish the two but presents a Gestalt (einheit or singularity) that every musician knows directly qua music and knows it cannot be presented by speech.

By adding the two unnumbered boxes I have wanted to suggest that we may now, owing to the revolutionary developments of twentieth-century verbalization, consider the possibility of extending the parameter of speech semantic variance *Abstract-Universal-Concept/Concrete-Particular-Percept* beyond the bounds of present fashions in musicology. I have already strained these bounds by the mere inclusion of reference to the "emptiness" of Buddhism and the fullness of the Tao, but would like still to carry it one step farther; for these seem to leave room for at least elementary verbal communication referent to music communication which sometimes seems to have something in common with these speech nonrationals but need not to be regarded as musically nonrational.

Both added boxes would seem to allow for the bearing upon the case in hand of nonverbal imagination and feeling. Verbalism, as represented by the chart, could be regarded as enfolded between the nonverbal, just as, in the chart itself, verbalism takes for granted that it enfolds, by the technique of naming, everything nonverbal, whether it can name it or not. The folding of the page to make a circular band with the two added boxes overlaying each other could be regarded as representing one kind of a cosmos—the circle or wheel—favored by some of the great religions on the assumption that the inspiration of one moment may accomplish as much as or more than a lifetime of studious application. The two ends need not meet, however, but could form a spiral. Or a parabola. Or, it could be regarded as crossed at all angles by many other such bands. This last mentioned kind of view contemplates the "uncomfortable" universes of antimatter, antitime, time going backward and sideways and allows for some of the so-called psychic theories in which some people put great store but which lie outside the understanding of this writer. Each of us has probably made up his world view, or had it made up for him, years ago. Both speech and music communicate much of whatever it may be: speech, by symbolizing it; music, by embodying it. But vision and tactility are also factors. Vision holds it at a distance, in a perspective. Words also hold music at a distance. Pictures, especially diagrams, sometimes draw it nearer. But perspective—that pushes it off in the distance again. Tactility is what we need to be more aware of. Closeness. Tactility holds us closest to what we try to communicate. It could, of course, be a stranglehold, but one would opt for an embrace or a dance. Which will you have?

In speech, the universals, both conceptual and perceptual, constitute one of the two best devices of language to escape from its own limitations. They function equally well in science, in criticism, and in poetry. But they have their limitations. They don't get along any too well with each other. And we—individually, socially, culturally, in every way—are bound in the chains of the orders we put them in. We look to them to free us even while they bind us down all the tighter, not only because we put too much trust in them but because we use them faultily. Humanity does not have to continue in bondage to this one system of communication and make only minimal use of the others. There are at least five to eight others (see Essay 1, fig. 4). Because they are musicians, musicologists know music. And music, though not a universal language, is without question more nearly universal in all senses of the word, including worldwide perspective, than speech.

Of all six, eight, or nine systems, music is in the best position to be the base for a critique of speech. Their phonologies and rhetorics are conspicuously homologous. Only one of the aims of musicology is more speech knowledge of music. Equally important is more music knowledge of speech. For it is only in terms of speech and its universals and particulars that we can direct the latter knowledge in pursuit of the former. There is no escape from the fact that musicology should be—even though it cannot yet be said to be—a speech discipline. One may play with the notion that it is not necessary for the musician to know anything about musicology. And though it may be that in the Western world and wherever the music and musicology of the West has been spread, too much preoccupation with musicology may do the musician more harm than good, the fact remains that every music known to us in the world is closely associated with the language and languages current in the cultures of which both are traditions. Everywhere we turn, speech and music are ineluctably related. They may not be necessary to each other; but they cannot be kept apart. Equal competence in both would seem to be too much to ask for either musician or musicologist. But a *sufficient* competence in the other can be asked of each. What is to be judged sufficient in the two cases would seem to be a matter of some importance to both. Certainly, it is as undesirable for the musician to be a musicological dilettante as it is for the musicologist to be a dilettante musician. The way out of the double risk would seem to be to balance the quantitative and the qualitative factors in both cases. This would mean, for the musician, a decrease in the quantity of musicological knowledge he can be expected to possess and an increase in its quality; and for the musicologist, a decrease in the quantity of musical knowledge of his own music and the increase in that of musics other than his own. For there are few things more futile than talking only about one music, one's own. By the very nature of the act—the inescapable necessity to deal with all particulars in terms of generic and abstract concepts—the particulars of one's own music masquerade as worldwide universals and, as an almost automatic reflex, distort not only one's understanding of one's own music, but of all others as well.

III

The Musicological Juncture:
Music as Fact

The situation in which we place ourselves when we talk or write about music must be regarded in barest outline as a sixfold complex that may be referred to as "the musicological juncture": (1) As students, each with our own singular competences and conceptual and perceptual banks of factual and valual behavior, (2) we meet, within certain limited extents of space and time, (3) in a particular biocultural continuum and social context, two of its principal traditions of communication, (4) of a music, (5) of a language, (6) and a subtradition, a musicology, the extents of whose spacial and temporal currencies are, in the constantly renewable collectivity of biocultural continuum, to best of our knowledge unlimited.

We have met the first two of these traditions, (4) and (5), as ordinary members of the communities in which we are born and live. As we have grown up, we have cultivated both, as ordinary carriers of the traditions of a culture; later, we may have cultivated the one as disciplined musicians; the other, as disciplined scholars. The subtradition (6) is a highly specialized speech study that can be entered upon only with a degree of competence in both of the traditions. This is a large order for one lifetime. Consequently, we do not insist that the musicologist be a virtuoso in performance or composition; but we do expect him to command a knowledge of and feeling for the making of music, in at least one music idiom, which we do not expect of the professional musician. Similarly, we do not insist that he command the encyclopedia of general (speech) knowledge; but we do expect him to use a language and the resources of speech to treat of a music more expertly than can the professional musician, the nonmusical or extramusical specialist, the general philosopher or anyone else.

While we cultivate them, these traditions do not stay still. They exhibit continuous more or less independent functional patterns of stability and change as wholes in themselves, among their individual components and within the overarching *Gestalteinheit* conceived as comprehending everything conceivable and perceivable. We can maintain any one particular attitude toward them to a limited extent only, because we ourselves do not stay still. Our individual and group actions with respect to what is continued and what is varied, what given more, what less emphasis, are prime factors in the musicological juncture and in the apprehension and valuation of the data and dicta of their study. We are ourselves data in the study we conduct. To the extent our conduct is exemplary—especially if it is expressed or referred to in words—we are dicta in the study. There is a given all-pervading dualism in the juncture: the limited operational range of the individual student versus the comparatively unlimited operational range of the biosociocultural continuum of which we become components; the two traditions (4 and 5) that we try to join by the subtradition (6); the concepts of these (which must be defined) versus their empirical referents (which must be described); the controlled objectivity with which we hope to regard the factual data versus the controlled subjectivity with which we may hope to inquire into the valual dicta; our limited carriage of the traditions versus the comparatively unlimited carriage of them by the collective of which we are members; and so forth. The reporting of these and several dozen other dichotomies in terms of only one of the traditions (speech) assures a speech bias. For the extent to which the other communicatory systems distinguish and employ this formidable roster has been little explored.

This presentation of the hazards of the musicological juncture may seem to barge unduly upon the domain of the professional philosopher, rather shortly after the explicit statement that the musicologist cannot pretend to be a professional philosopher, much less a professional in each of the dozen or more specialized philosophies—physics, biology, psychology, anthropology and sociology, linguistics, aesthetics, folklore, theology, and several more—which bear upon musicology. It might be supposed that application of some existing philosophical system—logical positivism or existentialism, structuralism or functionalism—might fill the bill for the musicological juncture. But no existent philosophical system has left any room for music as a means of communication on a par with speech in a speech undertaking. We must, apparently, accept the fact that the philosopher can pretend to no more competence in dealing with music than can the musicologist in dealing with philosophy. The conditions of the musicological juncture, however, require the musicologist to proceed by dealing with them all or else quit. To proceed we must adjust, in one way or another by intuition, imagination, or plain common sense, all the problems of philosophy, just as the philosopher, if he is to deal with music, must do the same with all the problems of musicology.

There is nothing new about this proposal but the acknowledgment of it; for it is precisely what both nonmusicologists and musicologists have done throughout history. But their fault has been and still is not to have admitted it. We are in a linguocentric predicament. The musicologist would seem to be in a stronger position vis-à-vis the philosopher (and by "philosopher" I mean also the natural and social scientist, value-theorist, expert in the history of religions, and so forth), for he is, as a rule, far more competent in the compositional process of speech than are they in the compositional process of music.

For the musicologist speech is a tool. This granted, the "problems of philosophy" become "dilemmas met with in the use of a language." Instead of risking "solutions" of them as "problems" that are full of philosophical dynamite that he may sometimes be unable to perceive, the musicologist will be wise to adopt purely operational adjustments of the various epistemological, lexical, grammatical, syntactic, and logical problems that he meets as dilemmas inherent in the linguocentric predicament, so that when one horn of a dilemma has been exploited as effectively as possible, the other shall be tried for what it is worth, the rule being to remain content with neither, but to accept the two as defining a range, gamut, or parameter of speech semantic variance between them over the whole of which both horns bear variably strongly or weakly. Naturally, the student must try to present his adjustments in manners as intelligible and acceptable as possible to musicians as well as to non-musicians. For it is the task of both to integrate the results of the specialized studies with the overall study of man.

For guidance of behavior in the musicological juncture, there follow, under four main headings, some suggestions that will be amplified elsewhere.

PREMISES

1. Music knowledge and feeling in music are to be distinguished from speech knowledge of and feeling about music.

2. Music knowledge and feeling are communicated in a music; speech knowledge of it, in a language.

3. Both kinds of knowledge and feeling are in themselves worthwhile seeking and are of equal importance to musicology.

4. To the extent he possesses both kinds of knowledge and feeling the musicologist may attempt to regard either pair in terms of the other.

5. The musicological knowledge of feeling for a music is a unique

kind of speech knowledge and feeling in that it must meet equally the criteria of music knowledge and feeling and speech knowledge and feeling.

AIMS

1. The immediate aim of musicology is (a) to integrate music knowledge and feeling in music and the speech knowledge and feeling about them to the extent this is possible in speech presentation, and (b) to indicate as clearly as possible the extent to which this is not possible.

2. The ultimate aim of musicology is to contribute to the general study of man what can be known of man as a music maker.

METHODOLOGICAL PRINCIPLES

1. Scientific and critical methods are to be regarded as complementary and interdependent, as are also, historical and systematic orientations and nonmusical and musical viewpoints.

2. Even as these three pairs of concepts are to be regarded as complementary and interdependent, so also are all correctly drawn dichotomies, ranges, gamuts, or parameters of speech semantic variance to be employed or implied.

PRACTICAL CONSIDERATIONS

1. Speech, ultimately, *a* language, is the communicatory agent or tool of musicology.

2. Music, ultimately, *a* music, may be one of many subjects dealt with by the communicatory agent and as such can be regarded as an item of attention in a number of diverse ways.

3. Music, independently of the communicatory agent (speech), is itself a communicatory agent.

4. A music communicates itself qua fact and value; but it does not "say" so.

5. The phenomenological and axiological aspects of a music are equally the concern of speech descriptive techniques in musicology.

6. The phenomenology of a music and that of a language can be commensurated.

7. The axiology of a music and that of a language can be commensurated, though probably to a lesser extent.

8. Both descriptive and valuative treatment of music in terms of speech take place in a biosociocultural context that can be termed "the musicological juncture."

9. The nature of the musicological juncture is such that the music of the world as a whole can be dealt with only as a speech concept.

10. Description of *a* music as a phenomenological referent is possible only in terms of those of its aspects that can be named and related as homologs, analogs, or heterologs of speech.

11. The terms in which these aspects can be described are, for the most part, integral elements of the general (nonmusical) technique of speech.

12. The use of these terms in the specialized treatment of music that is musicology tends to cast a music into the likeness of both the language which is the communicatory agent and of the predominantly dualistic nature of speech in general.

13. Speech descriptions and valuations of a music in the forms of a language qua a composite of aspects may correspond variably to the forms of a music in some respects but not in others.

14. The degree of correspondence between the speech report and the music reported upon will depend largely upon the homologs, analogs, and heterologs set up in the conceptualization of the two communicatory agents under the conditions of the musicological juncture.

15. A music, as an item described in a language, must be viewed from the standpoints and in the terms of the full roster of speech disciplines, and those relevant to a music must be translated into the terminology of musicology.

16. No one of these disciplines—least of all, one school of thought within any one of them—should be relied upon to give the whole story. Special care must be taken in the distinction between the phenomenology of the sense stimulus and the sense datum.

17. Gaps found in our speech thinking about music may be suspected of being areas of music thinking.

18. Allowance must be made for the various systems of tactile and visual thinking.

19. The relationships of the eight or nine systems of communication among men, tactile, auditory, and visual, are prime subjects for musicological investigation.

20. In our speech thinking we must not regard other communicatory systems as irrational or beneath notice solely because we cannot give a speech-rational account of them.

21. The extension, by analogy, of the devices of the speech compositional process into the speech report of the compositional processes of

the other systems of human communication is the only means of naming and relating them among themselves and with speech; but unless the result is merely to show the dependence of nonspeech communication upon speech communication and, so, to cast both the natural universe and the universe of man into the likeness of the idiosyncrasies of the speech compositional process, we must inquire into the limitations of that process.

22. Music is in a unique position vis-à-vis speech with respect to the identification of the limits of the potentialities of speech; for the identities, analogies, and heterologies of their respective compositional processes can be clearly plotted because those processes are enough alike to be associated intimately in song.

23. A prime—perhaps *the* prime—operational consideration in musicology is the principle of bidirectionality in the comparative semiotics of the two compositional processes, for without continual check upon the potentials of the speech process, with which the user of speech is usually more drunk than he realizes, its limitations are forgotten and the bias of linguistic solipsism perpetuates itself as the curse of Eden upon all that goes by the name of scholarship. Perhaps Adam and Eve sang to each other before they ate the apple (the word, that is, learned to talk).

A few words should be said about the relationship of musicological undertakings to the actual conduct of the music they deal with. There have always seemed to have been excellent grounds for a hearty distrust by musicians of all talking about music (except when they do it themselves). Conversely, there is the inescapable mandate of speech scholarship that there is nothing that cannot be talked about provided only it be done in the best way possible. The musicologist is the only one who can obey this mandate in talking about music. It is not the musician who commands him, it is he himself as a petitioner for attention of the world community of speech scholarship. And it is primarily to himself and to this world community that he is responsible, not to the community of musicians. But it is only to the extent that he is a musician as well as a speaker that he can function as a musicologist. And as a musician, he is equally responsible to the world community of musicians for everything that he does in his musicology.

To achieve maximal compensation for the speech bias inherent in the musicological juncture we must seek a common basis for the comparative study of the two systems in a third system—one other than an auditory.

IV
The Musicological Juncture: Music as Value[65]

It is our misfortune today that both the predominantly historical study of the professional, elegant, or fine art of European music which we know as *musicology* and the predominantly systematic study of the total music of the world which we know, perforce, as *ethnomusicology* have both been developed mainly as descriptive sciences. Neither has had a comparably organized critique. Neither has taken any cognizance of general value theory. Yet both have been bound by assumptive value judgments that, though quite different, are the more dominating for lack of explicit statement. These judgments hold apart the two branches of what eventually must be a single study and provide an almost impassible barrier to the integration of either with a comprehensive concept of the humanities as a whole.

Historicomusicology has assumed that the single European idiom with which it deals is the only one worth its serious attention. Other musics and the folk and popular idioms of the European tradition have been ignored or regarded variously as irrelevant, inferior, "bad," barbarous, or not music at all. To ethnomusicologists, from Stumpf, Abraham, von Hornbostel, with the possible exception of Sachs, down to the present day, this ethnocentric and class-conscious bias has been anathema. Yet a uniform approach to their field embodying another highly restrictive value judgment, discarded long ago by historicomusicologists, has been adopted uncritically by most ethnomusicologists and has been a prime conditioning factor in what is collected, studied, and published qua ethnomusicology. Another single value, purity or authenticity, has taken the place of the "good" music of the historicomusicologists: between two items one of which shows changing features, the apparently unchanging has almost always been considered the proper ethnomusicological datum. Only too often the former has not even been considered worth recording; sometimes its very existence has been deplored. This is ethnocentrism in reverse—broader, it is true, and not biased in favor of "own" music, but still ethnocentrism in the sense that change seems usually to be induced by outside influences, that is, by acculturation, and is therefore "bad." Thus ethnomusicology has tended to be archaistic rather than realistic in its approach to its field. Stability has been weighted against change.

To the student of a music not his own, changed or changing traditions in it have seemed the lesser value. Certainly they are more difficult to study. But to their carriers, change usually constitutes a reaching for higher values, even though this may later prove mistaken or overdone. Survival, continuity, stability, variation, change, diversification, consolidation, revival, decay, and other such concepts must be employed with care to avoid bias toward one or another. They refer to aspects of the equally valid holistic concept of the propensity for music-making, the musicality, of man: a universal behavioral continuum that the student himself personifies, emergent in him from prehistory and persistent through him and his contemporaries into the unforeseeable future.

I am not depreciating the achievements of this century of historico-musicology and ethnomusicology. Salvage, preservation, and study of survivals is a task of prime importance for both disciplines. If we do not know the relatively stable, how shall we measure change? If we do not have a single concept *music*, how shall we decide what are and what are not musics? But without a concept of value, how shall we order among the musics of the world the multiplicity of value systems which they are? What is value, anyway, and a value system? Shall we regard criticism as the valuing of fact or the fact of valuing? And what is the relation of music value to other values and to value in general?

Such questions can be dealt with properly only by a critique with a method as comprehensive and as carefully thought out as that of science. Although both methods were well launched by the ancient Greeks, Christianity put a stop to cultivation of that of science and developed its own overmastering value-theory and supporting dialectic in whose terms were settled, supposedly for good, all the scientific and critical questions raised by the Greek philosophers. Scientists from Galileo on had to fight a bitter, three-century war for independence from ecclesiastical value theory. But although on the whole the churches eventually lost the war with science, they seem to have held criticism to something like a draw.

Unlike the scientists, the critics never fought a united war of independence. Some remained in the church and maintained the essentials of the religious value theory intact; some declared and won doctrinal independence but maintained the value theory in modified forms. Criticism in the arts seems on the one hand to have been exploited and on the other to have "bored from within," with the result that the early puritanism of Christian religious organizations gradually gave way to increased use of the arts as vehicles for support and expression of religious value. Critiques of the arts, at first entirely subordinate to ecclesiastic value theory, gradually emphasized artistic value until they became separate, independent genres. By the time of Galileo public art criticism, as in the Artusi-Monteverdi controversy, was politically possible because it seemed to have nothing to do with ecclesiastic value-theory. Ecclesiastic value theory was not regarded as value theory; it was the Word of God, or at least of church doctrine.

Thus by the early eighteenth century, when letters, art, and music became recognized as appanages of the prosperous middle classes instead of a small number of princes, ecclesiastics, and nobles, critical activity was firmly split into two domains, an ecclesiastic and a secular, whose separation some tried to reason away, bridge, or unify, to no avail. For the split, like a geological fault, produced innumerable ancillary splits—separate literary, art, and music criticism—among which there has been no substantial connection.

What the founders of Christianity seem to have realized is that the art of speech—at least in the languages of the Western world—depends for its operation, wherever there is even a modicum of rationality, upon a recurring alternation of analysis-synthesis, synthesis-analysis, in which analysis, a splitting technique, and synthesis, a technique of joining the split parts, effect an appearance of one-to-one correspondence between the verbal symbols of speech and the apprehensions of our senses and feelings. The utter fragmentation of this apparent correspondence in Greco-Roman sophistry and the cynicism of Roman imperialism presented in crisis form a need and a demand to control what amounted to runaway verbal inflation. Assumption of the single, unequivocal supremacy of the Word—an unanalyzable, unsynthesizable, eternal oneness of primitive and ultimate value, knowable only by faith but backed by sufficient (verbal) propaganda and physical power, economic, social and political—met both need and demand. It endured intact for well over a thousand years and still carries enormous weight throughout the world Fact was subordinate to value, at least in theory.

It is neither necessary nor appropriate for the present undertaking to trace in detail the nearly two-thousand-year history of this split in the value theory of the Western world. Suffice it to say that music has always been valued in its own terms, that is, intrinsic to its making, as well as in terms extrinsic, contextual, to it, and as incidental or exemplary in studies other than of music. Over the centuries, however, general value theories have laid bases upon which music has been valued in accord with them in their respective terms. I list eight of these, to which I shall add, at a later point, a ninth.

SPEECH VALUATION OF MUSIC IN EXTRINSIC TERMS

1. *Denial of the reality both of the problem of fact versus value and of its constituents through the practice of a discipline designed to transcend belief in them.* Fact and value, and so any relationship between them, are illusions. There is a problem in man's enslavement to illusions which can be solved by discipline. The Rigveda seems to have been the fountainhead of this adjustment. The discipline of yoga taught escape from illusion by experiential union, physiological, affective, and intellectual, with the Brahman or ineffable. The supreme illusion was belief in individuality. To become nothing or to be neither something nor nothing, became the supreme value; a paradox, of course, but in which within a universe of illusion, one could believe or disbelieve as one chose. Music seems to have been ignored in the basic texts, though it is likely that the texts were chanted.

2. *Denial of the reality of the problem but not of its constituents; and postulation of a reasoned integration of them in "correct" or "wise" conduct.* This adjustment would appear to be made in the name of "common sense." Confucius was the outstanding exponent of this middle-of-the-road approach. One finds oneself in a situation in which the fact of a social and political authority is so unquestionable that a practical value adjustment to it seems inevitable. Successful adjustment is possible and can be achieved as the supreme value. Music has an honored place.

3. *Postulation of a reasoned primacy of value.* Idealist philosophy from Plato on has relied upon this adjustment of the dilemma. Reason is employed to establish and give order to value, especially the highest value or values, with fact in a secondary place or even shunned, as by Plato, because the attempt to attach ideas to the infinite multitude of facts would be an endless and frustrating task. Socrates took refuge in ideas of the just, the beautiful, and the good, and let the rest go; thus, he viewed all things teleologically rather than causatively, that is, in terms of the ends, or as we would say, the values, they served.

4. *Assertion of an unreasoned primacy of value.* The Judaic-Hellenic-Christian epos seems to have been a syncretion of the Judaic passionate mysticism, Greek intellectualism, and the Roman genius for social-political organization. Of course there were other ingredients, notably Orphic and Mithraic traditions. Reason, though not employed to establish the primacy of value, was employed to support that primacy and to order the facts of life in accord with the policies of the institutions set up to control private, social, political, and economic affairs. The relative dependence upon unquestioned assertion of value reasoned support of the assertion varied enormously. In Islam, in words such as those of San

Juan de la Cruz and Santa Teresa, and in the writings of Nietzsche, the role of reason is more subordinate than in, for example, those of Saint Augustine and the long line of Christian apologists, philosophers, and reformers of an idealist cast since his time. In the presence of control by doctrinal law, music throve to whatever extent the right hand knew not or ignored what the left hand did.

5. *Postulation of a reasoned primacy of fact.* This adjustment was stated clearly in Francis Bacon's First Aphorism: "Man, being the servant and interpreter of nature, can do and understand so much and so much only as he has observed in fact or in thought of the course of nature: beyond this he neither knows anything or can do anyting." Other early scientists adhered to this view. Music was interesting especially for the number relations it exhibits, but variously for its form and content. Merz classed music as unmethodical thought.[1]

6. *Assertion of an unreasoned primacy of fact.* As Western science became more diversified and specialization, in many minds, took the place of the comprehensive synoptic view, the primacy of fact was often taken for granted or as self-evident. Value became so subordinated that it was defined and used in terms of special fields—moral, aesthetic, economic, psychologic, and so forth. Often as not it was retained only in a technical sense as, for example, in economics as the measure of use and exchange; in the visual arts as the name for a characteristic of color; and in music for the relative length of notes. The tendency, outside of art criticism, was to denigrate music, especially in England and America.

7. *Search for a bridge between the poles of the problem.* This adjustment was preeminently the goal of Immanuel Kant, who may be regarded as the founder, in his *Kritik der Urteilskraft,* of "modern" critical method. The aim was to reason away the dualism and substitute a monism. The argument, as it deals with music, runs: music is one of the proper objects of aesthetic contemplation because (a) it is "free" beauty (a flower is another example), that is, without intellectual content (meaning, presumably, speech-intellectual content), and because (b) it is only in free beauty that man can see a unity in fact and value.[2]

8. *Acceptance of the case as a dilemma.* A few writers have tried to see both sides of the problem, without trying to reconcile them. As Thomas Mann has written so eloquently:

> Music is a great mystery . . . by virtue of its sensual spiritual nature and the amazing union it achieves between strict rule and dream, good form and magic, reason and emotion, day and night, it is without a doubt the most profound, most fascinating, and, in the eyes of the philosopher, most disquieting phenomenon. . . . Music is a theology of number, an

austere, godlike art, but an art in which all demons are interested and which, of all the arts, is most susceptible to the demoniac. For it is both moral code and seduction, sobriety and drunkenness, a summons to the highest alertness and a lure to the sweetest sleep of enchantment, reason and anti-reason—in short, a mystery with all the initiation and educative rites which ever since Pythagoras have been part and parcel of every mystery; and the priests and masters of music are the initiates, the preceptors of that dual being, the divine-demoniac totality of the world, life, mankind and culture.

Any survey of the enormous number of complex arguments being upon value in general (i.e., extrinsic to music) must disclose such extremes as blanket condemnation or prohibition of music by the Apostle Paul, early Islam, and some later Protestant sects, and the opposite, unexceptionable approval of all music without words, and the extreme permissiveness of contemporary American life. Discrimination has varied from the severe reasoning of Plato and the vehement affective bias of Nietzsche to the statistics of the psychological laboratory and the polls of musical taste taken by public relations companies. The contradictions among the manifest invalidity for musicology of some of their assumptions (such as the Kantian, that music has intellectual content, "no perfection of any kind, no purposiveness"),[3] together with the persuasiveness of their presentation, make confusing reading for students of music, excepting possibly the last two, the second of which effectively denies the problem and poses a dilemma in its place. But before either can be recommended for musicological consideration they will need essential qualification. (See, later, a ninth way of handling the situation.)

Now one would think, would one not, that with this incessant concern with value, both general and critical philosophy—not to speak of the galaxy of special studies—would have organized a general critical method comparable in comprehensiveness and precision and acceptable to a consensus such as that with which the scientific method has been accepted. But this was not done. Kant had injected the problem of value into nineteenth-century thought in such emphatic terms that it became, however, an increasingly absorbing concern of every branch of learning. Pietistic handlings were made by theologians from Albrecht Ritschl to Rudolph Otto; materialistic by economists from Carl Menger to Thorstein Veblen. But it was not until nearly the end of the nineteenth century that the concept of a unified value theory was adumbrated. Perhaps it was in part Nietzsche's "transvaluation of all values" that shocked students in every field to an awareness of the chaos in a situation in which they were all equally involved.

Around 1900 a philosophy of value, since known as the "Austrian," came into being through the work of Franz Brentano, Alexius von Meinong,[4] and Christian von Ehrenfels.[5] Under the names "general value theory" or "general theory of value," the predominant emphasis was psychological, as the members of the Austrian group were primarily psychologists. But nearly every facet of philosophic and humanistic thought became involved: epistemology, metaphysics, ethics, aesthetics, logic, scientific methods, and so forth. George Santayana,[6] W. M. Urban,[7] Hugo Munsterberg,[8] John Dewey,[9] and R. B. Perry[10] were among the first in the United States to carry on the work of the Austrians. In the *Postscript* of his first substantial volume, Perry sums up his view, of which the following quotations give a fair notion:

> There are three accepted classifications of values . . . the trinity of canonized values, known as the "True, the Beautiful and the Good"; or the tetrad in which to these three there is added the higher unity of God. This classification employs two principles: a triadic psychology, which divides mind into thought, feeling and will; and an absolutist philosophy, which affirms that these three acts define a convergent goal of aspiration. The absolute or God, when thought is Truth, when felt is Beauty, and when willed is Goodness. . . .
>
> A second mode of classification is that which, assuming values to be functions of interest, divides them in accordance with the several modalities of interest or the different relations which objects may sustain thereto. . . .
>
> The third mode of classification is that which adopts the divisions already made among the several moral or social sciences. . . .

Perry finds the first "is objectionable on several grounds"; the second, because it "tends to be excessively detailed and schematic" is "easy to make and likely to prove barren when made." His last words commit him to the third alternative in his second volume:

> A fruitful theory of value will accept those stable and well-marked unities in which the values of life are already grouped. The great *foci* of interest are science, conscience, art, industry, state and church. Perhaps there is no absolute reason why this should be so, but there is no denying the fact that it is so. . . .

A crisis seems to have been reached in the attempt to set up value-theory as a semi-independent division of philosophy on a par with epistemology, ethics, metaphysics, aesthetics. H. O. Eaton hazarded the opinion that "a value which is neither economic, ethic, aesthetic, nor any other of the specific types of value seems unthinkable."[11] About the same time, H. Osborne wrote of "The deplorable *imbroglio* in which philosophy of value is entangled."[12] J. W. Smith surmised "perhaps we had better abandon the value program altogether."[13]

The historic procedure, of course, has been to include consideration of value in the body of the comprehensive philosophical inquiry. This has been supplanted by inclusion in the main body of later twentieth-century scientific inquiry by many writers, among whom we may mention C. I. Lewis,[14] M. R. Konwitz,[15] D. J. McCracken,[16] P. W. Taylor,[17] and S. C. Pepper.[18] Pepper states plainly that "The Basis of Criticism in the Arts must ultimately lie in a complete philosophy" and it would be hard to disagree with him.[19] He presents an analysis of the valuing process showing

> the need of considering the thing we call a work of art as a nest of objects . . . that . . . consists . . . of three closely interrelated objects: First, the physical vehicle; second, the object of perceptual immediacy . . . third . . . the object of criticism.

this last being made possible

> by the process of funding, through which earlier perceptions fuse their contents with later ones making possible an intuitive sense of a perceptual whole spreading over a wide period of discrete stimulation.[20]

A physical vehicle would be the acoustic sound of speech or music—the *sense stimulus*. An object of perceptual immediacy would be the sound as apprehended and perceived by a listener—the *sense datum*. This would vary extensively, but a norm of amateur or of professional competency could be conceived. An "object of criticism" would include, in the case of music, an assemblage of discrete apprehensions and perceptions of the object of perceptual immediacy, funded in a frame of contextual relevance in which many factors bearing different weights have become fused in a single unified understanding of the nest in its relation to the valuer and to the situation in which the valuer values it.

While the search for a general or unified theory of value has lagged, the handling of the value situation in terms of special focuses or realms of interest in accord with Perry's third classification has become, since about 1940, a prime concern of many psychologists, sociologists, anthropologists, and other students of the humanities. Cross-disciplinary conferences and published anthologies of papers attest to a vigorous new approach. In spite of many technical neologisms that make difficult reading, they have direct bearing upon musicology. A very readable survey is by Clyde Kluckhohn "Values and Value-Orientations."[21] It proposes a definition: "Value is a conception, explicit or implicit, distinctive of an individual or characteristic of a group, of the desirable which influences the selection from available modes, means and ends of action." It is emphasized "that affective (desirable), cognitive (conceptive), and conative (selective) elements are all essential to this notion of *value*." The "desirable" is pointedly distinguished from the "desired."

The student of music cannot but be impressed with the enormous advance made in the study of value both as a semi-independent general theory and as an essential part of philosophy during the first two-thirds of the twentieth century. Its bearing upon musicology should be obvious. But the extent of the literature, its complexity, the increasingly unfamiliar terminologies and, above all, the vast extension of its viewpoint beyond that of the musicologist seem to have discouraged his interest in it. It seems virtually unknown to American musicologists, or, in cases where it is, must be regarded as irrelevant; for it remains unused by them. Yet the concern of criticism, whether of music or anything else, is value, is it not? And just as in science there must be many particular scientific methods, there must be at the same time one overall theory within which they may be distinguished and related, so in criticism we must accept the probability that there will be many specialized critical methods but eventually, we may hope, one overall general theory within which these particular methods will be distinguished and related.

The early twentieth-century burst of enthusiasm for "a" general theory of value may simply have been premature. Until the specialized theories of the arts can catch up with those of economics, theology, sociology, philosophy, and the others, it may not be feasible. However this may be, in any other than a superficial approach to a critique of music it must be obvious that the history of the first effort to formulate a general theory of value must be required reading for musicologists. R. S. Hartman has made a brilliant attempt to fill the bill by a proposal to scientificize value theory completely, but he limits himself to effable value alone.[22]

There is a question whether fact and value are solely speech constructs, whether homologs or analogs of them are factors in any other forms of human behavior, or whether there are factors in all human behavior of which the constructs "fact" and "value" are merely the speech counterparts of matters of attention seen through the specialized colored glasses, as it were, of speech. Musicology could make little if any headway under the first alternative; for its acceptance would mean that music fact and music value would be no more than what speech might say they were, with complete disregard of what the musician might understand they are. In the final analysis, the second and third are reducible to a single more basic proposition that will be stated in the concluding paragraphs of this Essay.

In approaching the statement of such a proposition, however, one runs into widespread confusion of fact and facts with values and valuation and, so, with value. Valuation, or value judgment, consists in a two-way relating of items that compel or are given our attention to ourselves and to other human beings. Such relating, when attempted, as here in a speech undertaking, is a speech operation that is always done *in a situation or context* (1) of facts of many kinds—physical, physiological, social, cultural, philosophical, and other; (2) of values, also of many kinds—individual and social, aesthetic and moral, pleasure and displeasure, preference and avoidance, attraction and flight, hope, anger, and fear, and so forth; (3) of a valuer in the presence of other valuers. The situation or context is entered by compulsion, by appetite for a giving of attention, or, usually, both. Attention is the meeting place of factual stimulation and satisfaction of valual appetite and ongoing aspiration. With respect to attention, facts are caused and causative; values, creatable and created. A dead body can neither undergo stimulation of attention nor exhibit appetite for it. At the receiving end of its parameter of variance, attention is visual, aural, or tactile. (For convenience and economy, I include olfaction, gustation, and surface touch, both outer and inner, in the single term *tactility*). In the broadest sense of the word, all items in a context stimulating or sought by attention are communicatory in character, though in a narrower sense they are communicatory only when produced for or by other human beings. In both cases, they are usually easily identified as objectively observable. At the producing end, appetites, promptings of our innermost thinking and feeling, moral, aesthetic, religious aspirations, are equally communicatory but less objective, though quite as "real" or even more "real." Once made, a valuation—especially if it is recorded or witnessed—can be regarded as a fact, that is, the act, the statement, or the evidence of the valuation, not the value expressed in the act, statement, or evidence.

SPEECH VALUATION OF MUSIC IN INTRINSIC TERMS

Coming, then, to the question whether intrinsic or textual value can be distinguished in music through expression in (speech) literary form, it must be admitted that no such survey as I have hazarded of the literary expression of extrinsic values can be made. Agreement seems general that "musical criticism," as at present known, has tried to do this. In earlier days it was closely associated with literary criticism itself. To quote Saintsbury it has been an exercise of "that function of the judgment which busies itself with the goodness and badness, success and ill-success of [musical] literature [and its public performance] from a purely [music-] literary point of view"; which is to say it is "pretty much the same thing as the reasoned exercise of [musical] taste" expressed in words rather than music, by musicians and musical amateurs engaged in the concert life of the well-to-do bourgeosie of the Western world. It has been wholly "particular and actual."[23]

While we still await a history of this musical *Fachkritik* comparable to Saintsbury's compendious work, useful handbooks by Armand Machabey[24] and Max Graf[25] are readily available, as are articles on the subject in the standard dictionaries and encyclopaedias of music.[26]

I propose, therefore, a ninth way in which the dilemma of fact versus value may be adjusted for musicology.

9. *Acceptance of the problem of fact versus value as a dilemma of the linguocentric predicament inescapable in speech communication, but denial of it as a factor in music communication.* Must we conclude, then, that in terms of the speech description of music-fact and music-value further investigation of value by musicology is a fruitless task? I believe not. We must admit the limitations of speech and stay within them. And we may often arrive at results whose truth or untruth it may be difficult or impossible to demonstrate (in terms of speech). May it not be, simply, that the typical or normal act of producing music is at once both factual and valual? Surely, in all optimal cases the note Y is the "best" choice a composer or improviser can make in a situation. His best is not produced in a vacuum but in two related contexts: one, intrinsic to music, the tradition in which he operates, some of whose norms he has represented, others he has re-presented in modified ways; the other, the bundle of traditions or culture of which the music tradition is one. If a consensus comes into being among the effective judges of intrinsic value to the effect that this "best" has exceeded the norms of the tradition, has enriched its repertory, and has extended its capabilities, a work may take its place as a masterwork. If it merely meets the norms but does not seem to aid the growth of the tradition, it may still be valued as nourishing its vigor and serving its continuity. If it falls short of these requirements it may be forgotten or kept in storage as a datum for statistical studies, doctoral dissertations, or research for the maintenance of academic status.

But note: in all these cases, as well as in the many that fall between them, the producer himself has functioned as a judge of music value. Every act of composition, performance, and improvisation is a critical as well as a phenomenological act. *The prime critic of music is the producing musician.* For him the music-critical act can be entirely free of the speech-dilemma fact versus value. But to the extent that he talks about music or allows speech-thinking to intrude in or influence his music-thinking, to that extent he is in thrall to the verbal dilemma intrinsic versus extrinsic and must accept the linguocentric predicament in which he has placed himself by entering the musicological juncture.

Elsewhere I have dealt with the phenomenology of the juncture, music as fact. I restate it here in the same six-fold pattern with respect to the axiology of the juncture: music as value (1) in itself; (2) in terms other than itself.

1. The student himself, with the particular value inclinations his since birth and cultivated by him through training and experience.

2. The value inclinations, individual and collective, of persons with whom he has close contact as teachers and colleagues, and of those to whom he addresses his talking and/or writing about music.

3, 4, 5. The valual potentialities of two traditions and one subtradition of communication which he has inherited, cultivates, and transmits, respectively, a speech, a music, and a musicology.

6. The general value structure and value functions of the music-cultural continuum that he enters, lives in, and departs from.

NOTES

1. J. T. Merz, *A History of European Thought in the Nineteenth Century* (Edinburgh and London: W. Blackwood, 1896-1914).

2. Immanuel Kant, *Critique of Judgment,* trans. J. H. Bernard (New York: Hafner, 1951), sect. 16.

3. Ibid.

4. Alexius von Meinong, *Ueber Annahmen* (Leipzig: J. A. Barth, 1902).

5. Christian von Ehrenfels, *System der Werttheorie* (Leipzig: O. R. Reisland, 1897).

6. George Santayana, *The Sense of Beauty* (New York: Charles Scribner's, 1896-1936).

7. W. M. Urban, *Valuation: Its Nature and Laws* (London: S. Sonnenschein and New York: Macmillan, 1909); idem, "Value, Theory of," *Encyclopaedia Britannica* (Chicago, 1946).

8. Hugo Munsterberg, *The Eternal Values* (New York, 1909).

9. John Dewey, "Theory of Valuation," *International Encyclopedia of Unified Science,* Vol. II, pt. 4 (Chicago, 1939).

10. R. B. Perry, *General Theory of Value* (Cambridge: Harvard University Press, 1926); idem, *Realms of Value* (Cambridge: Harvard University Press, 1954).

11. H. O. Eaton, *The Austrian Philosophy of Values* (Norman: University of Oklahoma Press, 1930).

12. H. Osborne, *Foundations of the Philosophy of Value* (London and Cambridge: The University Press, 1933), p. 1.

13. J. W. Smith, "Should General Theory of Value Be Abandoned?" *International Journal of Ethics,* LVII, 4 (July 1947), 274-288.

14. C. I. Lewis, *An Analysis of Knowledge and Valuation* (La Salle, Ill.: Open Court, 1946).

15. M. R. Konvitz, *On the Nature of Value: Philosophy of Samuel Alexander* (New York: King's Crown Press, 1946).

16. D. J. McCracken, *Thinking and Valuing* (London: Macmillan, 1950).

17. P. W. Taylor, *Normative Discourse* (Englewood Cliffs, N.J.: Prentice-Hall, 1961).

18. S. C. Pepper, *The Work of Art* (Bloomington: Indiana University Press, 1955).

19. Pepper, "Some Comments on Professor Kahn's Paper," *Journal of Aesthetics,* IX, 1 (Sept. 1950), 51.

20. Pepper, *The Work of Art,* pp. 30 ff.

21. Clyde Kluckhohn, "Values and Value-Orientations in the Theory of Action," in *Toward a General Theory of Action,* ed. Talcott Parsons and Edward A. Shils (Cambridge: Harvard University Press, 1962).

22. R. S. Hartman, *The Structure of Value* (Carbondale: Southern Illinois University Press, 1967). (See especially pp. 307-313 and bibliographical references.)

23. George Saintsbury, *A History of Criticism* (Edinburgh and London: W. Blackwood, 1948), 1:3-4.

24. Armand Machabey, *Traité de la critique musicale* (Paris: Richard-Masse, 1947).

25. Max Graf, *Composer and Critic* (New York: W. W. Norton, 1946).

26. H. H. Stuckenschmidt, "Musikkritik," *Musik in Geschichte und Gegenwart* (Kassel: Bärenreiter Verlag, 1961), 9:1130-1147; Winton Dean, "Criticism," *Grove's Dictionary of Music and Musicians,* 5th ed. (New York: St. Martin's Press, 1955), 2:529.

27. Charles Seeger, "On the Moods of a Music Logic," *Journal of the American Musicological Society,* XIII (1960), 224-261.

28. E. M. Forster, "The Raison de Etre of Criticism in the Arts," in R. F. French, *Music and Criticism: A Symposium* (Cambridge: Harvard University Press, 1948), p. 30 passim.

V
On the Moods of a Music Logic[57]

Throughout the history of the Western world we can trace persistent search for a rationale of its music. This has been sought as well in the inner organization of its compositional process as in the outer organization in the communities that have cultivated it and even in that of the cosmos, of which music has sometimes been conceived to be a model or reflection.

In the musicology of the West the inner order of its music, its form, has been most often conceived as design, a term borrowed from the speech treatment of visual art, less often as logic, a term designating a factor in the speech treatment of speech itself.

The concept of design brings out the structural and spacial aspects of order in music. It seems to be more the tool of the student of the already produced product than of the producer of it and more successful in treating the sound than the movement of music. Customarily, its point of departure is the whole of a music cursus which it divides by a technique of analysis into movements, sections, parts of sections, periods, phrases, half-phrases, measures, motifs, and individual notes. The farther this process of analysis is carried into the music microcosm, the weaker it becomes. If not by the time the level of the section is reached, surely soon after this, it becomes a mere catalog of fact, not an accounting for fact.

The concept of logic, however, brings out the functional and temporal aspects of music order. It seems to be more the tool of the producer of music than of the student of the product. Its point of departure is the smallest unit of form and views the compositional process as one of synthesis. Thus, it parallels the production and reception of a cursus, from the minimal initial unit or mood of music-logical form, into the measure, the part of a phrase, the phrase, the double-phrase, period, double period, part of a section, section, all the way to the product as a whole. Here again, at the level of the section, the point has been reached where synthesis seems to be a prescription in speech that is belied by the music process supposed to fill it out.

Clearly, a gap exists between any effective analysis as design and any affective synthesis as logic.

To the musicologist the two concepts should seem equally valid. Both require identification of units of form: design, in an order from large to small; logic, from small to large. What the concepts refer to surely is, in the hands of the competent musician not too dominated by speech-thinking, equally one single collection of maximal units divisible into medial and medial into minimal, and of minimal units combinable into medial and medial into maximal.

Once the maximal unit has been established for design, as for example, a symphony in four movements, or the minimal, for logic, its initial measures or so, a vast number of possibilities of intension and extension present themselves. The degree of uncertainty in a comparatively stabilized idiom, cultivated within a small, homogeneous society with few or no acculturative impacts is naturally less than in a rapidly changing idiom cultivated in a highly diversified society and across political boundaries. For example, in Turkey Creek, North Carolina, around 1900, the predictability of the successor to the melodic pattern or mood delivering "In scarlet town" (which continues "where I was born") was undoubtedly higher than that of the second measure of Brahms's Symphony no. 2. But even in this latter case, there are limitations: the probability of the fortissimo sounding of a solo gong, or the second or third movements being in D major, triple meter, and allegro non troppo, could be confidently stated as zero.

With the intension of analysis as design and the extension of synthesis as logic into the body of a product, the degree of uncertainty increases, that is, the uncertainty in the speech report of the progress of the two speech concepts. We cannot assume that the separate functioning of the two concepts in a speech rationale of music is the same as the integration of the two—or whatever must be the music process so referred to—in the actual operation of a music rationale. To the best of present knowledge, no documentation of the music compositional process has been made. Beethoven's sketchbooks provide a vague clue. The rules of, and classroom work in, harmony and counterpoint are more specific; but these are framed within such artificial limits and are so heavily encased in verbal forms that their acceptance as even prototypes of a traditional process outside the classroom is questionable. Indeed, their impact upon the strong creative urge of early youth may account for the rather large amount of adult composition which seems controlled less by musical considerations than by speech concepts of what music should or should not be.

The present undertaking proposes, therefore, that the units of music design and music logic can be regarded as identical, and that they can be presented in a speech rationale as a single, partly closed system, equally of patterns of design and moods of logic. Ideally, a completely new terminology should be invented for the presentation of such a system. But mindful of the resentment that often greets such innovations, I shall concentrate upon its treatment as a logic, using a minimal vocabulary of terms borrowed from speech logic. This is done for three reasons. First, although the concept of design has been conventionally the more exploited in connection with the study of musical form, the general concept of logic has been given in recent years far more comprehensive and precise general theoretical development. And, a logic is a pre-requisite to an overall rationale. Second, the term *design* has been used more for pedagogical purposes, especially in inexpertly verbalized courses in "music appreciation." Third, the term *logic,* in referring to the compositional processes of both speech and music, implies an approach in the order in which products are actually presented to a receiver and, so, received by him, that is, from a beginning, through a cursus to an end.

THE SPEECH-CONCEPT OF A MUSIC-LOGIC

If we use the term *logic* to designate the musical device that results in or characterizes the inner order of music as known to its makers, this must be in a sense consistent with its use in designating the speech device that results in or characterizes the inner order of speech as known to *its* makers. We must distinguish what, if any, procedures of a music logic show homology, analogy, and heterology to them. And we must always bear in mind that the presentation of the results of our observations and reflections will be in terms of speech, not of music.

There is a double hazard here. The first is epistemological, semantic, and terminological. As we have seen, musical counterparts of some concepts essential to speech logic are easily found and customarily widely used, such as: knowledge, thought, reason, order, meaning, form. Divergence in their understanding, controversy arising from it, and dependence of these concepts (in speech) upon others for which counterparts (in music) are not usually sought, such as quantity (in the sense of universal and particular), quality (affirmation and negation), truth and untruth, are confusing factors.

The second hazard is methodological. The musicological juncture, in which traditions of speech and music meet to form the subtradition of musicology, poses a unique philosophical situation: the report upon one technique of communication in terms of another. Music is reported upon by speech, but speech is not reported upon by music. In this one-sided relationship, there is, thus, no direct check upon the former. Music can be studied as a datum in the physical universe by the extramusical or nonmusical sciences, but this yields the nonmusician's speech knowledge about music and can only serve as a partial check upon the speech report about the musician's knowledge of music. This can, of course, be submitted to the consensus of musicians above-mentioned. But when musicians attempt to understand or deal with it they have to use speech. And despite the nearly unanimous consensus of musicians in the making of music, as soon as they begin to talk about it the consensus might as well not exist. They react variously, as do nonmusicians, from one of the three positions cited above. What is talked about tends to take on the characteristics of the technique of talking.

I hope I have shown that there is no perfect escape from this linguocentric predicament. We enter it voluntarily, but only too often forget it involuntarily. If we stay in it, the best we can do is to temper it by exploring each one of the horns or alternatives of its dilemmas and then to state clearly the nature of the best adjustment among them that we can devise.

I can find units of music-logical form in the simple, but not in the compound, functions. These can be employed in all four branches of the technique, namely: (1) the single melody or sonal line; (2) successive combinations of such lines; (3) simultaneous combinations of lines; and (4) successive combinations of simultaneous combinations of lines. It is to this last category that most of the productions in the Occidental fine art of music belong. But even a single, unaccompanied melody or melodic line exhibits a multilinear music-logical organization in that one or more units of form or moods can be presented both simultaneously and in succession in different extensions. Thus, in example 1, a single mood

EXAMPLE 1

of the torculus-porrectus type ($\wedge\!\vee$) in minimal (motival) extension and in medial (phrasal) extension provide a twofold music-logical process in the blues "When I was single" and a threefold, in the first sixteen measures of the violoncello and bass parts of Brahms's Symphony no. 2.

Octave transformation is indicated by dotted lines. The unit $\wedge$ and its contrary $\vee$ may be regarded as fragmentary with respect to $\vee\!\wedge$ and $\wedge\!\vee$.)

Considered together with the first horn part, we have in the Brahms excerpt a sixfold process, presenting the same unit in variance both of direction and extent of progression.

EXAMPLE 2

Considered together with the first flute and first clarinet parts, which fill in the silences in those of the horns, the same torculus-porrectus type of unit is presented in the form of pitch levels in medial extension (see ex. 3). In the first four tone beats, these instruments present the second (a climacus-scandicus type) of the two moods upon which the essential stuff and logical process of the whole work is built.

EXAMPLE 3

A speech logic, in contrast, presents, in the actual succession of its terms, propositions and the more extended processes of development, a single, unilinear (or, from a musical point of view, monophonic) cursus. It does so, however, sub specie a vast traditional accumulation of speech-logical constructions, relations, and inference, which serves as a counterpart of the internal order and repertory of a music tradition. This accumulation seems to have such integrity, independence, and grandeur that it has fully earned the title "universe of discourse." It is not a universe of sounds. It has been built by sounds that name things (the "named") and can be learned only through sounds. It is a universe of speech-named things divorced from any particular sound and easily believed to have an existence entirely apart from all sound. So convincing can this belief be that poetry, oratory, and mystical contemplation can make out of it a veritable polyphony of ideation. But the aim of logic is to be employable in a single-line cursus.

Correspondence between this universe of discourse and the physical, phenomenal, external universe that is known through the other senses as well as through that of sound, is a main preoccupation of all (speech) philosophies, both scientific and critical. Strangely enough, musicology has not posed a universe of musical discourse. Why it has not is hard to explain, for the lack of it means that when music is spoken of it can be envisaged only as located in one or another of the several speech universes, but not in its own. And since only the most rigorously disciplined mind can keep even two speech universes reasonably well separated, music often becomes thought of as an empirical datum in the one or an immaterial, gossamerlike unreality in the other; or, more commonly, as some confusion of the two. So the musician is told "what music is." Sad to say, he only too often believes what he is told, for he is rarely skilled enough in the use of speech to realize that it is speech logic alone that is responsible for the confusion. Thus, if the confusion is to be clarified, musicology should take a fresh view of speech logic.

SPEECH LOGICS AND MUSIC LOGIC

The classic, textbook, Aristotelian logic that still serves in everyday life and in most musicological literature is mainly a technique that deals with structural concepts arranged according to canons of procedure solipsistically known as "laws of thought," the assumption being that there is no thought but speech thought. These laws of thought should perhaps be restated here, since not all musicologists have kept them in mind from their university days. They are three: (1) of identity—what is, is; (2) of contradiction—nothing can both be and not be; and (3) of the excluded middle—everything must either be or not be.

As far as I know, no musical counterparts, comparable laws of musical thought, or canons of music-logical procedure, have been proposed. I would say that only the first, *identity*, has any relevance to the music process itself and, then, restated as "what can be shown to be can be said to be."

For the law of contradiction, I would substitute a law of seriation. Of no product in the Occidental music can it be said that it contradicts itself, another music product, or anything at all. By the term *seriation* I designate a technique by which any unit of music-logical form can be transformed into any other by traditional norms of procedure. Potentially, the resources or functions of the technique exist in the tradition, that is, in the consensus of living carriers, as a single, unbroken series. Take, for example, two conveniently short units such as the initial measures of Schubert's well-known Symphony in C Major and the scherzando transformation of those of Strauss's "Till Eulenspiegels lustige Streiche." Presented in immediate succession, they apear to be two very different and unrelated entities, and can be so treated. Connected, as in example 5, it is obvious that they belong to one single

EXAMPLE 4

series—the single series to which all music motifs belong. A cursus in

EXAMPLE 5

which a number of units of such or even less diversity occur in succession without the traditional music-logical connection that would relate them would not be held to be highly organized from a music-logical viewpoint.

For the third law, that of the excluded middle, I would substitute a law of *compensation*. The typical product of Occidental music consists of some factors that must show a high degree of variance, while others may show a very low degree of variance or none at all. Pitch and proportion are of the first type, tempo and dynamics of the second. In the well-organized cursus, variance of one kind is compensated for by a compensatory variance. This process tends to establish a center or axis about which the two kinds of variance take place and with reference to which this may be organized. Movement toward this center or axis may be designated *centric;* away from it, *decentric.* Once we distinguish the concepts of the six functions, their relevance to the sonal-temporal materials of speech and music, and their variance and invariance, the next most important pair of concepts is that of centricity and decentricity. In their terms we can trace the selection and molding of raw materials through generations of traditional communication into the manipulated materials of a highly elaborated and diversified art. It may not be an exaggeration to say that centricity-decentricity is one of the principal governors of the compensation of variance and invariance.

The traditional speech-logical device in which the laws of thought find application is the syllogism. In its simplest form, this is a cursus of three sentences, superficially not unlike the three-phrase blues shown in example 1. For example, the famous textbook syllogism "Socrates is a man. All men are mortal, etc." is presented in English in almost exactly the same number of phonemes (40) as the musemes of the blues (36). But here the resemblance ceases. The three sentences (propositions) must comprise three words that are names (terms) joined by three verbs in such a manner that each term occurs twice in the three propositions. Thus, the terms a, b, and c, are shown variously in the relationship $a = b$, $b = c$, $a = c$, according to certain rules that need not be detailed here, the objective being to effect a conclusion that is either true or false. Propositions are classified in terms of quantity and quality as

universal	affirmative	(*A*ffirmo)	A
	negative	(n*E*go)	E
particular	affirmative	(aff*I*rmo)	I
	negative	(neg*O*)	O

There are 64 (4x4x4) conceivable moods, that is, ways of combining these four kinds of proposition in the syllogism. According to Jevons, 53 of them break the rules, leaving only 11 that can be considered "good forms of reasoning."[1] Other authorities accept various totals. As some will remember, a charming bit of academic folklore "B*a*rb*a*r*a*, C*e*l*a*r*e*nt,

Darii, F*erioque prioris, etc.*" seems to allow 19, but by excluding repetition, 12. Thus, the truth or untruth of the conclusion depends upon (1) consistency with the premises (the first two propositions) and (2) correspondence with empirical observation. Because of the importance of this second factor, the classic logic can be regarded as an applied logic. There are 64 basic quaternary moods in the present music logic; all are equaly valid (see table 6).

It might be expected that a speech logic differing so profoundly from the music process might give varied and irreconcilable accounts of it. That it does, and the fact that opposite speech rationales of music produce contradictory music logics is attested to by such controversies as whether musical scales are based upon the harmonic series and whether music can communicate any content other than itself. It seems strange that such problems are still regarded not as the speech problems they are but as music problems, which they certainly are not, considering the remarkable progress in the development of speech logic since Pascal's adumbration of a logic of probability and especially since Boole's open challenge of the supremacy of the Aristotelian logic in 1854.[2]

Boole's "pure" logic was not proposed to supplant the resources of the classic logic, but rather to extend and show them in their proper perspective, and to provide a "more perfect theory of deductive reasoning."[3] The classic logic provides "no satisfactory theory of relation,"[4] or of the factor of probability. Boole accepted the laws of thought and the syllogism only as "formal laws of judgment whose real office is to determine the forms of necessary propositions." They cannot, he believed, be regarded as "ultimate laws of all thought" because they cannot be regarded as "principles of reasoning."[5]

From this initiative, two separate operational logics have been developed.[6] One, the algebra of logic, involves expression of speech logic by algebraic symbols, a largely untraditional speech; the other, logistic, involves expression of the basic assumptions of mathematics by traditional speech. Both, apparently, are still in an exploratory stage of elaboration. According to Bertrand Russell, they run from Boole through the work of Peano, Cantor, Weierstrass, Peirce, and others to Whitehead and Russell himself.[7] Suzanne Langer looks forward to integration of the two in a single, unified symbolic logic.[8] All seem to be concerned mainly with general and abstract, that is, purely endosemantic, concepts such as classes, sets, series, relatives, and so forth, viewed as functional rather than structural factors, entirely free of reference to the empirical universe. Thus, a pure logical process may be logically true but empirically false. Its truth lies solely in consistency with its premises. The universe of speech discourse posed by such logics would in this respect seem to be homologous to a universe of musical discourse as envisaged here. Both would be endosemantic, although presumably ectosemantic application might be found in another system of communication so like yet so different from speech.

If I am correct in my understanding of the nature of these new speech logics, they are much better suited to formulation and presentation of a speech rationale of music, especially of a music logic, than is the classic logic. It is possible, however, that until the two branches are integrated, as Langer hopes, we might find ourselves in a worse situation than we are at present if we were to depend upon one of them to the other's exclusion. Their very precision might tempt us to trust them more than any speech technique based upon only one term of a dichotomy should be trusted.

This caution is to be taken the more seriously in view of the recent development of communications theory. Whatever passes from a producer of music to a receiver is surely a communication. The highly successful implementation of general communications theory by symbolic logics plus the fact that it is only too easy to forget that all speech logics, symbolic or nonsymbolic are speech techniques, might still further consolidate the assumption that music communication is only a variety of speech communication and, so, subject music to even more control by the "dictatorship of the linguistic" than it suffers from at present. For example, speech-communication theory is being developed at the moment with special attention to what is known as "information." What is sought under this designation is what is unknown, that is, new knowledge, alone. Such techniques might prove valuable in experimental composition, since much of it seems to be motivated by speech concepts. But the vast body of music-making is closer to the main stem of the tradition, in which continuity through *re*-presentation of the old and known is at least as important a factor as variation of it by presentation of the new.

COMPOSITIONAL FUNCTIONS—DIRECTION AND EXTENT OF VARIANCE

In presenting the units of music design qua moods of a logic in a unified, partially closed system, I shall not describe them in terms of universal and particular, for they are both; nor in terms of affirmation and negation, for they are neither; but in terms of the variance and invariance of progression of the four simple functions or resources of the compositional process, without whose full participation a sound signal is not a music signal and therefore not a music message, that is, music. The criteria of truth and untruth, so essential to the classic, applied speech logic, will find no place in this sytem, nor in the system of their combination in the music compositional process. Development from initial melodic materials, so characteristic of the works to which the ascription "music logical" may properly be made, certainly resembles the consistency with premises in the operational logics. A music logic would thus appear to be a pure logic. And it seems an unnecessary complication of our vocabulary to designate any factor in such a logic as truth or untruth.

Variance of the simple functions may be plotted in terms of *direction* and *extent* of progression.

Variance of direction. The parameters of the four simple functions permit variance of progression in only one direction or its opposite. A single formula can thus express variance of direction by any or all of the four. Pitch may rise, dynamics become louder, tempo faster, proportion increasingly divided (contracted). I shall refer to this direction of variance as *tension* and shall indicate it by the sign plus (+). Pitch may fall, dynamics may become softer, tempo slower, proportion less divided. I shall refer to this direction of variance as *detension* and shall indicate it by the sign minus (−). Invariance, that is, maintenance of a given pitch, dynamics, tempo, or proportion, will be referred to as *tonicity* and will be indicated by the sign equal (=). Choice of these terms seems justified by two classes of evidence: first, to produce higher pitches and louder sounds, strings and membranes are submitted to greater tension; second, increase in pitch, loudness, tempo, and divisions usually requires more muscular and other psychosomatic tension. The reverse holds for decrease of these functions. In most short "pieces," tonicity characterizes a single level of loudness and tempo functions. It can be effected in the pitch function over and above, intermittently or throughout its variance by the implications of the hierarchic organization of mode. Similarly, tonicity can be effected in proportion through the rhythmic modality implicit in metrical organization.

Variance of extent. Variance of pitch and proportion is articulated, that is, used, in measured quantities or degrees. That of pitch is the more precisely measured. The relationships among its degrees and their relationship to a traditionally or conveniently fixed point within the parameter are embodied in norms of the tradition. The measured quantities or degrees ("note values") in the parameter of proportion are precisely measured in their relations to one another, in a particular context; but there is no traditional, fixed point of reference in the para-eter, but only in a particular notational schema. Variance of dynamics and tempo, however, are not articulated but staggered; and at that, only roughly. The stages *ff, f, mf, mp, p, pp,* and so on, are about as vague as the superscriptions largo, adagio, lento, andante, moderato, allegretto, allegro, presto. The sliding scale of the metronome provides very accurate prescription and description of tempo; but the relationship of metronomic beat in general time and music beat in music time is not clear. There is a question whether a sense of "absolute" time exists among us comparable to the sense of "absolute" pitch.

In most measured music, however, a tempo is set by the speed of beat adopted at the inception of a performance. This may give it a point of reference, axis, or centricity for that cursus as a whole that can, especially in tempo giusto, serve as a rhythmic tonicity quite as firm as the pitch tonicity commonly recognized in the concept of tonality. But this has no generality and is valid only for a particular performance. To best of present knowledge, the limits within which the tempo of any particular composition may be varied have never been defined. The limits of pitch variance are most closely defined; but those of dynamics are wide open. (A counterpart of the metronome for prescription and description of dynamics in decibles could easily be devised, and might serve as an aid to our rather unstabilized discrimination of dynamic levels.)

The compound functions of tonal density (timbre or tone quality) and rhythmic density are not used in Occidental music in any measured way. The parameter of tonal density is without any articulation or fixed point of reference whatever; even its limits are undefined. No units of form are discernible. (Modern technology could provide electronic aids that might enable us to locate points of reference and rough classes of tone quality.) Rhythmic density presents an even more difficult problem. While the three tonal functions are easily separated, the three rhythmic functions are not.

COMPOSITIONAL FUNCTIONS IN MINIMAL EXTENSION

A unit of music-logical form can be conceived as being comprised by one single component. In minimal extension, this would be a single tone beat. It can exhibit the tonal functions pitch, dynamics, and tone quality, but neither their variance nor invariance as a progression. It can exhibit no rhythmic function whatever other than mere occurrence. In a cursus it can be used in an organized way in a context where there is variance and/or invariance of all six functions (1) as a factor in incremental and decremental transformation of a unit of sufficient components, (2) in phraseological diversification, (3) as pedal point or drone, and (4) as an *idée fixe.* Such a unit could function as a music-logical form only by contingency and should be regarded as *protomorphic* in character.

A unit of music-logical form can be conceived as comprised by two components. In minimal extension these would be two tone beats. A single tonal-rhythmic progression would be formed, showing variance or invariance of pitch and dynamics. A single duration would be established for tempo and proportion, but neither their variance nor invariance could be shown. Like the unit of one component, but to a lesser extent, the unit of two components could function as a musicological form only by contingency, but could be regarded as unary or *mesomorphic* in character.

A unit of three components—three tone beats—can constitute two progressions and meet the requirements for a complete, independent unit of music-logical form or mood in both direction and extension. Both variance and invariance can be exhibited in each of the four simple functions. It can be regarded as binary and *holomorphic*—a music morpheme or musems. Together with the protomorphic and meso-morphic units, it can account for the detail of the compositional process of some fairly extended construction. By identity of initial and final tone beats, a rudimentary tonal centricity can be established. By the falling of both initial and final upon a down beat, a rudimentary rhythmic centricity can be established.

If to this three-tone beat, two-progression tonal-rhythmic unit we add a fourth tone-beat unit, yielding a three-progression, ternary morpheme or museme, we shall have at our disposal, I believe, a set of basic patterns of musical design or moods of music logic sufficient for most purposes of synthesis in composition and of analysis in study of the occidental music. By the falling of both initial and final components upon a down beat a wide variety of meters can be established. Moods of five or more components (four or more progressions) can usually be considered compounds of two and three progression units, but occasionally can be formulated to advantage as separate units (see XII, below).

The dual reference to these units, as on the one hand comprised by components (tone beats) and on the other by relations (progressions), is admittedly cumbersome. It is, I fear, the irremediable disadvantage of the only kind of speech presentation that the consensus to which the present undertaking is addressed can accept and the only kind I can make. It is a compound, not an integration, of a logistic (a description of a music process in traditional speech) and an algebra (a description in symbols and graphs). Thus, what may be a single, unified system in the hands of the musician must be dealt with in the technique peculiar to the art of speech separately, in two sets of terms. For speech must first analyze what it deals with as a many before it can synthesize it as a one or vice versa. To suppose that the one or many synthesized corresponds either exactly or in no manner at all to the many or one analyzed is, as I previously pointed out, both naïve and unreasonable. Such procedure must be borne in mind as a condition of the musicological juncture which one must either accept or reject. Obviously, it is accepted here.

COMPOSITIONAL FUNCTIONS IN MEDIAL AND MAXIMAL EXTENSIONS

Conception of compositional functions in these three classes of form or mood (protomorphic, mesomorphic, and holomorphic) in minimal extension implies their employment in variance and invariance in medial and maximal extension. Upon these higher levels of construction, an extended cursus may be viewed in many different aspects, such as key, mode (both tonal and rhythmic), tonality, tessitura, dynamic level, tempo pattern, and so forth. If only one mode, key or meter, and so forth is used, the medial and maximal mood will be, in these respects, protomorphic. On some instruments, such as the clavichord and spinet, the dynamic level of hundreds of pieces may be invariant and the loudness mood protomorphic throughout. The same may be true of the tonal mode of many pieces, especially for childrens, but many folk songs are bimodal and thus, in that respect, mesomorphic.

Exposition of a basic set of binary and ternary music-logical moods, which will serve a music logic in a manner analogous to that in which the syllogism has served speech logic, will be made here in minimal extension only. Its development in medial and maximal extension may be remarked on from time to time, but should be treated more at length in a separate paper. The exposition will be divided into twelve steps. Steps I to III will deal with variance of the four simple functions in *direction* of progression, and Steps IV to XII, with variance in *extent* of progression. It is hoped that after the necessary research has been completed, the two compound functions, tonal and rhythmic density—since they are defined in terms, respectively, of the two pairs of simple functions—will fit into the pattern here outlined.

The word *mood*, as used here, has two well-established meanings. On the one hand, it designates the form of the syllogism, in which connection it might have been replaced by its cognate *mode*, except that the latter has perhaps too many meanings in musicology already. For this reason, too, it has seemed better to borrow the former for musicological use. On the other hand, the word *mood* denotes a more or less stable affective state, departures from which we call *emotions,* that is, "moving out of or away from" a mood or another emotion; a process rather than a state. The difference between one person using a speech-logic mood and another using a music-logic mood is that the former optimally maintains an invariant tonicity of affective mood, never submitting to an emotion, while the latter is free to—indeed, must, if he is at his best, musically— feel in one-to-one correspondence not only with the intellective but also with the affective variance-invariance of the music message he is producing or receiving.

FORMATION OF THE BASIC (MINIMAL) BINARY AND TERNARY MOODS BY VARIANCE OF DIRECTION AND/OR EXTENT OF THEIR CONSTITUENT PROGRESSIONS

I. *The sequence, enchainment or stream of progressions.*
   A. Let δ indicate the direction of a progression by any simple function and o, an opposite direction.
   B. If δ is a direction of tension, then o will be one of detension; similarly, if δ is a direction of detension, the o will be one of tension.
   C. Then, δδ and oo will indicate the possible binary orders and δδδ, δδo, δoo, and δoδ, the possible ternary orders of variance in direction of the basic (minimal) moods of compositional form.
   D. Each order of variance will, therefore, yield two moods, according to whether the initial progression is tense or detense. In either case they will bear to each other the relationships of *recte, contrarie, retro,* and *retrocontrarie.*
   E. Invariance of direction will be dealt with below, here and there, as modification of the patterns of variance.

II. *The mood as a Gestalt: its tensity, tonicity, and detensity.*
   A. Moods tend to be characterized by the sum of the tensions and detensions of the progressions that constitute them, as tense, tonic, and detense.
   B. Thus, in table_1, moods *A* and *C* must be tense; *a* and *c,* detense. The rest may be tense, detense, or tonic according to the extent of direction represented by the sum of the tensions and detensions of the separate progressions.

EXAMPLE 6

Binary

tense		detense
+ +	δ δ	– –
+ –	δ o	– +

Ternary

+ + +	δ δ δ	– – –
+ + –	δ δ o	– – +
+ – –	δ o o	– + +
+ – +	δ o δ	– + –

III. *Centricity and decentricity of the mood.*

    A. If the initial and final components show the same pitch, loudness, place on the down beat, or relative duration, the mood will be regarded as having primary centricity (=) with respect to the function concerned.

    B. If the initial-medial or medial-final components show any of these identities, the mood will be regarded as having secondary centricity with respect to the function concerned.

    C. The more identities of functions in this respect, the more centric may the mood as a whole be said to be.

    D. If the variance of a function shows a tense progression between initial and final, the mood will be said to have plus decentricity (+); if detense, minus decentricity with respect to the function concerned (–). Secondary decentricity may be ascribed in the same manner.

        Comment. The four functions may all vary in the same direction, or each may show variance or invariance inpendently (see VI). A centricity-decentricity factor in larger extension may outweigh one in smaller.

INFLECTION OF THE TWELVE BASIC BINARY AND TERNARY MOODS BY VARIANCE IN DIRECTION OF TONAL PROGRESSION AND IN EXTENT IN RHYTHMIC PROGRESSION

IV. *Graphic representation of the twelve basic moods in minimal tonal extension.*

    A. Table 1 shows a schematic representation of the twelve basic moods of example 6 with minimal extension of direction of tonal progression, with centricity where possible.

TABLE 1

Twelve Basic Moods in Terms of the Simple Tonal Functions

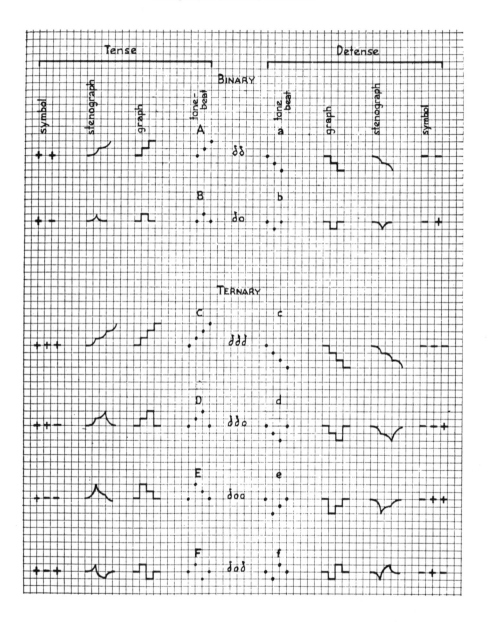

Comment. The transformation of the sixfold formula of step I into twelve moods of step II results in a complete self-contained set in which all recte, contrarie, retro, and retrocontrarie transformations are included. Those designated by the same letter, upper and lower case, are one another's contraries. *A* and *a*, *C* and *c*, *F* and *f*, are also one another's crabs and their own contrary crabs. *B* and *b* are their own crabs and each other's contrary crabs. *D* and *D*, *d* and *e*, are one another's crabs. *D* and *e*, *d* and *E* are one another's contrary crabs. Comparison of this dozen with the average dozen moods of the syllogism accepted as valid is interesting; but its significance, if any, has escaped my notice.

B. Example 7 shows a notational equivalent of table 1 in the function of dynamics alone, in terms of progressions and levels.

EXAMPLE 7

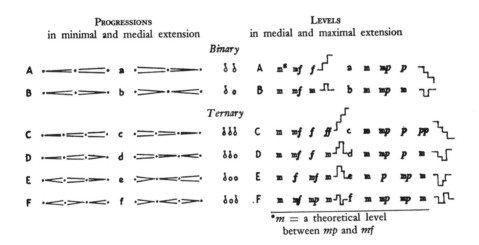

PROGRESSIONS
in minimal and medial extension

LEVELS
in medial and maximal extension

*m = a theoretical level between mp and mf

Comment. The negligible development of dynamics as a music-logical factor by Occidental music should not deter us from seeing the compositional possibilities of such use. The patterns in example 7 are familiar enough in minimal and medial extension.

Short symphonic movements often show clear-cut dynamic mood in maximal extension, as for example do many of Haydn's Menuettos, the type represented in table 1 as *b*.

V. *Graphic representation of the six basic moods and their contraries in minimal rhythmic extension.*

It may be well to repeat that the three rhythmic functions are not as easily abstracted from one another as are the three tonal functions. The understanding of their nature has always been complicated by two factors: first, intrusion of the classical theory of (speech) versification, in which the foot was organized in terms of quantity or relative duration of long and short syllables, as opposed to the later development of organization in terms of quality or stress; second, confusion of tempo beat and accent.

There is a discrepancy between general and musical spacetimes. In general space, we can move in any direction at will; but in general time, in only one, which we usually designate "forward." The musical sound signal, of course, is an event in general spacetime. But it is also an event in music timespace. We move in music space very much as we do in general space. But by the establishment of a particular tempo and its periodic pulse or step, we move in music time in quite a different way from that in which we move in general time. In the first place, we can set a music time, that is, a tempo, at will, provided only it is within the parameter of variance characteristic of the tradition. In the second place, we can retard or accelerate it at will; we can begin a cursus, interrupt it, stop it and begin it again as we wish, or present it backward.

To remain within the scope of the present undertaking, the following dispositions will be made:

A. The pulse, *Takt*, step, or downbeat follows immediately each bar, *whether or not there is a tone there to deliver it.* Representation of the twelve basic moods in terms of tempo can be given separately, as in the case of dynamics; but it is best to represent them in terms of proportion as enclosed by bars defined by tempo. The higher elaboration of the rhythmic functions, unlike that of the tonal, can be carried out only in terms of the two, jointly.

B. Table 2, a counterpart of table 1, shows the proportional moods as progressions within a single measure defined by downbeats. All common and some uncommon forms of poetic foot are represented, as are also the six rhythmic modes of medieval theory. These moods are all given here in rhythmically centric form.

TABLE 2

TWELVE BASIC MOODS IN TERMS OF
THE SIMPLE RHYTHMIC FUNCTIONS

Tense   Detense

BINARY

A   Pyrrhic   Mode II   a   Spondee

B   Iambus   Mode I   b   Trochee

TERNARY

C   Tribrach   Mode VI   c   Molossus   Mode V

D   Anapest   Mode IV   d   Antibacchius

E   Bacchius   e   Dactyl   Mode III

F   Amphibrach   f   Amphimacer

C. Example 8 shows the notational equivalent of table 2 in the function of tempo alone, in a manner similar to that in which the function of dynamics was shown in example 7.

EXAMPLE 8

PROGRESSIONS				LEVELS			
in medial and minimal extension				in medial and maximal extension			

Binary

A	*ac. ac.*	a	*dec. dec.*	A	M*	pm	f		a	M	mm	s	
B	*ac. dec.*	b	*dec. ac.*	B	M	pm	M		b	M	mm	M	

Tenary

C	*ac. ac. ac.*	c	*dec. dec. dec.*	C	M	pm	f	F	c	M	mm	s	S
D	*ac. ac. dec.*	d	*dec. dec. ac.*	D	M	pm	f	M	d	M	mm	s	M
E	*ac. dec. dec.*	e	*dec. ac. ac.*	E	M	f	pm	M	e	M	s	mm	M
F	*ac. dec. ac.*	f	*dec. ac. dec.*	F	M	pm	mm	M	f	M	mm	pm	M

*M = Moderato; pm = piu mosso; f = faster; F = still faster; mm = meno

Comment. The beat is regarded as the rhythmic counterpart of the tone; the tempo established by the downbeat serves for rhythmic centricity as does the final of a mode for tonal centricity; both kinds of centricity consist in the recurrence of a center or axis: the rhythmic upon invariant, periodic recurrence (iteration), the tonal upon variant, imperiodic recurrence or inference of such a center or axis: "modulation" within the rhythmic centricity can be effected either with or without change of metrical signature, as can that of the tonal centricity with or without change of the key signature.

The moods shown in example 8 are barely detectable in minimal extension as factors in the rhetoric of rubato. Elsewhere, I have called attention to the probability that except in tempo giusto rubato is the rule rather than the exception, so that this music-rhetorical factor is a concomitant of music logic in contrast to speech logic, which has (or should have!) nothing to do with rhetoric. In medial and maximal extension, more use is made of tempo than of dynamics as an ordering device. The movements of the romantic symphony, for example, were distinguished from one another as much by their tempo moods as by their tonality. Thus, example 9 shows a typical example of mood *e,* as in example 8.

EXAMPLE 9

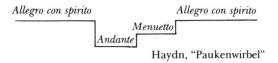

Haydn, "Paukenwirbel"

VI. *Variance of relationship among the four simple functions.*
   A. Variances of pitch and dynamics are usually parallel, but they can be used in complete independence. Thus, a *B* pitch mood is usually accompanied by a *B* dynamic mood and is not often found with a *b* dynamic mood. When it is, such opposition (decentricity of relationship) is usually a music-rhetorical effect, for example, the rapidly ascending-decrescendo scale in the strings, twelfth measure before the end of Strauss's *Don Juan.*
   B. Variances of tempo and proportion are usually interdependent, but rarely completely independent. Yet opposition is extensively used by composers, although perhaps not as commonly as parallelism.
   C. Enchainment of a proportional mood is commonly effected in three manners (cf. the *ordines* of medieval theory), as in example 10: (1) elision—the final tone-beat of one presentation is considered the initial of a successor, as in example 10 (a); (2) immediate succession—the final tone beat of one presentation is followed immediately by the initial of a successor, as in example 10 (b); (3) delayed succession—the final tone beat of one presentation is followed by a rest before presentation of a successor, as in example 10 (c). Proportional mood *C* is used as a paradigm.

EXAMPLE 10

D. I can find no evidence that, except when verbalizing, musicians have sought or ascribed one-to-one correspondence between similarly designated tonal and rhythmic moods. Table 3, however, shows a single tonal mood (*D*) in eight rhythmic moods, and a single rhythmic mood (*D*) in eight tonal moods.

TABLE 3

COUPLING OF SIMPLE TONAL AND
RHYTHMIC FUNCTIONS

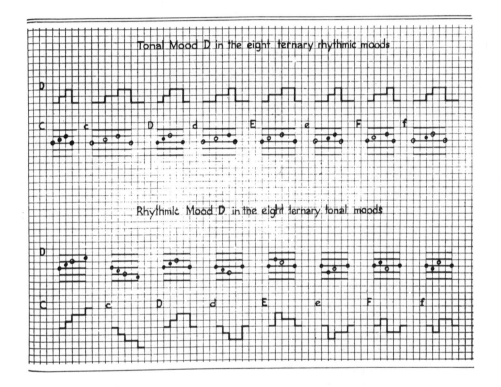

VII. *Variance of progression in the tonal moods in medial and maximal extension.*

A. Provided the directional order, that is, the shape, of the mood be maintained, any or all progressions may be varied in extent without change of mood.

B. Each of the twelve moods, therefore, will be known in one or more versions. Of each version, there may be countless variants.

C. Moods *A*, *a*, *C*, and *c* can be realized in only one version each. Example 11 shows six of the many possible variants of the single version of mood *A* in the pitch function.

EXAMPLE 11

D. Moods *B* and *b* can each be realized in three versions—one centric (=), two decentric, a plus (+), and a minus (−). Three of the many possible variants of each are shown in example 12, using mood *B* as the example.

EXAMPLE 12

E. Moods *D*, *d*, *E*, and *e* can be realized in five versions—one centric, four decentric. Three of the many possible variants of each are shown in example 13, using mood *D* as the example.

EXAMPLE 13

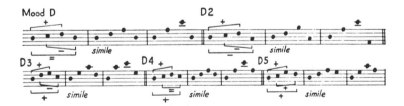

F. The terms *centricity* and *decentricity* have been used here with reference to melody (melodic curve of a line) alone. Thus, a variant of mood *C* whose final component is one or more octaves above the initial component is not regarded as having melodic centricity. Depending upon the definition of the concept of mode, it might or might not be regarded as having modal centricity. It certainly would have centricity with respect to tonality, if this were imposed by a context, real or implied.

G. Any octave progression or relationship within a mood can be given greater or less weight in terms of modality or tonality according to the positions of the components in the rhythmic structure of the context.

> *Comment.* Octave progression is not to be confused with iteration (successive unison). If there are any doubts—and one meets them occasionally—compare (a) and (b) in example 14. If more convincing evidence is needed, try performing the first four notes of Beethoven's Symphony no. 5 in octaves, as at (b). Note that (c) and (d) are harmonically identical, but melodically highly variant.

EXAMPLE 14

b) Beethoven, Symphony No. 8, first movement, measures 100 ff.

VIII. *Variance of progression in the rhythmic moods in medial and maximal extension.*

A. Tempo is rarely varied in minimal extension in Occidental music. Frequent changes of metrical signature might, with suitable augmentation and diminution of proportion, produce rapid changes of tempo; but often as not they are subordinated to an overall tempo, as in the Finale of Stravinsky's *Le Sacre du printemps*. The tempo variance in the third movement of Brahm's Symphony no. 2 is a pattern of design, but owing to the derivation of its melodic content from the initial moods of the first movement, it is a logical mood also. In contrast, the building of the climax in the third act of *Tristan und Isolde* before Isolde's entrance has marked logical structure of proportion, even though it is dominated by a single tempo process of *stringendo.* But the tempo is quite dependent upon the proportions.

B. Proportion, however, is highly elaborated in minimal extension, but compared with the elaboration of pitch, its articulation is quite primitive. It is tied to the powers of 2, with ½ augmentation by dot, but no diminution. Rhythms of 2 against 3, 3 against 2, 3 against 4, 4 against 3, and more complex rhythmic intervals (polyrhythms) must be used independently, or be superimposed upon the power-of-2 system. Because of the clumsiness of notation, they are not much practiced except in fast tempos, where their peculiar characteristics are obscured.

C. Transformation may be effected by lengthening and shortening progressions (duration of component tone beats), provided the form of the mood as expressed in shorts (∪) and longs (−) is preserved. Thus, mood *B* can be varied as in example 15.

EXAMPLE 15

Mood B

D. Extreme transformation of this sort is likely to break the mood into smaller units, or to combine two into one larger unit.

EXAMPLE 16

Mood C

IX. *Formation of a complete set of versions of the basic tonal moods in medial and maximal, as well as minimal, extension.*

A. Decentric forms of the centric moods shown in tables 1 and 2 (*B*, *D*, *E*, *F*, and their contraries) can be formed by extension and/or contraction of the progressions, provided only the directional pattern be maintained.

B. Two kinds of secondary centricity may be found in the ternary moods: one, between the initial and third tone beats; the other, between the second and final.

TABLE 4

COMPLETE SET OF VERSIONS OF BINARY
AND TERNARY TONAL MOODS

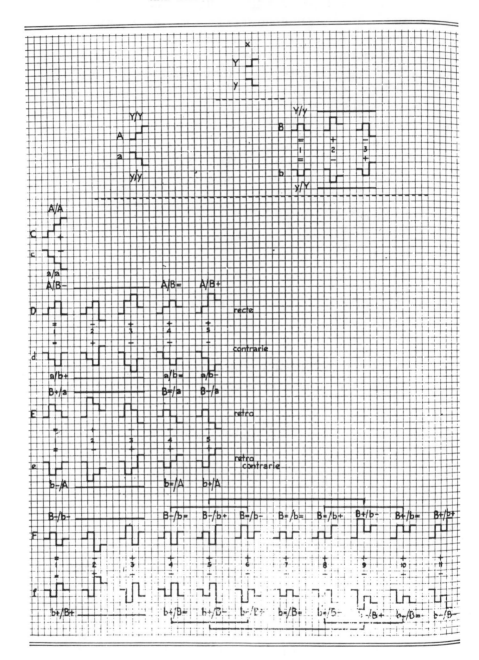

TABLE 5

COMPLETE SET OF VERSIONS OF
BINARY AND TERNARY RHYTHMIC MOODS

◡ = Minimal metrical unit	❙ = Unsounded pulse
‿ ≃ ◡◡	❙ = Sounded pulse
‿‿ = ◡◡◡	(attack or release)

BINARY MOODS

Duple meter		Triple meter		

(rhythmic mood notation symbols)

TERNARY MOODS

(rhythmic mood notation symbols)

... sim ... sim ... sim ... sim ... sim

... sim ... sim ... sim ... sim ... sim

ETC. ‿‿ TO ‿‿‿

C. These additional moods and their contraries—40 in all—and the original six and their contraries yield a total of 52 fully morphic moods. If we view as a single aggregate the total roster of simple, primary or, as I pefer to regard them, "primitive" forms of music composition (including the protomorph and two mesomorphs) we have a total of 55.

Comment 1. There must be no ambiguity in the understanding of the concept *progression.* Any variance of a simple function (and eventually of the compound, when at last we find ways to identify and chart orders in their parameters) constitutes a progression. Naturally, the distinction, identification, and naming of variance will vary with the scope of the attention given and the extent and direction of what is attended to, just as looking through a low-power microscope will not disclose as much detail as looking through a high-power instrument, though it covers a larger area. In notated music levels of attention are usually easy to establish. Analysis or synthesis can be made upon any level from the shortest to the longest note, or upon whatever note values there are in between. What is an inessential or passing note upon a long-note level may be an essential note upon a shorter- or shortest-note level. With the new electronic techniques of music-writing upon charted graph paper, arbitrary levels may have to be set according to whether the scope of attention is general (coarse), detailed (fine) or whatever. This point is especially important in connection with the protomorph. This is definable as one indeterminate extension of direction only—anything from a microsecond to an hour or more, from near zero decibels to the maximum endurable, from a "pure" tone to the most complex noise, from nearly zero proportionality to an envelope for an extended composition, as by the (East) Indian tambura. In most cases, if the extension is more than minimal, there is likely to be variance, which will be in a mesomorphic or holomorphic form. This is especially noticeable in protomorphs sounded by instruments whose attack is different from what follows the attack, or whose sustaining of an extended sound is uneven. Upon a level of coarse attention, the first four measures of the slow movement of Beethoven's Symphony no. 7 is protomorphic in pitch, loudness, and tempo, but affords two possible analyses in proportion: one, an alternation of a ternary mood $|-\cup\cup|$, and a binary $|--|$ (*e* and *a* in table 2), once repeated; the other, two quintary moods $|-\cup\cup--|$. Upon a level of fine attention, a metrical accent may be intended or understood to have a slight stress, that is, increase in loudness upon the first beats of measures, and the down-bow may produce a slightly different tonal density (tone quality) from that of the up-bow. The barbarism of considering the two two-four measures to be one four-four is not to be excluded.

Comment 2.   Any individual mood can be considered to consist of components *added* together to define a unit of logical form, or as a unit of a pattern that can be *divided* into its component parts. In both cases, the mood must be regarded equally as a Gestalt (unique whole) and as an assembly of components, disassemblable in as many ways as it is assemblable. The order adoped here might be termed *genetic* in that each class of unit is conceived to imply, or to contain the nuclear or germinal conditions for, the formation of the next more elaborate unit. Thus, for example, mood *A* may be considered formed by elision of a mesomorph *Y* with a successor *Y*, and mood *a*, similarly, by two *y*'s. The binary moods being formed thus by simple elision, it is not surprising that the ternary can be formed of some, but not all, combinations of binary moods by double elision, a quaternary set by triple elision of some ternary, and on and on, ad infinitum. Example 17 shows ternary mood *D1* in terms of double elision of binary moods *A* and *B*−. A full set of secondary syntheses and analyses of Mood *f8* will be given in XI, *Qualification of the mood.*

EXAMPLE 17

D. In each of the moods in which a centric version is found (*B, b, D, d, E, e, F, f*) there is only one; and of all possible double elisions, those that form the centric are the only ones that yield two decentric as well—a tense (+) and a detense (−)—three, in all. Other double elisions yield only one apiece—a tense or a detense.

X. *Increment and decrement of the mood.*
   A. Increment of mood may be prefixive, interpolative, or suffixive. It may range from minimal, which leaves the mood intact, to maximal, which converts it into another mood.
   B. Minimal increment may be effected by iteration of one or more components as in example 18. Multiple iteration can

EXAMPLE 18

become a logical factor in itself. Beethoven was especially skilled in the use of multiple iteration; in Symphonies nos. 3, 5, and 7 it is a primary music-logical factor.
   C. Passing-tones, especially when filling skips with intervening degrees, are medial in transformation of the mood when unaccented; and maximal when accented (see ex. 19).

EXAMPLE 19

D. Accessory tones, especially when contrary to the progression, are more transformative. When accented, they can change the identity of the mood.

EXAMPLE 20

E. Increase in incrementation usually means increase in transformation.

EXAMPLE 21

F. Interpolation of rests tends to break up a mood (see ex. 22).

EXAMPLE 22

G. Decrement of a mood may be initial, internal, or final. Even minimal decrement transforms a mood into another (see ex. 23).

EXAMPLE 23

XI. *Qualification of the mood.*
    A. Apart from the factors essential to the definition of the mood, its versions and variants, there are several factors that do not define or transform it, but operate in a manner I shall term "qualification." They serve to delineate, underline, or emphasize aspects of the mood which are selected by the composer for logical transformation and development.

B. The resources available for qualification of the mood are almost limitless, since they comprise the almost uncharted parameters of tone quality and accent as well as those of the four simple functions. Many of them, lacking either historical, systematic, traditional, or logical formulation, remain music rhetoric until such form is given to them. Some others, however, approximate such formulation. Among these is what is more or less precisely known as "phrasing."

C. Viewed in its simplest formal aspect, phrasing is concerned with the connection and disconnection of the components of a mood. Staccato may be considered tension of the tone beat and progression complex; détaché, its tonicity; legato, its detension. It is largely by these simple means of variance that a mood is presented as an indivisible unit, an assembly of smaller units or, in its highest form, as a Gestalt constituted by both unity and diversity. The bond between a music logic and the resources of elementary phrasing is shown in example 24. Genesis of more complex units from simpler ones would be shown by brackets, as in example 17; but since it exactly parallels the resources of simple phrasing, slurs are used to indicate legato. Components not within a slur may be considered either staccato or détaché. Mood *f8* is used as the paradigm.

EXAMPLE 24

Mood *f8*

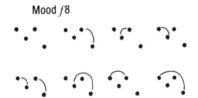

D. One of the aspects of the mood most susceptible to qualification is that of centricity-decentricity, or, more precisely, the implications thereof. With respect to rhythm, a normally duple or triple mood in a cursus with a triple or duple signature may effect quite drastic qualification. With respect to tone, the matter is more complicated, simply because the pitch function is so much more highly organized. Strictly speaking, a single binary or ternary mood in minimal extension cannot define mode, key, or tonality. The tradition-conditioned ear will tend, however, to infer or impute to it a mode, key, or tonality, especially when it initiates or closes a phrase. It may be in accord with, opposed to or in ambiguous relationship with the mode, key, or tonality established in medial and maximal extension by the cursus of which it is a component. Take, for instance, mood *b1* as shown in example 25. The conserva-

EXAMPLE 25

tive ear, as well as that of the adept of the twelve-tone row, will probably infer or impute a major or minor mode and a key of *C*, with even a possible tonality of *C* in the offing. But although the continuant might support such inference or imputation, it might instead oppose it as in example 26:

EXAMPLE 26

Furthermore, each continuant mood in the cursus may have like or unlike centricity or decentricity. Each of these possibilities is probably gauged in accordance with the tradition by all of its well-trained participants. The various tensities, tonicities, and detensities of the individual moods, the relationships among them and to the features of the complete process in which they participate, constitute some of the most characteristic concerns of musical thought, reason, and logic. The mere classificatory convenience that labels 26(a) "*A*-minor," 26(b) "*F*-major," and 26(c) "Dorian" only too often distorts understanding of the melodic process. For example, any one of these three may have to be revised when the succeeding moods are known. Two tunes may have the same final and the same general overall classification with respect to mode, key, and tonality but have entirely different inner makeup in these respects. Or, they may have different finals and have practically identical inner makeup and relationships. Mood centricities and decentricities, even in minimal extension, should be seen, therefore, as building tensities, tonicities, and detensities within the larger centricities and decentricities in the cursus.

E. One of the prejudices that even the well-trained carrier of the tradition of Occidental music must guard against is, however, that every self-contained or complete cursus must have a formal end. Not least among the less common forms is the circular melody, whose last phrase leads back into the first. Such melodies are likely to be at least bi-modal. Another example is the fading-away into toneless speech in singing of the ballad, or into brief, inessential, almost listless, abbreviation or irrelevance, as in much jazz performance. Some competent improvisation may not even have a beginning or ending.

XII. *Moods of more than three progressions.*

A. Table 6 shows the basic quatenary moods in both tonal and rhythmic graph form. Their synthesis and analysis follow the procedures for formation of the ternary moods, the order being determined by triple elision. Centric versions are possible for all but *G* and *g*.

B. Full tables of the more complex moods are hardly worth compiling, owing to the sheer multitude of versions and variants, and it is doubtful whether any composer worth his salt would ever need to use one. Musicians probably keep them in mind by processes of musical thought; it is only the speech presentation of them that is complicated. When musicology becomes mere bookkeeping, it may gain an author academic preferment, but not even musicologists read him.

C. One example might be given of transformation among these more complex moods that will be familiar enough to any reader. It occurs at the end of Stravinsky's *L'Oiseau de Feu*, II Tableau, lento maestoso. The four-measure phrase first presents two moods that would probably be designated by most students as quatenary *g* and ternary *f10*, quarter notes on offbeats regarded as passing or auxiliary notes. After six full presentations, the slow 3/2 changes to 7/4 allegro non troppo giving each note, formerly varying from whole, dotted half, half to quarter notes, uniform value. The quatenary

TABLE 6

Basic Quatenary Moods in Terms of the Simple Tonal and Rhythmic Functions

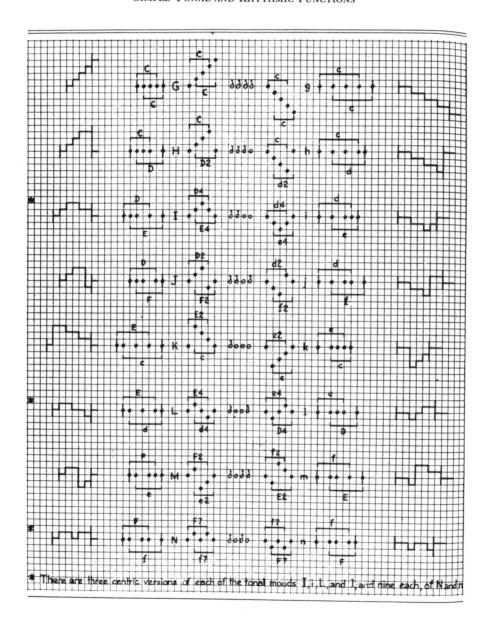

* There are three centric versions of each of the tonal moods I, i, L, and l, and nine each of N and n

mood promptly becomes quintary and the ternary, 'senary (see ex. 27).

EXAMPLE 27

* * *

June 1976.   Now that I revise slightly and condense this essay written twenty years ago, I feel that comparative (ethno-) musicology has advanced to a point where it would support a proposal that a universal music lexicon could be organized along the lines of such a music logic as I have presented in the foregoing pages. The various musics of man would be found to use this lexicon in accord with their respective music grammars and syntaxes. These would vary from the almost completely random to the highly organized music systems characteristic of the most diversified and extended cultures of man.

I envisage such a lexicon as comprising three levels: (1) the proto-morph −, the mesomorph ⌐ and the five binary and ternary holomorphs

;

(2) the four transformations and possible techniques of enchainment (ellision, separation, diversification of rhythmic and tonal patterns, etc.), (3) the relative independence of and dependence upon the binary and ternary moods by the quatenary, quintary, senary, and other such more elaborate structures.

The grammars would comprise the tonal and rhythmic modes, their scaling, intonation, traditional ways of transforming and enchaining the moods peculiar to each music; the syntaxes, the formation of half-phrases, phrases, periods, sections, and so forth. The employment of linguistic transformational devices should be compensated for in equal measure by music transformational devices.

The spreading of the nuclear theme in Javanese music over extended periods, the rhythmic patterns in African drumming, and the elaborate *tala* of Indic rhythm would seem to constitute promising subjects for investigation.

NOTES

1. W. S. Jevons, *Elementary Lessons in Logic* (New York: Macmillan, 1914), p. 137.

2. George Boole, *An Investigation of the Laws of Thought* (London: Walton & Maberly, 1854).

3. Ibid., p. 242.

4. F. B. Fitch, *Symbolic Logic* (New York: Renard Press, 1952), p. 3.

5. George Boole, *Studies in Logic and Probability* (London, 1852), "Note in Editing" by R. Rhees, p. 25.

6. P. W. Bridgman, *The Logic of Modern Physics* (New York: Macmillan, 1927).

7. A. N. Whitehead and Bertrand Russell, *Principia Mathematica* (Cambridge: Cambridge University Press, 1910).

8. Suzanne Langer, *Introduction to Symbolic Logic* (Boston: Houghton Mifflin, 1937), p. 18.

VI
Toward a Unitary Field Theory
for Musicology[75]

An imaginary interrogation by
Boris Kremenliev and a student

Kremenliev: This is a student of mine, Jim Yost. He has run across an abstract of a paper of yours and wants me to tell him more of the idea it presented. I couldn't tell him. Can you tell me? Apparently, you never published it in full.

Seeger: I don't remember just what was in that abstract.

Yost: Here it is: *Bulletin of the American Musicological Society*, 9-10 (June 1947, as of June 1944 and 1945), page 16. You read it December 27, 1944.

S: H'm . . . It was not a very good paper. Curt Sachs remarked afterward it was interesting but he didn't understand it.

K: What did you say?

S: I don't remember. Something to the effect that now that I had presented it I wondered if I understood it also.

K: You talk quite lucidly, but I find your written prose difficult reading.

S: People do. That's because it is difficult writing.

Y: Is that why you never published it?

S: Partly. I've rewritten it several times but not with any finality.

K: Perhaps you could talk it now. . . . We could record our questions and your answers.

S: Fair enough. Talking is just as much composition as writing. It is likely to loosen the organization, and that is precisely what holds one up in writing.

K: Begin!

Y: As I understand it, you tried to present in one hour of admittedly speculative inquiry a comprehensive outline of the whole domain of musicological endeavor in a unitary field theory. What I want to know is where did you begin. As you have said, if you start with the foundations, things look one way; if you begin with the objectives, another. If you take a structural approach, you foul up your functional analysis. If you start with facts, you never get to values. And so forth.

S: You have been reading something else but musicology.

K: He is switching from linguistics to musicology.

S: I hope he will bring a lot of the former to the latter with him—we need it—and that he will not be too horrified at my manhandling of speech communication.

Y: What discipline does not need to be looked at from outside as well as from inside?

S: We'll get along.

Y: Where, then, would you begin an exposition of your theory?

S: In the middle. And then work outward in all directions.

K: What is the middle in musicology?

S: As I see it, the musicological juncture—the situation you put yourself in when you start to use one means of communication, speech, to deal with another, music, in the middle of things.

Y: And there you find yourself in the pedicament that you call "linguocentric."

K: He's been checking on you.

S: Good.

Y: Would you say that you find yourself committed to a basic bias for which there is no corrective?

S: Yes. No hundred percent corrective. By reference to nonlinguistic checks scientists have shown the bias can be reduced by approximately fifty percent with respect to fact; but the approximate half remaining may operate virtually unchecked with respect to value.

Y: You have argued that correctives for value bias can be developed.

S: Modifications, yes. A search for them would seem to be a first order of business facing not only musicologists but also the human race in general and our own society in particular. But bear in mind that however much you may reduce it, the linguocentric predicament remains a universal condition of the use of speech. The primary semiotic bias is reflected in the dozens of secondary logical biases commonly referred to as "the problems of philosophy." There is no escape from these problems but to stop talking and writing or else to accept them, as biases, in every statement of them and in every proposed solution of them.

K: That seems to mean that no one can believe anything that anyone says. Must I be a cynic?

S: You would then be one of the most biased of all creatures.

K: Suppose I propose that I have solved all the problems?

S: Then you would be one of the most enchanted in the magic castle of speech bias.

Y: Suppose I challenge your statement that the problems are insoluble?

S: Look at the history of philosophy.

K: Then the best we can do is to doubt everything but still search for something to hang onto?

S: You would qualify for the moderate skepticism now rather generally the fashion.

K: And you too.

S: Agreed, except that with respect to value I am a believer, as everyone else is.

K: Then why is it not just as easy for you to talk and write about music as for ay of the rest of us?

S: Let's go back to the musicological juncture for an answer to that. . . . You are a musician. You can make a fresh and hitherto unformulated attack not only upon the common bias of all speech communication but upon the dozens of minor biases or problems. You still must start with shaky assumptions, but you admit it, for you have a resort not available to the philosopher.

K: What is that?

S: You know music; he doesn't. Look at the job as an exercise in comparative semiotics. Speech communicates referent to what is not speech. Doesn't music communicate referent to what is not music?

K: Of course it does.

S: What, then, is the relationship between the two kinds of reference? And the two kinds of referents—between what is not speech and what is not music?

K: That is precisely what we all want to know.

S: Yes. We all say "music is this, music is that." We try to *say* how music does what it does. But that puts us right back in the linguocentric predicament. How do you know music is *this* or *that*? Doesn't it do *what* it does? Can't you check?

K: Against what?

S: Your music knowledge.

K: But that would be pure subjectivity.

S: No, merely inexpressible in words. . . . It is true that speech and music are very unlike in many ways; but they are very like in others. One can try to use agreement upon the latter to help agreement upon the former's *account* of the latter.

Y: You two could stay bogged down in problems of musicological epistemology until 1984. I'm looking for relevance.

S: How about a nonproblem approach I have never tried before. . . . There seem to be two broad categories of reasoned speech usage: one, of common sense; the other, of learning.

Y: Wait a minute! What do you mean by "common sense"?

S: A kind of speech usage in which referents may be freely talked about without defining the concepts used in the talking.

K and Y: But we shall need definitions!
                  must have

S: All right: a modified common sense—uncommon common sense. Definitions as requested. . . . Most people talk about music in terms of common sense. Most musicians do, too. But they have music learning, that is, direct music knowledge and music feeling far beyond that of non-musicians. Some nonmusicians, however, are learned in fields of specialization other than music of which some aspects of music are data.

K: For example?

S: Among them, mathematics and logic, the physical sciences, the biological sciences, psychology, anthropology and sociology, economics, political science, philosophy, ethology, aesthetics, folklore, belles lettres, poetics, comparative religion, mythology, mysticism, ecstatics. They contribute the vast majority of words and ways of using them by means of which we talk about music. . . . But to continue, nonmusical specialists can, therefore, talk learnedly about some aspect of music in ways often as incomprehensible to musicians and to other specialists as to non-musicians who are not specialists of any kind. But they may still talk of music as a whole in terms of common sense. The musicologist must try to comprehend as much as possible of all these ways of talking and to integrate them in such a way as to reconcile the diverse viewpoints, orientations, methods, and aims involved.

K: It is too bad that we cannot talk about music in strictly musical terms.

S: True. But our lexicon of strictly musical terms is very limited.

K: We may have to invent a metalanguage.

S: I feel that one is on its way. It has a competitor in an equal tendency to mathematization.

Y: Over and beyond the lexicon, there is the use of its components in the sentence. In talking, one cannot use a music grammar, or music syntax, if such there be. One must use, as you put it, the characteristic formational apparatus of the particular means of communication. It is this, as much as the lexicon, that tends to cast whatever speech refers into likeness of itself.

K: Look here. We are going to spin this interrogation out of proportion if we don't come back soon to the basic question: what is a unitary field theory for musicology? Starting with a definition of musicology might be a good idea.

S: Over the years I have said musicology is this and that, but I have never drawn the lot together in one knot.

K: Oh, come now, Charles—if you're going to talk about a unitary field theory for musicology you'd better start with a clear definition of the study.

S: Yes, I suppose I must. Let's approach it this way: will you admit that every human being looks outward from his own body as well as inward into it, as it were—partly consciously, partly unconsciously—and that you and I, as typical literate Americans, can give highly conceptualized accounts of how things look to us, how they are related among themselves as fact, and how we relate them to ourselves as value?

K: I don't know how safe it is for me to commit myself to anything you propose without thinking it over pretty carefully, but I'll risk this one.

S: Good enough. The product of this outward and inward looking is sometimes referred to as a "world view." We can speak of each scholarly discipline as incorporating a particular world view of its own, and of each student devoted to its cultivation as incorporating an individual variant of that view.

K: Can you say what is the particular world view of musicology?

S: In order to do so I shall have to point out that while it is easy to say that the product of our outward and inward looking is our world view, yet when we come to talking about any particular world view we find that on the one hand we have a concept that is easy to define and on the other an empirical referent that is difficult to describe. But I will try. First, solely for convenience and economy, let me substitute for the functional term "world view" a structural "universe," referent to "what is viewed."[1]

K: Then according to this disposition of the semantics, you will refer to what the world view of musicology refers as "the universe of musicology."

S: For the moment, yes. Now what is inside that universe?

K: You're going to tell me.

S: A number of universes.

K: How many, and what are they?

S: How many have we already involved ourselves within this conversation?

K: Let's see. There is the physical, phenomenal, "external" universe. And the universe of discourse in whose terms we are talking about it. What others?

S: How about a universe of music? If there is a universe of speech, which is one way men communicate by mediums of sound, why should there not be one of the other ways of communicating by sound—music? As musicians, we know that music communicates something that speech does not. Is not music as much involved with what is not music as is speech with what is not speech?

K: That sounds reasonable.

S: Three universes, then. How about a fourth?

K: What could that be?

S: When you run into a snag in what you are writing about or are composing, don't you ever feel that there is a fund of knowledge, feelings, and purposes rumbling around inside you that is definitely yours and no one else's. It is variably auditory, visual, and tactile, but it is not quite in the order you could wish it to be so as to enable you to clarify the passage you are working on; and that by exploring it a bit deliberately or resting and letting yourself dream you either solve the problem satisfactorily or give up and make a fresh start?

K: Of course.

S: Was this exploring or dreaming all in words or notes?

K: Of course not. Some of it was in auditory images, some visual, some, as you say, tactile—matters of touch, inner as well as outer. Or even smell and taste. But they are kinds of touch, too. You're not able to identify all the factors. Lots of them are beneath the threshold of consciousness.

S: Or above the lintel.

K: Precisely.

S: Something like another universe, no? Modesty forbids your saying it is as comprehensive as the atomic-galactic universe the physicists are talking about. But while they are exploring theirs, it is, in a sense, in their heads, is it not? While you are exploring and dreaming yours, you know that there are lots of things in it that are not in theirs. And, naturally, there must be a lot of things in their heads besides the physical universe that they study. These universes of individual human beings are quite extraordinary. They not only involve our heads but the rest of our bodies, especially what we refer to so poetically as our "hearts." There are universes of individual feeling as well as of individual thinking and, above all, of feeling our thinking and thinking our feeling.

K: Very pretty, though not very scientifically expressed.

S: No, mere common sense. But I doubt any scientist would gainsay it. . . . Well, that gives us four universes in whose terms we have already talked and customarily do talk about music. How about a fifth?

K: My god, how you complicate matters?

S: No, simplify them—a good simplification always shows how complicated you had already made things. How did we ever get around to talking about music?

K: I suppose our ancestors started us off, way back. Oh, I see what you are driving at: a cultural universe.

S: Magnificent. Let's be content with these five for the moment—speech, music, individuality, culture, and physics—although there are others, some of which I'll have to mention later. It is on these five universes and one other that I expect you to name that I would build a comprehensive definition of musicology. I would put it: musicology is (1) *a speech study,* systematic as well as historical, critical as well as scientific or scientist; whose field is (2) *the total music* of man, both in itself and in its relationships to what is not itself; whose cultivation is (3) *by individual students* who can view its field as musicians as well as in the terms devised by nonmusical specialists of whose fields some aspects of music are data; whose aim is to contribute to *the understanding of man,* in terms both (4) of human *culture* and (5) of his relationships with the *physical universe.* A prime methodological postulate would be that there is a limited compatibility between the semiotics of speech communication and of music communication, so that its findings, when sought with sufficient rigor, will constitute a comparative study of the communicatory processes of the two arts and a potential factual and valual view of speech, by the musicologist as a carrier of a tradition of music, no less than a factual and valual view of music, by him as a carrier of a tradition of speech.

Y: That covers a lot of ground. Now, how does your theory unite it all?

S: Let's look at the five universes we were just discussing. I'll represent them as circles and identify each with the capital letter of its name, thus:

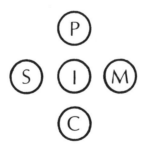

FIGURE 1

K: Well, what next?

S: There is one very curious relationship among the five: each includes all the others.

K: Oh, come now!

S: Yes, indeed.

Y: But the inclusion must be quie different from one case to another.

S: Surely. Let's represent them in the manner made classic by the textbooks in logic, thus:

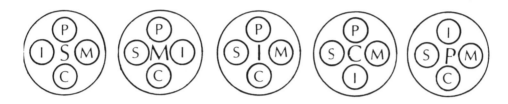

FIGURE 2

Inclusion S is representational, symbolic, semantic. By naming the other four—and itself—by relating the names (endosemantically), by relating the named (ectosemantically), by relating the relationships among the names and the relationships among the named, and by relating the lot to ourselves, it includes the other four in the sense that it includes speech knowledge of them (which is quite a different thing from the sense knowledge of them). Where value cannot be attributed to the named—as to electrons or galaxies—the correspondence of names and named and the relationships among each can be very close, as by mathematics and the natural sciences. To the extent that value must be attributed to the named, as by the humanities, the correspondence becomes less and less close until, in myth and in mystical and ecstatic verbalization, the correspondence may become specifically denied, as in "what I want to say is ineffable; it is beyond words." *Inclusion M* is presentational, embodied, semiotic but not symbolic. Music does not "mean" what is not music; it identifies itself with it. As I have put it elsewhere, "It does not say so; it does so." It cannot particularize or generalize. It can affirm but it cannot deny. *Inclusion I* is experiential, solipsistic, aesthetic. It is the individual man who senses P, carries C, makes S and M. *Inclusion C* is axiological, consensual, valual. The other four are products of traditions that are members of the bundle of traditions that make up the variant ways of collective living that we call "cultures." Cultures, too, exemplify world views. In them are embedded the dearest values of their carriers. They are impressed upon the soft wax of the growing child's individuality and, thus inherited, are cultivated and transmitted to future generations. *Inclusion P* is phenomenological, existential, factual. The other four universes are phenomena in it. . . . There is continuous interplay among these five universes, and especially between the consensuses of C and the solipsisms of I.

K: Is any such comprehensive view of musicology generally agreed upon?

S: Oh, no. Take the articles on the subject in the five leading dictionaries, lexicons, and encyclopedias published in the 1960s.[2] I find myself in substantial agreement with them as far as they go; Wiora's, in *MGG*, is the most comprehensive. The trouble is that they begin and end in the middle of the subject, though they do not state or define it as such. They don't inquire into or speak of the need to inquire into the foundations of the study—that is, its necessary assumptions—nor do they treat or speak of the need to treat of its aims and methods beyond service to the routine pursuit of a profession. I should hasten to say that François Lesure in the *Encyclopédie Fasquelle* does write eloquently of this lack of concern. "Le but suprême," he says, "serait évidemment de découvrir ce que le musical nous enseigne de l'homme, qui soit différent de ce que le langage, la religion ou le droit nous apprend de lui. Le jour où, même partiellement, on aura atteint ce but, on pourra dire que la musicologie sera en possession d'une méthode." ("The ultimate aim will clearly be to discover what music teaches us of man that may differ from that which speech, religion or law tells us of him. The day when, even partially, this aim has been attained, one may be able to say that musicology is in possession of a method.")

K: The implication being that it isn't a discipline until it has aims beyond itself and a method for reaching them.

S: I would suppose so.

Y: How does your definition relate to these authors'?

S: A concept and its empirical referent are so closely bound together that it is not worthwhile to push the distinction between them too far. But at any given time it can be important to know which of the two one is talking about. A definition such as mine is more of the concept of musicology than of any particular or general existing practice. All five of the authors whose articles I cite have addressed themselves to a concrete empirical situation: students of music who want information relative to their particular study. This may or may not be the authors' decisions, but it probably accords with their editors' wishes. Musicology is presented therefore, as a relatively isolated study and primarily in its aspects as the historiography of the fine art of European music, an ongoing professional activity the vast majority of whose adepts are strongly disinclined to stop and ask what their initial assumptions are, on what ground they are traveling, where they are going, and why they are cultivating it.

Y: If their definitions are limited, how does yours fit into your broad schema of the five universes?

S: First and most generally, half of musicology is the view of music from outside. No one disputes the scholar in any prime discipline when he says that his discipline underlies all study. Of course it does. They all do. But surely, it is a grave methodological error to assume that any one of them underlies more deeply, is the base or the heart of the lot, to the subordination of the others. They are inextricably interdependent. What is more, as they are all speech disciplines. . . .

K: What? Mathematics?

S: Yes, mathematics is a kind of language—more nearly universal than any other. I won't argue with you if you call it a metalanguage. There is plenty of authority as well as logical support for the inclusion. A metalanguage is still a kind of language. . . . As I was saying, all these studies are speech disciplines, bound to the formational apparatus of the speech compositional process and its bias. And that apparatus is all that any discipline, even musicology, has available to deal with the music compositional process and its formational apparatus.

K: But if musicology is a speech discipline like all others, where does music come into its practice?

S: As a speech discipline, musicology must conform with the essentials of the universe of speech communication; its reference being to the universe of music communication, it must conform with the essentials of that universe also.

K: Now at last I begin to feel we are getting down to the subject of this interrogation.

S: Right, though we're still laying the ground upon which a unitary field theory, as a speech construction, can rest as securely as possible, that is, so as to be as believable as possible both as speech knowledge and feeling and as music knowledge and feeling. Both arts flourish in an identical environment, are molded by that environment, and contribute to the molding of it. The two can be and are intimately associated, as in song. There are many analogies between the forms in which the sound employed by each is cast in its respective compositional processes. Thus both can be studied by the same methods and by the same laboratory devices.

K: How so?

S: Because the study is carried on in the terms of speech. Speech can function only within its own peculiar parameters of semantic variance.

The studies we referred to a minute ago, for example, are no more than somewhat arbitrarily marked off areas of the parameter of speech semantic variance defined by the limits "logic" and "mysticism."

K: Hold on, now; I don't follow you. What is a parameter of speech semantic variance?

S: It is a term I have coined for the purpose of finding, in the art of speech, a counterpart or homolog of what we know in the art of music as a "gamut" or range of pitch variance from low to high. We might regard the ranges of loudness, speed, and duration variance as gamuts, too; but as you know we have increasingly come to use the term *parameter* for them and for the term *gamut*, as well. It is by the variance of pitch, loudness, speed, and duration of musical events—and, above all, the variance of tonal and rhythmic densities—that we produce the homolog of speech meaning that some call "music meaning" or, expressed with less speech bias, "music communication." To compensate for the inevitable bias of speech presentation, musicology must find, whenever it can, a bias of music presentation. As speech "looks at" music, so, music must "look at" speech. Our terminology must reflect this. Speech can be viewed as relying upon a veritable orchestra of gamuts of meaning, each defined or limited—as are the gamuts or parameters of the music compositional apparatus—by antonyms, opposites, polarities, or whatever you want to call them.

Y: But the music "meaning" is in the sound and the actual arrangements of it presented by the music maker, whereas the speech meaning is in what the sound stands for, represents, or symbolizes.

S: Yes. I won't stop here to suggest qualifications of both statements. Suffice it to say, an accurate plotting of the homologs, analogs, and heterologs postulated by musicologists if of highest importance to the believability of its results.

Y: Which is the more important in musicology: speech or music?

S: It is, I believe, a grave methodological error to assume that one is more important than the other. There is something of a Copernican twist to be made here. Neither speech nor music should be conceived as revolving around the other, but rather, like some double stars that astronomers tell us about. They revolve around each other, now one, now the other given or imposing more weight, ever eluding our best efforts to keep them in equilibrium. Musicology is to be seen, then, as a 50-50 composite of speech and music. As speech, it must conform to the essentials of the universe of speech communication; its reference, being to another universe of communication, must conform to the essentials of that universe also. The use of speech is essentially the relating of its own universe to the universes it sets up in any particular undertaking. The ways in which we relate them and the relative emphasis we put upon them constitute our musicological world view. A field theory is a particular conjunction of universes—one that is constructed very deliberately and seriously.

K: Isn't that what scientists have been doing?

S: Not as comprehensively as musicologists must. Philosophers have been making unified field theories for their field—the aggregate universes of speech discourse—which is far more comprehensive than that of science, although they have not labeled it in this particular way. It will not readily be conceded that musicology poses a still more comprehensive field. A truly universal philosophy would include musicology. It would not limit itself to auditory communication alone; it would embrace also the arts of tactility and vision. But to expect full competence in all the arts by any one man seems, in the light of our present specialization of both knowledge and feeling, beyond possibility of realization. Perhaps teamwork could produce it. We'd have to wait and see.

Y: Your definition of musicology seems to differ from those of the other authors you mentioned, chiefly in that you emphasize so strongly the linguistic character of the study, the only partial compatibility of the semiotics of the tool and the material worked by it and, most surprisingly, that musicology must constitute a critique of speech. One other part of the definition interests me particularly: what do you mean by rigor? I have an impression that your use of this much-touted term is not the conventional one.

S: Unfortunately, it is not. Man has not distinguished himself in the rigorous use of speech learning. Conventionally, I know, in the West for the last three centuries, it has been customary to speak of the highly organized a posteriori, factual, inductive reasoning of science as rigorous—just as we must admit that the equally highly organized a priori, valual, deductive reasoning of the theology of our Middle Ages can be spoken of by the same term. The theology became intolerable in terms of the internal relations of speech communication, on account of the contradictions inherent in the limitation of search for speech knowledge of fact by the unlimited search for speech knowledge of value, with such negative results as inquisitions, persecutions, and religious wars. Now, at last, science is becoming intolerable in terms of the external relations of speech communication, on account of the limitation of search for speech knowledge of value by the unlimited search for speech knowledge of fact, with such negative results as the pollution of the environment and the threatened extinction, by that and/or nuclear war, of the civilization if not the life of man. I put it to you, as one of the many millions of educated men throughout the world, whether we are not facing a situation today which teaches us that neither separately nor in opposition can fact and value as traditionally used in speech be trusted. Is not the only possible check upon the extremism, that both represent and encourage, a revised conception of rigor in our use of speech by which the two must run *pari passu* as checks upon each other—as each others' complements rather than opposites?

Y: And you think that musicology, as you define it, can contribute to such an integration?

S: There is your relevance.

K: I hope you are right. But to go on: are there further differences between your definition and those of the other authors?

S: Several. One is their Europocentrism; another, their excessive historicism.

K: I suppose you mean as opposed to systematic study. You are familiar, of course, with Adler's table or *Gesammtgebäude* of musicology.[3]

S: Yes; it is the ancestor of all the dictionary descriptions of musicology I have cited and in significant ways the ancestor of much of my own thought, including my own field theory. Come to think of it, we should reproduce his table, for at least here in the Americas, little as it is read about it is less often seen. The authors I cited reduce it from a synoptic table to a list, usually of three to five headings. Wiora, in *MGG*, leads off with a first category of his own which extends Chrysander's original concept of the field of music as a whole (*das Ganze Gebiet der Tonkunst*)[4] to the field of musicology as a whole ("*Die Musikwissenschaft als Ganzes*") and lists the systematic orientation second, the historical third. German musicology shows an almost unbroken, though uneven, continuity of Adler's initiative.[5]

K: I wonder why so little attention has been given to the systematics of study in America. The trouble was, I suppose, that musicologists found themselves without the pale of academe. To get in, they had to conform to current fashion in dealing with the humanities, which was historical—the museum point of view. System was supplied from the outside by the natural and social sciences; from the inside, it was left to the conservatories and schools of music, where it became pedagogy without theory but still called *theory*.

S: It also ran into the tail end of the "make America musical" movement, the "good music" movement to promote the kind of music that was felt proper for the genteel American. W. S. Pratt in the leading article of the first issue of the *Musical Quarterly* expressed the prevailing view of Adler's systematics.[6] "This classification," he wrote, "is largely dictated by a knowledge of the kinds of publication that German scholarship has evolved. . . . Its systematic division is less useful than the historical. The das Gesammtgebäude[1] also:

senschaft.

II. Systematisch.

tellung der in den einzelnen Zweigen der Tonkunst zuhöchst stehenden Gesetze.

A. Erforschung und ründung derselben in der			B. Aesthetik der Tonkunst.	C. Musikalische Pädagogik und Didaktik	D. Musikologie (Unter-
urmo- ik il od. ich).	2. Rhyth- mik (temporär oder zeitlich).	3. Melik (Cohärenz von tonal und tem- porär).	1. Vergleichung und Werthschätzung der Gesetze und deren Relation mit den apper- cipirenden Subjecten behufs Feststellung der *Kriterien des musika- lisch Schönen.* 2. Complex unmittelbar und mittelbar damit zusammenhängender Fragen.	(Zusammenstellung der Gesetze mit Rücksicht auf den Lehrzweck) 1. Tonlehre, 2. Harmonielehre, 3. Kontrapunkt, 4. Compositionslehre, 5. Instrumentationslehre, 6. Methoden des Unter- richtes im Gesang und Instrumentalspiel.	suchung und Ver- gleichung zu ethno- graphi- schen Zwecken).

Hilfswissenschaften: Akustik und Mathematik.
Physiologie (Tonempfindungen).
Psychologie (Tonvorstellungen, Tonurtheile und Tongefühle).
Logik (das musikalische Denken).
Grammatik, Metrik und Poetik.
Pädagogik
Ästhetik etc.

ständigste Übersicht über das musikalische Unterrichtssystem der Griechen enthält;
der vollkommen deckende Ausdruck im Deutschen fehlt.

Musik.

II. ΠΡΑΚΤΙΚΟΝ - ΠΑΙΔΕΥΤΙΚΟΝ
(Unterricht oder praktischer Theil).

	C. χρηστικόν (Compositionslehre)			D. ἐξαγγελτικόν (Ausübung oder Execution)		
λοποιία dische osition)	g. ῥυθμοποιία (rhythmische Composition oder angewandte Rhythmik)	h. ποίησις (Poetik)	i. ὀργανική (Instrumental- Spiel)	k. ᾠδική (Gesang)	l. ὑποκριτική (dramatische Aktion).

1885.

2

CONSPECTUS OF THE RESOURCES OF THE MUSICOLOGICAL PROCESS

I. WORLD VIEW

Its formation by response to and appetite for communication,
and
for communicating in traditional norms of semiotic behavior

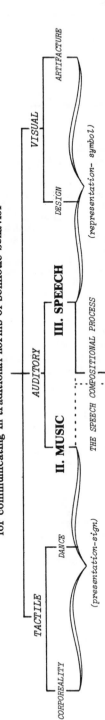

TACTILE   *AUDITORY*   *VISUAL*

CORPOREALITY   *DANCE*   **II. MUSIC**   **III. SPEECH**   *DESIGN*   *ARTIFACTURE*

(presentation-sign)   *THE SPEECH COMPOSITIONAL PROCESS*   *(representation-symbol)*

The formational apparatus provides a class of discrete event in the physical universe consisting of a single sound-line that names, relates names (endosemantically), relates the named (ectosemantically), relates the relations, and relates the lot to the producer and/or his fellows. Its study comprises five branches: phonology, lexicon, grammar, syntax, rhetoric. The event occurs in general space time—a single, given, frequency-amplitude, continuum, entirely independent of man's control. When funded within and/or produced in terms of the traditional repertory or universe of communication of a particular language or language family, each event defines its own exemplar of speech space time—a single, man-made, discontinuum, entirely within man's control. A universe of speech communication may be conceived as a synchrony of ideation, more multitary than unitary, that serves as part of the reference and, hence, of the context of each discrete event in the two space times, viz.:

Mathematics Logic	Physical Sciences	Biological Sciences	Anthropology Sociology Psychology	Economics Political Science	Philosophy Communication Theory	Ethology Aesthetics	Belles Lettres Poetics	Religion Folklore	Myth Mysticism Ecstatics

THE MUSIC COMPOSITIONAL PROCESS [1]

The formational apparatus provides a class of discrete event in the physical universe consisting of single and/or multiple sound-lines that do not name, that is, that do not symbolize, represent, but embody, present. Its study comprises a phonology basically identical with that of the study of speech in the principal concepts and laboratory devices employed; but the music analogs of the speech lexicon, grammar, syntax, logic and rhetoric (only recently so named) are heterologous and possibly complementary in most respects. Like the speech event, the music event occurs in general space-time—a single, given, frequency-amplitude continuum entirely independent of man's control. When funded within and/or produced in terms of the traditional repertory or universe of communication of a particular music or music family, each event defines itself as

application of musicology to comparative, ethnological research is surprising and must be set aside as arbitrary." Yet on the next page he says:
"Musicology, if it is to rank with other comprehensive sciences, must
include every conceivable scientific dimension of musical topics." You
throw away your cake and eat it too. Harap and Hibbered supported this
view.[7] Indeed, as late as 1946 the leading article in a new musicological
journal could begin "La musicologie est une science historique qui a pour
object la musique et qui embrasse l'ensemble du phénomène musical
sous ses aspects *théorique* (mathématique des sons), *physique* (émission du
son), *esthétique* (l'étude des formes) et *philosophique* (essence de la musique
et son rôle psychologique et social)." ("Musicology is a historical science
that has music for its object and views the sound of music in terms of
theory [mathematics of sound], *physics* [emission of sound], *aesthetics* [study
of forms] and *philosophy* [essence of music and its psychological and social
role].")[8] This represents a considerable shrinkage of Adler's broad view.

Y: Albert Wellek seems to be the only man who has produced a substantial book specifically using the title *Musikphyschologie und Musikästhetic:
Grundriss der Systematischen Musikwissenschaft.*[9]

S: The trouble is, though, that Wellek makes psychology the base or
heart (*Kernstuck*). Walter Wiora has kept close track of him.[10] But even in
1953 neither the International nor the American Musicological Society
would have anything to do with systematic or comparative musicology as
organized or organizable approaches, orientations, or entitites on a par
with history. Occasional contributions to both subjects were, I must say,
accepted courteously as initiatives of individual scholars, both here and
abroad.

K: There is still confusion regarding the relationship of historical and
systematic orientations, and ethnomusicology. I know that you have distinguished them by pairs. Could you now distinguish the trio?

S: I have consistently pled for their unity.[11] In 1935 I proposed that
historical and systematic orientations of study "are complements—not
mutually exclusive opposites—of each other. One leads continually and
inevitably into the other. Their rapprochement is the most pressing task
of present day musicology." In 1951 I proposed "that distinctions
between historical and systematic orientations in musicology may best be
made upon the basis of two related concepts of spacetime, general and
musical: the historical viewing music as occurring in general spacetime,
the systematic, in music spacetime." I related the two concepts under
seven headings: occurrence, provenience, identity, continuity, control,
measurability, and variability. Where archeological, iconographic,
organographic, written, and/or sound-recorded data exist, historical and
systematic musicology go hand in hand—the more comprehensive the

treatment, the more history becomes a history of system(s) and system, a system of history (histories). Where no such data exist study must be mainly systematic—extensive prime research is being done under such conditions, and its classification under Adler's heading "*II. Systematisch.D.*" is not inapt—but historical reconstruction by comparative methods and speculative hypotheses are very much in order.

K: Much equally prime research is being done today in the study of music as diversified, as elaborate, and as extended as that of Europe and with vast unexplored data of all five kinds you cited. And that takes us to ethnomusicology. What about *that*?

S: In 1960 I proposed: "Two meanings of the term 'ethnomusicology' are current. One equates the prefix 'ethno-' with the adjective 'ethnic,' meaning 'barbarous, non-Christian, exotic'; the other, with the prefix 'ethno-' as in ethnology. The former implies that the study now known as 'ethnomusicology' is limited to musics *other* than the student's *own*; the latter, that it is limited to the cultural functions of music. Both of these meanings lead to unacceptable situations when applied to a musicological discipline *as a whole*: the first, because, in accord with it, if the study of a student's own music is to be known as musicology the same music studied by another student who does not carry its tradition, must be known as 'ethnomusicology'; the second, because no relatively independent academic discipline can be expected to confine itself to the view of a thing *in a context* to the exclusion of the view of the *thing in itself.*"[12]

K: Doesn't your definition of musicology run into Mantle Hood's, of ethnomusicology, in the Harvard Dictionary?

S: Not head on. They ultimately merge. Hood was very careful to put it: "Ethnomusicology is an approach" and goes on to say "to the study of *any* music, not only in terms of itself but also in relation to its cultural context." He was also careful to say, "Currently, the term has two broad applications: (1) the study of all music outside the European art tradition, including survivals of earlier forms of that tradition in Europe and elsewhere; (2) the study of all varieties of music found in one locale or region, e.g., the 'ethnomusicology' of Tokyo or Los Angeles or Santiago would comprise the study in that locality of all types of European art music, the music of ethnic enclaves, folk, popular and commercial music, musical hybrids, etc.; in other words, all music being used by the people of a given area." The implications of this second approach are inescapable: if the given area were Europe, its ethnomusicology would include what is currently known as "musicology," that is, the history of the fine art of European music; if the given area were the world, Hood's view of the field would coincide with mine. I feel quite comfortable with that eventuality and I believe Hood does, too.

K: Isn't it curious that once in the academic saddle American music historians have given no more than lip service to any concern but that of the history of the fine art of European music? Oh, there are individual exceptions; but I speak of the generality.

S: Yes. It is a pity that with so few exceptions music historians have withheld themselves from this large part of their field and that ethno-musicologists have done the same with respect to the ethnomusicology of the music of Europe *as one whole*. Until these two tasks have been undertaken upon a substantial scale for quite a few decades, the study of music will not have arrived at the degree of maturity reached by the study of language more than a hundred years ago.

K: In Europe they seem not to worry about the distinction between musicology and ethnomusicology as much as we do in the United States.

S: That's right. Constantin Brailoiu gave it the *coup de grace* in his attack upon the first of the two applications listed by Hood when advanced in 1954 by Manfred Bukofzer.[13] And the situation continues to change in both Europe and America. The Society for Ethnomusicology was organized after preparatory years 1953-1956. Madame Clercx-Lejeune, herself, took the initiative in 1954 by organizing the first *Colloque de Wégimont* of the *Cercle International d'Études Ethno-Musicologiques*. By 1960 in the United States, historicomusicology was wooing ethnomusicology. In 1960 the president of the American Musicological Society sent out a circular letter to members urging more attention to systematic musicology.

Y: To shift the conversation somewhat, do you expect your unitary field theory could be expressed in mathematical terms as physicists do theirs?

S: Only in part. Mathematization of linguistics is already well under way, and musicology follows linguistics in many respects. The lexicon and grammar—even syntax—of a well-established current music tradition might be even more susceptible to mathematical expression than might be the analogous functions of its most closely associated language. But we must remember that linguistics is only a descriptive, not a valuative, study.[14] It does not comprehend value theory, criticism, moral or speculative philosophy, ethology (ethics), poetics, comparative religions mythology, folklore, and other integral factors of all language use. As I have defined it for you, musicology comprehends the musical counterparts of all these and other studies. Their mathematization will undoubtedly be attemped, but I would not venture now to speculate upon its outcome.

K: One of the things that bothers me most about musicology is its avoidance of any attempt to reason about its critical method, its values.

S: It bothers me too.

K: There certainly is as much feeling and valuing as thinking and observing in musicology as in music. But the rationale of the relating of the two pairs of concepts is as remote from our musicology as it is from most scientific inquiry. How is it that you haven't made a universe of value?

S: That is the sixth universe I expected one of you to mention. You can make a universe of value out of four of our original universes, S, M, I, and C, all of which are valuative, that is, value-giving with respect to P, which—except for some religious teaching by which we, as musicologists, are not necessarily bound—is neither valuative nor value-giving. Thus, SMIC = V and can be related as follows:

FIGURE 3

K: How can you comprise such a diversity of items under the single concept "value"? What do you mean by value?

S: Take a full breath . . . Hold it . . . Hold it . . . You are a brave man . . . Longer . . . Relax . . . Don't lock your throat; keep it open . . . Do you begin to feel that there is nothing in this world that you want more than to take a breath? . . . Ah, there you go. Now you know what is meant by at least one class of value, the biological.

K: Whew! But that was just a physiological reaction to a breaking of habit. . . .

S: Like hunger, thirst . . .

K: Yes.

S: . . . tension of work or loneliness, lack of a mate and children, need to be yourself, to be in company with one's kind, to be part of a group joined in some common activity, to live in an organized society of a particular kind, to defend its traditions, to make music . . .

Y: Are you trying to make us admit there is no difference between fact and value?

S: Oh no. Rather, to admit that we relate facts to ourselves and ourselves to facts variously, and that it is this two-way relating that we call "valuation"—a function whose end products we generalize as the structural concept "value."

Y: Isn't there a borderline between the psychophysiological reflexes and the "canonized" values beauty, goodness, and love?

S: None that I can distinguish: between the basic physical intrusions upon our attention and our highest "spiritual" aspirations—the being of ourselves and the believing in our individuality or even in a universal individuality, as all monists do—no borderline. But between the direct, unmediated kinds of knowledge of value—as in music—and the indirect, symbol-mediated knowledge of speech communication relating to value, we must be careful to fix a borderline of utmost clarity. With you, I know, I need not dwell upon the distinction between speech value and music value; but I might have to remind you, as I must also continually remind myself, that the speech account of music value is not to be confused with music value as the musician may know it—we must not confuse the word with what it stands for.

K: Then what do we mean by the term *value* in speech communication about music?

S: It's a construct upon the same level of abstraction as our five original universes—and equally necessary in the art of speech. But as with the other five, definition is hazardous unless you have defined the terms you use in the definition—which takes a lot of time. To the extent that value is involved in musicology, I have had somethng to say about it in my "Preface to the Critique of Music"; but I hesitate to recommend your looking this up until my rather extensive revision of it is out. For purposes of our present discussion I can, however, paraphrase some of it. I will begin somewhat circumscriptively by pointig out that a growing literature upon the subject has been accumulating since before 1900, although reference to it in twentieth-century musicology is rare. W. M. Urban has said that some regard it as "the greatest philosophical achievement of the 19th century." In the context of our present discussion, I propose that *valuing is the relating, by a living organism, of itself to what is not itself and, equally, of what is not itself to itself, with a view to the continuance of its individuality*. Value is the relationship so set up.

Y: I'm still confused.

S: We have to talk about music in terms of fact and value, but that is looking at music from the outside—we must also look at music from the inside.

K: How do you look at music from the inside?

S: You know! That is what the musician does—in making music. Strictly speaking, you don't look; you just make music.

K: Of course.

S: When we talk we must say "that is musical fact" or "that is musical value." But music makes no such double statement. Its facts and values go out in a single package.

K: Some composers do separate them. They might even say to themselves, "These are facts, I think I'll give them such and such value. No, that combination sounds old-fashioned. I'd better rearrange them so as to be more contemporary, more avant garde, or what not."

S: Oh—that is what I call "musicological composition." It's exceptional.

K: In the sense that we speak of "the exceptional child"?

S: Perhaps. But let's go back to our universe of values,

which for present purposes can be shown as

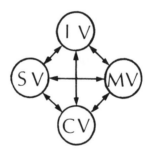

FIGURE 4

where SV stands for speech value, MV for music value, IV for individual value, and CV for cultural value. There are, of course, visual value and tactile value. And value as a pure concept remains valid. Individual value (value to the individual man) can be described in the same terms in which we can describe the minimal functions of the music event. I won't press that point now. Suffice it to say: you don't relate anything to yourself as value unless it either engages, or you give it your attention. It may be zero value, as far as you are concerned. Supposing we agree that minimal attention, whether induced or sought, rates a one percent value. From there on, increasing incidence, intensity, and duration of concern (three more gamuts) can range from pleasure, interest, absorption, devotion, to complete dominance of what might be a nearly hundred percent value upon being in love, experiencing the beautiful, or "god-consciousness." An opposite gamut of negative value would run from complete ignoring of something to pain, evil, hate. The parameter of cultural value (CV) would mirror the individual (IV) except that the teleology would be the continuity of the culture to be itself; hence the adjustments that individuals and cultures must continually make between the desired and the desirable, the want and the ought.

Y: I'm still confused. You distinguish between fact and value, and define valuing as the relating of fact to our own individuality. Are we then facts or values? If valuing is relating, it seems the things related— the individual as well as what is not himself—ought to be facts.

S: We can regard ourselves and be regarded by others as facts in the universe of fact (fig. 2, inclusion P) and as values in the universe of value (fig. 3).

K: Oh, I see. Like those gamuts of semantic variance you talked about earlier, there is a gamut of fact/value. But isn't there a point along this gamut where one becomes the other, or at least where they, as thesis and antithesis, are synthesized Hegelwise?

S: Not as I see it. Hegel taught that the thesis and antithesis are mutually interdependent and interpenetrate; his synthesis was a third term showing this. I prefer to accept the principle of complementarity announced by Niels Bohr in 1933, with the proviso that it is valid for our universe S regardless whether or not corresponding referents can be found in universe P. My idea of a gamut or parameter of semantic variance is one of structural lexical antonymity within a functional linguistic frame. Structurally, a parameter is defined in terms that are lexical constructs that are each other's antonyms, opposites, polarities, or what not. Functionally, it is defined in terms of grammatical and syntactic (and if spoken, also rhetorical) operations in which you move first in one direction and then the other, as for example, to value fact or to factualize value as in speaking of past valuations. I do not like to consider any gamut or parameter in either speech or music as a path that permits only head-on lexical collisions, but rather as a line that is given grammatical, syntactic, and logical width by a second parameter, depth and other dimensions by a third, fouth, fifth, sixth, and any successive gamuts involved in any particular undertaking.

K: Give me an example.

S: Well, we customarily regard the pitch gamut as a line of frequencies running roughly from +20 to +4000 cps., upon whose length we may proceed in either direction or stay still. A gamut of loudness, roughly 1-120 decibels, gives the parameter breadth; in the metaphor of visual representation that we have adopted, loudness is at right angles to pitch. The two ineluctably form (or are formed by) a third gamut of tonal density which gives depth. Adding the gamuts of speed and duration of events and of rhythmic density, we have the minimum six dimensions for the smallest musical unit. The speech parameter fact value can be viewed in a similar manner. As I see it, both fact and value are operational over the whole gamut that they define, but variously with respect to the variance of the other parameters involved. It is of highest importance always to bear in mind in which direction you are moving on the parameter, whether you are valuing fact or factualizing value.

Y: You still haven't answered my question: Which are we, fact or value? Or both at once? Now one, now the other? Now more, now less one than the other? Or neither?

S: What a persistent man you are! Now you have laid us out upon one of the most heavily traveled parameters of speech semantic variance—the ancient battlefield of soul versus body. As bodies, we are facts, no? Phenomena in the physical universe P. As knowers and feelers of our own separate individualities—and, if you insist we have them, our souls—we are values: to ourselves, in our individual universes I, to others like ourselves with whom we come in contact, in theirs and our common sociocultural universe C. And as upon each of the hundred-odd parameters or semantic battlefields, the battles fought are with the other parameters as weapons—especially, as in this case, with those of either-or-ness, all-or-nothingness, existence-nonexistence, subjective-objective, inclusion-exclusion, logic-mysticism, appearance-reality, determinism-free-will, and so forth, weapons each of which we grasp to flail our adversaries with and to maintain our positions. Before giving you my answer to your question, it might be good to mention five of the traditional positions taken by some of the most notable contestants who have fought upon this field. I'll represent them in the same way as before, as concepts, in circles large and small. It is to be understood that universe P is the universe of fact. To read the diagrams as referent to ourselves, imagine an I in front of each P and V.

Diagram 1 represents the position on the parameter taken by Plato. Concepts or ideas—beauty, truth, goodness, love and their ancillaries wisdom, justice, law, and so forth—are the few eternal and real values that can be reasoned about. Facts are too numerous, tenuous, and transitory to be reasoned or talked about. *Diagram 2* represents Bertrand

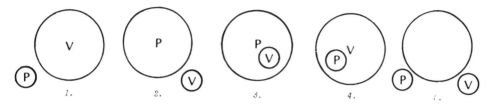

FIGURE 5

Russell's position. Value and values are entirely subjective, they cannot be reasoned about. *Diagram 3* represents Max Scheler's position.[15] Values are entirely objective facts that can be reasoned about. *Diagram 4* represents the position of several religions, most particularly Christianity. There is one supreme value: God. All others—and facts, too—derive from it. *Diagram 5* represents the position of classic Hinduism. Both fact and value are illusion: "The aim (value) of existence (fact) is nonexistence," but even better to become neither something nor nothing.

K: Now for your own position on the parameter.

S: Both fact and value are primarily speech concepts; as such, they belong to the universe of speech discourse. So I will use my earlier diagram of that universe (fig. 2, inclusion S), modifying it thus:

or, more appropriately,

FIGURE 6

In reference to not-speech, speech must use either fact or value. Of course, speech communicates much that is not in the words used, but rather in the way they are used and especially if spoken, in the way they are spoken, the tone of voice, its modulation, the speed, the loudness, the accent, and the accompanying gesture, facial expression, bodily tension, poise or relaxation, and so forth.

Y: How many gamuts, parameters, scales, or hierarchies of value have we got now?

S: Let's not try to count them. There are many more.

Y: Science gives us a more or less ordered universe of fact, but it seems to me that your universe of values is a vast chaos.

S: That is just what it is. The best we can do is to conduct ourselves in it in the most orderly way we can.

K: Granted. But if we should, do you think we could ever lay out the varieties of value as well as we have laid out the varieties of fact?

S: What is the layout of fact as of 1970?

K: Oh, you know: physical, biological, psychological, anthropological, and all the rest of the great academic disciplines.

S: All of these have bearing upon the inescapable necessity of every living organism to value.

Y: Can you seriously propose that animals, birds, fishes, insects value?

S: To the extent that any of them feed and defend themselves as individual beings—and especially if they mate discriminatingly—I can see no reason for withholding the name of the function. They certainly have many of the same problems we do, for example, the conflict between individual and social values. The mass suicide of lemmings is probably a valuative act.

Y: Do you suppose it was largely from anxiety regarding the position one takes upon this parameter of speech semantic variance that the nineteenth century finally resulted in the formation of the so-called Austrian school of general theory of value?

K: I should think that musicology might have something to say about general value theory. There is no anxiety in music.

S: Agreed. If dance can be said to be the art of being, surely music is the art of well-being and speech, the art of anxiety. Speech can hurt; music cannot. You state the case for serious examination by musicology not only of general and specialized speech theories of speech value but also of the world views of which they are essential and molding factors.

K: How did you become interested in such an unpopular topic?

S: It's too long and personal a story to be told here. Suffice it to say that when I was a very small child, that is, before I was five or six, my father became interested in astronomy. He had a good pair of binoculars and a popular book on astronomy with some good illustrations. He showed me how to see the satellites of Jupiter and he told me of enormous orbs, many times the size of the earth or the sun, hurtling through enormous spans of space and time. I was so impressed that I took to waking up several times with the same dream—very beautiful but terrifying.

K: A nightmare, eh? You should have been an astronomer!

S: Oh no. There was, I admit, an element of objectivity in my memory of the dream, but it was primarily a deeply subjective involvement, more emotional than intellectual. The latter was probably the awakened rationalization.

K: How so?

S: The stars and planets were beautiful peach-colored orbs and half-orbs seen against a sky-blue background and in some way moving tragically. It was I and only I who could keep the universe from destroying itself. I had only my own hands, and I was failing.

Y: Have you never thought of making a *Gesammtgebäude* for your unitary field theory?

S: I have made dozens. Here is the latest (see foldout), with much credit due to Adler's broad theory.

K: Why haven't you published one?

S: By its nature, such a schema is static and makes the field it represents—a dynamic, functional thing—appear static. Furthermore, it tends to make us view the study as a structure. True, the individual product of study—the book, the monograph, the paper—is a structure. But it is also a functional thing, a step in the musicological process. Then again, two-dimensional drafting dangerously oversimplifies. Three dimensions would be better, but that is beyond my ability. Music itself is four-dimensional. Musicology adds a fifth. In limiting myself to the two dimensions of the conspectus, the best I can do is to ask you to begin at the top and as you read down to remember that you are tracing your own progress over the terrain. When you come to a fork, you must decide which path to follow first but not to stay on it so long that you forget to go back and follow the other fork; for it is the drawing of the two together that is essential to the reading of the table.

K: If I can judge from a limited reading of your papers, you have spread yourself rather widely over your conspectus.

S: I wish the coverage were wider.

K: On examining it, I am somewhat confused as to exactly what you intend to cover under many of your terms.

S: For instance?

K: Systematics, historics, arbitrage.

S: Under the heading "Systematics" I gather all scientific and critical, musical and nonmusical, studies for which some aspect of music is a datum and may appear to have valual implications together with their analogs in the music compositional process as musicians know them. Under "Historics" I include not only universal history and evaluation but general histories, general histories of music, and the mass of special histories, both musical and nonmusical, that may appear to have valual implications. Under "Arbitrage" I gather the more or less collective operation of arbiters of musical and nonmusical taste—an indeterminate aggregate that bears variously upon the valual aspect of the act of music making.

K: What is a music event?

S: Anything that we accept or propose qua music, lasting a split second or an hour.

K: And that word *density*?

S: The number of events plus the relative energy with which they are produced within any specified time and place.

K: Semantic density bothers me.

S: No wonder! It took me a long time to find a term to denote the valual diversity and strength of a composition or performance. By the way, did you know that the word *value* derives from the Latin and Sanskrit roots *val-* and *bala-*, meaning strength, health, power? Hence, economic value.

K: Well, enough of that. Your conspectus is, I take it, a kind of road map. It doesn't tell you how to drive, though.

S: No, it doesn't and is not intended to. As you say, it is a kind of map of the field. How you behave in it is another matter, not structural but functional.

Y: Don't you expect your theory must await empirical verification, as must that of the physicists?

S: No. Because at least half its concern is with value, and because value must by definition be, in terms of my reasoning, ultimately nonempirical, it does not provide for verification.

Y: What, then, is to recommend it over against other field theories that might be proposed?

S: As far as I can see, only its possible greater usefulness in ordering musicological work.

K: We might have to examine a lot of them before choosing any one as best suited to our individual purposes?

S: Yes. That is precisely what we do now.

K: How so?

S: Each of us, to the extent he commands what he may regard as an ordered world view, has supposedly some kind of field theory. Much of it he will have learned from others. Its unitedness or unitariness will most likely, under present conditions, be found to be weak or nonexistent. The concern I emphasize is how well it is organized to comprehend the greatest number of factors and to order their interrelationship to best advantage in the particular orientation, scope, method, and aim of each individual man's work.

K: You simply offer your theory, then, as so far the most comprehensive and ordered as a unit.

S: And explicitly presented—yes.

K: It is not proposed for final acceptance?

S: By no means. For me, after I have completed presentation of the functional aspect of the case, that is, how best to drive the principal roads on the map that is my conspectus, it may be very close to what is final. There is, of course, the possibility that other musicologists might also find it so. I wouldn't even want to guess the probabilities. But I would expect that each person who would accept it might modify it to suit his particular world view. What I would most hope for would be a rather general acceptance of its essential factors.

K: You'd have to spell these out for me before I'd know just what you mean.

S: That is what I hope we shall do in the sequel to this interrogation, which should be a kind of manual of "How to Drive the Musicological Chariot, Model 1970." I shall have to add three more universes—one each for dance, painting, and sculpture. You can throw in drama, drawing, and architecture for inclusion, respectively, in the three. That gives us, in place of our two-dimensional road map that is our conspectus, a nine-dimensional world view through whose miraculous domain the musicologist may drive at his pleasure. I shall try to reduce the number of controls of the vehicle from the theoretical more than a hundred parameters of speech semantic variance to a bare minimum of two or three dozen that are primary and essential for general theory, which is what I am dealing with here. Specialized research may lock these in place in advance by assumptive adjustments so as to leave the student leeway in the use of the secondary for precision in research in the field, the laboratory, and the study. The key methodological principle will remain, however, that sound research into the microcosm is best assured by as comprehensive and balanced an outlook into the macrocosm as one's world view can provide—and vice versa.

Y: Just one more question before we break off. What has all this to do with contemporary composition—Cage, Stockhausen, aleatory, serial, improvisational, computed, electronic, and so forth.

S: Oh, those are some of the things you see, hear, and feel as you drive over the terrain schematized in the road map. I should warn you in advance that important as these are they will be only a minute part of the total scenary: for the vast majority of the music-producing and music-consuming population of this earth have not and may never know of their existence. They may, however, have an influence far beyond the small universe in which they have been born and flourished up to this day. They have added two categories of music to the already rich variety of musical experience—musicological music and antimusic. Business enterprise has added a third, a nonmusic that sounds like music but isn't, that is Muzak.

K: What, precisely, do you mean by "musicological music"?

S: Composition that is planned in advance and worked out in detail for the most part verbally and only then "realized" in sound that can be presented in the traditional fashion inherited from the nineteenth century—at a public concert, for which tickets may be put on sale for seats in a hall, with performers on a stage, most likely of an evening, and for which announcements are made in advance and reviews are hoped for later in newspapers or, nowadays, over the air qua music.

Y: How do you feel about musicological composition?

S: As a musician, I am variously repelled, offended, bored by most of it. In contrast with other music of the present and the past it seems anemic, without guts. But as a musicologist, it interests me enormously. In fact, I have amused myself often in this sort of enterprise.

Y: And antimusic?

S: That is the child of musicological composition. Although it began with Marinetti and Antheil, Cage's 4′32″ (or is it 4′33″) was the first immortal example. Speech has provided us with antimatter and antitime; why not antimusic?

Y: What is the borderline between music and mere sound?

S: I'd rather not try to fix one. Let's leave that to musicians and their audiences for the moment.

Y: At the present rate, it looks as if both may become increasingly musicologically minded.

S: Surely. But right-about-faces have not been unknown in music as in world views of vast populations. To some, the chance of the persistence of the unaccompanied voice may be about equal to the chance of its being stilled forever by the ecological crisis. But all this has to do with the manual of how to drive; for it is how you drive that enables you to discover details too small for inclusion on the road map without making it cumbersomely larger.

Y: And popular music?

S: I wouldn't be surprised if the hitherto almost rigid borderline between composition in the fine, elite, or professional art of music and in that of popular music might be broken down. For one thing, improvisation is increasing in both. The vast rewards, financial and other, in popular music will eventually attract academically, even musicologically, trained composers. Makers of some of the now almost innumerable kinds of so-called pop music are borrowing freely from the elite concert repertory.

K: And from cross-cultural, "ethnomusicological," sources.

S: That, too, is already on the way in both idioms.

K: I see you have provided for this in your conspectus.

S: It would not be worth much if I had not. We can probably expect hybridization to become more and more general.

Y: There will always be some who downgrade and void it.

S: Yes, and some who will upgrade and make the general do things no one else ever expected it could.

K: It seems to me, my friend, that the techniques of talking and writing you outline are so complicated, and that there is so much disagreement among authorities about what is fact, what is value, and what is meant by almost every other word we have to use, that there isn't much use in trying to talk about music seriously at all. Better just make music and give up musicology.

S: If that could be done I should be all for it. But what are the chances that it could be?

K: None at all, I suppose.

S: Well, there you are. That is precisely the justification for a more rigorous musicology, even though we know its reliability must necessarily fall far short of what we wish. As musicians, we have to defend ourselves against the shackling of music by speech prohibitions, fads, prejudices, good and bad intentions based upon innumerable different biases, dozens of other misrepresentations—and sheer ignorance. As musicologists we have the same hazards to meet and the same ingrained tendency, even necessity, to go to extremes. Between the neo-Baconians, who claim that the only things that can be known are facts, and some who, like F. S. C. Northrop, claim that all knowledge of fact is based upon sense data that are sheer mysticism, there are also an indeterminate number of variant views. If we are going to build a musicology that will be as reliable as possible and engage the widest possible consensus among our fellow students, we must use the principal concepts involved in it in some kinds of middle-of-the-road senses. Such senses would represent compromise between their applicability to the object of our study and the most acceptable usage of the language current in the society in which we live, whether or not studies extrinsic to music approve. My reduction of the elements of the speech process to the four steps (1) naming, (2) relating names, (3) relating the named, (4) relating the relations among the names to the relations among the named, is a step in the direction of agreement.

K: Nonmusicologists—and perhaps musicologists, too—may call that simplistic.

S: Of course they will. It is; it cannot be otherwise. A less pejorative term would be *reductive*. But see what an intelligible pair of definitions it allows: fact is defined by the degree of correspondence between the relationships among the names and the relationships among the named; value, by the relating of facts to ourselves—ourselves as affected by the impact of forces from outside ourselves and as being, ourselves, forces with appetites to live and purposes in living that act upon our environment.

K: Again simplism.

S: Yes. It has to be. And thank heaven, if it keeps us out of the intricate controversies of the more than a dozen *Hilfswissenschaften* that musicology must rely upon.

K: Provided only that your approach serves our purposes.

S: Yes, I propose it only as such. And I plead extenuating circumstance. Simplism with respect to music is admittedly inevitable in every nonmusical study and has always been tolerated benignly. It is high time that simplism with respect to nonmusical studies were admitted to be inevitable in musicology—and tolerated, also benignly.

K: Will this procedure not produce merely one more jargon where already there are too many?

S: Of course. We can try to keep ours down to the underlimit of what is commonly derided as "gobbledygook," but we cannot entirely escape the hazards of the predicament we put ourselves into when we propose to talk about music, any more than can students in other fields escape the hazards peculiar to the predicaments they put themselves into in talking about their subjects of study. Any more questions?

Y: A lot, but only one that I can put into words at the moment. It is a double one. First: is the field you speak of really not the total music of man but rather the total talking about it? Second: what is unitary about your theory of it? The more we have talked, the more we have talked of talking; and the more we have divided, rather than unified.

S: True. That is the way this kind of talking has to be done.

K: You know, of course, that this is a highly unconventional way of handling the matter.

S: Who knows it better! But it isn't as unconventional as your words would seem to make it. It is only the few new names and the concept of the ranges of variance that are not in common use. The dichotomies that define them are hoary with age; they have been wrestled with by every philosopher, scientist, and critic in our history as well as by poets and mystics. The proposal that speech and music, between them, define a parameter of speech semantic variance between logic and mysticism may be hardest to accept. As I have said, perhaps too often, it is chiefly because of the written word and written note that we do not more bear in mind that speech sings and music talks to greater extents than we realize.

K: What is unitary about your theory, then, is to blend the conventional verbalization of music with a novel musicalization of speech so that opposites are not necessarily mutually exclusive and so that mysticism takes an ordered place on a par with logic . . .

S: . . . which implies that the field of musicology is, after all, one of talk rather than of music. But then I remember that the musicologist can say things about music (because he is adept in both the intrinsic and extrinsic views of music) which neither the musician nor the nonmusician can. I find myself, therefore, regarding the field of musicology somewhat as shown in this kind of diagram:

FIGURE 7

You understand, I am sure, that I do not imply that the musicologist can know the whole of either universe, S or M, except as concepts. It is within the area of the overlapping of their empirical referents that he can be most logical. He must feel free to speculate and use poetic imagery and metaphor, and even mystical reference, in trying to link the areas of the two universes outside their overlapping with the area of the overlapping. Of course, the boundaries themselves are so vague as to be largely imaginary.

K: So—your musicologist is to be poet and seer as well as scientist and critic.

S: All the better, if he can be.

Y: What occupies the blank spaces above and below the two over-lapping circles?

S: I was wondering whether you would notice them. . . . We cannot, I believe, omit consideration of the bearing of vision and tactility upon musicology. Seeing and touching are operative in music in ways secondary only to hearing. I would like to think they are equally relevant to talking about it. That is why, in my conspectus, I make my first break-down of communication the threefold classes: Tactile, Auditory, and Visual. As I have pointed out before, the advantages of considering them (1) as three identifiable media that sometimes act together, sometimes separately, and (2) as three related ways in which an overall "mind" always acts, appear about equal to the disadvantages.

K: Then music is not even half the total field of musicology.

S: We must, however, resist its looking that way, for there are other ways in which we must look at the case—in terms of focus, for example, which is clearly upon music rather than upon other elements in the picture. Then again, the intensity of the student's concentration upon this focus must lead him to try to bring to bear upon the situation as much as he can from inside music, to balance the overwhelming amount of what comes from outside it. When you cast up the final account, you will find musicology is about equally a critique of speech and of music.

K: It begins to look to me as if your instructions of how to drive the 1970 model musicological chariot would turn out to be something of a broad guide to live and let live—a more or less complete philosophy.

S: I wouldn't pose them as a philosophy, for I do not pretend to be a philosopher. I admit I have trespassed upon the domain of philosophy but as one who looks at it more from the outside than from the inside, whereas the traditional role of the philosopher has been the opposite. But as a guide to musicological living and letting live it expresses fairly well my present view. Music has been the prime discipline in my life, and for me the prime function of musicology is to interpret this discipline to fellow carriers of my own and other cultures so that it will fit my own music and other musics as well. Then eventually the lot may be viewed empirically as well as conceptually as one coherent system.

EPILOGUE

S: Now that we see the foregoing interrogation in page proof, Boris, how do you feel about its publication?

K: Well, it certainly doesn't conform to customary styles of dealing with topics such as you have touched upon. As you said it would, it has the randomness of common sense, but sometimes the reasoning belies this. The two don't always fit together very well. But I'd let it go as it stands.

S: It is clear, though, is it not, that I propose a world view has its roots, and a field theory must be regarded as much in terms of common sense and feeling as of reason?

K: Oh, yes. And as you say, common sense, feeling, and reason are not mutually exclusive opposites. But the questions you have had me ask do not explore as many of the possibilities of disagreement with your propositions as they might.

S: Touché. And I am sure that some who know you well will be surprised to find you asking some of the questions you do. Indeed, it was because it would have been absurd to attribute some of them to you that I had to invent Jim Yost. . . . How do you feel about it, Yost?

Y: Out of respect for my elders I soft-pedalled a lot of questions.

S: For example.

Y: For one: shouldn't you have taken more specific pains to justify pursuit of musicology at a time of crisis such as the present? For another: is not the role of morality, theology, and religion too hidden in your conspectus? How about *satyagraha*? And where does musicology relate to the threats of our ecology?

S: I would have welcomed any of these questions.

K: Might they not belong more to the manual how to drive than to the road map?

S: I would prefer to handle them that way. What frightened me years ago (and still does) when I first faced the questions you pose, Yost, is man's ever overtrusting of one system of communication, speech, and his steady depreciation of all the others qua communication; for speech alone poses the conditions of our lives in terms of problems, while its domination of us and our affairs is possibly the biggest problem of all. How can we expect to solve all problems in terms of the biggest problem of all—that of the linguocentric predicament—is quite a problem. As a problem, I believe it is insoluble.

Y: In an address at the 14th Nobel Symposium last year a speaker is reported to have lent his support to the theory that man's inhumanity to man is evidence of a genetically aberrant evolution of our species and that our use of speech reflects this. So, man is committing specicide. Now you come along and tell us, virtually, that it is our misuse of the art of speech that lies at the base of all our troubles and that it is mainly— surely not only—by a revision of our habits of verbalization that we may hope to escape from the dilemma they have put us in. Is this not perilously close to raising ourselves by our own bootstraps? Might not the misuse of speech also be the result of such aberrance?

S: For my part, until biologists present conclusive evidence that some genetic process such as the RNA-DNA syndrome operates in man in a way markedly different from the way it does in all living organisms, I see no reason to assume that the aberrance is genetic and therefore probably irremediable. It might as plausibly be sociocultural and therefore re-mediable. This could be the case if our prehuman ancestors developed, from a single set of sound signal types such as those of present-day non-human primates, two sets—one that exploits distinction and problem-posing (speech), the other (music) that does neither. As to the bootstraps, I fear we are so deeply imbedded in the linguocentric predicament that we shall have to pull ourselves out by those bootstraps or not at all. Fortunately, the problem approach is not our only recourse. In addition to the viewing of (speech) concepts as mutually exclusive competitors in determinative wars of words that better us in some ways but worsen us in others, perhaps more, we can view them as compensatory factors in a technique ruled by principles of indeterminacy and complementarity. Such a technique would set stringent limits upon its own authority by acknowledging that speech is only one of a consortium of six or nine systems of communication available to us. As you know, for thousands of years some philosophers have sought development of this latter approach, the dialectic, as an alternative to or an adjunct or corrective of logic, which is the technical implementation of the problem approach. By its very nature, its service is to mediate, reconcile, harness together the dichotomies, trichotomies, and other problem-generating devices of speech logic. Common sense, as I see it, is a random alternation of logic and dialectic, reason and mysticism, perception and intuition, knowledge and imagination, with random intrusions of other means of communica-tion. The problem approach is preeminently suited to fact thinking and, so, to the great natural and social sciences; the dialectic, to what *under-lies* the sensation, perception, and cognition of fact and what *lies beyond* it that defines purpose, will, and conation. It is, characteristically, the method of criticism. During the last three or four centuries of the West, value thinking has been subordinated to fact thinking. Consequently, the development of logic has far outstripped the development of dialectic, which, in turn, has often partaken of a not quite orthodox, a dissident, even a revolutionary character.

Y: What are the six or nine members of your communicatory consortium?

S: I list them near the top of my conspectus under the three media, channels, or avenues of communication: tactile, auditory, visual. By "corporeality" I refer to body-to-body contact as in combat and coercion, handshaking and grooming, to courting and copulation. By "design" I refer to painting and drawing; by "artifacture," to sculpture, architecture, and the production of material objects from pottery jugs to statues, tents to cathedrals, pointed sticks to computers, G-strings to jewels.

K: You believe, then, that all of these, music and dance, too, function as communication, not only *with* mediation of speech but also *without* it.

S: Yes. They can and do, do they not?

Y: I notice that your titles II and III, music and speech, are connected with a dotted line; music and dance, by a brace.

S: By that I indicated that the semiotics of music and speech differed from that of music and dance. In music and speech we use one and the same sensory means, channel, or avenue—audition. In both, we use an internal musculature—the voice or vocal mechanism—to communicate by making sound audible in the immediate space around us and in the immediate time span of our lives. The spacetimes and mass energies of music and speech are paradromic. That is why they can be so intimately associated in song. They divide rather evenly most of the sound-making resources of the voice but share some of them. For example, both can be spoken of as well in terms of level of intonation, loudness, and density of sound (timbre), and of speed, relative duration, and density of rhythm (movement), as in terms of lexicons, grammars, syntaxes, and rhetorics. I have chosen to indicate this spacetime, mass energy, tonal rhythmic, relationship of music and speech by a dotted line. The semiotics of music and dance, however, are only half paradromic—in time, but not in space. Both, as do all the other means of communication, function in the same general (outward) spacetime. The dancer's own space—the space his body occupies—is always his, however he may move in general spacetime. He uses another of our three media, tactility. The prime sensation of the dancer is the touch of the ground upon and the air in which he moves, the speed and relative durations of the movements he makes. In many respects, the rhythmic density of dance can be identical with that of music. The movement of dance is, however, mostly with the outer musculature, not an inner, as with music. Spatially, however, that is, in terms of mass, the semiotic medium of dance is quite, though not, of course, totally, different from that of music. To regard singing as a dance of the vocal chords may be a bit fanciful; and in dance there is sound, especially at higher energies—of the breath, the feet upon the ground, the swish of clothing, the jingle of ornaments.

K: You feel that the counterpart of the sound space of music is, in the dance, the body space of the dancer, touching the ground, the air, itself, another dancer, or even artifacts such as swords, shields, wands, clothing, and natural objects?

S: Yes.

K: How about instrumental music?

S: A real composite of all three media. A musical instrument is an artifact; the musician dances upon it—even with it, as may a dancer, too. . . . Please bear in mind that the categories I am dealing with are not to be regarded as mutually exclusive opposites. One can see and touch a speaker or a musician, hear and see a dancer, touch and hear many artifacts. We all know the difference of sound of a pencil and a book falling upon the floor . . . but to keep this epilogue from excessive length, let me revert to the main reason for its being. A curious aspect of the linguocentric predicament is that in dealing with the manifoldness of scientific fact speech has formed a remarkably unitary logic, whereas in dealing with the ineluctably unitary individuality of the particular human being it has had to endure a manifoldness of none too compatible dialectics, all of which require a philosophical sophistication to which few, if any, musicologists may aspire. In adding one more to the lot I am not pretending to make a contribution to philosophy but to adapt the art to speech to its use by musicologists in the study of music. From an orthodox speech viewpoint this may seem to be a preposterous undertaking and may be regarded as sciolistic; but I aver that in view of the unique nature of musicological work something of the sort is a prerequisite for research that strives at once for the utmost in both comprehensiveness and precision.

K: You haven't given us much of a notion how your dialectic works.

S: No. I have gone as far as to propose that viewed qua a problem, that is, as a case to be handled by logic, the linguocentric predicament is insoluble, but that a modus vivendi for individual and collective man under the present conditions of his domination by the art of speech might be: (1) to develop the dialectic to an extent comparable to that to which he has developed logic (not forgetting, of course, that logic can be viewed as a kind of dialectic and dialectic, as a king of logic); (2) to develop our axiology until it is on a par with our phenomenology; (3) to impose strict limits upon the relevance of speech and not-speech; (4) to depend more upon the other systems of communication and in the course of so doing to free them of some of the inhibiting bonds we have imposed upon them through speech. How this might be done is what I must try to show in the manual how to drive the musicological chariot Model 1970, or "What every young person should know who contemplates marriage—of speech and music."

NOTES

1. Earl W. Count, "Myth as World View," in *Culture in History* (New York: Columbia University Press, 1960), pp. 580-627; Karl D. Uitti, *Linguistics and Literary Theory* (Englewood Cliffs, N.J.: Prentice-Hall, 1969), pp. 1 ff.

2. Walter Wiora, "Musikwissenschaft," *Die Musik in Geschichte und Gegenwart* (Kassel: Bärenreiter Verlag, 1961), IX, 1191-1203; François Lesure, "Musicologie," *Encyclopédie de la Musique* (Paris: Fasquelle Editeurs, 1961), III, 268-269; Hans-Gunter Hoke, "Musikwissenschaft," *Musiklexikon*, ed. Horst Seeger (Leipzig: VEB Deutsche Verlag für Musik, 1966), II, 186-196; Hans Heinrich Eggebrecht, "Musikwissenschaft," *Riemann Musik Lexikon* (Mainz: B. Schott's Söhne, 1967), III, 615-618; Willi Apel, "Musicology," *Harvard Dictionary of Music* (Cambridge: Harvard University Press, 1969), pp. 558-559.

3. Guido Adler, "Umfang, Methode und Ziel der Musikwissenschaft," *Vierteljahrschrift für Musikwissenschaft*, I, 1 (1885), 5-20.

4. Friedrich Chrysander, "Vorwort und Einleitung," *Jahrbücher für Musikwissenschaft*, I, 1 (1863), 9-16.

5. See for examples, Hugo Riemann, *Grundriss der Musikwissenschaft* (Leipzig: Verlag von Quelle und Meyer, 1914), which devotes its first four chapters (pp. 1-112) to systematic musicology and its fifth to history (pp. 113-148); K. G. Fellerer, *Einführung in die Musikwissenschaft* (Berlin: Bernhard Hahnfeld Verlag, 1942), which is exclusively systematic, dividing music as a field of research into two sections, I. *Die Grundlage der Musik*, II. *Die Musik in ihre Wertung*. The *Hilfswissenschaften* function as they may in reference to any relevant item.

6. W. S. Pratt, "On Behalf of Musicology," *Musical Quarterly*, I, 1 (January 1915), 1-16.

7. The prejudice against the German terms *systematik* and *systematisch* seems to persist among writers in English, as, for examples, Louis Harap, "On the Nature of Musicology," *Musical Quarterly*, XXIII, 1 (1937), "I do not believe that formal classification (except for the initial separation of historical and systematic studies) is of much importance, except as it serves some practical purpose, such as the formulation of a list of courses for the musical curriculum" (p. 20); Lloyd Hibberd, "Musicology Reconsidered," *Acta Musicologica*, XXXI (1959), " . . . Adler's opposition to a 'historical' and a 'systematic' section (*Teil*) is unsatisfactory" (p. 27).

8. Suzanne Clercx, "Definition de la musicologie et sa position a l'égard des autres disciplines que lui sont connexes," *Revue Belge de Musicologie*, I (1946-1947), 113-116.

9. Albert Wellek, *Musikpsychologie und Musikästhetic: Grundriss der Systematischen Musikwissenschaft* (Frankfurt am Main: Akademische Verlagsgesellschaft, 1963); see also "Begriff, Aufbau und Bedeutung einer systematischen Musikwissenschaft," an address presented at the meeting of the Gesellschaft für Musikforschung at Rothenburg in 1944 as reported in *Die Musikforschung*, I (1948), 67; and see also "Gegenwartsprobleme Systematischer Musikwissenschaft," *Acta Musicologica*, XLI, 3-4 (July-December 1969), 213-235.

10. Walter Wiora, "Die wechselseitige Fundierung der Historischen und Systemati-schen Musikwissenschaft," an address presented and reported at the meeting of the Gesellschaft für Musikforschung as above in n. 9. See also his "Albert Wellek's 'Grundriss der Systematischen Musikwissenschaft und die Verbindung von systematischem mit historischem Denken,' " *Die Musikforschung,* XIX, 3 (July-September 1966), 247-260.

11. Charles Seeger, "Systematic and historical orientations in musicology," *Acta Musicologica,* XI (1939), 127-128; "Systematic Musicology: Viewpoints, Orientations, and Methods," *Journal of the American Musicological Society,* IV, 3 (Fall 1951), 242-243.

12. Charles Seeger, "Semantic, Logical, and Political Considerations Bearing Upon Research in Ethnomusicology," *Ethnomusicology,* V, 2 (May 1961), 77-80.

13. Constantin Brailoiu, *Les Colloques de Wégimont: Cercle International d'Études Ethno-Musicologiques* (Bruxelles: Elzevir, 1959), Premier Colloque 19-26 September 1954, pp. 35-36.

14. John Lyons, *Introduction to Theoretical Linguistics* (Cambridge: Cambridge University Press, 1968), p. 1.

15. Max Scheler, *Der Formalismus in der Ethik und die Materiale Wertethik,* 5th ed. (Bern: A. Francke AG, 1966), pp. 29 ff.

VII

The Music Compositional Process as a Function in a Nest of Functions and in Itself a Nest of Functions[69]

The disposition to communicate by means of auditory signals seems to be a trait of many species of insects, fishes, birds, and mammals. Some have fairly elaborate sets of signals. Peter Marler writes: "It begins to appear that a repertoire of from about ten to about fifteen basic sound signal types is rather characteristic of non-human primates as a whole."[1] We may suppose that paleosocial man communicated by means of sets of auditory signals not too unlike those employed by nonhuman primates of our own day. Anthropologists assure us that direct observation has never disclosed the existence of a society of human beings in which two separate sets of auditory signals—a predominantly symbolic speech and a predominantly asymbolic music—have not been cultivated side by side. Historians, although they have no direct evidence that speech and music may once have been one and the same communicatory tradition, have found abundant evidence that the two arts have been associated in song among men from earliest recorded historical times.

When and by what gradual or sudden steps our presumably primate ancestors separated their presumably single sets of auditory signals into the two that we can trace back only a few thousand years, we shall probably never know. Tone languages, signal-drumming, the passing of meaningful spoken words into intonation of meaningless syllables in the exhortation of possession rituals, the attaching of particular speech meanings to bugle calls, ruffles and flourishes of drums, and the snatches of motifs and phrases in radio and television advertising—all these and more associations of the two arts in twentieth-century civilized life, cannot but impress one with a continuing interdependence and complementarity of the two arts. Not the least significant, today, are the novel auditory constructions produced by electronic means which are neither traditional speech nor traditional music, but are planned, often in great detail, (1) in terms of mathematical, logical, or even poetic language under (2) direction of imagination trained or at least accustomed in the composition of traditional music.

On the whole, the variance of the respective sound signals of the two arts, though substantial, is more one of degree than of kind, which is to say: it is upon parameters that can be studied with identical concepts and laboratory equipment. But the variance of the formation of these signals in discrete messages that can be received with the affects and understanding characteristic of the separate arts is more one of kind. It is not yet entirely clear how many of the concepts necessary in study of one of the two arts are valid in the study of the other. The formational difference is as clearly distinguishable with respect to the understanding as to the affect of the two diverse signal-message syndromes. For examples, one must study the tradition of a language before one can understand even a simple speech message, whereas, though a study of the technique of the making of a music message enhances understanding, it is common experience that a very substantial proportion of this content can be received without any study or even previous experience of the tradition that it represents. It is not surprising, therefore, that we are faced today with the question: how is it that there are many kinds of music but that they are not as mutually unintelligible to their makers as are the many kinds of speech that we call languages to their makers?

In spite of the proliferation of distinguishable traditions of music, through the lot of them runs a preconception that music, though not as the old cliché had it "a universal language," is at least less differentiated in its technical operation and more universally comprehensible than speech. An ambiguity in the use of words referent to music is knit into the very fabric of European languages. Scholars as well as the general public generalize and particularize the nouns *music, speech,* and *language* in quite different ways. We say we go to a concert "to listen to music." We do not say that we go to church or to the theater "to listen to speech" or "to listen to language." We may listen to *a* speech, but not to *a* music. We do not speak of a "piece of speech" or a "piece of language" the way we do of a "piece of music," as if it were a piece of pie.

In the Western world, music is talked about to a greater extent in terms of structure—concrete structures, at that—with immutable beginnings, endings, and inner construction. The *piece* of music is regarded more as a physical object than is the piece of speech, unless it be a formula, a poem, or a Gettysburg Address. Furthermore, the sociocultural functions of speech are well known. Almost anyone could list many, from prayer and exhortation to argument, through the management of daily life to information, entertainment, and gossip. Beyond entertainment, few could cite a social-cultural function for music other than to "pull people together" or to be liked or not liked. In many other parts of the world, first to be cited would be magic, ritual, ceremony, therapy, expression of the spirit of a people, usefulness in daily life.

Twentieth-century fashions of speech communication in the Western world—especially in dealing with the humanities—have tended to refer to matters of attention more easily in terms of structure than of function. Thus, we do not have descriptions or histories of musicality, which is a function of individual social behavior, or of tradition, which is a function of collective social behavior, but of discrete structures produced by these behaviors. Similarly, the generic term *music* tends to denote these and collections or repertories of them rather than the interplay of individual and social, musical and nonmusical functions in which selectivity, continuity, and variation are equally norms of a socially current tradition of music and the behavior of living carriers of that tradition.

I

In distinguishing, naming, and relating any matter of attention in the humanities, we must accept, I believe, as a necessary methodological postulate, the equal importance and interdependence of concepts of structure and function. By "structure" I refer in the present instance to such examples as the physical form of a particular artifact and of aggregates of artifacts, to the patterns of belief and behavior observed in the individuals who produce the artifacts and the patterns of population distribution and social class these individuals represent; by "function," (1) to the traditions or ways of making, using, believing, and doing things that have been inherited, invented, cultivated, and transmitted by these individuals; (2) to the relative intensity of the activity; and (3) to the relative dependence and interdependence of the traditions of a culture, and to their combined operation in the culture as a whole and in the living bodies of their carriers.

In the discursive use of language it is easier to identify, similarize, and differentiate structures than functions, as well as things in themselves as things in their context. Items viewed on a level of maximal discreteness, such as particular artifacts, are most easily structuralized. They are perceivable as facts, past or present phenomena in the physical, external universe of the senses. It is only a small additional step to the structuralization of classes of items, classes of such classes, and so on until the whole body of items of attention becomes viewed as a gigantic structure—a universe of *things*. Structures, small or large, seem to "stay still" while one contemplates them, especially when referred to in the isolation of writing or print. They are data—things given. One can observe them objectively. Thus, any tentatively mentioned whole can be most easily analyzed as a composite of many parts. And on, ad infinitum. Study that is mainly reliant upon structural thinking tends to be a posteriori, of what has been, of the past. The view of a field of study with emphasis upon structure tends to represent it as spatial, with fixed components, static, even its values. Observe the extensive and elaborate treatment of sound—the spatial aspect of music—in the so-called theory of Western pedagogy. A hundred books, articles, dissertations are produced relative to tuning, intonation, scales, modes, keys, chords, tonality, tone quality, to one upon any aspect of rhythm which is the temporal and essentially functional aspect of music. Melody—perhaps because it must be conceded to be made up as much by rhythm as by tonal factors—is rarely dealt with. Structural thinking encourages the backward glance, fact-finding, and concern with origins. History comes to be regarded as succession of events. Inevitably, music becomes a matter of many kinds.

It is more difficult to speak of anything in terms of function. Function has to do with action, movement, force, process toward an end. We cannot say we see, hear, or feel action, movement, force, or process. We have to say we see, hear, feel some structure, *thing*, or *things* as parts of a process, or as acting, moving, exerting force upon some other *thing* or *things*—ourselves or what not. It is not surprising, therefore, that distinguishing, naming, relating, and classifying functions in the art of speech has been done in terms of structures that are bundles or patterns of functions and that this has operated adversely upon the understanding of particular functions and of the concept of function in general. It is easier to treat any item of attention in terms of structures that reveal functions than in terms of functions that reveal structures. Thus, verbalization tends also to structuralize function. It becomes a *thing*. To offset this weakness in the technique of speech, the view of a field of study with deliberate emphasis upon function may attempt to represent it as temporal, with changing rather than stable components, dynamic rather than static. Functional thinking is dynamic, encourages the forward glance, value-thinking, teleology, purpose, and concern with ultimate ends. History comes to be regarded as a linear process upon which events are points and tradition, a function of a culture. In this view, music may be regarded for some purposes of study as functioning in a single unitary manner regardless of the culture in which it is found.

The wisest course to pursue in this predicament would seem to be first to give equal attention to the two alternatives and then to attempt to compensate for the overstructuralization caused by the art of speech by deliberate emphasis upon a functional approach to any item of attention.

This is the more important in musicology because the compositional process of music seems to be as predominantly functional as that of speech is predominantly structural. There is no evidence that music distinguishes—that is, isolates one item of attention from another—names, structuralizes, or classifies anything. There is no evidence that the feature of contradiction, essential in reasoned and discursive speech, is a feature of music. Truth, therefore, is neither a fact nor a value in it.

In short it would seem that while speech creates a predominantly structural universe music creates one in which the dichotomy of structure versus function is either integrated or not involved. If music creates a predominantly functional universe, we are impaled in musicology upon one horn of the dilemma presented by the dichotomy structure/function in that we are attempting to treat it in terms of discoursive speech which creates more easily a predominantly structural than a predominantly functional universe. We would structuralize music. This is precisely what conventional "theory" and history of music has long done. If music creates an integrated structural-functional universe or one in which the dichotomy is not involved (which seems the more likely), we are impaled upon the other horn of the dilemma. Better than treating the two antonyms, opposites, or polarities as a dichotomy would seem to be to accept them as the limits or, better, limiting areas of one of the two or three dozen most important parameters or variables of speech semantic variance. On such a parameter, speech about music would seem to operate in an area near the structure limit, music itself, in one near the function limit.

Ideally, mathematical speech, which is predominantly functional, would seem to be the most efficient instrument for dealing with music in terms of that art. The hazards there, however, would be: first, that few musicologists could hope to acquire the mathematical skill to use the instrument properly; and second, that instead of an overstructuralization of discursive speech, we would have an overfunctionalization by mathematical speech of something that in itself may be a blend of the two or something neither functional nor structural. What we should try to avoid is remaining Pythagorians *or* Aristoxenians to the end and missing the target of our study, music, for confusion of it with speech reports of it.

II

The following table lists some of the principal categories commonly found in music-technical and historiographical literature as points that are locatable on the parameter of speech semantic variance defined (or limited) by the terms *structure* and *function*.

TABLE 1

A. Extrinsic	B. Intrinsic
1. Geographical area	1. Own and not-own traditions
2. Culture area	2. Own and not-own tastes
3. Political area	3. Expert and less expert
4. Social strata	4. Creative and re-creative
5. Sex, age group, occupation, etc.	5. Written and unwritten
6. Social function	6. Self-made and made by others
7. Focuses of interest	7. Free and priced
	8. Traditional and nontraditional
	9. Music-technical functions

A.1. *Geographic area.* Consideration of music in relation to the broadest geographic category—the continental—yields only the broadest generalities, as, for example, in the acculturation of European and Amerindian and European and African traditions in the Americas, the penetration of Islamic traditions to Morocco, sub-Saharan Africa, and Indonesia, and of European traditions throughout the world. Of such acculturation we have, however, few carefully studied data. Geographic features such as elevation, natural avenues, and barriers of communication and movement, climate, flora, and fauna have direct bearing upon the making of musical instruments and the spread of music tradition.

A.2. *Culture area.* Eminently necessary in the categorization of music, this much-debated and little-agreed-upon concept of *area* in which a human population exhibits a uniform pattern of culture traits is difficult for musicologists to handle. Of special importance is the relative coincidence and noncoincidence of linguistic and musical culture areas.

A.3. *Political area.* Political and music areas have been generally assumed to be on the whole coincident, largely on the basis of European and American nationalism. The atmosphere in which claims or denials of nationalism in music are made is so foggy that although in common everyday parlance it is convenient to speak of German, French, Russian, or Italian music(s), the usual omission of the plural *s* of music would seem to acknowledge these as variants of an overall unit—European music. In contrast, the designations Japanese, Chinese, Korean, Indonesian, East Indian, music(s) discloses a need for the plural afforded by that final *s*. Current ethnomusicological usage tends, on the whole, to accept the blanket term *Western* music, but reject the counterparts *Eastern* and *Oriental.* "Our (National) Music" is, still, an epithet frequently met within the West. Sometimes it refers to one or another of the various kinds of music cultivated within national boundaries and, so, considered characteristic of the national *Geist* or Gestalt; but it rarely refers in a comprehensive and precise manner to the total music cultivated in a country; for there is much music that has never been and still is not studied upon the level and with the methods that others are studied. The rare references to total music in either musicological or ethnomusicological literature are in terms of concepts used only in broad surveys of an initial and exploratory nature.[2]

A.4. *Social strata.*   Classification by social strata is probably one of the most widely and ambiguously used at the present time. It is the fruit of a view of man and his ways of living "from above down," the viewer placing himself ethnocentrically in the position of "the above." Such a view might flourish in any highly diversified and elaborated civilization with coinciding, strongly maintained, political, cultural, and geographic boundaries. Specifically, here, it is a development of European academic disciplines that have observed the population of the Western world and its colonial extensions as consisting of one coherent, social-class structure, its primitive minorities, rural and urbanized majorities, and wealthy, educated minorities forming four social classes, low to high, scholars eventually considering themselves members of the last and highest class. Strictly speaking, a tribal society is not a social stratum. Only colonialism and the ethnocentric viewpoint of the colonizing society makes it seem so. It may, nevertheless, have no class structure and, so, constitute a single-social-stratum type of social organization. But within the hegemony of the conquering culture, it is, in effect, a lowest class—"the common people" or even pariahs.

Copious reference to societies in such extrinsic, nonmusic-technical terms has distinguished, named variously, and found useful the distinction of four categories of music usage—subtraditions or, as I shall name them here, "music idioms." To best of present knowledge, no generally agreed upon definitions of the lot have been arrived at. Neither historicomusicologists nor ethnomusicologists were involved in the conception or naming of these categories. Both have used them in offhand, uncritical manners, without special scrutiny. As a result, both find themselves embarrassed by having extrinsically conceived, uncritically accepted, and variously named, but possibly useful, baggage on their hands. The embarrassment is complicated by the fact that as conceived by the nonmusicologically minded, musicians and laymen alike, these often were functional categories. But musicologists have understood them to be more or less watertight structures, that is, repertories modeled after the written or printed repertory of the masterworks or monuments of European music amassed by historicomusicologists. The question presents itself, therefore: are these extrinsically conceived and named idioms valid in terms intrinsic to music?

In order to range the four extrinsically named idioms upon a common level and render them uniformly susceptible to a strictly nontechnical and musicological identification for later technical analysis, I shall propose (1) a set of four names as close as possible to present majority usage and (2) a method of distinguishing them from one another. It is to be noted that these four categories do not by any means cover the whole of the parameter of variance of world musicality or even of that of the area in which they have come into use. Rather, they block off certain segments of the parameter. The gaps between the four segments are conceived as filled by hybrids. Whether or to what extent this categorization is valid in the non-Western world remains to be shown. That it is of universal validity has been questioned by some scholars.

For present purposes, I shall accept the current naming the four idioms the tribal (rather than the primitive), the professional, the folk, and the popular, and I will try to find what music-technical support for them as I can.

A.4a. *The tribal idiom.*   Recognition of the idiom was first by travelers who distinguished it from their own music and referred to it as "savage," "barbarous," "un-Christian," and so forth. Its early collection and study was by anthropologists who gave it the name *primitive.* This term is so loaded with evolutionary, sociological, economic, political, aesthetic, and other biases that an increasing number of scholars would like to get rid of it. The commonest substitutes have been *nonliterate* and *folk.* The former means, of course, "speech nonliterate"; for "music nonliterate" would include the larger part of the population of the world, including its leading scholars, painters, poets, public administrators, and businessmen. The term *music of people nonliterate in speech* would be hard to handle. If I gauge correctly the best thought of current folklore scholarship, the conception of folklore of which folk music is an integral part, does not fit, as I shall presently show. Therefore, I urge abandonment of both in favor of the term *tribal,* for that is what the idiom is, namely, the music tradition carried by the members of a tribal society or by members of what must once have been such, as, for example, Eskimos.

That the concept, regardless of its name, is useful is attested to by the large literature relative to what it refers to and by the almost universal acceptance of some name for it. Regardless of the terms in which anthropologists may define tribal, primitive, nonliterate (meaning speech nonliterate) society, one of the features they will be most anxious to have understood is that the name refers to a very wide variety of social organization. Probably, this would range from the very primitive of the Ona or Yahgan Indians of Tierra del Fuego, through the larger, more diversified and extended cultures of the Andean highlands, Guatemala, and Mexico, to the complex tribal societies of Africa, which are more embryonic city-states or nations than tribes. I shall assume, therefore, that the concept "tribal music idiom" refers to a norm of music practice which can be correlated with the norm of social organization exemplified by such an aggregate. Acculturation may be supposed to have been in process for an indeterminable length of time in all tribal societies known at the present time or in our written history.

A.4b. *The professional idiom.*   The concept of the professional idiom, though it has no agreed upon name, is drawn from the long line of professional musicians, writers, philosophers, and poets of Europe from ancient Greece to the contemporary Western world. To its adepts it is simply "music" or, perhaps, "Music." German musicologists have spoken of "die hohe Kunst"; French, of "la musique savante"; Spanish, of "la música culta." Some Americans have referred to it as "cultivated music" or "art music." I find both of the latter terminology unacceptably solipsistic, class conscious, and ethnocentric. The American music industry has coined the odious, even more biased, term "serious music." I have adopted from time to time, in varying contexts, such slanted terms as *elite, elegant, genteel,* but have usually settled for the *fine art of music,* which is clumsy and permits only the bastard adjective *fine art,* which I have abandoned. In emulation of Standard English, we might use "Standard Music," but I have never encountered it. "Concert music" is, perhaps, a useful synonym, but gets us into trouble because it does not cover operatic and ecclesiastic genres. I understand the term *professional* in the sense of four of the categories listed in table 1 above: (B.3) expertness; (B.4) creativity; (B.6) exhibitionism (i.e., music made for listeners who do not, themselves, make it); (B.7) priced (whether by elevation of status and its prerequisites, slavery, wages, box-office receipts, or contract). There is also an unlisted criterion of importance in the understanding of the term *professional,* namely, that of deliberate, even formal, organization of the above four criteria.

The germ of the professional idiom can be found in existing tribal cultures in which there is sufficient diversification of social function and sufficient geographic and demographic extension to encourage individuality to the extent necessary to form at least two social classes: of rulers and of ruled. Status may be the prime criterion for the formation of a distinct professional music idiom; but presence in and distance from the seat of power must also be factors. Whether or not all members of a society can and do make music for themselves, a general tendency can be observed and has been recorded in the history of those societies that have recorded history: ruling classes have music made *for* them by the most talented and trained individual members of the society who can be recruited for the purpose; only rarely does a chief, a king, a noble, or a very wealthy person attain the competence of a professional musician.

The diversification and class-structuring of a tradition of the professional idiom probably conforms closely to the nature of the social-cultural context in which it serves. It may conceivably take place suddenly in the case of conquest of one society by another in whose resulting acculturation the conqueror might sequester his own cultural traditions from the conquered in order to heighten his status and confirm his hegemony. Two distinct idioms might also form by growth from within in the course of aggrandizement through war, trade, slavery, religious conversion, and so forth. One would not expect to find boundaries for the transition. Two distinct repertories might begin to come into being without substantial difference in idiom, but only in the skill with which they were presented. If not fully professional in a cosmopolitan sense, certain protoprofessional music idioms can be found in several African tribal societies today, as, for example, among the Abatusi (Tussi). In some tribal societies there are hereditary master drummers, just as there are hereditary musicians in the *gagaku* of the Imperial Household of Japan. The instruments may be larger and more elaborately made than the ordinary. Some are reserved for special occasions.

Wherever guilds of musicians are formed, one may expect to find secret techniques, symbols, and insignia of office which result from or are designed to encourage and guard the higher standard of professional expertness. These tend further to set the "higher" idiom apart from and differentiate it from the "lower." We may suppose that as the priestly, noble, and wealthy members of a society have organized themselves increasingly apart from the people, in compounds, castles and, finally, cities, and surrounded themselves with protocolar and military defenses, the professional musician has likewise set himself apart from the nonprofessional music-makers of the society and, as ruling classes, have come to associate increasingly with the professional musicians of those other societies. As tribal organization has given way to city states, nations, and empires, so the music made for a ruling class may become more like the music made for other ruling classes and less like that of its adjacent ruled urban and outlying rural areas.

Not seldom the ranks of the urban professionals have been recruited from the "common" people. These recruits may hardly be supposed not to have brought with them into the more or less esoteric community of professionals echoes of the traditions of their "common" ancestors. At the same time, echoes of the music of the palace, the salon, the boudoir, may filter down back stairs, through windows, and by more surreptitious avenues, into the ears of the carriers of these older traditions. Folklorists have termed the former path *ascent*; the latter, *descent.*

The more populous and extensive the political, economic, and social structures and functions, the larger must become the number of professionals and the size of their nonmusic-making audience in the city, and the larger the area around the city receiving echoes of the brilliance of the city professional idiom. As technology has increased the scope of the professional idioms, it tends to professionalize any other idioms with which it comes in contact.

In some instances, a professional idiom has obliterated its predecessor or predecessors. Mantle Hood reports that in Java the flow back or *descent* of the professional art into the mass of the people is so complete that there are no substantial traces of any other idiom—or were not until mass communications began to inseminate them. In other instances, as in the United States during the twentieth century, survivals of African tribal idiom, thought to be moribund, have flowed upward in an *ascent* penetrating nearly all levels of musical activity in the country.

Professional musicians inevitably compete ruthlessly with one another for favor of patrons or public. This puts a premium on exhibitionism, on variance of the tradition, and on emphasis of the social status of those who produce and consume the products of the tradition. To the extent that variance appears as novelty, what novelty cannot be developed from within the tradition will be borrowed from without, regardless of source.

A.4c. *The folk idiom.*   The name *folk music* is from the study of folk-lore—itself an adaptation (1846) of the German *Volkskunde* (1806), which designated the beliefs, lore, arts, crafts, and subculture of the peasantries of the European nations. Throughout the nineteenth and twentieth centuries, two traits have been distinguished in the folk idiom: one, survival or retention of features characteristic of the oldest cultural heritage and, specially, rural traditions; second, penetration or adoption of features characteristic of the latest professional innovations and urban traditions. Variance is as typical of the norms of the folk idiom as it is of the tribal and professional, but like the tribal, it lacks the deliberate, organized cultivation of variance and of difference from other idioms as ends in themselves that is such a constant factor in the professional. Furthermore, it seems reasonable to suppose that during unknown centuries of change in enclavement, racial intermixture, acculturation, and even shifts in geographic location, the music idioms of peasantries have changed less and retained more of the characteristics of tribal idiom and the myths inherent in it than have the professional. To students who are usually city dwellers, part of its attraction is its archaism, which has always been a prime value in folklore study. Thus, the tendency among students of folk music has been more to maintain the subjective, qualitative—even sentimental—approach toward the structures of the idiom than to emulate the objective, scientific approach typical of the anthropologist in his study of the tribal.

Along with this bias has gone a tendency, as B. A. Botkin has pointed out, to emphasize structure rather than function.[3] Since a similar bias has also characterized the approach of the historicomusicologist to the European professional idiom, it is surprising that the two groups of students have never, except in rare instances, come together until recently, and then in Europe rather than America. There are two good reasons for this. First, the archaism of the historicomusicologist has been directed to values that were new in their day, whereas that of the folklorist has been directed to values that were old in our earliest texts. One might suppose that the historicomusicologist would be in a far better position to develop a functionalist approach to what is contemporary with him. But strangely enough, it is folklorists who have tried the harder to achieve a functionalist approach in theoretical writing, while musicologists have not. Yet the cry of the antifunctionalist is still widely heard: "folk music is dying; in a few years all the really authentic singers will be dead and the young will have lost the tradition."

On the whole, those who try to form an integrated concept of structure and function have been less pessimistic. Although deploring corruption and shrinkage of the repertory of artifacts under the assault of the media of mass communications, they point to the spread, through these same media and the so-called folk music revival, of at least some of the essential norms of the idiom. With the prospect in view of an eventual extinction of tribal culture, one may venture the prediction that the folk idiom will, at least for a while, be the sole carrier of the most ancient cultural good that is not enshrined in the most highly sophisticated professional verbalization.

A.4d. *The popular idiom.*   To best of present knowledge, the name is without specific parentage other than the etymology "of the people," "liked by the most people," to which might be added "at the moment," this last being contradicted by the not rare retention among populations at large of outstanding successes that have a queer way of becoming referred to as "folk songs" even when they have run counter to any known folk idiom and stubbornly resist communal re-creation that would fit them into one, as, for example, "Silent Night." The popular idiom seems to have the vaguest content and limits, and the least inner consistency and coherence as a conceptual unit of any of the four idioms. Its genres are numberless, ranging from light opera, musical comedy, folklike and composed chorals and hymns, through the entertainment industry to schoolroom, sentimental, and parlor songs, to jazz, blues, calypso, high-life, hillbilly, rock 'n roll, and a hundred more. The other three idioms have been studied by specialists devoted to each of them.

No serious study has been made of the popular idiom. Folklorists and musicologists alike have regarded it as a kind of rubbish heap of commercially produced and distributed, easily dispensed with, and replaced commodities. Anthropologists, at least in the United States, have treated it with less disdain. But even its American adepts, by adopting the epithet "serious" for the professional idiom, seem thereby to regard their own product as "not serious." It has been variously referred to as "entertainment music" and as the "folk music of the cities." Carlos Vega calls it "mesomusic." There is truth in the city origin and point of diffusion. The term "commercial music" fits some but by no means all of it. And much production in the professional idiom is just as commercial. Certainly, it engages the largest financial support of any idiom in our day. Strangely enough, encyclopedias are only now beginning to commission articles on it as they do on the other three idioms.

A.5. *Sex, age group, occupation.* In many societies, certain songs are for singing and certain instruments for playing by individuals of one or the other sex only. Throughout the Western world, children carry traditions of music which can be considered folk songs. These are not learned from the elders, who have usually either forgotten or pay no attention to them. Constantin Brailoiu believed that traditions of children's songs were universal and exhibited music-technical traits in common.

Many occupations have had their peculiar music tradition. Tribal, folk, and popular idioms have been associated with work; popular and folk-popular, with politics. In highly diversified, extended, and elaborated societies, this has been accomplished by setting new words to old tunes. Modified, hybrid, and newly created tunes have been known to become current among groups of individuals engaged in a common occupation, especially soldiering and manual labor. Some have been handed down from the higher command or the boss. Others seem to have originated among the rank and file.

A.6. *Social function.* It is with considerable diffidence that I undertake to give any account of the social functions of music. They have been so variously presented that it is difficult to summarize them in a short space. The task of distinguishing, naming, and classifying them involves equal competence in both the social sciences and musicology, and nicely suppressed bias in favor of either. No one man has yet achieved such distinction. And ethnomusicologists have not yet learned to work in teams. I shall therefore resort merely to quoting the best and most recent list I have found. A. P. Merriam proposes a roster of "ten major and over-all functions, as opposed to uses, of music.[4]

1. Emotional expression
2. Aesthetic enjoyment
3. Entertainment
4. Communication
5. Symbolic representation
6. Physical response
7. Enforcing conformity with social norms
8. Validation of social institutions and religious rituals
9. Contribution to the continuity of the culture
10. Contribution to the integration of society

With two exceptions, it seems unlikely that anything approaching a one-to-one correspondence with any one kind of music could be found. One is the third function, entertainment, which comes as close as any one word to defining the norm "popular" music. The other, the eighth, validation of social institutions and religious rituals, could define several subfunctions; most accurately, perhaps, patriotism. Religious ritual would have to be broken down into several subclasses before it could correspond to such variances as the sounding brass and tinkling cymbal of an Earth-goddess ritual, plain song, the "St. Matthew Passion," or "Jesus Wants Me for a Sunbeam." Most "pieces" of music would, presumably, serve at least six of the functions and some, even more. All would have to be regarded as communicating something, if nothing more than its selected fraction of the tradition in which it was cast. If the meanest of the lot were fated to serve as a counterpart of the *Seikilos skolion* for musicologists of the thirty-ninth century, this fraction could communicate a lot. With ten such items one might piece together in the thirty-ninth century as fair a notion of the music of twentieth-century United States as we now have of that of ancient Greece.

A.7. *Focuses of interest.* Like the labor necessary in the organization and operation of a society, its principal aspirations—survival, procreation, health, status, possessions, and so forth—become divided and distributed institutions whose validation was classified as social function eight by Merriam. But the values that are coefficients of these aspirations have a currency over and above the institutions that have invoked, served, or pretended to serve them. The extent to which these values, expressed as they are in terms of speech and ranging from casual attention through grades of interest to the highest conceived by man, correspond to (speech) identifiable music structures, functions, or content, is a perennial topic for discussion. It would not be surprising if—once general and music value theories attain sufficiently mature statement to be compared—some degree of correspondence were to be established. For cross-traditionally, music is above all a value system, and focuses of interest are essentially valuative.[5]

B.1. *Own and not-own traditions.* That there are differences between music traditions is well known to the carriers of most traditions. They may not be able to describe their own or any other in words; but they know very well when they hear an example of either. By and large, to most people there are two classes of music: one's own and all others, indiscriminately.

B.2. *Own and not-own tastes.* Similarly, the differences of one's own and others' tastes are marked and known within one's own tradition. By and large, there are two classes: what one likes and what one does not like. The wider the experience, the more tolerance for the tastes of others and the wider one's own. Aesthetics and value theory, both branches of philosophy, have developed extensive theories of taste. The former limits itself to the exceptional expertness and creativity, to Art rather than art.

B.3. *Expert and less expert.* Except for its relationship to other categories, notably A.4 and A.8, this is one of the weakest criteria for classification of music. Variance of expertness in the carriage of a tradition is one of the commonest perceptions; but provided the difference is not excessive, an expert and an inexpert composition or performance is one of degree rather than of kind. Norms of expertness become established in any tradition carried by a sufficient number of individuals. Qualitative considerations in musicology tend to emphasize high degrees of expertness; quantitative, to take into account all degrees of expertness above a specific minimal level, below which a tradition is not considered recognizable. Quality and quantity are equally important to musicological study and any report upon a tradition in terms of either to the exclusion of the other is deceptive.

B.4. *Creative and re-creative.* European musicians, musicologists, and the general public have distinguished three types of individuals: composers, performers, and listeners. I shall consider under category B.6, below, the dichotomy of the first two versus the third. In the Western world composers alone are supposed to create; performers, to re-create. But in direct proportion to expertness, performers create "what is between or outside of the notes"; and in direct proportion to their recognition of the potentialities of the continuity and variance of a tradition, composers re-create it. In the non-Western world, within specifications of raga, maqam, patet, and the like, creativity is mostly or entirely in performance, the composer, as a separate individual, being often as not nonexistent or merely a name in the annals of the tradition. A tradition has no reality apart from the behavior that manifests it. Both creation and re-creation are essential features of it. Without creation and its incessant re-creation, there never could have been a tradition or, indeed, even a separate kind of auditory communication known as "music." Creation is always by individuals; groups do not create. It is customary to suppose that creation is always intrinsically or self-motivated; but that it can be extrinsically motivated is well known. A broad theoretical approach will do well to accept a norm of 50-50 relevance for motivation of these two kinds. That the criterion establishes two classes of music is to be doubted.

B.5. *Written and unwritten.* In the Western world, the distinction between written and unwritten ("oral" or, better, "aural-oral") tradition is one of the most important criteria for categorization of music. In the non-Western world, it is of negligible importance. The distinction has been widely exploited by students of folklore—especially in connection with folk music. Two common misrepresentations have attended its use: First, the word *tradition* has been associated solely with unwritten techniques, so that musics using these techniques—as, for example, folk music—are called "traditional" in contrast with those that use writing, which are implied to be nontraditional. This is absurd. Most professional composers and performers are as traditional as are most folksingers. Second, musics using writing are supposed not to depend upon oral-aural techniques. This is false. In the first place, writing can be learned only by oral-aural techniques; in the second, no conventional music writing can be read without them. Whether the electronic graph now being developed could eventually be read sufficiently well to render possible performance in an otherwise unknown tradition, remains to be seen. The parameter "written and unwritten" must, therefore, be restated as "unwritten and predominantly written." The categories dependent upon this criterion are valid only in the Western world and where its predominantly written traditions have become seeded. Even there, much music that is regarded as unwritten can be shown to have known influence of written sources. The criterion is handy but not dependable without qualification.

B.6. *Self-made and not-self-made but merely listened to.* If a majority of a population that can understand its native language could speak it in no way but a kind of baby talk, we would have a linguistic situation comparable to the musical state of affairs that actually exists in many parts of the Western world, as, for example, in the United States. How large this majority of nonproducers of music may be, we have no way of knowing. Even if we include as producers individuals with only moderate technical abilities, it seems unlikely that it could be more than 10 to 15 percent of the total population. Yet the total population is hearing each year an increasing amount and variety of music. This bifurcation of musicality which results in the division of two to three hundred million people into two classes, a producing-listening minority and a merely listening majority, has never been studied. The difference between the kind of music *heard* by the musically productive and the musically mute may be slight or large; but we know nothing about it. This matter will be taken up again later, under caption B.7.

B.7. *Free and priced.*   One might surmise that more music has been and is made without than with payment or expectation of payment; but there is no way of validating it. Instances of the buying of songs are not rare in nonliterate (that is, speech nonliterate), folk and tribal, as well as in modern cosmopolitan societies. More common, probably, has been the buying of the services of expert, creative individuals, either as slaves, traveling minstrels, "gentlemen of the court," and so forth. The question whether buying and selling of particular items or services results in a kind of music different from what is produced "for free" is an interesting one. For in the contemporary Western world, a very large amount of the production of music is bought and paid for. Publication, copyright, managerial enterprise, and mass communications have developed a music industry that more and more dictates the form and the content of an increasingly large production of music and the conditions under which it is consumed, which is to say "used though not used up." The term "commercial music," now widely used, may come to designate a recognizable genre, intrinsically different from noncommercial genres. And it might not all be what is usually equated with commercialism, that is, entertainment or popular music.

B.8. *Traditional and nontraditional.*   The romantic movement has finally reached what seems to be a logical conclusion—the presentation of sequences of sound in time which represent a thoroughgoing, deliberate attempt to move as counter to tradition as possible. To the extent that its presentations still involve composers, performers, on and off a stage, with instruments (however untraditional), before a seated audience that has bought or been given tickets, which expects to listen more or less quietly to "pieces" or "numbers" usually of a length shorter than the customary total duration of a concert, which applauds and reads reviews in the next day's papers—to that extent the presentation is still traditional. Whether the intrinsic characteristics of the presentations will be regarded as music by later generations or as a new art or craft with a relation to traditional music resembling that of photography to painting, remains to be seen.

B.9. *Musical functions.* Coming at last to the subject of function viewed as intrinsic to music, rather than as extrinsic to it, as in caption A.6, *Social function,* we may venture counterpart definition of the idioms (tribal, professional, folk, and popular) so widely used during the twentieth century in both general and scholarly reference to music. Many musicologists—even though they make use of such reference—deplore the categorization as unreal. The following definitions in terms intrinsic to music are presented for what they may be worth:

The tribal idiom is one in which we can observe or for which we may hypothesize no substantial traits other than of its own kind of idiom.

The professional idiom is one that usually differs from and excels any other idiom in its society through the exceptional expertness of its carriers, the verbal organization of a supporting ritual or theory, and the competition in production of new values of its products, in which we may observe and/or hypothesize traits of other idioms as well as of other manifestations of its own kind of idiom.

The folk idiom is one in which we can observe or for which we must hypothesize a norm in which there are equally retention of the most ancient traits and values from below and adoption of novel traits and values from above.

The popular idiom is one in which we can observe and may hypothesize a norm that exploits equally materials of both the professional and the folk idioms, but is less deliberate in the cultivation of expertness and new values characteristic of the professional idiom, and in the retention of ancient values characteristic of the folk idiom.

III

It will be observed that none of these definitions is technical. There must be in every musicologist's mind that the present music-technical lexicon and existing methods of factorial analysis cannot pretend to produce definitions of such broad, class-structural concepts. Some will contend that "musicality is one" and that the four idioms are nonexistent musically. In this connection we must remember that the term *music* is a word, a structure in the art of speech which, unless it is given specific qualification, will refer to a structure—"music," "the art of music," a piece or some such, all of them static, structurally conceived referents, all of them structures. Even if we pose these as having or defining functions, as being produced and consumed (in the sense, of course, of being "used but not used up"), these pieces of music, repertories of them—even the whole aggregate of them—remain objects, articles, commodities, monu-ments, static, structuralized. The continued distinguishing, naming, and classifying by techniques of (speech) analysis and synthesis brings even some musicians and musicologists to the point of believing that music is what speech tells them it is rather than of remembering what music has told them it is, at which point the signal message of music has only speech content and a not very specific one, at that. Thus Merriam voices a very general belief when he writes: "The fact that music is shared as a human activity by all peoples may mean that it communicates a certain limited understanding simply by its existence. Of all the functions of music, the communication function is perhaps least known and understood." The knowledge and understanding referred to here is, presumably, speech knowledge and understanding. And our author would have been correct from a musicological viewpoint if only he had inserted the qualification "limited *speech* understanding" and had added four words "least known and understood *in terms of speech.*" Can anyone, musician or nonmusi-cian, validly claim that the musician who is performing music in his own tradition or listening to it when performed by others does not know and understand what he is doing? Surely, this is absurd. The words *know* and *understand* do, as a matter of fact, conventionally refer to speech knowl-edge and understanding. And they can be used without qualification of a musicological nature in referring to anything else but another system of communication. Thus, in reference to music, the distinction between speech knowledge and understanding, and music knowledge and under-standing must be accepted, I believe, as an ineluctable postulate of rational dealing with music in terms of speech. If a musician or musicol-ogist cannot tell you *what* music knowledge and understanding is, it indicates not a lack of music knowledge and understanding but of speech knowledge and understanding. And if the nonmusician really wants to know what are musical knowledge and understanding, he has only (as I have put it elsewhere) to study music until he does know.

It is at this same point that the usefulness of the term *musicality* can be appreciated. Specifically defined as a disposition (a function) of social man to be able to do something called "music"—to produce discrete instances or, better, specific manifestations, of its activity—it is then susceptible to (speech) analysis and synthesis in terms of function rather than the other way around, in terms of structure. The two approaches can, in fact, be closely correlated. The necessary "elements" or "mate-rials" (all structures)—necessary, because without any one of them there can be no music—can be named *pitch, loudness, tonal density* (timbre, tonal quality), *tempo* (speed), *proportion* (relative duration), and *rhythmic density.* To produce a "piece" of music, minimal and medial sized tonal and rhythmic elements or materials (structures) are enchained so as to exhibit a certain *form* (noun, referent to a structure) traditional in a repertory (a structure). The same elements or materials can be regarded as necessary variables (functions) of a stream of sound in time that an individual or group *forms* (verb, referent to a function) into music in accord with a tradition of formation whose norms of style have evolved historically as a function of a culture and whose social functions can be listed by an anthropologist in terms extrinsic to music. Traditions are distinguishable from one another (1) in the selection of materials and (2) in the manner of forming them in discrete productions. In this joint structural-functional approach musicality is seen to operate in two opposite directions: outwardly, into the social continuum as known in terms of speech; inwardly, in development of the potentialities of the auditory signal, into the musical continuum, known directly as music.

IV

The summary of the categorization tells us a good deal about the *why* and the *what* of music. But the key question remains: *how* is the inward forming done and how does what is thus formed perform the functions attributed to it?

One common answer to the question is: the inner aspects are symbols, the outer, the meanings of the symbols, the things symbolized, as in speech: "music is a language." Another, not so common, but strongly supported and, to best of present knowledge, more reputable answer, is: music does not symbolize anything: "music is not a language."

Viewed in terms of structure, the first position seems untenable. No one has ever shown that music distinguishes a cat from a dog, black from white, true from false, good from evil, any two concrete phenomena or abstract concepts. Assuredly it does not name them. Continued association of particular speech symbols with particular musical structures can, to be sure, become conventionalized and may, like the bell for Pavlov's dog, serve as a substitute symbol. But it would be a substitute speech symbol, not a music symbol. Without continued association of the convention, the dog discovered the food was food and the bell was not food. The jingle of the ice-cream vending truck would quickly cease to mean "ice cream" to children if it came to dispense toothpaste. Association of the symbolism "Victory for the Allies" to the beginning of Beethoven's Fifth Symphony during World War II did not alter the music message or the music semiotic understanding of the work in any way whatsoever. Unusual dissonance, especially if insisted upon and not resolved in the approved fashion, has been long associated with evil, and in the early 1920s brought about the denunciation of Schoenberg's music by one conservative musician as "dirty, evil, of the gutter." Coincidence, however, of musical sounds and some natural sonal and rhythmic events in physical and cultural phenomena is not to be taken as symbolization unless words to that effect are involved, in which case the symbolization is in the words.

Viewed in terms of function, however, the first answer seems to be convincing in a general way, but it breaks down when specificity is attempted, while the second is widely challenged. There seems to be some correspondence between music and objectively observable functions—especially overt human behavior and affective states. One does not try to put a child to sleep with the "Walkürenritt" or to march a regiment of soldiers down the street to the "Liebestodt" or "Waldweben." The nature of this correspondence has been debated for several thousand years. Each position has been especially vigorously held since Johann Mattheson and his contemporaries impelled it into budding *Affektenlehre* of literary journalism. From his time on, German scholarship has dealt with them in a progressively professional way in the works of nearly every prominent musicologist, expanding them under the more comprehensive concepts of *heteronom* and *autonom* or dependence upon outer-direction and inner-direction.[6] English and American writers have dealt with them, on the whole, more individually and amateurishly. The most ambitious and detailed treatment that has come to notice is that of Deryck Cooke who presents an elaborate theory of correspondence, in the professional and popular idioms of the Western world, between emotional states and the factor of pitch, modified by volume and time.[7]

Elsewhere I have dealt at some length with the inward operation of the function of musicality.[8] This has been done with the specific purpose of expressing it in terms as suitable as possible to dealing also with the outward. For the inward function is the concrete evidence of the musical knowledge and understanding of the musician, upon which there seems to be complete agreement among musicians as long as they are making— and competently making—music in the tradition in which they have been trained. The outward functions are primarily those conceived by others than musicians, but also by musicians who try to express themselves in the art of speech. The hazard here, as I have already pointed out, is that the very nature of the vehicle, the art of speech, tends to force the musician, as it does the nonmusician, to deal with music in terms of things other than music and, so, to run the risk of misrepresentation. And it is precisely in these speech terms that there has been endless controversy. Clearly, the approach in terms of speech to the outward functioning of musicality must be done by an integration of the musical and nonmusical viewpoints. I would accept, as a necessary postulate of such an approach, a 50-50 weighting of the two to the extent, of course, that to those competent in both arts this seems possible. The key question, then, is how does the inward function of musicality operate?

The common error has been to cite a musical datum, for example, the ascending diatonic third, and immediately to correlate it with nonmusical data. Thus, the major third is said to symbolize or stimulate cheerful affects; the minor, sad. Soon all major and minor intervals, simultaneous and successive, and major and minor chords and tonalities, are similarly characterized. There is impressive evidence supporting such judgments. Some of the numerous exceptions can be explained away, as Cooke very discerningly does, by marked variance of volume (loudness) and tempo.[9] Another hazard is to deal with musical data, whether structural or functional, in terms of tension alone, or, as is perhaps more common, in terms of only two—tension and detension (relaxation). A third is to adduce the harmonic series in superior resonance but not that in inferior resonance. A fourth is to lay more stress upon the tonal than upon the rhythmic variables and to employ no clearly ordered analysis of the *necessary* or essential features of the auditory signal of music, so that a single process can be hypothesized in terms of which the variance of the lot can be referred to.

Unfortunately, musicology cannot, as yet, give a full speech account of the music compositional process. There remain two gaps in our knowledge. The necessary six variables of the auditory signal of music (necessary because without any of them there can be no music) are not all the same kind. Three are spatial—the tonal; three are temporal—the rhythmic. Two of each trio can be classed as *simple* functions: pitch and loudness, tempo and proportion. Their variance is upon a common parameter that can be scaled as a single series in which the forming of a discrete product can proceed (that is, vary) in either direction as upon a single line, from any point except the two limits, to any extent within those limits or remain unchanged (not vary). Thus, pitch can increase (ascend), decrease (descend), or remain fixed; loudness can increase (become louder), decrease (become softer), or remain stationary; tempo can increase (become faster), decrease (become slower), or remain unchanged; proportion can be increased (become longer), decrease (become shorter), or remain the same.

Of the remaining two—tonal density (tone quality or timbre) and rhythmic density (number of events per unit of time), the tonal is spatial; the rhythmic, temporal. Both can be classed as *compound* functions, consisting of integrations of their two respective simple functions. They define, together, the *density* of the music event.

The space and time referred to here are music space and music time. Music space is defined as the *simultaneously sensed* frequencies, amplitudes, and densities of periodic sound events from the highest and loudest limits of hearing to the lowest and softest recognizable as sound; music time, as the *successively perceived* frequencies, amplitudes, and densities of periodic events from the fastest and shortest (about 10 per second) to the slowest and longest—a limit still, to the best of present knowledge, undetermined. We do not know how low, soft, or slow, how high, loud, or fast, a particular discrete piece of music can be performed without becoming unrecognizable or so distorted as to lose its identity as a discrete piece or as a re-presentation of its tradition. Doubled or halved in pitch or in tempo, in loudness or proportion, a piece might still be recognizable in these two senses if previously known in its proper place in the parameters of all four variables; but without such previous knowledge, it might be rejected if there were a variance of more than a low percent in any variable in any direction.

The term *tone quality* then, refers to the relative density of a sound heard by us as simultaneous, that is, as *a* note. For each note is a complex of many pitches of varying loudness. One of the pitches is heard as the note, and the sum of the loudness of the lot, as the loudness of the note. Similarly, the relative density of musical events perceivable by us as successive, that is, as a single chain or stream of sound with sufficient proximity and coherence in time, is to be regarded as a single, overall event. Variance of both compound functions is strictly-controlled by competent musicians according to the norms of the traditions carried by them. Expression of this variance in terms of speech has been, so far, notably unsuccessful. Representation by symbols (as, for example, k^5, l^2, m^6, n^{11}, and so on, up to a dozen or so components, where the letters would denote pitch or tempo beat frequencies and the numerals amplitude or proportional "widths" or "lengths") would be extremely clumsy to handle. Representation of tone quality in two-dimensional graphs has been in use for some time, as by the sonagraph and similar devices. Representation of temporal density has not, to best of present knowledge, been attempted, except by Leon Knopoff who has been at work upon two devices: the one to yield a characteristic numeral for music-spatial density; the other, a characteristic numeral for music-temporal density.[10] Although conventionally the most crudely notated in any notation system, some contemporary ethnomusicological thought attributes to these two compound functions the overmastering features of any music tradition, in that upon random first recognition of a body of sound

qua music and before the details of pitch, loudness, tempo, or proportion can be specifically identified, the overall density of the body—an
integration of the two compound functions—can serve for instant
identification of it as belonging to a specific tradition and sometimes to
one or more of the categories listed above.

The inward function of forming, which is, after all, musicality in
concrete manifestation, is a *complex* one. Its adequate expression in terms
of speech would seem to be possible only, as here, in protracted verbalization or, more concisely, in terms of higher mathematics. Visual representation would have to be in at least three, but better in four, dimensions. The fact that the compound variables remain still clearly deline-
ated in only one respect, namely, in that of their nonvariance, would
seem to recommend postponement of the attempt to block out a
comprehensive theory of music in itself and in its context at the present
time. The reservoir of dependable knowledge is, however, enlarged by
the factor, too often neglected in both musicological and nonmusicologi-
cal approaches to music, of the music knowledge and understanding of
the inward operation of the function of musicality in the possession of
and used by competent carriers of all actively cultivated music traditions.
The only problem here is the expression, classification, and valuation of
these in terms of speech. The identities between the two arts can, of
course, be adequately dealt with in speech terms. The analogies fade
from dependability to almost mystical relevance. The complete differences or heterologies, some sufficiently distinguishable only to be
named, others unnamable and even undistinguishable in terms of
speech, constitute a large measure of the predicament anyone places
himself in when he ventures to talk about music, whether or not he is
aware of it. Clearly, the case invites formulation of hypotheses whose
testing may reveal new paths toward increased knowledge and understanding of both kinds (of speech and of music) and seal off futile,
long-standing preconceptions that burden us all. A set of such hypotheses will be presented here. It is to be borne in mind that their relevance is
to norms determinable by direct observation, in time present to the living
observer. Exceptions are to be expected. If they prove to exceed reasonable limits, the hypotheses will have to be reexamined.

Hypothesis I.   Musicality as we know it today is a universal human disposition to form auditory signals in discrete messages in accord with
particular traditions of inflection all six necessary variables of an auditory signal.

Hypothesis II.   Inflection of the four simple variables of an auditory
signal is upon a single uniform parameter and can be measured in terms

of direction and extent in any unit of form from the smallest to the largest, as +, =, −, or 0.

Hypothesis III. Inflection of the two compound functions, though not yet susceptible to fully objective speech analysis, can be defined concisely when in the second type of inflection, namely, nonvariance. But since they are both constituted by simple functions, and the single concept "density" seems applicable to both and is partially susceptible to speech analysis, the directions and extents of their variance in the same speech symbols used for the simple functions, it is assumed that the same symbols can be tentatively used for the inflection of tone quality and accent or emphasis.

Hypothesis IV. Any variable may be inflected in either direction to any extent or remain unvaried regardless of the simultaneous inflection of the others. Even a short, single sound-time line (melody or percussion line) may present, thus, a six-variable polyphony with inner relations of parallel, oblique, and contrary motion analogous to a six-part contrapuntal fabric, their leading being subject variously to (1) the exigencies of the inflections involved, (2) the requirements of the tradition, (3) the idiosyncrasy of the individual producer, (4) his adjustment to the culture and the society, (5) the occasion, and other extrinsic factors. Aural guides are almost automatically laid down by the tradition in the form of its potentialities relative to continuity, variation, and selection.

Hypothesis V. Any variable may be inflected in any way successively, regardless of the successive inflections of the others; but its continued inflection in either direction must, because of the limits peculiar to each, eventually end and be followed by inflection in the opposite direction. Thus, the principal units of form—minimal, medial, and maximal—will tend to level off, with approximately as many plus and minus directions. To the extent this leveling off discloses an axis around which the variance occurs, we speak of a factor "centricity," or nonvariance upon a higher level of form.

Hypothesis VI. There is a degree of correspondence between the minimal, medial, and maximal units of inflection of the variables, the form of the auditory signal, the kinaesthetic behavior of the producer and receiver(s) of any concrete music production and the norms of the tradition that it represents, which may be expressed by equating the signs +, =, −, or 0, with the words "tension," "tonicity," and "detension." To raise, maintain, or lower the pitch of a stretched string one may increase, maintain, or decrease the tension. To effect the same variance in the singing voice the necessary musculature must be tensed, remain the same (tonic), or be relaxed (detensed). To produce a louder sound, a steady loudness, or a softer sound, the string must be plucked, struck, or rubbed more strongly, with equal strength or less, and the voice provided with more, the same, or less air, with the corresponding involvement of the musculature. Increase, steadiness, or decrease in tempo, division, and tying of beats, requires a similar involvement of the musculature. We commonly regard a presto, scherzo, or allegro molto as "tense" upon the basis of the tempo alone and, similarly, a march as "tonic" and a lullaby as "detense." Very loud, strongly accented pieces tend to be similarly classed. On the whole, the Europe-derived music of the Western world, from the short song to the extended symphonic work, exhibits strong tonicity. The tensions are complemented by the detensions. Common exceptions are scherzos that begin pianissimo and end forte; movements that begin in the minor and end in the major, or vice versa; songs that end an octave lower or higher than they begin, and so forth.

By now, the argument will surely be brought forward that an art in which tension, tonicity, and detension constitute virtually the essence of its communicatory content must be not predominantly asymbolic but totally symbolic; for it obviously symbolizes the tensions, tonicities, and detensions of the human beings who practice it and those who receive, hear, or listen to it. Such arguments would, however, indicate a lack of understanding of what a symbol is. Any dictionary should show that a symbol is defined as something that stands for something else that it does not or is not believed or intended to resemble. The greater tension of a string does not symbolize a higher pitch, nor does a sudden loudness symbolize the tension of the muscles of those making or hearing it. It would be more to the point to speak of cause and effect or stimulus and reaction. For both a tradition of music and the producer of concrete manifestations of it embody the potentials that we refer to as "tension, tonicity, and detension," and it is reasonable to suppose that in the formation of a piece of music the composer and performer may, if he wishes, make use of whatever casual phenomena or stimuli seem to him best in each particular case. Each listener may, conceivably, go through a similar process of selection.

Such considerations lead me to propose three additional hypotheses, as follows:

Hypothesis VII.   There is a degree of correspondence between (1) the inflection of the variables of the auditory signal that is formed, in accord with a tradition of music, into a music message and (2) the kinaesthetic coefficients of the affective states and the processes of verbalization that are commonly referred to as "feeling" and "thinking." I use the term *coefficient* to denote "that which unites in action with something else to produce an effect" (Webster, 1960), or "cooperating to produce a result" (Oxford, 1947). In this case, the effect or result is what we observe, feel, or think (1) as an emotion or (2) as a judgment of or ideation relative to fact or value. The coefficient is understood to be the observable kinaesthetic evidence either of the emotion or the thought itself, or of an overt physiological correlate from which we infer it. The questions remain: can two different speech-named emotions have the same coefficients of tension, tonicity, or detension? And if so, can a music signal, message, or its content distinguish them? Or only paraphrase the coefficients?

Hypothesis VIII.   Music is to be regarded as paraphrastic or, better, paradromic to, that is, running alongside of, the processes of individual and social life as evidenced by observable and speech-reported behavior. As such, music might be regarded variously as a reflection of the behavior and nature of man; as a play with what he is not; as a discipline in what he wants or ought to be.

Hypothesis IX.   As a result of the interposition of speech reference into the conduct of the art of music by questioning its nature, its intrinsic and extrinsic functions, and the overall operation of the function of musicality, producers and receivers of music are offered three choices: (1) to subordinate the less widely cultivated disposition of making music to control and direction by the more widely cultivated disposition of making speech to whatever extent the latter can effect the former; (2) to make music as independent as possible of speech; (3) to work out a rational compromise in the relationship of the two arts, so that we may know, in terms of speech, and approve, in terms of music, what we are doing.

Various individuals and groups can be expected to explore variously the potentialities of these three choices. For musicology, only the third would seem to be acceptable. This would mean, in terms of the present paper, equal attention to and valuation of both speech and music knowledge and valuation, and extensive and unremitting comparative study of the compositional processes of the two arts. For, like as they are in the microcosm of the smallest units of form, at the other end of the gross parameter of the auditory signal-message-content syndrome the two arts are so unlike that it is difficult to pinpoint their diversity. For example, in the speech message there is a wide variance in the correspondence of the signal in whose terms its producer forms it and the content it delivers to a receiver who carries the same tradition as does the producer. In mathematics and discoursive speech, the content can be delivered by a totally different signal system, as in translation. In belles-lettres, oratory, and poetry, much is lost by such change. In some mystical expression, translation is impossible. In the music message, however, there is nearly a one-to-one correspondence of signal and message. Perhaps we had better say that the signal *is* the message, for any change, even slight, in the signal changes the content. Substantial changes may destroy it. For another example, the speech technique of symbolization automatically sets up a dualism—two discrete funded aggregates (1) of endosemantic reference known as the universe of discourse, and (2) of ectosemantic reference known as the sensory, physical, or phenomenological universe.

Both of these universes tend to be mainly structural in character as far as the discoursive techniques of speech customarily used in connection with the humanities are concerned. There is, thus, speech and not-speech. And for speech, there is music and not-music. Both are compre-hended in the sensory, physical, phenomenological universe and are dealt with in terms of the speech universe or universe of discourse. In contrast, the music technique of embodiment conceived as paradromic to the technique of speech, tends to establish what can be referred to in speech as a monism or, perhaps better, neither a pluralism nor a monism, both of which are speech terms, but rather a peculiar musical reality that is either both or neither of them. Can there be, for music, a not-music? It seems quite impossible. For if there were, it would imply that music could contradict, which clearly it does not and cannot do.

The conclusions would seem to be: (1) the extensive structuralization of music throughout the world by the art of speech and (2) the many social uses and functions it is said to serve (3) tend to blind one to the possibility that music functions in a universe of its own as well as an item of attention distinguished as a phenomenon in the physical universe and named as both a concept and as a percept in the universe of speech discourse. In this model of the case, music would not embody and would not communicate with respect to particular speech meanings, which is to say, referent in the universe of discourse or the universe of the senses, or thoughts or emotions distinguished, named, and classified by speech techniques, but would mainly paradromize—run parallel to the dynam-ics (tensions, tonicities, and detension) of what is not music, in the manner peculiar to its signal-message syndrome. To what extent the producer of any particular manifestation of it—a maker of any particu-lar piece of music—had or had not recognized a speech awareness of its correspondence to the coefficients of human perceptions, thoughts, or affects as recognized and reported in speech terms, or intended or did not intend a receiver to do so, will probably be the subject of endless debate. And would, perhaps, be beside the point.

NOTES

1. Peter Marler, "Communication in Monkeys and Apes," in Irven Devore, ed., *Primate Behavior* (New York: Holt, Rhinehart & Winston, 1965), p. 558.

2. Renato Almeida, *História da música brasileira* (Rio de Janeiro: F. Briguiet, 1926), and Gilbert Chase, *America's Music* (New York: McGraw Hill, 1955).

3. B. A. Botkin, "The Folkness of the Folk," *The English Journal* (College Edition), XXVI, 6 (June 1933), 451-469.

4. A. P. Merriam, *The Anthropology of Music* (Evanston, Ill.: Northwestern University Press, 1964), pp. 221-227.

5. R. B. Perry, *Realms of Value* (Cambridge: Harvard University Press, 1954), p. 8. Merriam, *Anthropology of Music,* p. 223.

6. Hans Conradin, *Ist die Musik heteronom oder autonom?* (Zurich: Dissertationsdruckerei Gebr. Leeman, 1940).

7. Deryck Cooke, *The Language of Music* (London: Oxford University Press, 1959).

8. Charles Seeger, "On the Moods of a Music Logic," *Journal of the American Musicological Society,* XIII (1960), 224-261.

9. Cooke, *Language of Music,* pp. 95 ff.

10. Leon Knopoff, "Some Technical Advances in Musical Analysis," *Studia musicologica* (Journal of the International Folk Music Council), 2nd pt., XVII (1964); VII, 1-4 (Budapest, 1965), 301-307. Taking off from the suggestion of Knopoff that tonal density might be calibrated, as are minerals, by their hardness, Mantle Hood, in his *The Ethnomusicologist* ([New York: McGraw Hill, 1971], pp. 117 ff.) suggests a hardness scale for all the essential functions or dimensions of the physical materials of music, simple as well as complex.

VIII
Prescriptive and Descriptive
Music Writing[54]

Three hazards are inherent in our practices of writing music. The first lies in an assumption that the full auditory parameter of music can be represented by a partial visual parameter, that is, by one with only two dimensions, a flat surface. The second lies in ignoring the historical lag of music writing behind speech writing, and the consequent traditional interposition of the art of speech in the matching of auditory and visual signals in music writing. The third lies in our failure to distinguish between prescriptive and descriptive uses of music writing—between a blueprint of how a specific piece of music shall be made to sound and a report of how a specific performance of any music actually did sound.

I shall deal here with the writing of only the simplest kind of music—unaccompanied melody. All three hazards have combined to render it probable that speech conceptions of melody have played an important part not only in the development of the technique of writing but also in the composition and performance of melodies in writing. And the conditions of the musicological juncture, the situation in which we attempt to communicate in the art of speech relative to the nature of the art of music and what it communicates, render certain that speech conceptions of melody may sometimes outweigh music conceptions of it, particularly in any discussion of the problem of music writing. We cannot, therefore, dismiss with a wave of the hand the questions (1) to what extent do our speech conceptions of melody correspond to our music conceptions of it, and (2) to what extent does the visual representation of melody condition both conceptions of it? While it is risky to think we can answer these questions definitively, we can at least bear them in mind and set ourselves seriously to consideration of ways and means of evading or offsetting the hazards of the task. I shall refer only briefly to the problem of multidimensional visual representation of melody, for technological advance, upon which we must depend for aid in this respect, has not yet overcome the difficulties in the visual representation of the composite melodic functions of tonal and rhythmic densities. And since we cannot conceivably escape from the limitations of the musicological juncture, I shall single out two speech concepts of melody, not as comprehending the total range of the problem but as underlying the two methods of music writing now available to us—the one prescriptive and subjective, the other descriptive and objective.

On the one hand, let us agree, melody may be conceived (verbally, it must be remembered) as a succession of separate sounds, on the other, as a single continuum of sound—as a chain or as a stream. Conception as a chain tends to emphasize structure and entities that move; conception as a stream, function and movement itself as a transmission of energy. Neither, of course, tells the whole story as the musician knows it. Both distort this knowledge to extents we cannot precisely gauge. For many of the links of the chain may be fused together, and the stream may run through successions of comparatively stable levels. And there may be breaks in both. Like so many speech constructions, these verbal constructions are not mutually exclusive opposites, but can be shown to have possibilities of serving as complements to each other. And the truth may lie somewhere between them.

Visual representations of melody as a chain is comparatively easily done by a chain of symbols; as a stream, by a curving line. Symbolization inevitably results in sharp distinction between music space (tone) and music time (rhythm) as separate, independent factors; lineation, in non-separation of the two, as overlapping, interdependent factors. Within the incomplete frame of the two-dimensional page, both symbolization and lineation depend upon certain graphic conventions of obscure origin. One, identification of elapse of time with occurrence from left to right on the page, possibly borrowed from speech writing, underlies both factors. Another, identification of height in pitch with height on the page underlies some symbolic and all linear music writing. Uniform vertical coordinates for elapse of time (indicating tempo) and uniform horizontal coordinates for height of pitch form the basic chart for the most recent developments of linear music writing known as "graphing."

The history of the fine art of European music shows that our conventional music writing was first a predominantly symbolic, second a predominantly linear, and third a mixed symbolic-linear notation. The Greek tradition, as made known to us most clearly by Alypius, was based upon the convention of representing elapse of time from left to right. Separate symbols for pitches of tones and for meter were placed accordingly. The accents and neumes of the early Christian era added the convention of identifying height of pitch with height on the page, but were linear in character, expressing movement rather than the points moved to and moved from. They seem first to have come into use to describe an existing practice of recitation. The notation became, however, more and more used for prescriptive purposes. First, ecclesiastical authorities and, later, composers began to specify exactly from where and to where movement was to go, and how long it was to take to do so. Addition of the lines of the staff and of the stems and barlines (prototypes respectively of the horizontal and vertical coordinates of the graph chart) were major steps toward the lineation of the graph; standardization of the notehead and the metrical flags and beams was a reversion to symbolism.

As we find it today, our conventional notation is still a mixed symbolic-linear music writing in which the symbolic element is the more highly organized and therefore dominates. It is practically entirely prescriptive in character. Emphasis is upon structures—principally of pitch and meter. It does not tell us much about the connection of the structures. It does not tell us as much about how music sounds as how to make it sound. Yet no one can make it sound as the writer of the notation intended unless in addition to a knowledge of the tradition of writing he has also a knowledge of the oral (or, better, aural) tradition associated with it—that is, a tradition learned by the ear of the student, partly from his elders in general but especially from the precepts of his teachers. For to this aural tradition is customarily left most of the knowledge of "what happens between the notes," between the links in the chain and the comparatively stable levels in the stream.

In employing this mainly prescriptive notation as a descriptive sound writing of any music other than the Occidental fine and popular arts of music, we do two things, both thoroughly unscientific. First, we single out what appear to us to be structures in the other music which resemble structures familiar to us in the notation of the Occidental art and write these down, ignoring everything else for which we have no symbols. Second, we expect the resulting notation to be read by people who *do not carry the tradition of the other music.* The result can be only a conglomeration of structures part European, part non-European, connected by a movement 100 percent European. To such a riot of subjectivity it is presumptuous indeed to ascribe the designation "scientific."

There are three ways out of the dilemma, for that is what it is, so rare is the carriage by any one person of more than one music tradition and so difficult the correction of the bias typical of that one.[1] On the one hand, we may increase the already heavy overload of symbols in the notation, with a resulting increase of difficulty in reading and but little, if any, gain in accuracy or objectivity. On the other hand, we may dispense with many of the symbols and extend the graphic potentialities of the notation. The handmade graph based upon the notation has its uses. But for purposes of formal description—our main concern here—the objectivity of the electronic reduction of the oscillographic curve, especially of the soundtrack of high-fidelity sound-recording, is vastly superior. As Bartók has said, "The only true notations [music writing is what he might have said] are the soundtracks on the record itself."[2] These, unfortunately, are legible only through laborious mathematical calculation. For, when large enough to be seen in detail by the human eye, they are several feet long per second. Electronic analysis can reduce or compress them automatically, as desired. Compression within a range of about 2.5 to 25 mm. per second produces a graph legible by anyone who can read conventional notation and is willing to practice.

The time has not yet come, of course, for abandonment of our conventional notation. It has come, I aver, for development of the graph. Structure and function are equally important methodological concepts. Prescriptive and descriptive uses of music writing are equally necessary and not necessarily incompatible. Musics surely differ from one another in their adaptability to one or the other kind of music writing. But surely, also, we may hope, they resemble one another in this respect. The important thing for study is to know objectively wherein they differ and resemble regardless of their being written one way or another. Furthermore, as a means of communication among people, music must be expected to have its subjective aspects. The least we should expect of the scholar is that he will not be a party to the passing off of his own subjectivity as someone else's or that he will fail to report objectively upon the subjectivity of that someone else. My recommendation for the foreseeable future, then, is to employ the notation and the graph concurrently.

Correlation of the graph and the notation depends in great measure upon recognition of their relative capacities and limitations. Both are based upon the conventions of identifying elapse of time with left to right on the page and height in pitch with height upon it. They differ in that spacing is irregular in the notation, but uniform in the graph. The comparative efficiency of the two methods of writing in handling the six principal functions of the single melody may be summarized as follows:

TONAL FUNCTIONS

1. *Pitch* is only roughly indicated, that is, within a half tone by the notation. The attempt to increase accuracy by superscription of additional symbols such as cents numerals, arrows, plus and minus signs,

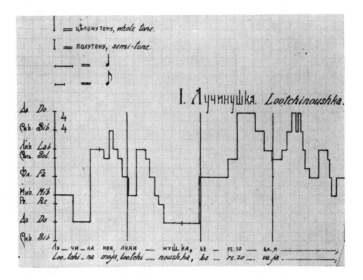

Hand graph, made by ear from phonograph recording. Excerpt of diagram 1, in *The Peasant Songs of Great Russia*, by Eugenia Eduardovna (Paprik) Lineva. Moscow, 1912. The vertical lines are music bars. Rectangular chart, in color, not reproducible.

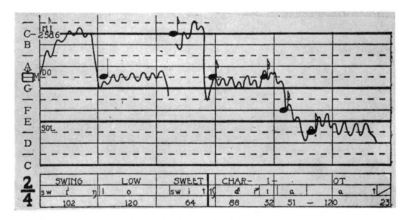

Hand graph, made by mathematical reduction of a "sound wave photograph." Fig. 29, in *Phonophotography in Folk Music,* by Milton Metfessel. Copyright 1928 by the University of North Carolina Press. Reprinted by permission. The light vertical lines are seconds; the heavy one, a music bar.

PLATE 1

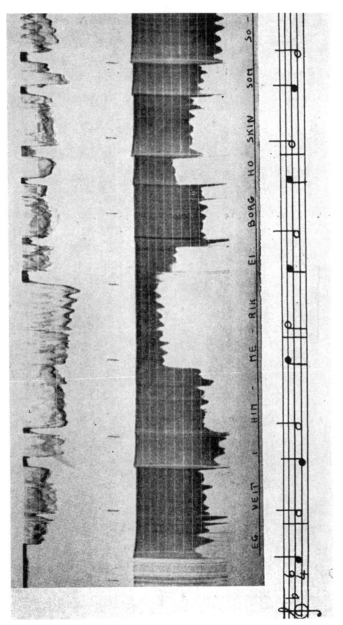

Automatic graph (oscillogram) made by electronic-mechanical reduction, photographed on film, of Norwegian folksong, sung by woman's voice. Excerpt of fig. 3, in *Photography as an Aid in Folk Music Research*, by Olav Gurvin, in *Norveg*, III (1953), 181-96. Reprinted with permission. Upper, shaded, outline shows intensity (amplitude); lower, white, outline, pitch (fundamental frequency) upon ruled, semitonal staff, with seconds marked by timer. (Enlarged?)

PLATE 2

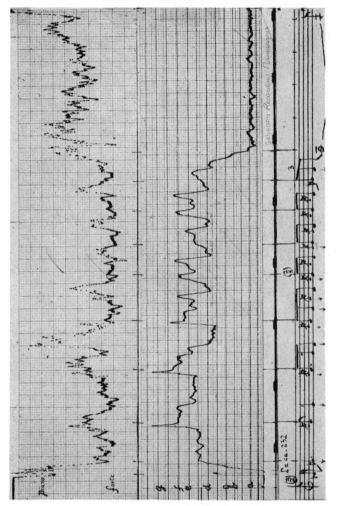

Automatic graph (oscillogram) made by electronic-mechanical reduction written directly on paper (see note 3), of Abatutsi Traditional Song, sung by man's voice. Excerpt of Band 16, in *Voice of the Congo, Riverside World Folk Music Series*, RLP 4002, recorded in Ruanda by Alan P. and Barbara W. Merriam, 1951-52. Upper, broken, line shows amplitude; lower, continuous, line, fundamental frequency, upon rectangular millimeter chart (green) with ruled, semitonal staff, and with seconds marked by timer. (Reduced)

PLATE 3

modifications of accidentals, and so forth, found in many ethnomusicological works is severely limited by the decrease in legibility. My present fundamental frequency analyzer, Melograph Model B, which is a mere Model T in the way of graphing devices, has a top discrimination of about 1/10 tone.[3]

2. *Amplitude* (dynamics) is only roughly indicated by the notation. My present amplitude graphs show changes in dynamics far beyond what the ear can detect.

3. *Tone-quality* (tonal density) cannot be shown at present by either method of writing except laboriously by instruments in or as the Sonagraph. Ample acoustic research has been completed and engineering applications are already in use permitting rough but meaningful graphs of tone quality. A practical device is still to be manufactured.

RHYTHMIC FUNCTIONS

4. *Tempo* or speed of event is only roughly indicated in the notation, even with the aid of the metronome. It is very accurately indicated upon the chart in both frequency and amplitude graphs by the analyzer I am using. The margin of error seems to be about 1/100 second.

5. *Proportion* is easy to read in the notation as prescription, but not always easy to read as a description in the graph.

6. When fed into a properly programmed computer, it can be easily read with perfect accuracy. Rhythmic density (number of events per unit of time) can be shown well by the graph produced by the analysis fed into a computer.

On the whole, the student will find the pitch and the beat more accurately shown in the graph than in the notation, but less independently delimited. As conceptions of verbal thinking, he will find both becoming less rigid and absolute. Also, he will find the gross formal aspects of melody more readily perceivable in the graph. But he will have some difficulty in fitting conventional terminology with what he sees in the graph. The problem is most clearly presented in all its complexity in the sung melody. For it is there that the tonal factor of vibrato meets the rhythmic factor of rubato head-on, in the most diverse and subtle manners.

First, let us consider the sung melody as a chain. From this viewpoint, vibrato and rubato are separate, unrelated factors.

Surely, all students of Occidental music know that the actual variance of the vibrato is an alternation of adjacent pitch frequencies and/or amplitudes customarily perceived, that is, musically thought of, by us as one salient pitch and/or loudness about the mean of the variance.[4] (Variance of tone quality in the vibrato is secondary and need not detain us for the moment.) It is this mean, not the actual, variance that we identify as a "note" and relate to a norm of our music theory such as a degree of a scale and, so, as a link in the chain. There are three main types of vibrato: (1) of pitch without loudness, (2) of loudness without pitch, (3) of both pitch and loudness.

Surely, also, all students of this music know that the actual variance of the rubato is an alternation of anticipation and delay (or delay and anticipation) of successive beats customarily perceived by us as one salient deviation from the mean of the variance, or tempo.

Operation of the vibrato is mostly below the threshold of deliberate control. That is, it is largely autonomic, customarily thought of as a characteristic of voice production, as, for example, of the single note or link in the chain. It can be modified—even acquired—by conscious effort, but not so much in terms of its actual as of its mean variance. Once acquired, it is set in its pattern and persists throughout the process of rendition, regardless of changes of overall pitch and loudness.

Operation of the rubato, in contrast, is mostly above the threshold of deliberate control. It is thought of as a characteristic of the sequence of notes or links in the chain. While factors of which we are largely unconscious are constantly deflecting it in minute ways, our deliberate control of it is mainly in terms of its actual variance with respect to whole beats and, in slow tempos, of divisions of beats. As to its mean variance, the Grand Tradition, as I received it from my most admired teachers, requires that it be (1) continuous in all but very strict tempos and (2) compensatory, for "the music should come out with the metronome at the end"—a quaint, but tenaciously held bit of musical folklore. The notation does not even attempt to show this; but the graph can submit it to an acid test. It can also show any unevenness in vibrato or rubato which is musically significant.

Now, the attack upon the next succeeding note in any melodic process, the more so if it is accented, long held, dissonant, or unusual in some respect, is very much a matter of deliberate attention and control on the part of the executant. But according to the acousticians, we customarily vastly underestimate (1) the extent of the actual variance of the vibrato, which may be commonly 40-200 cents, that is, from one-fifth to a whole tone; (2) its rate, which may be 4-10 per second; and (3) its irregularity in both respects. Such variances might be expected to modify the expectations of the singer, semi-automatic as they are, and occupied as he may be with the mean variance of the tone he is producing with the intention of arriving within the mean variance of beat required in the rendition of the melody he is carrying. Seashore and others have pointed out that singers—even the best—habitually overshoot or undershoot both upward and downward melodic progression. The fundamental frequency analyzer that I have been using shows this also. I would like, therefore, to advance the hypothesis that when the phase of the actual vibrato is in the direction of the melodic progression the establishment of the mean variance of the new note upon the beat expected is more likely to occur, whereas if it is contrary, the new note may not be established until after the beat, a slide being interposed. If the slide, which is typical of legato singing, is fairly slow or covers a wide interval, the graph may show little jagged points where the continuation of the vibrato may have forced an interruption of the progression. Overshooting and undershooting may also involve or be involved in difference in phase and progression. Thus, rubato may be influenced by vibrato.

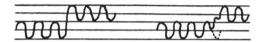

Schematic diagram of vibrato and upward melodic
progression, in phase (left) and out of phase (right)

Conversely, if the attack upon a higher or lower note is anticipated or delayed by rubato, a vibrato that might have facilitated a decisive attack may be upset. A slide or overshooting or undershooting may result. Thus, vibrato may be influenced by rubato.

It is only in the attack or release of substantial notes (links in the chain) that vibrato and rubato may meet head-on. A very common complication seems to result within the beat when the rate of actual variance of the vibrato and a division of the beat by articulated notes are within the 4-10 alternations per second of the vibrato and the 2-16 (approximately) of the beat division. For example, a vibrato of five actual variances per second will produce a very different rendition of a group of four sixteenth notes at a quarter = 60 from that of a vibrato of seven per second.

Next let us consider the melody as a stream, broken only by the necessity to take breath, as at the end of a phrase, or by the briefer closures of the vocal apparatus in enunciation of certain consonants, or the making of exceptional effects such as staccato, pauses, and so forth. From this viewpoint, vibrato and rubato are closely related factors in a continuum. For here, melody is not viewed as a jagged rising and falling but as a sinuous flowing along a course. In what may be the vast majority of cases the glide between levels, their overshooting and undershooting, and the various inflections given them are not exceptions to theoretical norms but integral characteristics of the stream, intentional and cultivated. Except in the most strict tempo giusto and marcato, which are rare in singing, the manner of proceeding between levels and of modifying the levels themselves are, then, often quite as important data for the student as are the levels themselves.

In instrumental performance, the collision (in the chain) or interplay (in the stream) of vibrato and rubato is modified or even broken variously by movements of fingers, changes in bowing or embouchure, and so forth, peculiar to each technique. Approximation of many of the devices of singing style above mentioned can, however, be noted in instrumental playing—as on the vina and sitar, the ch'in and koto, and even in our own banjo and guitar playing—where slide-fretting, pressing down on strings, "hammering down" and pulling them sidewise are common, as are tightening, relaxing, and shaping the embouchure on the trumpet, clarinet, and other wind instruments. The almost infinite variety of this interplay between and within beats defines more closely the fault so often found with the unskilled performer: that he rendered the notes correctly but left out what should have come between them, which is to say, he did not connect them in accordance with the appropriate aural tradition. Each of the many music traditions in the world probably has its own distinctive ways of connecting or putting in what should come between the notes. Conventional notation can give no more than a general direction as to what these ways are, as, for example, by the words and signs of portamento, legato, détaché, staccato, spiccato, crescendo, diminuendo, accelerando, rallentando, and others. In the graph they are all there for anyone to see in clear detail. If it causes us some trouble to find out just what the notational equivalents are, we must not complain that the performer did not render notes. Rather, we should be glad that instead of rendering notes he rendered music, and that we may set ourselves with greater assurance to the task of finding out what he did sing or play, without preconceptions that he meant to, or should, have sung notes.

At this point it is necessary to say a word of warning about the fetish of extreme accuracy in the writing of music. Physics can determine and engineering can reproduce incredibly small differences of sound and time. Psychology (and rare musical experience) can prove that human beings—not necessarily with talent or training in music—can perceive differences beyond 1/100 of a tone or of a second.[5] But the great music traditions, their practice by those who have carried them, and the phenomenological and axiological norms[6] incorporated in them were not determined by the exceptional human being. He contributes to them. We may never cease the controversy over how much. The same is true of our notation, which is, par excellence, a matter of norms determined by the vast aggregate of practice and codified by generations of workers. The graph, however, shows individual performance. Each graph, whether of the exceptional performer or the merest tyro, is unique. Norms can be arrived at by comparative studies of large numbers of graphs. But these norms may differ in many important respects from the norms embodied in the notation. Or they may confirm them. In any event, where the individual notation may give too much norm and too little detail, the individual graph may easily give too little norm and too much detail. It is well, therefore, especially in these pioneer stages of the development of the graph, not to look for too much detail or, better, detail too far beyond the norms of general practice, except for most carefully considered ends. For the present, I am inclined to set 1/10 of a tone (20 cents) and 1/10 of a second as fair margins of accuracy for general musicological use. Detailed study may go beyond these at the discretion of the student.

As a strictly musicological tool, the graphing apparatus brings to our existing notational techniques the needed complement to show "what happens between the notes" and what any departures from their theoretical norms really are in terms of musicological thinking. For lexicographical and many classificatory uses, the pitch-time graph will probably be the most useful. Used side by side with the amplitude-time graph, a beginning can be made in the all important exact study of performance style, especially of singing style, without which the infant discipline of comparative melodic research cannot hope to do more than half a job. But as yet, this can be only a beginning. For its full study, graphing of tone quality and visible speech, both now in advanced stages of development, will be necessary.

We are, then, at last nearing the time when scientific definition of the world's musics and comparative studies of them can and should begin in earnest. Extrinsic contributions in terms of culture history, of geographic extent, and of social depth are being made by anthropology, sociology, psychology, physiology, physics, and other nonmusical or extramusical disciplines. Musicology is hardly ready to attack the necessary definition and comparative study in intrinsic terms. We have not more than coined a word when we speak of the concept *music* or even *a music*. We do not even know whether our basic categories of music "idiom"—fine, folk, popular, and primitive (better, tribal) arts of music—hold everywhere outside of the Occidental culture community or even in it.

The volume of data now already at hand shows that in the near future we shall be compelled to adopt statistical techniques such as those being developed by anthropology.[7] These will increasingly employ the kind of thinking and operating that depends upon precise visual representation of the most detailed observation as well as of the most generalized synopsis or synthesis. Musicologists will have to learn to read the graphs of nonmusical sciences. And it is not impossible that nonmusical scientists might learn to read the music graph more readily than the conventional Occidental notation.

As a descriptive science, musicology is going to have to develop a descriptive music writing that can be written and read with maximum objectivity. The graphing devices and techniques, above referred to, show the way toward such an end. But it must be remembered that technological aids of this sort report only upon the physical stimulus to the outer ear. At present, too, it is possible to put into visual form only fractioned aspects of this, such as pitch and time, amplitude and time, and so on. One can conceive, though scarcely imagine, an automatic music writing that would comprehend the total physical stimulus in a single, continuous process of writing or reading. But even if this present impossibility were to be realized, we would still have to take pains lest the visual representation of the stimulus were mistaken for the full sensory and perceptual reaction of a person conditioned by the particular music-cultural tradition of which the stimulus were a product. For perception does not accept sensation without change. Put bluntly, "we do not hear what we think we hear." Just what is the nature of the change is one of the things we most want to know. For culturally unconditioned listening to music, unless by "wolfboys," congenital idiots, or the like, is not known to us. If the stimulus is a product of the particular music tradition that we carry, we perceive it as such. If it is a product of a tradition we do not carry, we perceive it as we would a product of the one we do carry, making such changes as we are accustomed to. Therefore, automatic music writing by such aids as those referred to must no more be taken for what we think we hear than most conventional notation. But even in its present pioneer stage of development, such writing must be accepted by us as a far truer visual portrayal of what we actually hear than is the notation. By comparing the two, we may achieve several useful ends: (1) we may learn more about the divergence of conception and perception in our own music; (2) we may take steps toward the discovery of how a music other than our own sounds to those who carry its tradition; (3) we may begin to correct our misperception of other musics than our own by cultivating our capacity for a universal musicality—surely, one would think, a prerequisite for musicological work. The automatic graph can serve as a bridge between musics—a common denominator, as it were, in support of such musicality. The physical stimulus constituted by a product of any music tradition is identical to those who carry the tradition and to those who carry another. It is the conceptions and perceptions of it by the respective carriers which may be different. There may be a clue here to the problem of what music communicates and perhaps an indispensable guide to the effort to develop a worldwide philosophy of music upon both rational and mystical bases—not on *either* one *or* the other.

NOTES

1. E. von Hornbostel, "Fuegian Songs," in *American Anthropologist,* XXXVIII (July-September 1936), 357n.

2. Béla Bartók and Albert B. Lord, *Serbo-Croatian Folk Songs* (New York: Columbia University Press, 1951), p. 3.

3. Charles Seeger, "Toward a Universal Music Sound-Writing for Musicology," in *Journal of the International Folk Music Council,* IX (1957), 63.

4. Carl E. Seashore, ed., *The Vibrato* (Iowa City: University of Iowa Press, 1932), p. 369.

5. See, for example, one of the most valiant attempts at descriptive accuracy using conventional notation (Bartók-Lord, *Serbo-Croatian Folk Songs*), in many of whose transcriptions there are passages in which it is difficult or impossible to decide to what extent the notes represent (1) unequal articulated divisions of a beat sung in strict time, (2) equal articulated divisions sung with rubato, (3) either of these with written out or partly written out vibrato, (4) an uneven vibrato, or (5) a vibrato that a less sensitive ear would hear as a single tone, i.e., whose mean, instead of actual, variance would be the musical fact.

6. The elasticity with which our notational norms are actually made to sound by competent professionals has recently been measured with great accuracy by Charles R. Shackford in "Intonation in Ensemble in String Performance—An Objective Study" (Ph.D. diss., Harvard University, 1954).

7. Linton G. Freeman and Alan P. Merriam, "Statistical Classification in Anthropology: An Application to Ethnomusicology," in *American Anthropologist,* LVIII (June 1956), 464-472.

IX

Music and Society: Some New-World Evidence of Their Relationship[43]

An aura of belief that society is influenced by music has hung about the art of music from its earliest days. Philosophers, statesmen, and even generals have praised, often extravagantly, the importance of music in the affairs of men.[1] Under authoritarian regimes, respect—even veneration—for music as a social force required no special apology. Since the days of colonial expansion and the industrial revolution, however, the spirit of free inquiry has sought a rational basis upon which the *raison d'être* of the art could be estimated. This is still in our day a moot question. Evidence of the belief is plentiful, but evidence of the facts to which it refers is lacking. In persisting in the belief—which many do—we are like the old preacher adversely criticized by his flock: we "argify and sputify but don't show wherein."

The converse belief, that music is influenced by society, is equally ancient.[2] More credible than the first, perhaps, in popular and learned minds today, it has been given increased attention during the last fifty years or so.[3] Music and society, we may agree, are both phenomena or functions of culture, so it is reasonable to assume that they have definite relationships both to each other and to the whole collection. Society being the more comprehensive concept, one might claim that music must be dependent upon it. Yet in spite of the reasonableness and its support by evidence of some of the larger events and processes of history, there seems to be very little tangible truth in it when we come down to details, even some rather large details. Causality—that when A happens, then B happens—is elusive. In less formal logic, we may search for correspondence. But it is difficult to show convincingly in what this consists or how it operates. Again, we cannot "show wherein." So we fall back upon the "great man" theory of history—that things happen because great men make them happen. Let us concede that sometimes they do. But there are many things, we all admit, which do not happen because great

182

men make them happen. It is with respect to these that the problem of music and society arises.

I must make clear the fact that I am about equally impressed with these two beliefs. As I see them, ultimately (and that means basically), the two are complementary and interdependent. Concerning the first—that music influences society—the outstanding laboratory in operation at the present day is, of course, Soviet Russia. As everyone knows, the Communist party is trying to persuade composers to write a kind of music that will have certain effects upon the Russian people, effects that will contribute to the social development of its policies. Political control of music for social, including political, purposes is nothing new. It operated in ancient Greece and in seventeenth-century Massachusetts. It was highly successful in the Roman Church (that is, in Western European society) up to about 1600 and in various sects of the Reformation. As for the second belief—that society influences music—the demographic explosion of the European culture over the rest of the world and its implementation by the electronic duplication of music offers an outstanding laboratory for testing the case. Here, the control, while it has varied in deliberateness, is a matter of written and other record.

Since data are lacking upon the Russian experiment, and since the occasion for this paper calls for emphasis upon the New World, I shall confine my remarks from here on to that aspect of our subject involving the second belief alone, citing such evidence as I can from both Anglo and Latin America. To clarify what must of necessity be an intricate presentation, I shall first define the senses in which I shall use some of the concepts I shall employ. This will be done in the form of eight observations.

Music in general and society in general.   While I have presented a subject of extreme generalization and wish to retain it as one to which I offer a contribution, I must admit that we cannot, at the present time, form a usable concept of music as a world whole, and so cannot show wherein the relationship between such a one and world society consists or how it operates. Rather, we must, as members of a society in which science presumably takes precedence over criticism, deal first with particular musics and particular societies.

A particular music in a particular society.   The music used by a particular society can be distinguished in a manner similar to that employed in distinguishing the language used by the society. Musicology is, of course, far behind linguistics in descriptive techniques, as well of qualitative as of quantitative factors. But as in the study of speech, the essential concept is that of tradition.[4]

Tradition.   Tradition comprehends those phenomena exhibited in the inheritance, cultivation, and transmission of a body of practice, or way of doing something, in a society. I shall view a music tradition as operating in three dimensions: in extent, throughout the geographical area occupied by a society; in depth, throughout the social mass; and in duration, throughout its span of life.

Society, culture, and the individual.   A society is constituted by a group of individuals; a culture, by a bundle of traditions. Anthropologists warn us that neither exists apart from the individuals that constitute the one and which carry the traditions that constitute the other. Conversely, neither does any individual exist apart from the society of which he is a constituent or the cultural traditions he carries.[5]

Acculturation.[6]   I shall regard acculturation as affecting any or all traditions that form a culture, including those of social organization. I shall regard it as operating not only in contacts between more or less distinct culture groups but also between more or less distinct social strata within each culture group, that is, not only in social extent but in social depth as well and, of course, over considerable duration of time.

Origins.   Since we cannot prove absence of prior acculturation in any group, we cannot logically entertain such notions as "pure" cultures and "pure" musics.

Integration and diversification.   In every culture and so in every acculturative process I will discern two opposing trends—one toward integration, the other toward diversification—often operating simultaneously in different phases not only of the culture as a whole but of one and the same tradition.

Identity.   A new and separate identity can be said to result when the diversification of a culture is more easily described in terms of its own characteristics than in those of its earlier acculturative components.

One of the reasons why efforts to deal with the influence of society upon music have run into what have seemed to be insurmountable difficulty is the fact that they have been conceived not only in too general terms but in terms of the music of the Old World. First, the essential acculturative components are not known. Second, the dates of the initial acculturative contacts are not known. Third, the diversification observed in process has already progressed far from its origins in prehistory.

The New World, on the contrary offers several advantages as a domain in which the influence of society upon music can be studied. First, the essential acculturative components are known—the continental traditions of America, Europe, and Africa. Second, the dates of the initial contacts are known—the discovery and conquest by Europeans from 1500 on. Third, a fresh process of acculturation began, and we can study it through written and other records, in both extent and depth, over a period of 450 years.

Our knowledge of pre-Columbian Amerindian music is built mostly by historical reconstruction. Not a single piece of written music remains. By and large, music traditions were probably of the nature of the idiom known as tribal or primitive and undiversified, except that in the more highly diversified cultures of the Maya, Aztec, and Inca civilizations there might very well have been something of the nature of a fine art, or at least prototypes of such.

European music is, of course, the one about which we know the most. By 1500 it was a highly diversified art. In extent, there were many national and regional variations similar to the languages and dialects of speech. In depth, at least two idioms, developed during the Middle Ages, were relatively stabilized and vigorously current in the fifteenth century: a fine and a folk art. Primitive idioms of the conquering countries of Western Europe were probably dead or dying, but in any case were not factors in the situation under discussion here.[7] A popular idiom— popular in the twentieth-century sense of being somewhat profession- alized, part oral, part written tradition of the urban middle and lower classes—had developed during the Renaissance and was an established one from the seventeenth century on.[8]

Our knowledge of African music resembles our knowledge of Amer- indian, even to the extent that we may speak of the possibility of the existence of emergent idioms of fine art. But it differs in this respect: Though African traditions came, in the main, directly to the New World from Africa, some may have come via Europe, where African culture had been transplanted to some extent well before 1500.[9]

We have, then, in our overall picture, one highly integrated and diversified culture with its highly integrated and diversified social and musical traditions—the European—forcibly joining two others, both of doubtful cultural, social, and musical integration, and with diversifica- tion probably only in extent. The military action, while socially only a fragmentary operation, was nevertheless socially motivated and socially affected and constitutes our first major evidence of the effect of social upon musical traditions. Had the conquest not taken place, *the music of the Americas today would be altogether different.*

But had it not been followed by colonization, the initial military action in itself might have meant little in the way of "subsequent changes in the original cultural patterns." For it was colonization that fixed conquest, that is, domination of European traditions as a permanent thing. And colonization is mainly a social process. Here, then, is a second major evidence of the effect of society upon music. Had colonization not been pressed continuously for several centuries, *the music of the Americas today would be an altogether different art.*

This is, of course, painfully obvious. It has to be stressed, however, because we so frequently forget that both conquest and colonization, although initiated in the past, are, as cultural and social processes, still operative in the Americas today. The conquest, affecting now only a few small resistent enclaves far from main cultural centers of population and highroads of communication, is virtually completed. We cannot say as much of colonization, the constructive part of the process of which the former was the destructive. It built a new culture community within whose form, colonialism, the subsequent changes in the original cultural patterns took place. The European became neo-European; the Amerindian, neo-Amerindian; and the African, neo-African. Continued acculturative and contra-acculturative processes gradually exhibited phenomena more correctly designated as Euro-American, Afro-American, for all three continental traditions underwent cultural change. Political independence gained from 1776 to 1898 and economic independence during World War II did not end the process of colonization or the period of colonialism. Rather, they stand as mileposts on the way to a destination, we may agree, which is already in view: emergence of a distinct subgroup of the Occidental culture community widely referred to as "American." This can only be regarded by us as a socially effected transformation. Individuals did, it is true, inherit, carry, and hand on the music traditions of their communities. But the whole 450 years is conspicuous for its lack of outstanding individuals, "masters," "great men."

The gross achievement of European colonialism in the New World may be summarized in the following skeleton formula:

1. ca. 1500, complete hegemony of Amerindian traditions:
    a) as a whole, unintegrated, though "families" can be assumed to have existed as they do today;
    b) probably socially undiversified, except by varying competence of individuals;
    c) with major acculturative processes relatively stabilized, that is, slow.

2. ca. 1950, virtually complete hegemony of neo-European traditions:
    a) highly integrated in extent;
    b) highly diversified by social class;
    c) with major acculturative processes highly destabilized by rapid change.

In tracing the effect of colonial society upon the music of the New World, I shall not attempt to discuss acculturation between Amerindian and African traditions. Too little is known about this phase of our subject.[10] Neither shall I pretend to handle as a whole the acculturation of all three sets of continental traditions. Overall integration has not proceeded, I believe, to the point where such a general subject can be dealt with. Furthermore, our musicological techniques, scarcely adequate for the analysis of acculturative processes with two components, cannot be expected to serve in those with three. I shall therefore divide my attention between a consideration of the spread of the neo-European hegemony, its transformation in different ways in different places at different times into a Euro-American hegemony, and the consequent interrelationships of the three acculturative components that, having survived within it, combine variously to form what some day we may be able to call an American music tradition, *sui generis,* though still a regional variant of the Occidental music community.

By and large, I believe we can say that during the colonial period there was music acculturation only when the extent, depth, and duration of social contact induced it. Where there was annihilation of the "receiving" group by the "donor" group, there was, of course, no music acculturation.[11] Likewise, acculturation was nonexistent or slight where the "receiving" group did not want to receive, or the "donor" group to give, but left the former in the wilderness or pushed it onto reservations.[12] Where there was reasonably humane treatment,[13] practical master-slave relationship, or sufficient preponderance of numbers in the receiving groups, these groups accepted a social status not unlike that of the European rural classes—tied to the land as serfs, or at best as small landholders, mainly relying upon oral music transmission. Their music gradually approximated the folk type of idiom, that is, an idiom made up of survivals of tribal idioms, on the one hand, and of the fine and popular idioms of the urban classes, on the other. This was true of both Amerindian and African traditions. With the loss of tribal organization, much of the *raison d'être* of tribal music disappeared. A consequent impoverishment of music tradition was bound to occur.

With respect to the European hegemony, we know that the same impoverishment took place. From the earliest days, traditions of fine and popular idioms were brought to both Hispanic and Anglo America.[14] But they could not thrive here, except in a few isolated spots where they eventually withered.[15] Fine instruments could not be housed or repaired. They could not be made. The magnificent church organs installed in many beautifully architected cathedrals of Hispanic America became unplayable for lack of care. After a brilliant beginning shortly after the conquest, music printing was so rare as to be practically nonexistent until the nineteenth century, and was limited even then.[16] In short, social conditions for the cultivation of fine and popular idioms as practiced in the mother countries existed to an almost negligible extent during the sixteenth and seventeenth centuries in the colonies. Music literacy, never high among populations at large, must never have reached more than a fraction of one percent. The majority of the colonists continued on, or reverted to, the folk level of oral transmission. This we may list as a third major evidence of the influence of social upon music traditions.

A trend to offset this impoverishment of music tradition was first set in motion by the increased opulence of the small class of colonial administrators and landowners. It constitutes a fourth major evidence of the influence of society upon musical tradition. The outstanding characteristic of this trend was that the well-to-do colonial or *criollo* tried to be more Spanish than the Spanish, more British than the British, and to set himself above and apart from the bulk of the population around him, in emulation of members of the ecclesiastic, noble, and merchant classes of the mother countries. Society in the large, more prosperous urban centers during the eighteenth century, patterning its values upon contemporary European fashions, called for the services of popular and fine arts of music.[17] Prior to this time, colonial musicians were solitary workers, few and far between. Many were immigrants. Some were professionally trained; others were not. But during the second half of the century, small groups of native composers began to produce chamber music and thoroughly secularized church music in such separated localities as Caracas, Venezuela;[18] Morelia, Mexico;[19] Pennsylvania;[20] Minas Gerais, Brazil;[21] and Santiago, Cuba.[22] The kinds of music written and the skill in composition employed in these widely separated regions bear striking resemblance. Certainly, these composers were, in the main, unknown to one another. But they acted as if they had held a convention, passed resolutions, and then entered upon a common program in a devotedly concerted manner.

This late-eighteenth-century wave of music composition was affected variously by the secession movements. In Venezuela it left no conspicuous following. In the United States and Brazil progress was steady. But everywhere, political independence started a rash of nationalism that developed with surprising uniformity in widely separate regions, quite out of communication with one another, thus constituting a fifth evidence that the occasion for the increased music activity was primarily a development of colonial society and only secondarily of the technical and stylistic competence of individual musicians, who rose to the occasion as well as they could.

Some of these embryonic nationalistic efforts were anti-British or anti-Hispanic in character. The only important difference was that North Americans adopted Germanism and South Americans *francecismo*.[23] Both took Italianism very seriously. But after 1900 this declined and the northerners compensated by turning more to France and the southerners to Germany.

Continued immigration of competent professional musicians, plus the growing nationalism, led to a succession of waves of music activity in the larger centers of the eastern United States, Mexico City, Rio de Janeiro, Buenos Aires, and Havana, into whose orbits neighboring areas of less concentration were drawn. Up to this time colonial music had been an echo, a dying echo, of the music of the mother countries. A new faith—that an American could write good music, in the European mode, of course—animated what we may call the first generation of republican composers, born around 1830. One gets the impression that Melesio Morales, Carlos Gomes, and Louis Moreau Gottschalk were not a little surprised at their faith in themselves. Certainly their public was. But there was no group feeling. Other than a common bond of colonial subservience to the mother countries, the group was entirely unintegrated and diverse.

A second generation, most of whom were born in the 1860s, first felt the vague necessity of "being American" in music itself.[24] Words of songs were in the vernacular; in some cases, direction for performance, also. But the music was still thoroughly European. Titles were often drawn from the American scene. So-called national music, more popular than folk, was harmonized in approved European fashion.

A third generation,[25] born in the 1880s sought more specifically to weave local popular and folk melodies into a fabric of a less conventional European character in such a manner as to give a semblance of nationalism or of that larger chauvinism *americanismo musical*. The distinguishing characteristic of this generation, however, was that it gave the individual a chance to be an individual and, for the first time in the history of American music, to know a group and so to transcend the group level. Carlos Gomes had succeeded in composing good Italian music. But Heitor Villa-Lobos and Charles Ives made some good music that, though it is mainly European in character, has indubitably something not European in it.

A fourth generation,[26] born around 1900, is still more homogeneous in its stylistic aspects, is more competent technically, and shows a degree of integration that practically obliterates distinction of nationality even though this is still potent as a selling point. Personal styles are well defined. Not one but a dozen men stand out above the group level. The effort is to reconcile nationalism and universalism—a somewhat dubious undertaking. Nevertheless, the non-European elements are more often evident.

A fifth generation, born for the most part before 1920, is more difficult to talk about, for it is very large and still very young.[27] But its output so far exhibits a homogeneity and integration that could not be—and, we know, is not—without a well-defined consciousness, not so much of nationalism as of America's taking its place in the large world of Occidental music. Most of this generation show an awareness of the importance of native folklore. But many avoid becoming slaves to the tunes of oral tradition. Rather, they are conscious of the idiom, its character, and its idiosyncrasies, and they consciously adapt their musicianship to it. If present progress continues, as it bids fair to do, we may still see leadership in the Occidental fine art of music shared equally by Europe and America before the century is out, as by one great music community, with a rich diversity of regional variations.

The last hundred years of composition in the fine art of music have not, then, developed purely in intrinsic terms. I have sketched them from the early colonial days, when the times made the man—or perhaps, to put it more charitably, gave him little or no opportunity to be a music man—to the present day, when men may attempt to make the times, or at least are free to give it a cogency, a characteristic flair, which distinguishes it beyond the dead level of colonial respectability.

At the same time that these five generations of composers were working—and not unknown to the last two—the large masses of the people were consolidating their own musical idioms in even greater unanimity of action.

On the whole, in those countries where a preponderance of Amerindian stock characterizes the population, the acculturation has been unspectacular and steady. What we know of their music today may have two or more centuries of relative stabilization back of it. Mexico and the Andean highlands early adopted and adapted the Spanish harp, the guitar of six, five, four, and three strings, and the violin. The music recently recorded by reliable collectors gives every evidence of having achieved an integration of regional styles and technic at least several generations ago. The folk life of these people is not something new. It is now assaulted by the radio, the phonograph, and the motion picture, and we may expect some rapid acculturation with considerable impoverishment of older idioms. However this may be, the effect of folk life upon the composers is so far slight, except in the works of Carlos Chavez, where it finds in some of his works its finest expression.

The case of the African tradition is more complicated. Drawn into the neo-European tradition, rather than blanketed by it as was the Amerindian, African traditions came into closer contact with a greater variety of European tradition than did the indigenous. The acculturation is more spectacular and varied.

It is interesting to note that of the three main elements in African music—the instruments, the solo-choral song, and the dance—only the dance was retained by the neo-African tradition in both Latin and Anglo America. In the former it survived openly; in the latter, clandestinely, until the resulting acculturation blossomed in jazz.

In the United States the instruments were virtually banned. But choral song developed, through what seems to be about 50-50 acculturation, a new genre—the spiritual. In the Antilles, Brazil, parts of Venezuela and Colombia, and some other areas, the instruments and solo song have lived, but choral song has not developed a product comparable to the spiritual.

Neo-African folk-music traditions have had little effect upon the fine art of music in the United States but have transformed its popular music. In Brazil and Cuba, however, neo-African traditions have permeated not only the popular but the fine art of composition, and maintains itself the while in exuberant varieties of form.

If the preceding argument can hold, there should be nothing strange in these striking differences. Deriving logically from two distinct types of society bred respectively in the Protestant and Catholic faiths, they constitute most impressive evidence of the relationship I have been examining.

The gathering together of the various strands that I have dealt with separately here and the weaving of them into a complete theory of music and society will have to be done by other hands than mine. As I have said before, not enough specialized studies have been made to warrant attack upon the overall problem at this time. We still lack descriptive techniques with which to discern in music itself evidence of the 'acculturative processes that we can trace so elaborately in the environment of music. The intrinsic, in any thorough study, must be exactly correlated with the extrinsic. Up to the present, it seems to me—as the foregoing analysis should show clearly enough—our knowledge of the environmental *pressure in upon* music in the New World can account for a vastly larger proportion of the acculturation phenomena than can our knowledge of the *push outward* of the vital music activity itself. Perhaps future music-technical studies may be better implemented. At any rate, the gross quantitative aspect of the music activity of the several billion human beings that have made up colonial society in the Americas these 450 years is a factor that our current musicological techniques simply cannot pretend to cope with. It is easy to say, "Oh well—society did it." But that is not my intention. I would prefer to be able to say, "Society,[28] that is, the anonymous activity of a multitude of individuals knowable by no other name, seems to have been responsible for this," and put it up to musicology to find in the music of those years the musicological data corresponding to or modifying the sociological data. In a virtually leaderless four and one-half centuries, our musicology, built upon the study of European leaders and the monuments they bequeathed us, can avail little. It is heartening and convenient, of course, that leaders are appearing, so that a man who may write a paper such as this in the year 2002 may have a somewhat more balanced scene to deal with.

Perhaps the history of America from 1500 to 1950 is a fairly normal picture of the earlier phases of grand acculturation processes. Perhaps these are predominantly social in character—the work of innumerable men whose small contributions form the indispensable base in terms of whose increasing stabilization recognition of contributions by individuals is possible and worthwhile. If this is the case—and I have a hunch it is—the more detailed study of music in the New World may have a healthful effect upon the study of the musics of other regions and of the total world situation.

NOTES

1. References, from Plato to Plekhanov, are, of course, numberless. For variety, see Charles Sayle, *In Praise of Music, An Anthology* (London, 1897).

2. Ibid.

3. Wilfrid H. Mellers, *Music and Society: England and the European Tradition* (London: D. Dobson, 1946), like the present paper, a regional study.

4. "Oral Tradition in Music," *Standard Dictionary of Folklore, Mythology, and Legend* (New York, 1950).

5. We must guard against both "either-or-ness" and opposition between the terms in the pairs of concepts "the society-the individual" and "the culture (or tradition)-the individual." After all, the distinction itself between the bundle and its constituents is largely one of convenience, when not of necessity. It is easy and possible to treat separately the outstanding individuals in a society and in a tradition of a culture. It is difficult, when not impossible, to treat all the individuals that are not outstanding. The exceptional individual who accepts as much as he can of his traditional role in society and of the traditions carried by the society, no less than he who opposes them, is an integral constituent of the society and a carrier of its traditions. There being no yardstick for the commensuration of the relative contributions of individuals and bundles of individuals,

we must be especially careful in historical handlings not to rely more upon the one than the other.

6. The term *acculturation* was defined in 1935 by a committee of the Social Research Council as follows: "Acculturation comprehends those phenomena which result when two groups of individuals having different cultures come into continuous firsthand contact, with subsequent changes in the original cultural patterns of either or both groups."—*American Anthropologist*, XXXVIII, 1 (January-March 1936).

7. George Herzog, "Some Primitive Layers in European Folk Music" (abstract), *Bulletin of the American Musicological Society*, nos. 9, 10 (June 1947), pp. 11-14.

8. Cf. jongleur, *Gaukler*, gleeman.

9. Richard A. Waterman. "African Influence on the Music of the Americas," *Acculturation in the Americas, Proceedings and Selected Papers of the XXIX International Congress of Americanists* (Chicago, 1952), pp. 207-218.

10. See, however, Geroge Herzog, "African Influences in North American Indian Music," *Papers Read at the International Congress of Musicology, Held at New York, September, 1939* (New York, 1944), pp. 130-143.

11. As, for example, in Cuba. See Fernando Ortiz, "La música y los areitos de los indios de Cuba," *Revista de Arqueología y Etnología*, series 2, vol. III, nos. 6, 7 (January-December 1948), pp. 115-189.

12. As, for example, in North America, Chile, and some parts of Brazil.

13. The Jesuits' treatment of the Indian, for example. See Serafim Leite, "A música nas escolas jesúiticas do Brasil no Século XVI, *Cultura* (Rio de Janeiro), I, 2 (January-April 1949), 27-39.

14. Pedro J. Grenon, "Nuestra primera música instrumental, datos históricos" (Buenos Aires, 1929); José Torre Revello, "Músicos coloniales," Estudios, *Revista Mensual de la Academia Literaria del Plata* (Buenos Aires), LXXII, 394 (December 1944), 392-414; Guillermo Furlong, *Músicos argentinos durante la dominación hispánica* (Buenos Aires: Editorial "Huarpes," 1945).

15. The most striking case is that of the cathedral in Mexico City, where a remarkable tradition of polyphonic music was maintained from 1575 down to the early eighteenth century. This has recently been investigated by Steven Barwick and reported upon in "Sacred Vocal Polyphony in Early Colonial Mexico" (Ph.D. diss., Harvard University).

16. Lota M. Spell, "The First Music Books Printed in America," *Musical Quarterly*, XV, 1 (January 1929), 50-54.

17. Rex D. Happer, "Status of Sociology in Latin America," *Intellectual Trends in Latin America,* (Latin-American Studies 1, Institute of Latin-American Studies, University of Texas, Austin, 1945), pp. 99-110: "Beginning about 1750 a tremendous ferment began to agitate the intellectual climate of opinion in Latin America." See also Harry Bernstein, "Some Inter-American Aspects of the Enlightenment," in A. P. Whitaker and others, *Latin America and the Enlightenment* (New York: D. Appleton-Century, 1942).

18. Juan Bautista Plaza, "Music in Caracas during the Colonial Period (1770-1811)," *Musical Quarterly*, XXIX, 2 (April 1943), 198-213.

19. Miguel Bernal Jimenez, El archivo musical del colegio de Santa Rosa de Santa Maria de Valladolid, siglo XVIII, *Morelia colonial* (Morelia, 1939).

20. A. G. Rau and H. T. David, *A Catalogue of Music by American Moravians, 1742-1842* (Bethlehem, Pa: The Moravian Seminary, 1938).

21. Francisco Curt Lange, "La música en Minas Gerais," *Boletin Latino-americano de Música,* VI (April 1946[7], 409-494.

22. Alejo Carpentier, *La música en Cuba* (Mexico: Fondo de cultura económica, 1946).

23. Jesus C. Romero, "el francecismo en la evolución musical de México," *Carnet musical*, Vol. V, no. 4, supp. 1 (July 1949).

24. Argentina, Julian Aguirre, 1869-1924; Brazil, Alberto Nepomuceno, 1864-1920; Cuba, Ignacio Cervantes, 1847-1905; Mexico, Ricardo Castro, 1866-1907, and Gustavo E. Campa, 1863-1934; United States, Edward MacDowell, 1861-1908.

25. Brazil, Heitor Villa-Lobos, b. 1887; Chile, Pedro Humberto Allende, b. 1885; Mexico, Manuel M. Ponce, 1886-1948; Uruguay, Eduardo Fabini, 1883-1950; United States, Charles E. Ives, b. 1874; Venezuela, Vicente E. Sojo, b. 1887.

26. Brazil, Francisco Mignone, b. 1897; Chile, Domingo Santa Cruz, b. 1899; Cuba, Alejandro García Caturla, 1906-40, and Amadeo Roldan, 1900-1939; Mexico, Silvestre Revueltas, 1899-1940, and Carlos Chavez, b. 1899; United States, Aaron Copland, b. 1900, and Walter Piston, b. 1894.

27. Argentina, Alberto Ginastera, b. 1916; Brazil, Camargo Guarnieri, b. 1907; Chile, Juan Orrego Salas, b. 1919; Cuba, Harold Gramatges, b. 1918; Mexico, Blas Galindo, b. 1910; Panama, Roque Cordero, b. 1917; United States, Samuel Barber, b. 1910; Uruguay, Hector Tosar, b. 1923.

28. See n. 5 above.

X
The Cultivation of Various European Traditions of Music in the New World[59]

A hegemony of European culture has been established in all but the least habitable areas of the New World. By hegemony I mean a continuing status of domination over two other cultures of continental magnitude which have flourished in the hemisphere. Before the sixteenth century, all three had functioned separately from prehistoric times. The European and African cultures had long interpenetrated to some, but now unknown, extent in both Europe and Africa. In the Americas the European and the Amerindian were thrown into contact with each other for the first time from about 1500; the European and the African, mostly upon the eastern littoral, more substantially and upon a larger scale than any previously known.

This hegemony has never functioned as an organized whole but is known in hundreds of apparently independent variants—continental, national, regional, and even local. Among them, enough common characteristics may be discerned to permit conception of it as a still expanding and consolidating factor in a vast area with certain far-reaching trends susceptible to some, though limited, predictability.

From the viewpoint of musicology, a culture may be understood to be a bundle of traditions; a tradition, a way of doing something that is inherited, cultivated, and transmitted by individuals associated in a society for many generations. Music traditions seem to have been well developed in all three of the cultures that came into continuous firsthand contact in the Americas. To the best of present knowledge, all three were highly diversified in geographical extent, but only the European in social depth. The African culture knew only what is commonly referred to as a "primitive" (better, "tribal") music idiom. The Aztec and Inca empires may possibly have developed, besides the tribal, prototypes of the idiom of the elite, learned, or fine art, but not a single notation is known to exist. The European knew at least three classes of idiom—a folk and a fine art, an emergent popular art and, probably, not a few survivals of a primitive or tribal.

European music traditions assumed a position of dominance over those of the other two cultures only gradually. We can speak, however, of such a hegemony as now for some time existent and increasingly exerting a function of consolidation of the other traditions, but also maintaining, at some cultural levels, extensions of European tradition that exhibit no positive evidence of contact with either of the other traditions, current though they be in its immediate vicinity.

We may view this hegemony in two distinct manners: (1) as a thing in itself that can be described and valued in its own terms, that is, in terms intrinsic to the techniques employed in its cultivation; (2) in one or more contexts, that is, in terms of studies other than of music and therefore extrinsic to the technique employed in its cultivation. The former might, unthinkingly, be designated the *musicological;* the latter, quite properly, because the principal contexts are those of the study of the races of men and their cultures, the *ethnomusicological.* I would prefer, however, to designate the former the *music-technical,* reserving the term *musicological* for the study in which the two views are integrated in a single, unified treatment.

In comparison with the study of European music in Europe, musicologists find two somewhat disconcerting factors in the study of the music of the Americas. First is the comparative scarcity of secondary, that is, music-historical, sources of an intrinsic nature—written, printed, organographical, or iconographical—before 1900.[1] The history of music in the New World up to that time must, therefore, be principally contextual in character. The factor of individuality—of producers, products, and verbal studies of them—which has conventionally engaged the attention of musicologists in both Europe and America finds no counterpart in the New World where, during the four centuries 1500 to 1900, even the few outstanding written compositions lie far below the run-of-the-mill contemorary European production. It is possible that a few figures, such as Louis Moreau Gottschalk, Carlos Gomes, and Edward MacDowell, might have received passing notice had they lived in Europe instead of Brazil and the United States. In the increasing roster of national histories of music, the attempt to spread the meager data into a semblance of the textbook of the history of (European) music smacks only too often of chauvinism. For in the Americas during those years, we are faced mainly with a vast anonymity—the ubiquitous currency of folk and popular idioms among the people at large. Probably, the numerous composers of popular songs, hymns, and *danzas* deserve more notice, but their names are only too often lost in obscurity, except in the United States where

sheet-music publication ensured wide distribution and copyright preserved the names of Emmet, Foster, Root, Russel, Work, and others.[2]

There was a vast anonymity in European music, too, at the time, in the
idioms of folk and popular music. But the choice first to build and
document the musical museum of Europe has so preoccupied the
attention of musicologists on both sides of the Atlantic that it has been
regarded beneath serious notice by the scholar. Consequently, value has
been identified mainly with individuality. The exigency that the values,
no less than the facts (artifacts), of a tradition accumulate and are funded
in its repertory and practice has never been faced in full, with the result
that the fundamental problem of the critique—the interrelationship of
the individual and the tradition, the particular and the general, the
judgment and the criteria upon which it is based—is left hanging in the
air while bias and whim are given free play.

That any production in a tradition must—to be in that tradition—
simply reaffirm, that is, *re*present, values already funded in it by predecessors of the producer seems incontestable. Many products, therefore,
are to be valued merely according to whether they do or do not
constitute generally acceptable alternative *re*presentations of values
already funded in the tradition. If, however, values are found in any
product that cannot be said to be already so funded, an accounting of
them must proceed upon the basis of one of three common theories.
According to the first, or "great man theory," the producer is conceived
as creating these new values; and, as the product enters the repertory,
the tradition is enriched by it. According to the second, the mechanist,
evolutionary, or determinist theory, the tradition is conceived as having a
momentum and direction of its own to whose cultivation the capacities of
a variety of potential producers with appropriate physical, educational,
and social characteristics must be assumed to be suited at various times
and places. Those that are available carry on the tradition. The third
theory avoids going to the extremes of mysticism or logic represented
respectively by the first two theories, admitting: (a) that both are
half-truths; (b) that their juncture is ineluctable; (c) that many factors,
probably unknown by us, will always be present; and (d) that we lack any
objective measure of gauging relative credit other than the consensus of
opinion of competent and interested connoisseurs. Proceeding upon the
basis of this third theory, we may conclude that: (a) the average credit
must be assumed to vary, in both Europe and the Americas, around a
mean of 50-50 individual and social; (b) where, as in Europe since 1500,
there is an abundance of individuality in the fine art, the index or
coefficient of value must be the individual producer or product; and (c)
although the producer may be credited with a major part of the new

value, the tradition is always due the major part of the old; (d) whereas in the folk and popular idioms of Europe and in all idioms in the Americas, there is little or no outstanding individuality but only a vast anonymity, practically all values must be considered social, even though admittedly created primarily by individuals in infinitely small contributions at times and places unknown. It will be readily understood, therefore, that the character of music activity in the Americas up to 1900 compels an approach in many ways different from that conventionally in use by historicomusicology. It must perforce be almost exclusively ethno-musicological, quantitative rather than qualitative, more concerned with tradition than with carriers of tradition, and with all four idioms equally under the increasing hegemony of traditions that did not grow to maturity upon the soil of the continent but were brought to it full-fledged throughout a period of four centuries and cultivated, often as not, in the frame of their continued and brilliant functioning in the distant, superior culture of Europe.

The second disconcerting factor in the study of the music of the Americas is the dearth of technical studies, especially the systematic, that is, those based upon the primary sources of data—the actual sound of the current traditions. After 1900, comparative musicology made rapid strides in Europe, especially in the collection and study of its own musical folklore and of the primitive musics of the world at large. These new techniques were admirably suited to application in the New World, as well to the idiom of its art as to its folk, popular, and tribal arts. Both direct (sound) and indirect (visual) sources are found in increasing abundance. But studies based upon them, such as Kolinski's of African survivals in Guiana,[3] Aretz's of folk music in Venezuela and several other countries,[4] Bayard's and Bronson's of the tunes of the Anglo-American ballad,[5] are exceedingly rare. Regional collection has spread over nearly the whole of the United States since Sharp's notable field trips in 1916-1918, but are rarer in Latin America.[6] Several governments—Argentina, Brazil, Chile, Mexico, Peru, Uruguay, and Venezuela—have growing archives. Organographic and iconographic work of distinction has been done by Alvarenga, Izikowitz, Ortiz, and Vega.[7] The only segment of the field in which collection and study has approached adequacy is that of the North Amerindians, begun by Fewkes and Gilman in the 1890s and carried on very actively today, though with many areas untended. Acculturation with various European and neo-European traditions has begun to be studied. The ethnomusicology of fine art should prove especially profitable. For the number and the competence of American composers has increased to a point where rivalry with the European begins to be envisaged. That such study might be a prelude—even a "proving ground"—for the even more important and difficult ethnomusicology of European music, that is, of all its idioms as a single unit—as they exist in intimate association in the context of its culture—should inspire both European and American interest in the music of the New World and its hegemony of European traditions.

I shall distinguish four contexts within which the many factors, both phenomenological and axiological, both intrinsic and extrinsic, which have molded the cultivation of European traditions of music in the Americas may be most briefly and rewardingly be grouped. These four are:

1. *Cultural dynamics*—the population explosion of Renaissance and post-Renaissance Europe.

2. *Transplantation*—the manner in which European music traditions were brought to the New World.

3. *Verbalization*—the kinds and extents of control to which music traditions have been submitted by speech traditions.

4. *Acculturation*—the kinds and extents of contact among the three continental music traditions.

Although a degree of temporal order may be ascribed to the four contexts, it must be realized that once the invaders took over the conquered Amerindian communities or set up new ones on their lands, all four must be regarded as concurrently effective down to the present day.

1. *Cultural dynamics.* Enough is generally known of the discovery, exploration, conquest, and colonization of the Americas to permit omission of detail here. This is not said to deemphasize their importance. Indeed, they are prime conditions for our discussion; for without them there would be no European traditions of music in the Americas. Suffice it to say, the grand historical processes they incorporate, while exemplified by individual men and women, can be envisaged by us here only as a mass social movement—one that has set a pattern now being carried out upon another plane by the mass communications made possible by advanced technology and large-scale capitalist enterprise.

1.1 In two respects, the body of traditions over which the hegemony of those of European provenance now rules with increasing strength is unlike any others of comparable size and development in the world. They, too, are hegemonies, but very old ones; their origins are lost in prehistory. But that of the Americas had a certain specious beginning in that its three components did first come into contact *in loco* at known dates. It did not spring Athena-like into resounding reality. There was a known time before which it did not exist and after which it did. And the means by which it came into effect was a superior technology and a social organization that aimed to use it for specific purposes.

1.2   The factor of origin—surely by now taboo in all general historical study—has some ponderable claim to legitimacy in the history of Americas. But it must be remembered that it is with the origin not of the components but of the hegemony of European traditions that we are concerned.

2. *Transplantation.*   Along with many other kinds of cultural good, European traditions of music were brought to the New World in three distinctly different manners. The first was inadvertent and incidental to other purposes of European man, from conquest, robbery, and propagation of religious belief, to freedom from religious persecution, pure adventure, and search for a better life. It would be unreasonable to suppose that the earliest soldiers, churchmen, later administrators, and immigrants did not bring with them a fair sampling of the socially and technically diverse music idioms contemporarily current in the mother countries from 1500 to 1960. The outstanding fact about this first manner of transplantation is that the idioms of the fine and popular arts of music introduced by it during the first century of colonial rule failed to survive or even leave any substantial trace. Conquest, though tapering off very gradually, was still in process until 1900. In the rough and tumble of pioneer and early colonial life, many customs and material conditions familiar in European life could not be maintained. Large rooms, fine instruments, their makers and repairers, teachers, students and, above all, substantial audiences of connoisseurs were, except in a few metropolitan centers, unavailable. Under the devoted teaching of a few of the earliest churchmen, natives applied themselves with enthusiasm to singing, playing, and even composing liturgical music. Scriptures and hymns were translated into Amerindian languages. But as colonial administrations became more bureaucratized it was made clear to the natives that the higher forms of European music were not for them but for and by the small handfuls of Europeans and creoles (persons of European ancestry born in the New World) who ruled them with increasingly iron hands. Even the most ambitious efforts to continue the grandeur of courtly life exhausted themselves. The most brilliant example was the "school" of choral singing and composition in the Cathedral of Mexico City (echoed in Puebla, Morelia, and Oaxaca) in which Spanish and, later, creole singers and instrumentalists were actively maintained from 1575 to the first quarter of the eighteenth century. Between 1556 and 1600, twelve substantial and well-printed books of liturgical music were published in Mexico. With the failure of the choral music installations, great and small organs were brought from

Europe—some of truly magnificent size. But it was not long before they became unplayable for lack of interest to keep them in repair.

2.1 As the increasing population of creoles assumed direction of affairs, the traditions thus introduced began to undergo certain subtle transformations, so that what might pass superficially as European is to be more correctly designated "neo-European." Just when a trend that could be called "American" emerged cannot be pinpointed. Perhaps one of the earliest instances might have been Pedro de Gante's teaching of the plainsong to Mexican Indians in his little school at Texcoco in the 1520s only a few years after Cortez's landing in Vera Cruz. However this may be, the two trends of neo-Europeanism, with its dependence upon Europe, and of Americanism, with its independence from Europe, have operated side-by-side down to the present day. There is good reason to infer that European folk musics throve under the circumstances so adverse to the other idioms. Not a few reports of travelers and records of popular antiquities and customs attest also a thriving acculturation of European and Amerindian, and European and African traditions among the people at large (see 4 below). In the creole segment of populations there was much loss of repertory. But what survived was retained with great tenacity, so that by 1900, when attention of serious students was finally directed toward it, vigorous and distinctively American folk musics were found from Canada to Chile. Such arts are not formed overnight and there is every reason to believe that their development, while subject to many fluctuations, was steady and could be accounted for step by step if only we had more detailed information.

2.2 The second manner of transplantation was effected by the deliberate and primary purpose of individual European musicians who removed themselves bodily *westward* with the express purpose of making a professional living in the newly opened lands. The history of immigrant religious sects, instrumental ensembles, Italian opera, and Spanish *zarzuela* companies that ventured into the wilderness, often becoming stranded, bears witness to the tough job of "making America musical" from-above-down.

2.3 The third manner of transplantation would be more accurately designated a "reinsemination," not by recently arrived Europeans but by creole Americans themselves. The intellectual ferment of the Englightenment (*Aufklärung*), Rousseauian social philosophy, the budding romantic movement and, above all, the increasing economic prosperity of the colonies which resulted in the wars of political secession from the mother countries (1776-1898) combined in the definition of a recognizably new type of culture that could be designated *Euro-American*—a concept that designates, perhaps, more accurately than the more common

American, the actual nature of the culture of the New World in contra-distinction to that of Europe.

2.4   With political independence in the offing and economic self-sufficiency assured, several of the colonies had already developed their own urban life and a prosperous bourgeoisie. Musically inclined individuals tended to deprecate the local folk music with its backwoods, Amerindian, or African flavor, and yearned for the ornaments of gracious living characteristic of the courtly and wealthy salons of London and Paris, Lisbon and Madrid. So, they reached back *eastward* to bring to the musically impoverished New World what they could of knowledge and skill in the popular and fine arts. In some of the smaller colonies, this was never more than an activity of single individuals. But in those with large concentrations of creole social life, individuals coalesced in groups during the ferment preceding or succeeding secession. Contemporaneously, in widely separated locales without any known intercommunication, surprisingly competent chamber music and instrumental-choral ecclesiastical pieces were composed from 1750 on as, for example, in Minas Gerais (Brazil), Caracas (Venezuela), Mexico City, Santiago de Cuba, and Pennsylvania (United States). Where political stability was achieved, as in the United States, the wars did not much disturb the steady advancement of the aims of such groups; but where it was not, fruition of these initial efforts was delayed for decades or even more than a century.

2.5   One of the most extensive and diversified of such group movements flourished in the United States. By the opening of the eighteenth century there was, to present knowledge, little music activity other than folk music among the people at large and congregational singing in the churches, which earlier had been publicly charged with being in a low state. Neither tradition—the folk nor that of the essentially popular hymnody—can be suspected of any acculturation with Amerindian or African traditions. Churchmen tried to improve matters by derogation of the folk music and by importation of contemporary British hymns. But the native musicality of the people did not respond. To some extent, patriotism was an issue. The tune of the imported hymn was to be carried by the sopranos. The American way was for the men (tenors) to sing it. Probably the natural wildness of pioneer life was a factor in bringing about a resurgence of the old Puritanism that found the British hymn too wordly. In the Great Religious Revival of 1800, quite a number of native semiprofessional tunesmiths were able to turn out a quantity of hard-driving, not too mellifluous choral settings full of chords without thirds, but with parallel fifths, fourths, octaves, and even seconds and sevenths, praising death and resurrection and damning worldly pleasures and the decadent ease of the cities. It was a music-reform movement from-below-up, largely rural, deliberately opposed to the more refined urban movement from-above-down. Thus the phenomenon of a war between two survivals of European music traditions in the New World got under way and lasted until well after 1900.

2.6   In spite of the opposition of the churchmen, English ballad-operas were introduced by the well-to-do bourgeoisie and were well attended since 1735—so well attended, indeed, that an American popular music theater can be traced from this beginning to its long, successful, independent career. Defeated upon both fronts, the churchmen finally allied themselves with the more intellectual urban, secular groups, one of which had already in 1770 achieved an at least partial first performance of the *Messiah* in Boston. So, by 1850, a well-defined pressure group, pledged to "make America musical" from-above-down instituted a third class of existing survivals of European music traditions by championing "good" music (i.e., the fine art) against the "bad" music not only of the rural shape-note hymn singers, their allied ballads, play-party, and fiddle tunes, but also the popular music of the cities.

2.7   Up to about 1930, the larger public, both rural and urban, looked with scorn upon this pressure group very much as had their ancestors upon the churchmen who wanted fashionable British music sung in their churches. It was snobbish and "highbrow." The battle might be still in full array, but quite inadvertently all three opposing camps had created among them a very sizable opportunity for economic exploitation. American businessmen, never slow to seize new openings, soon had not a mere music business but a music industry whose political, legal, and professional ties permeated public school education, the churches, music teaching, bands, choruses, and touring virtuosi throughout the land. With the tools—one might almost say the weapons—of mass communication, in their hands it was only a matter of three decades, from 1920 to 1950, for them to enter into full alliance with the make-America-musical pressure group and bring to almost total extinction the dwindling remnants of the shape-note tradition. More will be said about the diverse fates of these two efforts to organize control of an American music *sui generis* (from-above-down and from-below-up) in connection with the third context in which they can be viewed.

2.8   Another movement, in which commercial and intellectual leadership joined hands via mass communications has been the folk music revival of the mid-twentieth century. This (a revival properly speaking because the materials at hand had unquestionably survived *in loco*) had counterparts throughout the hemisphere as folklorism or *folclorismo* and will also be dealt with in the third context.

2.9   While there was no counterpart of the Great Religious Revival in

Latin America, the movement to reinseminate the idioms of popular and fine art from-above-down can be discerned in each of the twenty republics, though often upon such a small scale as to be a matter of individual initiative rather than of a more or less organized group as in the United States. One of the most effective was in Chile, where in the 1930s, a small band of musical leaders met annually in solemn conclave to burn "la mala música" in effigy.

3. *Verbalization.* The Greek civilization, from which the intellectual and artistic traditions of Europe and the Western world trace the main stem of their history, was a highly verbalized one. That is to say: of the various means of communication it relied most heavily upon speech— so heavily, indeed, that all affairs, the view of the universe, and man's understanding of his relationship to it, were dominated by language. Pure verbal constructions such as mind, thought, soul, were hypostatized as cause, integrating power, *raison d'être* of everything experienced, imagined, conceived or conceivable in speech. Thus, music, along with all other nameable things, was increasingly viewed in contexts formulated and expressed, and hence controlled, by means of speech. The historic controversy of the Pythagoreans and Aristoxenians attests to resistance by musicians to the domination of their art by speech, although only too often, by their own inept talk about it, they sank it still more deeply in that domination.

3.1   The Judaic civilization, with its immanence of a personal Yahweh, was quite as highly verbalized (see Gen. 1:1) but in a different way. Where the Greek was predominantly rational and logical, the Judaic was predominantly emotional and mystical. It remained for the Roman world to set the seal, under the impact of Christianity, upon the extraordinary feat of identifying the objective logos and phenomenological universe of the Greeks with the subjective "Word" that was in the beginning, that was *with* God, that *was* God (John 1:1)—surely a subjective notion of an internal, axiological universe of discourse transcending the phenomenological universe known through the senses. In this identification, which was a kind of linguistic prestidigitation, the art of speech was not only the means of communication between God and man, a second person in the Trinity, with a personal existence prior to its incorporation in Jesus of Nazareth, but even the Primordial Cause Itself. It was sacred. To misuse it was a sin. Although in its liturgical use it was intoned—and perhaps simply because it was thus intoned—the use of tones apart from words, as an instrumental music—was quite as worthless as wordless or silent prayer, or "speaking in tongues," that is, unintelligible sounds. Love, Saint Paul assured the faithful, was the supreme value and it could not be expressed by sounding brass and tinkling cymbals.[8]

3.2   This hypostasis of speech left music in an anomalous position, half angelic because of its traditional association with speech, half devilish because of its possible employment apart from speech—a conquered vassal as far as the elite, learned, or fine art of music was concerned, for more than a thousand years. Although we have little documentary evidence to prove it, vestiges of tribal idioms and proto-types of what we now call *folk* and *popular* arts of music probably flour-ished alongside the rigidly speech-formed and more or less speech-controlled music of the Christian churches, east and west, until this linguistic tyranny was relaxed and the flowering of both secular and religious music which took place in the sixteenth century defined the kinds of music which were brought to the New World.

3.3   At that very time, however, the Reformation and Counter-Reformation reimposed strict verbal controls upon music wherever they could enforce them. The ban upon all but hymn-singing (without instrumental accompaniment) was in full force in North America, and survivals of it are still maintained among some small religious sects. In the early days of the Spanish occupation, support and approval was given almost exclusively to the liturgy of the cathedrals and the larger churches. But with the failure of the first manner of transplantation and the spread of eighteenth-century secularization of church music from Europe to America, the old verbal restrictions became inoperative. Most governments now support secular music activity in some form.

3.4   It is significant that the two strong music movements in the United States during the nineteenth century (see above, 2.4-2.6) both made extensive use of speech propaganda. It is also significant that the rural, shape-note hymn-singing populism utilized the old scripture-quoting, hell-fire-and-damnation verbiage and ultimately declined to desuetude, while the urban, make-America-musical intellectualism adapted the new liberal speech formulations of the Founding Fathers and their Declaration of Independence to Pestalozzian educational techniques and ultimately won out, by judicious compromise and grad-ual relaxation of most of its own original verbal restrictions.

3.5   Another aspect of the verbalization of music can be seen in the rash of nationalism and folclorismo that swept the Latin American part of the hemisphere and found some, though less successful, following in the United States around 1900. This seems to have been an offshoot of the make-America-musical movement, which had its chauvinist side. Having observed that J. S. Bach and others utilized the religious folk song, *der Choral,* and German composers generally, from Haydn to Brahms, the secular, and that Russian and Spanish schools of composers had made national musics out of their respective folk musics, it seemed only natural for Americans to attempt the same feat by borrowing melodies from their native tribal and folk idioms, and weaving them as themes into great operas, symphonies, and chamber music. Thus, Carlos Isamitt (Chile) and Arthur Farwell (USA) both borrowed Amerindian materials; Alberto Nepomuceno (Brazil) and H. F. B. Gilbert (USA), Afro-American; and Manuel Ponce (Mexico) and Charles Ives (USA), Euro-American folk and popular tunes.

3.6   Naturally, these efforts gave rise to an antifolklore movement whose members claimed, quite justly, that both nationalism and folklorism were invasions of the domain of the pure international style by contextual factors. It is worth noting, however, that many of these latter are now showing an enthusiasm for serialism and composition in the twelve-tone row, which is manifestly based on speech postulates.

4. *Acculturation.*   Acculturation is not only a context within which music can be viewed but also a factor that can be viewed in the context of music. In the former case, we deal with music in terms extrinsic to it, that is, in terms of the study of culture; in the latter, in terms intrinsic to it, as hybridization, syncretization of music-technical factors.

4.1   Until the advent of mass communications, positive acculturation, that is, what we might designate "potential Americanism," of music tradition was typical of the areas most remote in either geographical extent or social depth (or in both) from the negative acculturation of neo-Europeanism whose stronghold was always in the bourgeoisie of the cities. Each tapered off as it neared the other. Mass communications have obscured but not obliterated these distinctions. In its simplest terms, acculturation envisages individual donors and receivers of traditions, who come into continuous, close contact. Donation may vary between the extremes of imposition by force and mere offering; reception, similarly, between grudging acceptance and enthusiastic appropriation.

4.2   The conditions under which one music supplants or rejects another two or more musics combine to various extents as a result of contact are still, however, obscure. Kunst has hypothesized a "defense power" in a music and accounts for the abandonment of their own traditional art by the people of the Island of Nias for that of the West by a lack of such a power.[9] This would imply an "offensive power" in the latter, in this instance the hymn-singing imposed by missionaries. The well-known manners of proselytizing employed by these often fanatic and bigoted persons, often allied with the police of colonial administrations, assures offensive power in the context sufficient for the abandonment.

The question of what intrinsic music-technical features can be adduced in support of such power or weakness in a music seems to be highly debatable. Kunst also cites the supplanting of the ancient music of south and east Sumatra by that of Java. Here, perhaps, no politico-religious verbalization was a factor. Perhaps the Sumatrans were seduced by the exact tuning of the components of the gamelan, the majestic 4 x 4, tempo giusto with its subtle divisions of beat and the structured form of the nuclear theme[10] just as was Debussy with its pentatonism. In the hands of a social class or professional or semiprofessional guild, a music may become obsolescent or stereotyped by cultish or other sociocultural restriction. Whether it may reach a point in its history where it is ready for new ideas, either from inside or outside solely for intrinsic reasons, is a question. I cannot see that any of these possibilities except outright force can properly be labeled *offensive* or *defensive*. Change is as normal as stability in any art. When, as a result of overall acculturation or inner development new modes of music communication impinge or are desired, change is normal. After periods of change, compensatory trends toward stabilization may be expected, and vice versa.

4.3   Under the hegemony of European culture in the Americas, the only instances of forced imposition which I can find in music traditions were in the United States. Both of these were motivated by groups of individuals operating in complete liberty and independence. Both were, at first, doctrinaire and intolerant. The movement from-below-up proselytized for its own membership alone; that from-above-down to convert the whole country to its tenets. Neither had an established church behind it; neither had or sought support from the government. The former died because it was, in the main, regressive in more ways than one; the latter won out largely because it was progressive, more flexible and, above all, more skillfully verbalized. Both, by the excesses of their programs and the attempt to obliterate the native folk music, inadvertently stimulated the folk music revival.

Pedro de Gante's (and many other musical churchmens') teaching of the plainsong and sixteenth century composition to Indians, though probably done by imposition of very strict discipline, was only to those who applied themselves through love of music and promised abatement of taxation. Unlike their northern Protestant counterparts, the Catholic priests were not unfriendly to the secular music activity of the faithful. The impetus to European-Amerindian music acculturation has probably continued in Latin America in a desultory manner, down to the present day, compounded, of course, with liberal infusions of Spanish and

Portuguese popular music, Italian opera, and diffusion of popular music from certain highly productive centers such as Havana and Mexico City, whereas in North America, such acculturation is negligible.

4.4   What one would like to know is whether, after fifty, one hundred, or several hundred years, would the people of Nias, Sumatra, or Mexico make European, neo-European, Euro-Niasian, Euro-Sumatran, or Euro-Mexican musics, or what could and probably would be called Niasian, Sumatran, or Mexican musics? Evidence from the New World now at hand points to the last-named possibility. Forced imposition of a music under tyrannical government of the people carrying the tradition of that music must be conceded capable of obliterating another music. One of the surest ways of effecting this result is obliteraton of the carriers of it, as was done by the Spaniards to the natives in the West Indies. But if enough of a population is left to live in reasonable integrity of its social institutions, an ancient music can last a long time against heavy odds. Mass communications, however, may still accomplish what the sword, slavery, and economic exploitation did not.

4.5   In the context of the culture of the New World, neo-Europeanism as a negative acculturative factor still holds sway in the fine art of music among very substantial segments of populations throughout the hemisphere. Such segments are constituted by (a) the more conservative patrons of music in whom the occupation is mostly passive listening with little or no active music-making; (b) music educators in the schools, colleges, and universities; (c) church music people; (d) the elite, avant-garde of the "international style" of composition and its surrounding cliques. In the activity of these segments, neo-Europeanism is to be clearly distinguished from Europeanism in the sense that the latter term can properly be applied to the music activity of Europeans in Europe. The activity of one creole generation has not been founded as much upon that of a preceding (creole) generation as upon that of a preceding European generation. It was upon the higher social levels that neo-Europeanism was deliberately antiacculturative; upon the lower, it was less so, permitting increasing positive acculturation. European leadership is still effective upon all these levels, but not that exhibiting acculturative trends, as, for example, Debussy, early Stravinsky, or Bartok, when folkloric. Recognition abroad—to be accepted on a par with Europe's best—is still the *summum bonum*. Negative acculturation is typical of the colonial mind. To a large extent it is status-seeking— social, economic, academic, even musical.

4.6   As alleged above, although data for systematic study of acculturation is now accumulating, techniques of study are adequate for little more than tentative orientation in such a survey as the present. Before we can state with assurance that such-and-such a factor is European or African or Amerindian, we must be able to describe each with one and the same procedure. When von Hornbostel wrote of American Negro songs that they "are European in style and pattern, they are American folk songs as far as they have originated amidst American folk and culture, they are African when sung by Negroes, and only then,"[11] he recorded an even more primitive phase of musicology known as comparative musicology. His statement, excellent as far as it went, does not allow for the fact that some of the styles and patterns are quite as African as European, that a very substantial proportion of the Afro-Americans in the United States have turned their backs upon Africa and rival the creoles in strictly European singing-style, while thousands of young Euro-Americans, caught up in the folk music revival movement, are studying field and studio recordings of singing more African than von Hornbostel ever heard in the United States, and sing the Negro songs with more African singing-style than do many Negroes.

In closing, it can be said by way of summary that two major trends have been emerging more and more clearly during the past thirty years.

The first is a result of the all-pervading influence of mass communications. These are instruments of oral, but even more of *aural,* transmission. With music literacy at a very low level—perhaps 5 to 10 percent ability to sing the skeleton notation of a simple folk song at sight—they serve the double function, first, of vastly expanding the variety of music intake of the hundreds of millions of people in the hemisphere, and second, by a compensatory contraction, of taking a leading part in the molding, out of this chaos, of the rudiments of a continent-wide music vernacular that might, through further expansion and contraction, eventually be a factor in the formation of a worldwide vernacular—a musical *lingua franca* or "pidgin music." In the process hundreds of ancient local and regional musics may be obliterated or modified beyond all semblance of archaic traditions now known. To some students, the prospect may be appalling; to others, inviting, according to the value system involved.

The second important trend is toward an eventual merger of Neo-Europeanism and Euro-Americanism in partnership with Europe in a single, integrated Occidental music. For some time, music has been flowing eastward as well as westward. The Atlantic Ocean is now less of a barrier than were the Alps or the English Channel before the advent of steam locomotion. Barring only the cataclysm of another world war, the political and economic independence already gained and the cultural independence almost within our grasp may still revert to a far more effective and desirable interdependence.

NOTES

1. G. Chase, *A Guide to Latin American Music* (Washington, D.C.: Library of Congress, Music Division, 1945); *Handbook of Latin American Studies* (Cambridge, Mass., 1939); C. Haywood, *A Bibliography of North American Folklore and Folksong* (New York: Greenberg Press, 1951); L. H. C. de Azevedo et al., *Bibliografia musical brasileira* (Rio de Janeiro, 1952); see also n. 2.

2. Histories of music within nations have been published for Brazil (R. Almeida, L. H. C. de Azevedo), Chile (E. Pereira Salas), Cuba (A. Carpentier), Mexico (O. Mayer-Serra, G. Saldivar, R. Stevenson), Peru (R. Stevenson), United States (G. Chase, J. T. Howard), Uruguay (L. Ayestarán).

3. M. Kolinski, "Musicological Analysis," in Melvelle J. and Frances Herskovits, *Suriname Folklore* (New York: Columbia University Press, 1936).

4. I. Aretz, *Bibliografía,* Boletín del Instituto de Folklore 3 (1959), 273.

5. S. P. Bayard, "Prolegomena to a Study of the Principal Melodic Families of British-American Folk Song," *Journal of American Folklore* 65 (1950), 1-44; B. H. Bronson, "Toward the Comparative Analysis of British-American Folk Tunes," *Journal of American Folklore* 72 (1959), 165-191.

6. O. Alvarenga, *Música popular brasileira* (Rio de Janeiro, 1950); I. Aretz, *Música tradicional argentina* (Buenos Aires, 1946) and *El folklore musical argentino* (Buenos Aires, 1952); C. Vega, *Panorama de la música popular argentina* (Buenos Aires, 1944).

7. O. Alvarenga, *Catálogo ilustrado do Museu Folklórico* (São Paulo, 1950); K. G. Izikowitz, *Musical and Other Sound Instruments of the South American Indians* (Götenborg: Elanders-boktrykeri aktiebolag, 1935); F. Ortiz, *Los instrumentos de la música cubana* 1-5 (Habana, 1952); C. Vega, *Los instrumentos musicales aborígenes y criollos de la Argentina* (Buenos Aires: Ediciones Centurión, 1946); see also n. 6.

8. E. Werner, "St. Paul's Attitude Toward Music," *JAMS* vol. 13 (1960).

9. Jaap Kunst, *Music in Java* (The Hague: nijhoff, 1949) I, 4.

10. Mantle Hood, *Patet in Javanese Music* (Groningen, Djakarta: J. B. Wolters, 1954) 3 passim.

11. E. M. von Hornbostel, *American Negro Songs, Int. Rev. of Missions* 15 (1926), 748-753.

XI
Music and Musicology
in the New World 1946[34]

It might be appropriate at this time to present a brief report upon the state of the union of our twin subjects of interest—music and musicology. Such a report should distinguish between the fields themselves, the relationship between them, and the workers who cultivate them. It cannot ignore the relationship of both fields and all their workers to the culture, of which the former are integral elements, and to the bearers of that culture, among whom the latter are to be numbered. This is a large order. So I shall touch only the high points in leading up to my main objective, which is to list some of the things to be done now that comparative peace is restored in the world—things that can be done more readily if we have a better understanding, able to agree upon some plans of action and to cooperate in the promotion of them.

I

In placing a geographical limit of the New World, I am covering, I think, the largest area for which we may presume to have at this moment fairly comprehensive and dependable knowledge, together with reasonably good chances of carrying out plans of development. Neither our music nor our musicology developed exclusively within this area, much less (as might be assumed) within any national boundaries. Both stem, in the main, from Europe, from which we are only in these days effecting our declaration of cultural independence. But of music and musicology in Europe since 1939 we know little, except that both have suffered great losses of men and materials. I am glad to be able to say that the International Musicological Society still maintains its Bureau in Basle, and that *Acta Musicologica* has been kept current, though we have not seen an issue since 1941. But there is little I can add.

As far as the Orient is concerned, we know no more than ever of the relationship we are discussing here—and that is almost negligible. To the best of my knowledge, research in the field of Oriental music was at a standstill during World War II. The only progress that has come to my notice is a survey made by Richard A. Waterman during the summer of 1944 of bibliographical materials in the United States relating to the music of the Middle and Far East.

Much as I would like to make a report worldwide in scope, it appears that the New World must, therefore, be our present frame of reference. It so happens that it is a surprisingly homogeneous region in this respect, its many parts having developed along the same general lines, though with little or no contact among themselves. The only important qualitative difference between Anglo and Latin America, which should be mentioned in connection with our present discussion, is that in the former there is something of a schism between musicians and musicologists—a schism we are, happily, on the way to healing. It has been due, I feel, to two conditions: first, the extreme compartmentalization of culture in the United States, and, second, the late development of musicology as a formal discipline in our universities. In Latin America, where the quantity of musical and musicological activity is much less, there has been less compartmentalization.

II

When I refer to the relationship between music and musicology as a "union," I refer to what, I believe, must be regarded as a fact. The matter has been thrashed out quite thoroughly, ever since Guido Adler's opening gun, over sixty years ago.[1] It is generally known that theory of music follows closely upon the heels of practice; but it is not so commonly admitted that it sometimes precedes and accompanies practice also. Musicology prepares and tends the rails upon which the trains of music run. A single example may be cited—concert repertoire. The older works have been discovered and prepared for performance by musicology. The newer works are, most of them, heavily influenced by historico-musicology, ever since under its influence Erik Satie invented the Muse with one eye in the back of her head. The interlacing of music and speech about music, however, has become so habitual that many people are still confused when faced with the necessity of distinguishing between music and musicology, or of defining their relationship. I should, perhaps, point out three fallacies that have clouded thought upon the matter, especially during recent years.

The first fallacy is to regard one's own particular brand of music or musicology as the whole of either. The specialist—and most of us have functioned as specialists—must, of necessity, employ a narrow view in the conduct of his work. It is only by adding together the many narrow views that we get a broad view of the field of music or musicology as a whole. The whole, however, we must remember, is something more than the mere sum of its parts. Equally important are the relationships among the parts. This does not make the broad view better than the narrow view or vice versa. It does make it required reading.

The second fallacy is to set in general a higher value upon value than upon fact, or vice versa. Quality and quantity are conditions for each other's existence and are not commensurable.

The third fallacy, a corollary of the second, is to let determinations of value color our determinations of fact. Thus, the positions that only "good" music is music, or the musicology of "good" music is musicology, are untenable, as is also the position that only the contribution of something new to music makes one a musician, or the contribution of something new to musicology, a musicologist.

III

Coming now to the music of the Americas, how are we to say "what it is" in order to say "it is in such and such a state?" A panorama of seven headings may serve to outline a conception of the nature of the total activity within an area. Let us say that such activity consists of:

1. The traditions—music culturally evolved ranges of forms and contents inherited, practiced, modified, and propagated, as, for instance, the Amerindian, the European, and the African, the acculturation among them and the products that embody them—all inherited from cultures antedating the dominant Euro-American.

2. The idioms—variations in type of usage of traditions upon different cultural levels or to serve different social functions, as, for instance, survivals of the primitive or tribal art derived from Amerindian and African sources, and the folk art and popular art derived from Europe, the hybrids among these and the products that embody them.

3. The methods of transmission—oral, written, and mixed oral and written, and education both formal and informal.

4. The quantitative distribution among the population of the traditions and the idioms.

5. The qualitative factors employed in evaluation of traditions and idioms, particular products of these, and their distribution, by area, social stratum, and so forth, with reference to style and manner.

6. The development of services to the traditions and idioms, as, for instance, through publication, library, implementation (including radio,

film, phonograph, etc.), management, property rights, organization of special fields, and so on.

7. The integration of the traditions and idioms in the culture, as, for instance, their relative autonomy and dependency, and their control from within and without.

IV

Amerindian music traditions survive—how unchanged since the advent of the Europeans we do not know—in more or less isolated spots throughout the hemisphere. In acculturation with European traditions, they are particularly strong in Mexico and throughout the Andean highlands. European traditions, without substantial acculturation, are especially strong in Anglo American and in Argentina, Chile, and Uruguay. They are dominant in all cosmopolitan areas and in rural sections depending upon these areas economically and socially, throughout the hemisphere. African traditions survive in comparatively pure form in some localities, and enter widely varied acculturation with European traditions along the eastern coastal islands and littoral from southern Brazil to the United States, and in some other sections such as the coast of Peru. Known examples of acculturation between Amerindian and African traditions without European influences are rare, but it would not be surprising if they proved eventually to be more common than at present supposed.

Folk music has not been generally distinguished from popular music up to the present time, except in the United States, Argentina, Mexico, Chile, Brazil, and by some students in other countries. There is reason to believe that the idioms are distinct in most localities, but collection lags. Strangely enough, some areas are reportedly "without singing" or "without music." This remains to be checked, for often it means only without the fine art of music.

Oral traditions serve the vast majority of the populations of Latin America as in Anglo America. Music education is authorized by law in most countries, but, as in the United States before 1900, the curse of solfège lies heavily upon it. Fine instruction, especially in the technique of the pianoforte, is to be had in the larger centers outside the United States, but in strings and woodwinds, the situation is not as favorable. Fine-art music depends, in Latin America, upon government subsidy to an extent unknown in Anglo America. It is a question whether fine-art music is practiced by more than 2 percent of the population outside the United States, or by more than 5 percent in it. The outstanding production of the hemisphere is, undeniably, in the idioms of popular and folk music, and in the hybrids of the two, such as hillbilly, of which there are parallel varieties in Latin America.

Overall integration of the various traditions and idioms among themselves and in the culture has come to be noticed by musicians and musicologists in several places. Brazil led off around 1900 and has achieved what may be the most advanced position today, with Mexico running a close second, and Argentina third. Cuba, while Caturla and Roldán lived, bid fair to lead with Brazil but seems to have lost its wind with their deaths a few years ago. Cuban popular music, along with the Mexican and Brazilian, and United States jazz, have made the outstanding successes.

Professional organization is weak or nonexistent in most areas outside North America. Conspicuous exceptions are the professional unions that established and maintain the Mexican Symphony Orchestra and the Colon Opera and Philharmonic Orchestra in Buenos Aires. Publication has wavered, being strongest in Argentina. Phonography is weak everywhere outside of the United States as are libraries, instrument manufacture, merchandising, and concert management. The copyright and performance right situation is anarchic. Strong efforts are being made to improve it. The Pan American Union has called an Inter-American Conference of Copyright Experts to meet in Washington in June. Two rival groupings of rights-collection societies—FISAC (Federación Interamericana de Sociedades de Autores y Compositores) and a putative Pan American Council to be allied with CISAC (Confédération Internationale des Sociétés des Auteurs et des Compositeurs)—will meet before or after the conference in an effort to adjust their differences. ASCAP (American Society of Composers, Authors and Publishers) has contracts with both. Of interest to composers and authors is the report that publishers are entering the Latin American societies of authors and composers, as in ASCAP.

So much for the external forms. The content of Latin American fine-art music bears a close resemblance to the content of United States composition of that kind. There are the usual epigones of European leaning, conservatives, liberals, folkloristic experimenters, twelve-tone-rowers, and others. In this particular idiom of fine-art music, we have indeed "one world." Folk and popular idioms represent more of a breakaway from European tutelage and have, interestingly enough, much wider and healthier roots in the populations.

V

Coming now to the musicology of the hemisphere, one significant difference between Anglo and Latin America is to be noted. In Latin America, the word "musicología" is used in the broadest sense, designating any talking or writing about music that is serious and reasoned. Music critics, teachers, authors of solfège and harmony books, and so forth, may be referred to as "musicólogos." It is in this sense that the word is used in Spain and Italy, and there are examples of such use in Germany and the United States.[2] In both Germany and the United States, a stricter definition has also been widely held. Otto Kinkeldey has phrased it "Musicology, a word formed by analogy with philology, theology, psychology or biology, is used to designate the whole body of systemized knowledge about music, which results from the application of a scientific method of investigation or research, or of philosophical speculation and rational systematization, to the facts, the processes and the development of musical art, and to the relation of man in general (or even animals) to the art."[3] It is in the spirit of this definition that the American Musicological Society was founded and has flourished. The importance of the difference between this view and that of Wolf appears upon closer examination, especially when we consider who is a musicologist. Glen Haydon has put it clearly when he says: "Every trained musician knows a good deal about music, has a more or less well-organized, systematic knowledge of music; but we do not ordinarily regard him as a musicologist unless he devotes himself particularly, through the application of scientific methods, to the advancement of our knowledge concerning music."[4]

The danger—if, indeed, it is a danger—in the very broad understanding of the term has been voiced by Curt Sachs: "Any girl that manufactures a newspaper article by transcribing Grove's Dictionary without too many misspellings presents herself as a musicologist."[5] A good many of the members of the American Musicological Society feel the same way. Having gone through a long fight to secure recognition for the study of music as a scholarly discipline and still suffering from something of an inferiority complex, one feels some nervousness about the use of the term "musicologist," as applied either to oneself or to someone else. For myself, I might ask: Could we not take these vagrant yearnings on the part of strangers to "belong," or offhand to improve themselves, with something of a smile? There is a good precedent for this. For some time, a log of silly people have been labeling themselves *psychologists*. But psychology remains a worthy name for a scholarly discipline. And bona fide psychologists still allow themselves to be designated as such.

In the interests of harmony and cooperation, especially between musicians and musicologists, but also to enfold some who would avoid the latter designation or be satisfied with the vague *musicographer* (a term commoner in Latin America than in Anglo America), I would like to propose a restatement of the view that seems in substance to represent the best thought of our field—one that I present here to our membership for their consideration. The object of this presentation is to show, in the form of a series of operations, the steps of a process which are begun by musicians and musicologists in common, but which arrive at a point where the two part company.

Let us say that musicology comprises five operations, as follows: (1) use of the art of speech; (2) to study the art of music; (3) in a deliberately methodical manner; (4) for the advancement of knowledge *of* and *about* music; and (5) of the place and function of music in human culture.

Clearly, the serious musician performs all the first three operations in the normal, everyday course of his professional life. So does the musicologist who, it must be remembered, is practically invariably a well-trained and experienced musician to start with, just as the average musician has been well trained and experienced in the use of speech—including, I should add, the writing of it and original composition in it.

In operation three, there is undoubtedly a divergence of emphasis. The musician is not, as a rule, trained beyond the average man in the deliberately methodical use of speech, whereas the musicologist must be. To the musicologist, deliberately methodical use of speech means rigorous application of scientific and critical methods. There is no difference *in kind* between the commonsense of the average eduated musician and the uncommon commonsense of the trained musicologist, but there is a difference in the extent of its refinement. As our distractingly loose-jointed educational system is gradually tightened up, the gap may be drawn together until the difference that impresses us now may eventually be scarcely noticeable. But even before then, we hope, the professional musician will cease to tolerate much of the trash that now serves him in lieu of source material and texts. He will have come to require higher musicological standards in these tools and will not bristle up, as he does now, at the mere mention of the word *musicology*. Similarly, it is to be hoped that the musicologist will unbend, at least to the extent that he will do something effective toward the improvement of these sources and texts that, after all, are used now for the making of our future musicologists just as much as our future trombonists, music appreciators, and music businessmen.

With respect to operation four, the type of systematization useful to

the practicing musician may be quite different from the type of systematization required by the musicologist. The emphasis of the musician will
be rather strictly limited to such knowledge *of* music as will serve the
practice of an instrument or composition or the teaching of some
technique. The musicologist will pursue *both* kinds of knowledge and
will, it is hoped, investigate the relationship between them—especially to
ascertain whether there is not, in the actual practice of music, an element
that bears a relation to other elements in music something of the same
relation that musicology bears to ordinary talking about music.

With respect to operation five, it may be said that this is exclusively a
concern of musicology. If the practical musician goes this far, he will, as
Haydon says, practically become a musicologist.

The essential differences between the musician and the musicologist
are, then: (1) the degree of refinement of the art of speech in dealing
with music; (2) the degree of emphasis upon the two kinds of knowledge
involved; and (3) the aim of the whole undertaking. As a corollary to this
last, it may be pointed out that the musician is more or less bound to
confine his activity to the class of music he values most. The typical
attitude of the musicologist is, however, to be able to submerge his own
taste preferences at will, in order to be as objective as possible in the
study of other people's taste preferences, or, upon occasion, to study
music data as free as possible of all critical considerations whatever.

VI

If the outline I have given of the relationships of music and musicology and of musicians and musicologists is reasonably correct, there
would seem to be no obstacle to cooperation among us toward some of the
objectives I shall presently list, except, possibly, the feeling among some
highly specialized workers that they have not the time nor the desire to
become directly involved. There will probably always be a certain
number of musicians and musicologists who simply cannot afford to
dilute their chosen activity with consideration of views other than their
own. There is every reason why we should encourage a just proportion
of such activity in the realm of pure music or pure scholarship and give
consideration to those who pursue it. All I would ask is that those who
choose this path give us their blessing and criticism if and when they feel
able to give it. We need their work, and we should protect in every way
their doing of it. But there will always, I presume, be but a small band of
workers inclined to and worthy of such tasks. For the rest of us, the

obligation to see not only our small field of immediate activity but also as large an overall view as possible is a mandate of our times which we cannot shirk.

Few fields of activity in the United States are so highly organized as that of music. This organization is, however, entirely in terms of compartments. Overall organization is not yet beyond the discussion stage.

Organization of music activity in Latin America is, as I have said, rare, and spotty at best. Professional organizations, such as the MTNA, MENC, NASM, MLA, and AMS, do not exist, though some tentative beginnings have been made. Existence of a low-pressure area close to a high-pressure one points toward certain definite results. Already a number of specialized promotional activities have begun to emanate from the United States toward Latin America. From there, it may be assumed, they will go on to penetrate other regions. In the United States these particular compartments operate under certain conventional checks and balances evolved in the course of the development of music activity upon a nationwide scale. In Latin America some or all of these checks and balances are lacking. I do not feel comfortable about the situation, either with respect to its effect upon the rest of the world or to the effect upon music activity in the United States. For the development of external relations without the checks and balances, of which I speak, will inevitably upset the conventions of checks and balances within the United States.

Like our industrial life, our music life is passing gradually from control by private enterprise, under terms of "free competition," to other kinds of control. Government is mixing in, and large power groups are emerging. Whether these may act as checks and balances to government, or become allied with it, is a question. I am not here concerned with the morals or wishful thinking of the situation. I want only to say that it is my considered opinion that the type of knowledge and experience, and the type of aims and purposes represented in our societies, are types necessary to keep the situation I have alluded to on an even keel and oriented toward the best interests and aspirations not only of music but of cultural democracy. Unless we give expression to this knowledge and experience and these aims and purposes on a sufficiently high level of discussion, we stand not only to lose a considerable portion of our present autonomy as artists, scholars, and teachers, but also to come increasingly under controls most unpleasant to us as individuals and unsuited to the fields we serve.

I come now, therefore, to consideration of some of the objectives for whose realization a higher degree of organization, based on better understanding among musicians and musicologists, is necessary. The list is divided into two sections, the first comprising what may be called internal affairs, the second, external affairs.

1. *In internal affairs, our knowledge of music should be culture-wide, world-wide, and homogeneous.*

    We need:

    a) Encouragement of study of non-European musics through the setting up of fellowships, special grants, and the organization of expeditions, utilizing the most improved sound recording and photographic devices. We should have detailed maps of the musics of the world.

    b) Systematic collection of music materials on a world scale, with archives in principal regions, equipped with mechanical notation devices and music-technical indices.

    c) Research in the history of non-European musics.

    d) Research in contemporary music acculturation processes throughout the world, in terms of traditions and idioms, their morphology and ecology.

    e) Research in the effects of music upon individuals and groups.

    f) Research on existing and potential controls of music, both from within and from without the art.

2. *In external affairs, our knowledge of music in its relation to other things should be brought up to the standards of our knowledge of music as a thing in itself.*

    We need:

    a) Closer relationship with the study of culture and with social planning.

    b) Closer relationship with the field of music education in the primary and secondary schools, and in the teacher-training colleges.

    c) Closer relationship with the music industry.

    d) Closer relationship with government in respect both to internal and external relations.

    e) Development of international relations in the fields of music and musicology, both regional and worldwide.

    f) Study of the economic bases of music activity.

Some of these objectives, and certainly the whole list of them, will seem a long way from the daily task of many musicians and musicologists. But as I have said, it appears that the time has come when few of us can afford to tend our home garden as if it were a thing-in-itself, independent of the rest of the world. I know well that we have to spend most of our time just tending our garden if we expect any crop at all. But I am quite as sure that we shall have to spend increasing amounts of time and effort for the protection of our right to tend that garden. Cooperative effort will take less of our time than individual effort. And it can gain us far greater results. That is why I urge it. This means that planters of cabbages, even if they do look down upon planters of onions, and vice versa, should conceal their feelings. The policeman on the beat may not like either of them personally, nor they him. They may look down on his occupation, as he may upon theirs. But it would be better if each would try to see the value of the other's occupation. As Enriques has said: "The end for which we ought to strive today is education which shall enable the workers in any field whatsoever to understand better how the object of their own activity is subordinated to more general problems."[6] To which we might add: "and how the techniques of their many separate fields can be welded together for the solution of these general problems."

Toward such ends let us work in company.

NOTES

1. Guido Adler, "Umfang, Methode und Ziel der Musikwissenschaft," *Vierteljahrsschrift für Musikwissenschaft*, vol. 1 (1885).

2. Johannes Wolf, "Musikwissenschaft," in *Das Atlantisbuch der Musik:* "Der Begriff Musikwissenschaft umschliesst das Wissen von allem was sich auf den Ton bezieht" (Berlin-Zürich, 1937).

3. Otto Kinkeldey, "Musicology," in *The International Cyclopedia of Music* (New York, 1939).

4. Glen Haydon, *Introduction to Musicology* (New York, 1941), p. 1.

5. Curt Sachs, "The Music Historian," *Music Educators Journal*, Vol. XXXI, no. 6 (May-June 1945).

6. Federigo Enriques, *Problems of Science* (New York, 1914).

XII
Music and Class Structure
in the United States[50]

The phenomena to which I shall direct attention seem to exhibit two large historical processes that have been taking place throughout the New World since the advent of Europeans. The first has accompanied prolonged contact of *masses* of individuals carrying different musics. To this process the term *acculturation* has been given. For lack of music-technical and culture-historical terms with which to designate such large, comparatively ill-defined, almost amorphous aggregates of tradition, we have no alternative for the moment but to distinguish them by the country or continent from which they entered the acculturative process. The second has accompanied the prolonged contact of these same individuals in the new societies thus formed, but in their roles as members of social *classes* carrying different music-social traditions, or music idioms, that is, classes of music usage commonly referred to as primitive or tribal, folk, popular, and fine arts. To present knowledge, no special designation has been given to this other than subacculturation. Obviously, it crosscuts what is ordinarily referred to as acculturation, distinguishing in terms of social depth certain aspects of the total music culture—an abstract concept never concretely perceived. By and large, primitive and folk traditions are carried by rural, and those of popular and fine arts by urban, people. In the New World this second process may have been a factor in the catastrophic phase of conquest, settlement, and consolidation, but as colonialism has given way to political, economic, and cultural independence, it has become the major factor in music activity, known as enculturation—learning to modulate behavior to the ongoing syncretism of inherited tradition, very much as it has been in the Old World for many centuries.

For the sake of brevity, I shall not dwell upon acculturation within the United States of three continental musics—Amerindian, European, and African. Suffice to say that during the colonial era an effective hegemony of neo-European music traditions was established on the North Ameri-

222

can continent in which survivals of Amerindian tribal traditions have been negligible, though thriving still in some Indian reservations, and in which African traditions, though not apparently surviving in tribal form, may be regarded as substantial acculturative components. Rather, it is with the inner relationships, or subacculturation, within this hegemony that may better be designated *Euro-American* and may some day justify the name *American* already so freely given to it that I shall be concerned. I shall distinguish three music-using groups or classes as basic to the discussion. Each is understood to be definable as well in terms of the particular music idiom carried as in those of the social behavior of the individuals involved in the production and consumption of it. By the term *consumption,* of course, I mean *used* but not *used up.*

From this viewpoint, the colonization of what is now the United States may be regarded as a dual effort: on the one hand, unconscious and immediate, to transplant a culture; on the other, conscious and ultimate, to form a new social order, or at least a more or less drastic modification of that known by the colonists and later immigrants before they crossed the Atlantic.

Traditions of class structure survived the conditions of pioneer life but in attenuated form. Peculiar variations of them were fostered. Every fresh wave of immigration brought additional impulses to invention of the new or to survival or revival of the old. Thus, acculturation was constantly offset by contra-acculturation. The wound suffered by the culture was a major one. We need not ask whether it has entirely healed, for there is abundant evidence that it has not.

The traumatic character of our cultural life in general has been and still is evident in our use of music; for conditions of pioneer life shattered many of the traditions of European music brought to the New World. These were of a music highly diversified in itself and in its social functions, whose chief idioms varied greatly in various regions of the European continent but in each region were well integrated with one another and with the several class structures that framed them. Broadly speaking, these idioms were: (1) a folk art, mainly oral in transmission; (2) a fine art, mainly written in transmission; (3) a popular art, hybrid of the first two, about equally oral and written in transmission.

The folk art seems to have survived in the colonies upon a broad basis of general social use, both urban and rural. Apparently, there was considerable shrinkage in repertory. But what did survive was held more tenaciously than in the mother countries, a phenomenon observed in colonial societies elsewhere.

The fine and popular arts, however, could not be given the professional cultivation and patronage, the material plant and equipment that had serviced them in the mother countries. Training in the various disciplines was impossible. Elite audiences did not exist. Consequently, these idioms did not flourish in the colonies for the first century of their history or very widely during the second. Indeed, even as late as 1800 they seem to have been employed only in attenuated form by some scattered individuals such as Thomas Jefferson, Patrick Henry, Benjamin Franklin, and their like in the larger cities and plantations, and in a few churches and such atypical religious communities as the Ephrata and Moravian. As a normal function of a music-cultural continuum, they fell far behind their counterparts in contemporary Europe.

European traditions of music in the United States suffered, then, not only the wounds of social, political, and religious protest and of geographical transplantation, but also the deprivation of three centuries of traditional interclass and interidiom relationships through which the art flourished normally in Europe.

The tug-of-war between the development of a neo-European class structure and cultivation of a classless, Euro-American, equalitarian society is well known and, it seems to me, still continues to be a factor in the course of American civilization. Extension of trade and industry has favored the former; extension of the geographical frontier, the latter. By 1750 a sufficiently large urban class of status, wealth, and fashion began to require something more than a musical art upon a folk level. It was the "Quality," the most well-to-do, of the pre-Revolutionary period which first expressed dissatisfaction with the only form of music formally recognized as "music"—psalm-singing—and had proposed as remedy the weekday singing school. The Great Awakening of 1730 had given some popularity to a first effort to "make America musical." In the centers of wealth and fashion it became bogged down, however, by the type of music recommended, which consisted exclusively of composed, usually British hymns.[1] Their secular counterpart, British musical comedy, found instant favor.[2] Both increased, at least temporarily, the prestige of an upper class and of the individuals composing it and constituted a contra-acculturative trend toward old European and away from new American ways of making music.

Extension of the geographical frontier encouraged in the rank and file of the population an opposite reaction, especially in the singing schools. As George Jackson has put it, "the Revolutionary War and its accompanying antipathy to all things British lent impetus to the tendency to desert the old imported (hymn) tunes and to substitute for them the newly fabricated domestic article."[3] The newly fabricated article was a mixture of secular folk song (oral) and popular hymnody written by native, amateur musicians. It constituted the earliest printed record of substantial creative achievement in music in the United States.[4] Disdained by the urban churches, the movement became oriented toward the rural population and implemented the great religious revival from 1800 on—an acculturative trend, democratic and equalitarian, replete with protest against the worldliness and wickedness of the cities. Thus the stage was set for a century of sociomusical conflict between poor man's and rich man's musics which has been resolved only in the mid-twentieth century.

While awareness of both musical and social implications was not entirely absent in the two above-mentioned importations of British music, nothing of the nature of a concerted plan can be seen in either. Such a plan can, however, be seen in the next phase of the conflict.

By 1800 the increasingly prosperous urban upper classes had already begun to experience a revulsion from the more utopian philosophies of equalitarianism which had sparked the struggle for political independence. Becoming better acquainted with contemporary European life and more conscious of the stigma of the colonial trauma, they began to yearn for cultivation of such fine arts as were customarily approved by royal, noble, clerical, and wealthy classes on the other side of the Atlantic. With less active commercial relations overseas, the new society might still have evolved in due time a fine art of its own, native in character and rooted in the soil of American life. But the Atlantic community was already a cultural reality. The industrial revolution had spread to America. The increased disturbance and tempo of living rendered the slow, unself-conscious development of homespun arts unacceptable. The emerging managerial avant-garde was in a special hurry to fill the gap left by two centuries in a culture whose values, to their minds, could be predicated solely upon those of Europe and not at all upon the variations of those values currently expressed in the rude nonconformity of rural, backwoods and pioneer America.

The manner in which this aspiration was pursued with respect to music is interesting—certainly quite a variant of that in which Spanish and Portuguese Jesuits had wooed the Indians of South America[5] and quite the opposite of that in which American writers from Thoreau on attacked their own aspect of the general problem. From about 1830, a small vanguard of private citizens, allied with some European musicians who had emigrated to the New World, set themselves with almost religious zeal to "make America musical" in the exact image of contemporary Europe as they saw it.[6] This deliberate and concerted, though outwardly unorganized, effort to plan and direct the music activity of the Euro-American hegemony in the still culturally colonial republic took two directions. Unlike its eighteenth-century pedecessors, it did not confine itself to mere reformation of church singing. On the one hand, it sought to create large orchestras and choral organizations, chamber music ensembles, and audiences for famous European virtuosi, on the other, to increase the music listening capacities of the population through music education in the public schools.[7] The movement was thus democratic in aim but demagogic in manner of attaining that aim.

No such quick success as that which followed the introduction of the popular idiom attended this far more ambitious objective. The public ready to pay for a fine art of music was still very small. The cost of operations was all out of proportion to box office receipts. Talent had mostly to be imported. Profits for outstanding soloists were ample, but livelihood for the rank and file performer was wretched. To the masses of the population, by then confident in their belief in an American way of life that excluded music, the elite arts appeared as something foreign—a luxury of the idle rich, an affected and unnatural waste of time.[8] Nevertheless, advancement was steady, although until after 1900 the music education movement bogged down in the boredom and difficulty of solfege (note-reading) and of dull, genteel textbooks.

The objectives of the make-America-musical missionaries were supported by a substantial number of less dedicated persons. Realization was general in small towns as well as in large cities and their fringe communities that deprivation of the finer things of life had occurred and should be remedied. Church and school groups, German singing societies, and even the literary clubs that came into being in the small towns were active in a similar way. Assemblies such as the Chautauqua and numerous lecture bureau circuits flourished. Second-rate Italian opera troupes were occasionally heard in most cities. Like their more sophisticated big-city cousins, the small-town semirural groups saw their job as both constructive and destructive. But comparatively ignorant of the fine art, they fostered mainly the only other they knew—the popular art that had taken firm root among the middle and lower classes of the cities. To the urban missionaires this was anathema. Along with the singing school and its spawn of shape-note hymns, they fought it as "bad" music. Thus the two elite groups were at loggerheads with respect to what was good, but in agreement upon one thing that was bad, the folk art with its repertory of the Anglo-American ballad, love song, game song, and fiddle tune, a style of performance employing the "natural" voice and devoid of exhibitory stage techniques except in fiddling.

Scarcely noticed by these self-appointed do-gooders, a powerful group of allies of both gradually formed among the music publishers, instrument makers and concert managers which we have come to call the music industry. Its birth and growth were concurrent with the make-America-musical movement. It had no slogan. It was undoubtedly directed by men interested in music and often by amateur musicians of ability. But its main reason for being was to make money. This "sell-America-music" group operated in a very small way until the 1840s, when it hit the jackpot with the minstrel show. The instant, nationwide success of this first native variant of the music theater rested not only upon the excellence of the "Ethiopian" songs of such men as Foster and Emmett but also upon the peculiar mixture of satirization and sentimentalization of the lowest socioeconomic class, especially its southeastern segment composed more or less equally of Negro slaves and poor whites. It allowed the whites to think they were socially above the Negro, even though both were poor, downtrodden, and unschooled. It offered ready compensation to the musical and cultural superiority-inferiority complexes of the cities.

Thus began the drive to make the once new American way of musical life become the old. To the missionaires' views, both urban and rural, the old way had to be supplanted. To each, only their own brand was good—all others, bad. To the backwoods, still almost untouched by the drive for urbanization, the "old-time" music was still good; the new, to the extent it reached them, was foreign and therefore to be wondered about and ignored.

The critical point in the evolution of these crosscurrents of changing traditions and of the groups carrying them came around 1900. About that time, a socioeconomic music class structure, reverting more and more toward the European model, was close to crystallization. The continental frontier had given way to a new type of frontier determined by social depth in which distance from elite urban and small-town influences was a dominating factor. Numerous social and cultural pockets, islands, or slums were formed: in the city by concentrations of large masses of recently immigrated laborers and in rural areas by the bypassing of main lines of communication. Although it became apparent that the dream of a classless society had less and less counterpart in reality, the dream itself remained very intense. Indeed such was its hold upon the verbal consciousness of the bulk of the population that it became imprudent to propose in a serious way that social classes ever existed in the United States. The very concept of social class was "un-American" and could only be entertained by a foreigner or by one under domination of foreign, hence dangerous ideas. Mass attitudes involving this myth had long been enhanced, as we all know, but its almost equally widely expressed contradiction, as, for example, in the society and fashion pages of the newspapers, by the prominence given to news of royalty and nobility, wealth and status, and in contacts between individuals of different social classes, when hair-trigger reactions of superiority-inferiority could be expected, ranging from "I'm as good as you are" to "You're as good as I"—rationalizations of the existence but undesirability of classes.

It is significant that the make-America-musical movement, highly authoritarian in its operation, and composed as it was of members of the well-to-do classes (or those who aspired to be), was thoroughly imbued with this paradox. To this almost religious brotherhood, music was of only one kind: "good" music, which was to say, monuments of the European fine art or well-meant imitations of them. In this sense, music (meaning good music) was not a class good for a few, but a universal good for all mankind. Before the altar of the concert stage all men were equal and all music divine. But face any of these protagonists with folk or popular music! If it were European it might pass. But if it were American, it was not music at all. Thus European and neo-European urban fashions in the written fine art were authoritatively pitted, in the *name* of democracy, against the truly democratic, but unwritten (or badly written), Euro-American and emerging American folk and folk-popular idioms. The adherents of the make-America-musical group, with its fine art, were comparatively few, but they became highly organized and very aggressive. The sell-America-music group, with its popular art, likewise was secure in its profits and urban compactness. The rural population that carried the folk tradition was large. But owing to its seclusion in the vast reaches of the countryside, it was not, during the nineteenth century, extensively subjected either to being converted to "good" music or being sold the "bad."

The first break in the dike that walled off the folk from the fine and popular arts was discovery of the Negro spiritual, hailed from the 1870s by the missionary group, the general public and, eventually, by the music industry, as "America's only folk music." The minstrel show had served as the foot in the door. Actually an Afro-Euro-American folk product, the spiritual was known to city dwellers in versions heavily doctored with devices of the fine and popular arts, either by Euro-American musicians or by Afro-Americans who wished to work away from Africa toward eventual identification with the European and neo-European world.

Two events of prime importance occurred during the first half of the twentieth century. First was the appearance of a brand-new factor—the mechanical and, eventually, electrical projection of music. Second was the transformation of the two pressure groups: from a musically esoteric, idealistic, contra-acculturative segment of the population; from a narrow commercial opportunism. The sell-America-music businessmen acquired a surprising amount of idealism, with many partially sincere slogans of social service, and with a degree of group consciousness. Having spent the first half of his professional life as an active member of the missionary group and taken part in the early 1930s in this transformation, it is understandably difficult for me to regard with objectivity factors that even in the 1950s began to be seen in perspective. Perhaps both groups would have effected their own transformation unaided. Without a doubt, some of the motivation and responsibility for the improved state of affairs has been owing to a degree of mature inner growth in both. However that may be, it seems to me that it was the sell-America-music group, composed of manufacturers, merchants, bankers, and engineers, which by large-scale exploitation of the new means of mass communication served as the catalytic agent in bringing together not only the art and the industry but the three principal music idioms I have distinguished and the classes consuming them and, in musical terms at least, set back the nearly successful drive to create a purely neo-European music class structure in the United States. Big business was—at least until about 1950 (since then it has become more and more autocratic)—more of a democratizing than an authoritarian agent in music.

The individuals constituting this second pressure group were, like the make-America-musical missionaries, either drawn from the upper middle class and elite of wealth or were self-made candidates for such status, mobility between classes always having been a salient characteristic of American society. These men, too, were interested in just one kind of music—the kind that would make money in large-scale production and distribution. From 1900 on, anything that would sell, from Caruso to Doc Boggs, from Verdi to Gershwin, was put onto rolls, cylinders, discs and, finally, tapes and film. The sales acceptance and resistance of every possible market were surveyed, analyzed, and developed by all the new devices of publicity and advertising. Since the majority of the earlier buyers of these commodities were members of the urban middle and lower middle classes, the bulk of the output of the factories and shops was, at first, the music these classes knew and wished to know—the popular idiom of the day.

One of the largest—perhaps the largest—single market became the public school. The music materials demanded were not necessarily what the children wanted but rather what the teachers wanted. Teachers were drawn mostly from the lower middle classes and from small-town, do-gooder environments. The idiom preferred by them was the kind of popular music that shied away from folklore and had yearnings, rather low-grade, it is true, for the "finer things of life." It is not surprising, therefore, that the conflict between the two main pressure groups rose to great intensity during the early years of the century, between the high-brows with their good or classical music and the lowbrows with their bad but eminently marketable commodity. To the former, the issue was clear: God against the Devil. To the latter, there was practically no issue. It could be laughed off. For the profits rolled in faster and faster.

But it was not long before the sheer magnitude of commercial operations began to require the know-how and experience in formalities of platform art possessed alone by professional musicians. And these, in turn, began to cast covetous eyes upon the possibilities of the new gadgets as they approached ever greater technological perfection and their employment became fantastically lucrative. With a little compromise on both sides and to mutual satisfaction, both financial and artistic, individual members of the make-America-musical group entered the large corporations. These, in turn, gave more and more time and space to the good and classical, which eventually acquired the preposterous designation of "serious" music. And thus, the new gadgets that at first were feared as marking the death of the fine art became the authors of a new life for it.

Dramatic evidence of the turn of events had already been afforded in the years following 1907 when the Music Supervisors (now, Educators) National Conference, the large professional organization of teachers of music in the public schools and teacher-training colleges, formally abandoned authoritarian leadership of the make-America-musical group for the more democratic opportunism of the sell-America-music group. Instead of offering school administrators an upper-class, intellectual, divine, quasi-European art, the Conference tried to find out what the administrators would buy and pay for in the way of music. This turned out to be the somewhat old-fashioned, middle-class popular music of the day. By giving them this in quantity and at the same time allowing the "good music boys" to work within such a frame as best they could, a revitalization of music education in the schools took place, the magnitude and quality of whose effect upon the use of music in the United States can scarcely yet be estimated. A small host of other music organizations, now banded together in the National Music Council, gives uniform evidence of the turn of affairs. Even the usually recalcitrant Musicians' Union gives signs of eventual cooperation. A few diehards of the authoritarian school still keep up the battle against bad music. But the gap between the highest of their values and sound business practice is narrowing steadily, hedged around by codes of ethics arrived at by compromise between national professional and business organizations.

This rapprochement of the urban music idioms and the new services that exploited them had left the rural population and its old-time folk songs and dance tunes to one side, despised if not ignored by the make-America-musical group, by most of the music industry, and by the schools. Here again it was the second of these, the music industry, which showed its leadership. Discovering a market in the backwoods and great open spaces, it first sold phonographs. By the 1920s it was putting favorite folk and folk-popular songs and dances, both white and Negro, on discs. The process was repeated with radios and radio programs in the 1930s. But it was not until the 1940s that the folklorists, the WPA, and the Library of Congress were able to persuade the urban music intellectuals to accept the native Anglo-American folk music.

It is important to stress the fact that neither of the urban pressure groups gave back to the rural areas exactly what they had taken from it. A general rule in the subacculturation of music idioms seems to be that the receiving (or taking) class must add something of its own to the products of the donor (or taken from) class before the process of giving back has gone very far. "Giving back" seems to be a kind of translation, subtly undermining the existing integrity of the music material, its tradition and cultivation by admixture of urban innovations. In the first flush of discovery, it is true, some commercial recordings of uninfluenced (authentic) folk music and jazz were pressed on commercial discs. But it was not long before platform graces—to begin and end with a flourish, to dramatize, to make more precise and "slick," in short, to exhibit the quaint or strange rather than to communicate the common—began not merely to project a mixture of what already existed but to create new, hybrid genres. Thus, hillbilly, commercial jazz, and country and western old-timey music have bade fair to smother their prototypes and have attained the status of subidioms in their own right, partly by sheer quantity production that in turn has established new mass tastes. Paralleling these creations of the commercial group, later discovery by the missionaries of the same prototypes resulted first in a rash of symphonic and concert jazz and second in "city-billy" folksinging aimed directly at the urban audience and audience participation, especially of youth groups. Thus the despised or ignored rural folk and folk-popular music, on the way to dying out in the country, became artificially reinseminated in the cities. And thus, gradually, the last borders of music class which had threatened to become Chinese walls between the various music-using groups began to be overridden.

The net result as I see it, might be said to be that the United States is beginning to come of age musically speaking. It has done so by swinging more than a little way from the imminent congelation of a neo-European social-economic music class structure and turning again toward the equalitarian mass use of what may be the embryo of a single integrated vernacular based upon nationwide intake of mass communications. True, a minority of sophisticates at one end of the scale may absorb a maximum quantity and variety of intake. At the other end, divers minorities may absorb minimal music communication services. But in between, the vast majority of the population must be absorbing an ever-increasing quantity and variety—an indiscriminate sampling of everything that is delivered by tens of millions of loudspeakers—and becoming increasingly devoted to and dependent upon it. From a situation in which music values were imprisoned in mutually exclusive compartments of an increasingly rigid class structure, we seem to be moving into one in which the formation of a unitary music idiom may be taking place.

But accounting for the field under consideration here on a basis of intake alone results in only a half picture. We can say that progress in intake measures up fairly well to the objectives of the early pressure groups. While it is risky to compare music with speech functions in any society, some notion of the music situation in the United States today can be had by picturing a community of its size in which only a very small minority could repeat the words of other people, though most could listen to talk, and in which writing and reading were highly developed by a few and 96 percent or more were generally illiterate. It is hard to believe that there is not in each individual a deep-lying relationship between consumption and production, by him himself, in such cultural traditions as he carries—between passive and active, re-creative and creative carriage of them. Yet in America today, the vast majority of the population is virtually incapable of using either a normal oral music tradition on the one hand or an effective music literacy on the other. Few persons, whatever their economic, educational, or social status, can perform any music beyond the level of the simplest item of near-folk or folk-popular repertory, that is, of a six-year-old competence, in any but a mongrel mixture of styles. Such is the imbalance of our educational system that though the majority of the population can and does pronounce sentences expressing moderately individualized, that is, creative, thought and feeling, a minority perhaps as small as a fraction of one percent can or ever does express its musical counterpart, a simple melody made up of commonplace formulas and clichés not exactly quoted from another person's expression in a written text. What a strange society it would be if the only kind of speech communication were in pronouncements by professional, student, or amateur elocutionists of complete prose or poetical compositions by a few masters! The combination of a countrywide commonalty of a comparatively high individual intake within a very low individual output presents precisely such a picture for the art of music in the whole of the Western world. In the United States the mass of the population exhibiting it may be more than 96 percent of the total and cuts clean across every other variety of class structure—an across-the-board leveling of the tendency that I have suggested as crystallizing around 1900. The elite executive and the dowager millionairess no less than the five-and-ten clerk and the gangster belong alike to a single mass—it is hard to call it a class—of music impotents.

What this may mean in terms of the relationship of music and society in the predictable future poses a lot of questions. I shall ask only one of them here: does a music-social structure based upon quantity of mass music communications taken in by individuals rather than upon the quality of products put out by them have any significance in the study of American civilization as a whole?

I cannot answer by reference to any massive reservoirs of dependable knowledge. Music has not yet been studied as a communications function in Western civilization. Its relationship to speech—complementary, compensatory, or antidotal—has scarcely been distinguished as a subject for study. Musicologists have spent very little time—and that, only recently—upon development of techniques of description of any music other than the monuments of the European fine art; and of that little only in a symbolic, not a descriptive, sound-writing. Furthermore, as in the rest of the humanities, techniques of prediction have not been and probably cannot be developed as they have been by the natural sciences. The best we can do with the contemporary situation is to assess the relative weight of the principal factors and leave formation of opinion and plans for action to those who will make happen that which will happen.

It will have been observed that the foregoing discussion has been descriptive in character. But the activities described have value in themselves. They happened because individual human beings held opinions about what could and should happen, opinions about what was valuable to the individual and to other individuals. The values sought were of two kinds—quantitative and qualitative. Contrary to the view of many judges, I aver, these two were not mutually exclusive opposites but rather necessary complements of each other and played equal parts in the activities of both pressure groups. The make-America-musical group, with its eyes consciously set upon the quality of the monuments of the European fine art, found itself more and more concerned with the quantity of performers, concerts, and ticket buyers. The sell-America-music group, with its eyes consciously set upon the quantity of goods sold and of profits accruing, found itself more and more concerned with the taste preferences—that is, quality judgments of buyers. Surely, it must have been recognition of a common aim and of the interdependence of their activities that brought the once hostile viewpoints and groups together.

Now that this integration has taken place, it can be seen as typical of a general trend of history. The old tradition of democratic individualism has become overlaid by a democracy of pressure groups. Where formerly the individual worker functioned within a framework of responsibility to an individual employer—or, in the case of the musician, to individual employers or patrons—his activity was molded and directed by the value system that has been built in the course of the give-and-take of intimate personal relationships in close physical proximity of time and space. In cultural and social crises of greatest tensity, such as those accompanying the dissolution of the Roman Empire, the consolidation of the U.S.S.R. or the religious wars of the sixteenth and seventeenth centuries, this give-and-take among individuals has always given way to group relationship between musician and patron in which control—even up to 100 percent—was vested in the latter as a *control group.* As crises have leveled off, control has gradually reverted to the 50-50 give-and-take between individuals which can be considered normal for more stabilized cultural and social relations, as, for example, of the nineteenth century in the United States.

By its very nature the pressure group is an aspiring control group. The complexity of a highly industrialized society and above all, the very nature of mass communications technology, has facilitated the fusion of apparently opposed pressure groups, at the same time opening the way for the proliferation of smaller control groups. Within this framework, individual personal relations between music-producer and music-consumer are no longer the rule. Portentous structures of administrative and executive personnel intervene. Operational streamlining exerts an almost irresistible molding force upon every producer, his repertory, his presentational style, the very idiom he employs. Custom, at the receiving end, similarly molds the tastes of consumers of the streamlined product.

At the moment this is written, control from inside and outside the art of music seems to be in fairly even balance and the results acceptable to most people concerned. Formation of a universal music idiom, differentiated only by the occasion of its use, the skill of the producer, and extent of education of the consumer might be expected to result.

Two eventualities must be weighed here. The one refers to the possibility, already evidenced, that increase in consumption of music by individuals automatically stimulates increase of production by them. The evidence is found in the enormous increase in amateur music-making from folk-singing and recorder-playing groups of young people to school, college, and community orchestras of symphonic proportions. (The national association of the last-named alone numbers upward of a thousand members.) The other refers to the possibility that the control groups of radio, TV, publication, management, and education may be halted in their present trend toward amalgamation in one supreme, corporative board of control and may be held as a set of competitive control groups upon a higher plane as it were, expressing there— perhaps even representing in a formal manner—the main or essential divisions of normal collective thinking and feeling as, for example, those of a left, a center, and a right. To some, the supreme control group may appear inevitable. To others, it may occur that there may be built in, as it were, in the deepest cultural traditions of the United States—perhaps also of other Occidental countries—sets of checks and balances not unlike those overtly expressed in the political Constitution and now for some time operating in various economic and social legislation. I hope that this may be the case. If it could be shown that there is some solid factual support for the surmise, we might shed light not only upon some of the darkest corners in our civilization in general but also upon some age-old questions such as why do people make music and what is the function of the art of music in a culture overwhelmingly dominated by the art of speech.

NOTES

1. Irving Lowens, "John Wyeth's Repository of Sacred Music, Part Second: A Northern Precursor of Southern Folk Hymnody," *Journal of the American Musicological Society*, V (Summer 1952), 114-131.

2. As, for example, in the little theaters of Boston, New York, Philadelphia, and Charleston, S.C. See O. G. Sonneck, *Early Concert Life in America, 1731-1800* (Leipzig: Breitkopf & Härtell, 1907) and *Early Opera in America* (New York: G. Schirmer, 1915).

3. George Pullen Jackson, *White Spirituals from the Southern Uplands* (Chapel Hill: University of North Carolina Press, 1933), p. 9.

4. The distinguishing characteristics of the patent or shape-note hymn are: a setting in three voice-parts (though four are often found) any or all of which may be sung by men, women or both men and women, with the melody in the middle (tenor) voice, utilizing a high percentage of folk materials, the added parts, the bass and treble, being conceived contrapuntally, i.e., more horizontally than vertically, so that quite surprising chordal structures result, some archaic, some novel, in which dissonance, forbidden in orthodox writings, abounds and chords without thirds, parallel octaves, and fifths are common.

5. Guillermo Furlong, *Los Jesuitas y la cultura rioplatense* (Montevideo: Urta y Curbelo, 1933); Serafim Leite, "A música nas escolas jesuíticas do Brasil no século XVI," *Cultura*, I (January-April 1949), 27-39.

6. In Argentina, Brazil, Cuba and Mexico there were counterparts of this North American movement; but they were so much smaller and less able to operate, that

development of integrated regional and national musical arts is possibly farther advanced than in the United States, where the bond to European fashions was more strongly supported.

7. Outstanding among the leaders of this movement were the Masons (Lowell, b. 1792 and William, b. 1829), Theodore Thomas, b. 1835 and the Damrosches (Leopold, b. 1832, Frank, b. 1859 and Walter, b. 1862).

8. For a more detailed account of the early history of the movement, with ample documentation, see James H. Stone, "Mid-Nineteenth-Century American Beliefs in the Social Value of Music," *Musical Quarterly*, XLIII (January 1957), 38-49.

XIII
Contrapuntal Style in the Three-Voice Shape-Note Hymns of the United States[23]

George Pullen Jackson has traced for us the bonds between the tunes of many shape-note hymns and the secular folk tunes of America.[1] The question at once presents itself: what do the extraordinary settings of these hymns owe to printed sources and what to predominantly oral traditions?[2]

I shall consider here only the three-voice choral settings of the type published during the first three-quarters of the nineteenth century in such famous collections as *Southern Harmony, Sacred Harp, Kentucky Harmony, Harp of Columbia, Missouri Harmony, Social Harp,* and the like.

These collections present a distinctive style of choral composition. It is not, in any orthodox sense, a harmonic style. The tones sung by the various voices upon any given beat are not conceived of as being fundamentally a unit—a chord. Instead, each voice added to the tune is related to it independently of the relation between the tune and the other added voice. Thus these pieces may be said to show a definitely contrapuntal style.

The melody is given to the tenor or middle voice, and the relation between each of the two added voices is separately considered. John G. McCurry, editor of the *Social Harp,*[3] has explained the process thus:

> After you have written your tenor, then commence your bass by placing your notes a proper distance from the tenor, and be careful always not to place any note within one degree of the corresponding note in the other part, or within seven degrees, it being within one degree of the octave. Also avoid ninths, as they have the same effect as seconds and sevenths. Any two notes of the same name will make an agreeable sound, you may place notes in unison if you see proper. The intervals that produce harmony (when sounded together) are thirds, fourths, fifths, sixths and eighths, or unison. Those that produce a disagreeable sound are seconds, sevenths and ninths. . . . After having written the

237

base and tenor, commence the treble by observing both parts already written; be careful not to place any note on the next sound to the notes in either part that are already located.

The "vertical" tonal units usually form conventional triads. Often, however, one or even two of the three constituents are absent. Or, they take the shape of chords built in fourths or fifths instead of thirds (with resulting intervals that contradict the rules). This is especially noticeable at cadences and semicadences, where the final chords tend to dyadic rather than triadic character, omitting a third and often the fifth also (see ex. 1).

EXAMPLE 1

As might be expected, these tonal units do not function as do chords in ordinary harmonic writing. The process preparation-dissonance-resolution is conspicuously absent. Add to this the fact that women customarily sing any tenor or bass part an octave higher and that men sometimes sing the "tribble" an octave lower, and it will be seen that results which seem very unconventional to us may be achieved.

The employment of only three voices, the setting of the tune in the middle voice, and the strong "horizontal" line of the melodic writing need not, of necessity, produce anything unusual in the way of style. Entirely orthodox music can be written within these limitations. But the style of the three-voice shape-note settings of which I speak are outrageously heterodox, violating such basic and centuries-old prohibitions as those against:

1. parallel fifths, octaves, and unisons
2. parallel fourths between outer voices or between upper voices without a third in the bass
3. unprepared and unresolved dissonances
4. cadences on $\frac{8}{4}$
5. crossing of voices

Were these violations only occasional, one might easily pass them by. But they are so frequent that they clearly constitute essential elements in the style.

I shall give three examples of this practice. The first is the widely known "Wondrous Love." Jackson quotes the tune as given in *Southern Harmony, Good Old Songs, Primitive Baptist Hymnal,* and *Olive Leaf.* I give a facsimile of it (ex. 2) as it appears in *Harp of Columbia,*[4] in seven "shapes." A signature of two flats is to be understood, since the rectangular note "law" which concludes the bass part is placed upon G. The E-flat in the tenor in measures 6 and 18 is, however, sung as an E-natural. Jackson reports this *musica ficta* as current practice. The Archive of American Folk Song in the Library of Congress has at least two records showing it—one from Virginia, the other from Alabama. I have seen this setting in several different systems of "shapes," but never any other setting of the tune. The editor's directions assure us that the metronome may be set at about ♩ = 96.

If my blue pencil, rusty these many years, serves me aright, there are here twenty-five parallel fifths, fifteen parallel octaves, and two parallel unisons. When sung with the characteristic nasal voices of the Southern singers and with the numerous but inimitable little slides, trembles, catches, and other ornaments that cannot very well be written down in our system of notation, the effect is one of highly stylized but admirable performance.

Another good example is "Romish Lady." Jackson quotes the tune from the *Hesperian Harp.* I give it in facsimile (ex. 3) as it is printed in *Southern Harmony,*[5] in four-shape notation. It appears in other collections—always, in my experience, in the same setting, though in different shapes. The metronome may be set at about ♩ = 60.

EXAMPLE 2

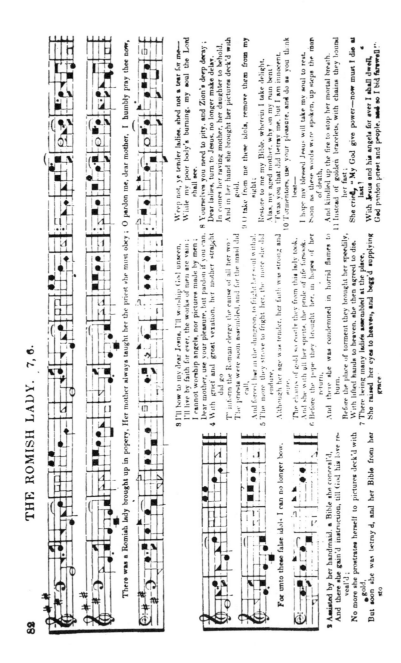

THE ROMISH LADY. 7, 6.

82

There was a Romish lady brought up in popery, Her mother always taught her the priest she must obey; O pardon me, dear mother, I humbly pray thee now,

For unto these false idol- I can no longer bow.

3 Assisted by her handmaid, a Bible she conceal'd,
And there she gain'd instruction, till God his love reveal'd;
No more she prostrates herself to pictures deck'd with
gold,
But soon she was betray'd, and her Bible from her
sto

3 I'll bow to my dear Jesus, I'll worship God unseen,
I'll live by faith for ever, the works of men are vain;
I cannot worship angels, nor pictures made by men:
Dear mother, use your pleasure, but pardon if you can.
4 With grief and great vexation, her mother straight
did go
T' inform the Roman clergy the cause of all her wo-
The priests were soon assembled, and for the maid did
call,
And forced her in the dungeon, to fright her soul withal.
5 The more they strove to fright her, the more she did
endure,
Although her age was tender, her faith was strong and
sure.
The chains of gold so costly they from this lady took,
And she with all her spirits, the pride of life forsook.
6 Before the pope they brought her, in hopes of her
return,
And there she was condemned in horrid flames to
burn.
Before the place of torment they brought her speedily,
With lifted hands to heaven, she then agreed to die.
7 There being many ladies assembled at the place,
She raised her eyes to heaven, and begg'd supplying
grace

Weep not, ye tender ladies, shed not a tear for me—
While my poor body's burning, my soul the Lord
shall see.
8 Yourselves you need to pity, and Zion's deep decay:
Dear ladies, turn to Jesus, no longer make delay.
In comes her raving mother, her daughter to behold,
And in her hand she brought her pictures deck'd with
gold.
9 O take from me these idols, remove them from my
sight:
Restore to me my Bible, wherein I take delight.
Alas, my aged mother, why on my ruin bent?
'Twas you that did betray me, but I am innocent.
10 Tormentors, use your pleasure, and do as you think
best—
I hope my blessed Jesus will take my soul to rest.
Soon as these words were spoken, up steps the man
of death,
And kindled up the fire to stop her mortal breath.
11 Instead of golden bracelets, with chains they bound
her fast;
She cried, "My God give power—now must I die at
last?
With Jesus and his angels for ever I shall dwell,
God pardon priest and people, and so I bid farewell."

"The Romish Lady" as it appears in *Southern Harmony*
Philadelphia, c. 1847.

EXAMPLE 3

"Wondrous Love" as it appears in the *Harp of Columbia*
(Knoxville, Tennessee, 1849)

Plentifully supplied with parallel fifths and octaves, this setting is especially to be marked for its emphasis upon the interval of the fourth. The parallels in measures 1 and 2, 6 and 7, 16 and 17, and the fourth-chord (C-sharp, F-sharp, B) in measures 2, 7, and 17 gives it a peculiar character. The astonishing coincidence of two parallel octaves and two parallel unisons in measures 14 and 15—at a semicadence—is not by any means rare.

My fourth example is "Parting Friends," from McCurry's "Social Harp." The metronome may be set at about ♩ = 96.

EXAMPLE 4

"Parting Friends" as it appears in McCurry's *Social Harp*
(Philadelphia, 1868)

Also well supplied with parallel octaves, fifths, and fourths, this setting exhibits semicadences on $\frac{8}{4}$ chords in measures 3 and 17.

The following excerpts will serve to illustrate some of the other devices employed (ex. 5):

EXAMPLE 5

Social Harp (1868)
Heavenly King (p. 20)

EXAMPLE 6

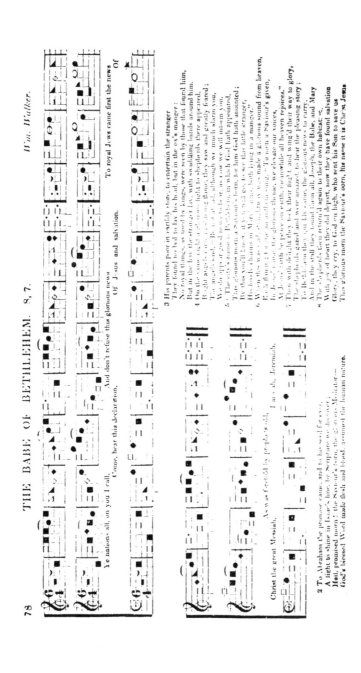

"The Babe of Bethlehem" as it appears in *Southern Harmony*
(Philadelphia, c. 1847)

EXAMPLE 7

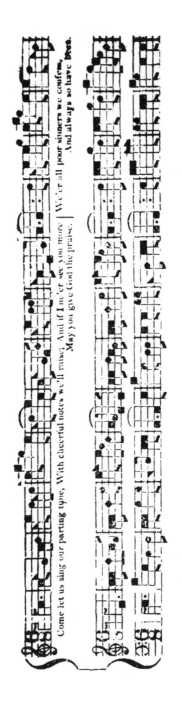

"Milton" as it appears in *Knoxville Harmony*
(Pumpkintown, Tennessee, 1838)

There are those among us, I regret to say, who evidently regard practice of this type as the work of ignorance, error or, perhaps, lack of musical feeling. It is true, there are typographical errors in the shape-note books. The musical skill and editorial capacity of their compilers varied greatly. Sometimes it was considerable. There are collections, however, full of academic "mistakes," which do not achieve the style of the above quotations. Compare, for instance, the two settings reproduced below as examples 6 and 7. The first, "The Babe of Bethlehem," from *Southern Harmony* maintains the high level of craftsmanship for which the collection is justly famous. The second, "Milton," is from the little-known *Knoxville Harmony* that, as most of its pages show, was not of the grand style.

It may be we are unable to say in many cases whether it was by design or accident that a particular departure from academic procedure has been made. The fact, however, that these settings (excepting, of course, those of the type of "Milton") and others like them appear practically unchanged in edition after edition and are still sung letter-perfect in many localities today must lead us to accept the printed page as faithfully representing the intentions of the composers and the appreciation of the millions of singers who have sung these songs for a century or more.

Curiously enough, in some books the prefaces (containing "full expositions of the rudiments of music") give rules forbidding parallel fifths and octaves. The same books contain "Wondrous Love" and other settings like it. With our own experience in music-teaching practice in mind, we should, I presume, find it not difficult to account for this seeming paradox.

It is further to be noted that in modern re-editions—even of the most admired originals—the three-voice settings have in most part given way to four-voice treatments. Often as not, this is done by the simple device of adding an alto. According to Jackson, one editor, S. M. Denson, announces that he has composed 327 alto parts, presumably to improve the old songs and give them additional life.[7]

Other more sophisticated musicians have, strangely enough (for they protest admiration for traditional lore), abandoned entirely the old settings and substituted new voices in the manners of Brahms or Vaughan Williams.

Personally, I would as soon change the tunes as change the settings. For here is true style! There is a rigorous, spare, disciplined beauty in the choral writing that is all the more to be prized for having been conceived in the "backwoods" for which many professional musicians have such scorn, and in the face of the determined opposition of sophisticated zealots in no small number, from Lowell Mason down to those of this very day.

Would it not seem to be a matter of interest, not only to scholars concerned with the study of American culture but also to musicians concerned with the development of the art of music in the New World, to inquire into the origin of this curious musical style, how it developed, and what was and is its function in the total field of music in America?

Obviously, our forefathers brought with them to this continent a fair cross section of the cultures of their motherlands, including the idioms of art music, popular music, and folk music. There is ample historical evidence that in early days practice of the fine art of music was necessarily curtailed in the colonies and that the popular art did not flourish extensively. But immigration was continuous, and professional musicians and amateurs of the fine art of music and of popular music arrived in steadily increasing numbers. It is known that some continuity in the teaching and performance of both art music and popular music existed from early in the eighteenth century. It may not be too much to say that until very recently—say, up to World War II—this had the character of being imposed from without in emulation of envied European fashions rather than of being developed from within upon the existing premises of New World culture. Four-voice hymn-singing, however, with the melody in the highest voice and orthodox harmonic (chordal) writing, was well known before 1800 and has increasingly dominated the field of written music.

Historical references to folk music, however, are slight. Transfer from oral to written tradition (as in the early "songsters") has not been enough investigated to have provided us with much year-to-year evidence of the state of folk music in the New World. From evidence of survival in our own day of over a hundred ancient British and Scottish ballads, and of a wealth of related folk-music materials, and the development of some new, apparently local, forms, it would appear that folk music has functioned healthily throughout our three centuries of Anglo-American culture. Other—minority—European language groups (German, in the middle Atlantic States; French in the northeast, down the Mississippi, and along the Gulf; Spanish along the southwestern border and in Florida) have defined some regional variations.

Cultivation of these folk arts, almost entirely through oral rather than written tradition, would seem to be a development from within the fabric of New World culture. While we must, of course, look to European hymnody for ancestors of our shape-note style (some round-note hymnals, as far back as 1800, be it said, also exhibit it), does it not seem possible that we may discover more than a little of its nature and hence its ancestry from the living descendants of our largely unknown folk history?

In our culture as a whole, an initial simplification, enforced by the conditions of pioneer and colonial life, gave way to a consequent elaboration. Current notions of evolution have dubbed this "progress" and its reverse—complex to simple—"regress." Owing to the fact that the more archaic music appeared to have attained a special importance in some cultural islands such as the northern woods and the southern mountains, some observers have been tempted to associate folk music, oral tradition, and such phenomena as shape-note singing, with the moribund elements of culture and so with regress.

Our present knowledge lends considerable support to this view. For example, a very large number of shape-note tunes, of the related but unprinted revival hymns and other materials of strictly oral tradition, and, indeed, of American folk music in general, is pentatonic. If Yasser is correct in his theory that pentatonic tonal systems represent a more primitive development in the evolution of musical art than do heptatonic, the problem would to a large extent be solved almost mechanically.[8]

Certainly, the resemblance of the shape-note settings to some thirteenth-century music—especially the *Conductus*—is striking. Compare, for example, the following "Ballade Style Conductus" (ca. 1200) given to me by Dr. Leonard Ellinwood:[9]

EXAMPLE 8

A · ve vir-go vir - gi - num, ver-bi car-nis cel - la

The old singing-school teachers had not, of course, the historical knowledge that could rationalize a revolt against orthodox four-voice harmonic writing in such a form as that of the three-voice shape-note style. The explanation might very well be that, along with the borrowing of secular folk tunes (which practice Jackson has shown to have been

common), borrowing of a prevailing convention in the polyphonic performance of these tunes may have taken place. We would expect to find,
however, traces of such practice in present-day secular folk music and in
the branch of religious singing that functions along lines of oral rather
than written tradition.

Interestingly enough, this is just what happens. Both White and Negro
spiritual singing in two and three voices is common; in four voices, rare.
Current hillbilly singing also shows two-voice and three-voice improvisation. The interval of a fourth is very prominent, occurring often upon
long-held tones, on accented beats, where urban conventions, both of art
and popular singing, would call for a sixth or a third. Parallel fourths are
common, parallel fifths and octaves also. Especially to be noted are the
sudden and, to sophisticated ears, unaccountable unisons and octaves
in places where a full harmony would be expected. The tendency to
close upon chordal structures of fifth and octave only is also often
encountered.[10]

The fact that similar material is to be found on commercial recordings
should attest, to some degree, to its being a widespread convention and
not merely a rare discovery of seekers after the quaint or antique.

To have pursued the matter thus far, even without adequate documentation, broadens the problem beyond the scope of the present effort.
For if, as I feel it is, the contrapuntal style of the three-voice shape-
note hymns is part and parcel of the general Anglo-American folk-
music idiom of the New World, the question still remains: how did it get
that way? While something may be said for the theory of cultural regress,
it is too mechanical and contains too many untenable implications to rest
with. On the one hand, we cannot accept invariable harnessing of the
notion of progress with movement simple to complex, nor of regress
with its opposite. On the other, we cannot accommodate a view that our
widespread and dearly loved popular music—from blues, swing, and
boogie-woogie to hillbilly (all largely of folk extraction)—is regressive,
with the view, which all accept *as if* true, that the culture of the New
World (and particularly of the United States) is essentially progressive in
character. Is it not possible that cultures sometimes get somewhat bogged
down in complexity and have to simplify in order to maintain their
feeling that they are going ahead? May this not hold true of certain
strands in a culture, whether or not the culture as a whole acts in the
same way?

It would seem that history rarely presents to us such a simple set of
data as the one-way theory of cultural regress might attempt to account

for in toto. It is true that by 1800 (or, for that matter, still in 1900) musical learning and practice in America presented no development comparable with that of Europe at the time. Immigrant traditions had become stilted and garbled, *re*productive rather than productive.

Be it said to the credit of the people, dissatisfaction with the "state of singing in our churches" was chronic from before the Revolution. One senses a conflict between the state of singing and the state of learning. People were continually popping up with new methods by which either or both could be improved. New methods were in the air. A new method of government and social organization was in process of being tried out. A new religious revival was evolving. Curiously enough, our first musical rebel, William Billings, announced about this time a declaration of independence from traditional limitations in music.[11] Indeed, the patent-, character-, or shape-notes themselves were invented about 1800 in a similar spirit in the field of music teaching—an effort to free the ordinary man from bondage to the high priests of the musical profession and their difficult notation. Did this innovation create the style of the three-voice hymns, or did it serve to organize, for wider distribution, a fait accompli frowned upon by the cultured but supported strongly enough by the multitude to enable it to persist in spite of this? Is there a European prototype of it?

Now, it is a curious but significant fact that European art music since before 1900 has employed increasingly a number of devices, including parallel intervals, which characterize the hymns I have been considering. The restrained melodic line and the spare tonal fabric have been gaining more and more adherents. Harmonic (chordal) writing is not so strongly dominant as it was fifty years ago. If one likes to play with the theory of cultural regress, how about its opposite "cultural advance-guard"?

The old singing-school teachers—Ananias Davisson, B. F. White, William Walker, W. H. and M. L. Swan, John G. McCurry, William Hauser, and the rest—had no small hand in the making of America. Their books have sold in the tens of millions of copies. Often, a single book served (and sometimes still serves) as the sole written music source of a dozen or more intensely musical people over many years. During their heyday, European art music was undergoing the heavy upholstery of Wagner and Brahms. Though we have no reason to believe the American shape-note composers knew of the work of the Germans, they nevertheless mark the first turn away from the then prevailing trend of late romantic music.

It was not until the 1890s that Erik Satie (probably ignorant of the shape-note hymns) made, within the framework of "art" music, the first determined turn toward the spare and austere fabric, though foretokens of it are to be found in both Berlioz and Mussorgsky. The music puritanism of Satie and the neoclassicists is, of course, a very different kind of thing from the music puritanism of the American hymn-writers. But the technical function is very like.

There is, then, something about these three-voice shape-note settings that is not only centuries older than their day, but a good half- or three-quarters of a century in advance of it. May we not hope that sometime in the near future adequate study will be made, not only of the technical processes they exhibit but also of the sociohistorical processes of which they were a part?

NOTES

1. G. P. Jackson, *Spiritual Folk-Songs of Early America* (New York: J. J. Augustin, 1937). See also the same author's *White Spirituals in the Southern Uplands* (Chapel Hill: University of North Carolina Press, 1933). In his article, "Buckwheat Notes," published in the October 1933 issue of *The Musical Quarterly,* Dr. Jackson described the nature of the shape-note systems.

2. I have asked Dr. Jackson if anyone is investigating this phase of the field in which he is the principal authority, and he tells me that he knows of no one besides myself who has expressed an interest in it. I am, unfortunately, in a position that allows me neither time nor opportunity in which to undertake the necessary research. I am broaching the question here simply because I feel that it is an important one. If, then, as a result of the brief exposition I shall make, some competent student should investigate it, my present objective will have been gained.

3. *Social Harp.* Published by S. C. Collins for the proprietor John G. McCurry (Philadelphia, 1868).

4. *Harp of Columbia,* edited by M. L. Swan (Knoxville, Tenn., 1849). There is a facsimile reprint of the edition of 1867 called the *New Harp of Columbia* (Nashville, Tenn., 1921) (procurable from L. D. Schultz, 1126 Eleanor St., Knoxville, Tenn.).

5. *Southern Harmony,* edited by William Walker (Philadelphia, ca. 1847). There is a facsimile reprint of the edition of 1854 by the Federal Writers Project, Works Progress Administration (New York, 1939).

6. *Knoxville Harmony* (Pumpkintown, Tenn., 1838).

7. *Original Sacred Harp* (Denson Revision) (Haleyville, Ala., 1936). This is NOT the original *Sacred Harp* but a revision of it.

8. Joseph Yasser, "A Theory of Evolving Tonality" (New York: American Library of Musicology, 1932).

9. Florence, Biblioteca Medicea-Laurenziana, MS. Pluteus 29.1, folio 240.

10. See, for instance, the following discs in the Archive of American Folk Song in the Library of Congress: no. 188B2 "God Moves on the Water" and no. 502B "Dig my Grave," both about to appear in transcription in John and Alan Lomax's forthcoming *Our Singing Country*; see also, Resettlement Administration recordings deposited in the Archive, no. 239B2 (10 in.) "I wouldn't mind dyin' if dyin' was all," 3241A1 "Little

Marg'et," the singer, Bascom Lamar Lunsford, tunes his banjo in three fourths and one second, giving rise to some unusually good opportunities for parallel fourths in the accompaniment. I have been told upon good authority that this is a usual tuning for the five-string banjo in the low country of South Carolina.

11. William Billings, *New England Psalm-Singer* (Boston: Edes and Gill, 1770), pp. 19-20 ("To all musical Practitioners").

XIV
The Appalachian Dulcimer[53]

The Appalachian dulcimer, dulcimoor, or dulcymore is known to folk-lorists as an instrument in fairly general use since 1900, and probably for some time before that, by musically nonliterate rural and small-towns-people in the mountains and foothills of southeastern United States, stretching from southern Pennsylvania to northern Georgia, Alabama, and Mississippi, taking in West Virginia, the western counties of Mary-land, Virginia, and the Carolinas, and the eastern parts of Kentucky and Tennessee.[1] It is a fretted cordophone, in my experience usually a little less than a meter long, from 120 to 200 mm. at its widest and about eighty to 100 mm. in depth (pl. 1).[2] It is made of local woods such as pine, spruce, poplar, hickory, birch, maple, and walnut by rural woodworkers with simple hand tools. Owing partly to the encouragement of rural handicrafts by urban trained social workers during the last fifty years, and partly to the nationwide folk music revival movement in the cities since 1940, a number of makers have found a market among urban amateurs. I have, however, never known of a factory made instrument. Nor have I ever come across evidence of its use, prior to this revival movement, as a parlor or concert instrument, as was, not seldom, the true hammer dulcimer or whamadiddle throughout the United States during the eighteenth and nineteenth centuries. The Appalachian dulcimer may be classed as a folk instrument in the strict sense of the term. Until the present writing, its making and its use have taken place within the currency of an oral tradition of music and no printed directions for its manufacture or notations of its playing have appeared.[3]

In figure 1, I give rough outlines of the front views of the five shapes of which I have personally known enough specimens to be able to state that these five, at least, are traditional. A sixth is of a specimen reliably reported by Bryan. The side views are alike, except that in some cases a mere stub takes the place of a scroll at the end of the peg-stock or a handle appears at the opposite end.

The instrument is constructed in two sections. The first is represented in the outlines by cross-hatching. In many specimens this consists of a single piece of wood running the full length of the instrument, serving at once as peg-stock and scroll, finger or fretboard, tailpiece with or without the occasional handle and, often as not, as endblocks within the second section over which the first is shaped to fit and be glued. Sometimes section one is made in two, three, or more separate pieces, glued, pegged, or even nailed together. Section two consists of a shallow soundbox that protrudes symmetrically on each side below section one. The front and back of the soundbox are flat and of single boards. The two sides are single boards bent or shaped in one of the several outlines shown.[4] On some instruments there are small buttons, usually three, on the back to hold the soundbox a few mm. clear of a table.

One common type of construction is especially interesting. The part of section one that serves as fretboard is hollowed out so as to form, in end cross section, an inverted square U, to each of whose edges a side of the front is glued, the part of the front under the hollowed out part of the

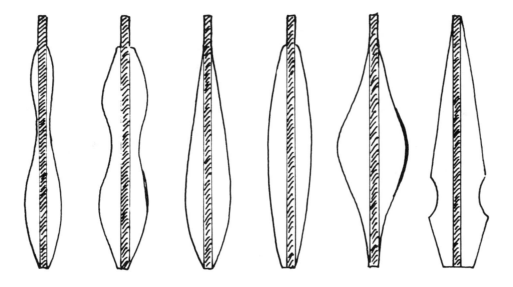

FIGURE 1

fretboard being cut out. The fretboard serves, thus, not only as a bridge by which the vibrations of the strings are transmitted to each side of the soundbox but also as an integral part of the soundbox itself. As on all the dulcimers I have seen, this type of construction also has no separate bridge. The strings pass over two nuts, an upper and a lower, consisting each of a piece of hard wood, bone, or metal set into slots in the fretboard, with notches so that the strings run parallel to one another. A cross section of this type of construction is shown in figure 2.

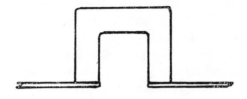

FIGURE 2

The dulcimers that I have seen have had three or four metal strings, rarely five. I have heard there are instruments with more. The strings are normally thin, .001 to .002 of an inch. Bryan recommends guitar G and E. I might add B.

The most common tuning of the three-string dulcimer seems to be to set the two highest strings on the instrument's right[5] in unison, the third a fifth lower as in figure 3*a*. Bryan gives the tuning in figure 3*b* as common for the four string instrument. His experience that the A tuning is most common confirms answers given to me by informants who claim that they tune the dulcimer "to the same note as the fiddle," but meaning an octave lower and varying sometimes as much as a fourth in either direction.

a   b

FIGURE 3

The frets are placed either under the chanterelle (melody string or strings on the instrument's right) alone or across the whole fretboard. They are usually arranged diatonically: T-T-ST-T-T-ST-T-(T) for two octaves and part of a third. This might imply that the basic tuning were for a mixolydian mode. But upon historical grounds as well as in view of the type of music mostly played, the intention is obviously to set a conventional major with the tonic at the third fret.

The commonest manner of playing the Appalachian dulcimer is for the player to hold it crosswise upon his spread knees or back down upon a table or chair in front of him with the peg-stock to his left. This might be called right-handed or normal practice.[6] Mercer shows a photograph of a woman playing the dulcimer with the butt end in her lap, the back propped up against a table in front of her. A turkey, goose, or other quill is held in either hand—in the right, to sweep back and forth or in one direction only over all the strings, a little distance above the lower nut; in the left, to press the chanterelle down upon the fretboard so as to intone a melody while the other strings sound as drones. The quill held in the right hand may be slit an inch or so from the end to make as flexible a plectrum as desired. An index finger or guitar pick will also do, while any hard, smooth, little stick, piece of bone, or even a thumbnail may serve for the left hand as a "noter." Only once have I seen the dulcimer played with a bow. The player, in Marion, Virginia, in 1936, volunteered that he was "the only one" who played it so. Eaton, too, says this is rare. I have heard of players who fret several strings at once with their fingers. Bryan cites this as "the most complicated" manner of playing and says that chords may be produced and the strings plucked as on a psaltery. But I am not convinced that this is traditional in the United States, though further research may prove it to be. Certainly, it is very rare. Some urban performers play a countermelody on the instrument when they sing to its accompaniment. But I have not been able to convince myself that this is traditional, though it must be admitted the effect, when well done, is pleasing. Usually, voice and dulcimer either alternate or sound the melody in unison or at the octave. Rarely, a guitarlike strumming is used.

The timbre is thin, metallic, soft, and may well be described as twanging or even buzzing. A vibrato is possible on tones of sufficient duration. Indeed, depending upon where the pressure of the noter is brought to bear—in the middle of the fret square, close to, or upon the fret—upon the height of the fret, upon the breadth of the noter and upon the amount of pressure down upon the string—considerable variety of intonation is possible at any fret. The gliding of the noter over the string allows, perhaps it would be more correct to say almost compels slurring. Though the tone fades quickly, staccato is not characteristic of the instrument. The dulcimer is for the individual or the intimate group, not for the crowd; for the night rather than for the day, though in the hands of a skillful player, tunes lively enough for the square dance, ordinarily carried by the fiddle, can be rendered.

Obviously, the Appalachian dulcimer is not, in the accepted sense of the word, a dulcimer at all, but a fretted zither (*Griffbrettzither*), belonging to a well-defined subclass upon which the melody is played on one string (or several in unison or even parallel thirds) while others sound as drones. This subclass is well represented in European organography, especially in the northern region, by the Icelandic *langspil,* Norwegian *langeleik,* Swedish *hummel,* Lowland *Noordsche balk,* German *Scheidtholt,*

and French and Belgian *bûche* or *épinette des Vosges*. It is related on the
one hand to the *tromba marina* or nun's fiddle and on the other to the
hurdy-gurdy or *organistrum*. Specimens can be seen in most large instrument collections in both Old and New Worlds. Praetorius,[7] Claas
Douwes, the *Encyclopédie Méthodique*, Boers, Mahillon, Thuren, Norlind,
Panum, de Jong, Vanderstraeten, and others describe their tuning and
manners of playing in such detail that the European provenience of the
Appalachian dulcimer and of the manner of playing it is clearly marked.
As I write this, there comes to hand through the kindness of Curt Sachs,
an outstanding monograph, Stig Walin's *Die Schwedische Hummel*.[8] Besides meticulous description of forty Swedish instruments, their histories, references to them, careful acoustical measurements and report
upon forty-five others from northern European countries, nearly all
reproduced in fine halftone front views, Walin gives a survey of the
European field as a whole, without getting entangled in the controversial
background of Asian ancestors or the foreground of American descendants, the latter of which he did not know.

Walin distinguishes three form groups: (1) with straight sides all
around, (2) with a bulge (*Ausbauchung*) on the left side, (3) with bulges on
both sides. He points out that all specimens in his third group and four
of the twenty-eight in his second, are made in two sections, one of which
is fitted on top of the other.

The Appalachian dulcimer obviously belongs to Walin's third form
group. On the basis of the preceding verbal description, it would seem to
have no feature distinguishing it from its European prototypes. Indeed,
pictured as played by Otto Malmberg not long before his death in 1921,
Walin's No. G 35, although belonging to his second form group, could
easily be taken for the American instrument, except for the fretting with
the fingers of the left hand instead of with the noter. For the lack of right
bulge might not be remarked or even considered of much importance
(pl. 2*a*).

Three questions most commonly asked about the Appalachian dulcimer, and most worth considering here, are: (1) from what part of
Europe was it brought to the New World; (2) what, if any, are its distinguishing features; and (3) how did it get its name?

As to question 1, Niles and Thomas claim its prototype was brought
from England. Shoemaker states that Mercer discovered evidence of
similar provenience (I have not been able to trace this) but goes on to say:
"The French Huguenots in Berks, Lehigh and Lebanon Counties
brought a unique instrument to Pennsylvania, the dulcimer, 'dulcimore'
or Hackbrett, as it was variously called." Campbell and Eaton favor a
German provenience, citing the trek of German-speaking immigrants to

Pennsylvania southwestward along the ridges and through the valleys of the Appalachians, a well-established fact still attested to by the prevalence of Germanic family names throughout the region today. Eaton also cites the Highland copying of spinning wheels from Pennsylvania models of German provenience. In extension of these opinions it should be remarked that there was heavy Scandinavian immigration into Pennsylvania throughout the nineteenth century. The Dutch were early settlers in Delaware, New York, and New Jersey in localities close to the borders of Pennsylvania. It is interesting to note that in defense of the theory of British provenience the use of the Appalachian (often called the Kentucky) dulcimer to accompany the singing of the British ballad is often adduced. The very few recordings of dulcimer playing deposited in the Archive of American Folk Song in the Library of Congress indicate that as of 1940 this was, to the contrary, very rare.[9] C. J. Sharp, who made his extensive field collection of survivals of British song between 1916 and 1918 in the very heart of what has been known as "dulcimer country," states in the Introduction of his monumental work: "I came across but one singer who sang to an instrumental accompaniment, the guitar . . . ," though he was informed that accompaniment by the dulcimer (which he describes briefly) was practiced in Kentucky.[10] Maud Karpeles, who accompanied Sharp on all three of his trips, states in her Preface to the same work: "The dulcimer . . . we saw and heard only in some of the Kentucky mountains-schools and never in the homes of the people, where it is evidently but rarely to be found." This testimony, coupled with the apparent absence of any trace of this type of instrument in the British Isles during the colonizing period, would seem to prejudice the theory of British provenience.[11]

With respect to the claim of French Huguenot introduction of the instrument into Pennsylvania, I do not know upon what data Shoemaker based his statement or whether it is relevant, for presumably he refers to the true hammer dulcimer. European evidence seems to point the other way. All the French bûches or épinettes that I have seen were small, rectangular, and of Walin's first form group, that is, without bulge. To the writer in the *Encyclopédie Méthodique,* the instrument was so "tres peu connu" that he describes its German counterpart, the Scheidholz. Mahillon describes a single specimen in the great Brussels collection. Choquet reports but two in the collection of the Paris Conservatoire. Walin details five of French origin. Four belong to his first form group; the fifth is not classified. Interestingly enough, a surprising number of the specimens now in museums were made by one Fleurot in Valdajol, a fact that certainly points away from a well-distributed folk tradition in France. C. Marcel-Dubois, of the Musée National des Arts et Traditions

Populaires (Paris), who possesses an épinette by Fleurot much like one in the National Museum in Washington, D.C., also made by him, assures me that this type of instrument is, in her experience, known only in the extreme east of France.[12]

The most cogent support to the theory of German provenience is borne by the collection of Pennsylvania *zitters* made, documented, and reported upon by Henry C. Mercer and now housed in the Museum of the Bucks County Historical Society in Doylestown, Pennsylvania. It consists of seven plucked- and five bowed instruments (pls. 3 and 4) in good or fairly good states of preservation. To be sure, like the French variant of the family, they are examples of Walin's straight-sided first form group. But unlike that almost miniature variant, they are full-sized and about the same length as the average Appalachian dulcimer. Unfortunately, most were bought from secondhand dealers and are consequently without pedigree whatever; others were gifts. The information about them was sketchy and did not antedate the middle of the nineteenth century. Similar specimens have been found in the attics of old houses and some have been acquired by municipal, county, and other museums, and by private individuals. Eventually, we may hope, some will turn up with more detailed documentation. Mercer, a brilliant amateur student of local history, knew of their European provenience and was in touch with such collectors as F. Scheurleer and J. W. Enschede in Holland. He diligently sought local informants and interviewed them in detail. Several bore witness that both plucked and bowed zitters were played by members of the Mennonite sect[13] to accompany hymn singing, not in the church, but in the home, as is still the *psalmodikon,* a Swedish variant "invented" by one J. Dillner in the early nineteenth century and used by Scandinavian Americans in some North Central states. Mercer gives excellent descriptions of the playing of the instruments and assumes that the Kentucky dulcimer is related to them.

Obviously, it is a far cry from the almost primitive Pennsylvania zitters with their straight sides, fretboard, and soundbox all in one, to the more elaborate Appalachian dulcimer with its often hollowed-out fretboard and symmetrically built out soundbox. If we are to hypothesize a connection between them, might we not reasonably expect to have some evidence of the existence of transitional or intermediate forms? Perhaps the shelves of local historical societies and museums may still reveal such. Mercer, who evidently combed the antique shops of southeastern Pennsylvania quite thoroughly during the early part of the century seems to have found none. John Cummings, curator of the Bucks County Historical Society and himself an expert woodworker, has offered the ingenious suggestion that given a verbal order, but no model, to make a stringed instrument of the zitter type, a Kentucky fiddle-maker, for example, might readily have adapted his customary procedures to the occasion and produced a mutation such as the Thomas type, or an ancestor of it, which, when seen by others, might have given initial impetus to the distinctive design of the Appalachian dulcimer. It might even have been purposely designed to meet the needs of music-loving people who would prize it not only for its resemblance to the beloved fiddle but also for the greater ease with which its playing could be mastered. However this may be, it is of course pure speculation. The Pennsylvania zitter remains, at this writing, probably entirely out of use and as only one possible ancestor of the Appalachian dulcimer.

Attention was called as long ago as 1917 by Josephine McGill, to another possible ancestor of our instrument. And Maud Karpeles published a reminder of its almost forgotten existence fifteen years later. "The history of its [the dulcimer's] introduction into the mountains," she continues in the text already quoted, "is obscure, but it may be noted that a similar instrument, catalogued as a German zither of the eighteenth century, is exhibited in the New York Metropolitan Museum of Art (Crosby Brown Collection of Musical Instruments, no. 988) and if this classification is correct, it is possible that the instrument was introduced by the early German settlers, who drifted into the Mountains from Pennsylvania."[14]

This CBC 988 (briefly reported on by Walin as VG No. 33) is no transitional or intermediate form, but a full-fledged specimen of what I have been designating the Appalachian dulcimer. This can be seen in plate 5, where it is pictured by the side of one of three dulcimers made before 1938 by Nathan Hicks of Rominger, North Carolina, and which is now in my possession. The resemblance to the Thomas instrument pictured in plate 1 is striking enough. The Hicks instrument, which is representative of shape 2 in the outlines given in figure 1 and is among the most common to be found in current use, could almost be a copy of CBC 988.[15]

If CBC 988 is German, then the Appalachian dulcimer is a direct importation and there is nothing more American about it than there is about the guitar or the hammer dulcimer. The variations of its shape as pictured in figure 1 could not be considered significant acculturative phenomena, any more, for examples, the five-string banjo and the Trinidadian steel pan.

But is CBC 988 German? Unfortunately, Emanual Winternitz, director of Musical Activities of the museum, tells me, neither the agent of the Crosby Brown family who acquired the instrument for the collection nor the editor of the catalog whose description I quote in full above, left more documentation than that published, except that it was acquired before 1889. We have, thus, no record of where it was made or bought. The description "German, 18th century" may be reasonably correct if it was acquired in Germany. But it might as well have been bought elsewhere in Europe or even in the United States. Here, at least, almost any seller would readily swear that his "granpappy's pappy" brought it over from Germany "more'n a hunder years gone." Yet if it came from Germany, why are not specimens of like patterns reported—and commonly reported—from European museums? According to Eaton, James Edward Thomas, maker of the instrument shown in plate 1, was born in 1850 in Letcher County, Kentucky, began making dulcimers in 1871, and died in 1933 after turning out about 1,500 of them. And he was by no means the only maker.[16] True, for every dulcimer one might have run across in the last twenty-five years in the Highlands, one might have found a dozen fiddles, a dozen banjos, and two dozen guitars. But in contrast to its neglect in Europe, cultivation of the Griffbrettzither in the United States seems to be comparatively vigorous.

It is worth noting that of the fourteen other exhibits, listed by Walin as of *deutschsprachigen Gebiet* (his nos. VG 23-26, 28-32, 34-38), none belong to his third form group with Ausbauchung on both sides. But all Appalachian dulcimers seen or reported upon (to my knowledge) do. Only one of the German zithers, and that belonging to his first form group, shows heart-shaped sound holes. Yet, for example, of his five Danish specimens (VG 6-10), two belong to his second and three—the only ones in his non-Swedish section—to his third form group. (Perhaps we should explore the possibility of Scandinavian provenience.) And of his five Norwegian instruments, three show heart-shaped sound holes on the front, as do three of the French specimens pictures.

If the wood of CBC 988 can be identified as German, our only doubt of the provenience of the Appalachian dulcimer might be that it had been fashioned in Pennsylvania from a piece of imported furniture, reworked along some such lines as those suggested by Cummings. Painting of a formalized wood grain upon natural wood was common in Pennsylvania in early days. There remains, of course, the chance that even if this wood were identified as American, CBC 988 might still have been fashioned in the likeness of a German original, now unknown. The trouble is that the geographic origin of poplar wood, I am reliably informed, is very difficult to determine. Discovery in Germany of only one such instrument, or, upon opening up 988, of internal evidence of German manufacture, would dispel the above doubts.

As things stand at present, then, the European provenience of our instrument is clearly established in all but minor detail. I consider the claim of German eighteenth-century origin of CBC 988 open to question, but the

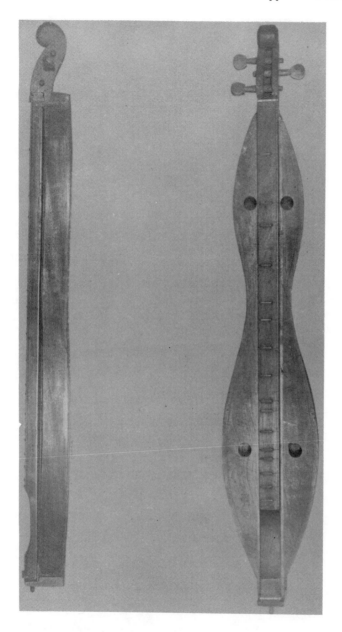

Pl. 1. Appalachian ("Kentucky") Dulcimer. MS label on back of lower right sound hole reads: "Manufactured by J. E. Thomas Jan, 25 1918 Bath Ky." Presented by Loraine Wyman to the Bucks County Historical Society, in whose Museum, Doylestown, Pennsylvania, it bears the number 18514. Photograph by Maddox Photo Studio. Courtesy of the Bucks County Historical Society.

Pl. 2*a*. Otto Malmberg playing the hummel. Reproduced with permission of the author from Stig Walin, *Die Schwedische Hummel* (fig. 84). Courtesy of Nordiska Museet.

b. Jethro Amburgey playing dulcimer of his own manufacture.

c. Jean Ritchie playing dulcimer made by George Pickow. Photograph by Barratt.

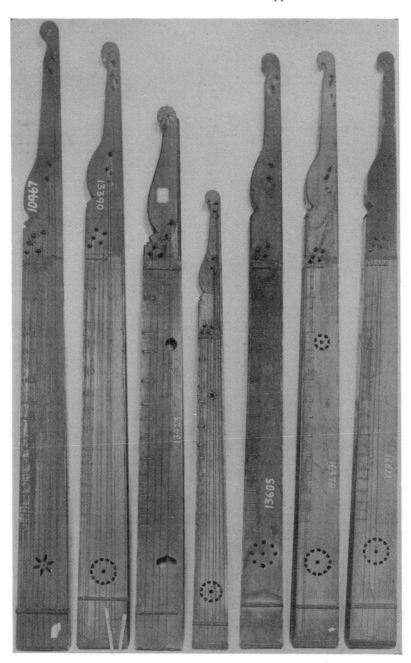

Pl. 3. Pennsylvania plucked *zitters*. Phograph by Maddox Photo Studio. Courtesy of Bucks County Historical Society.

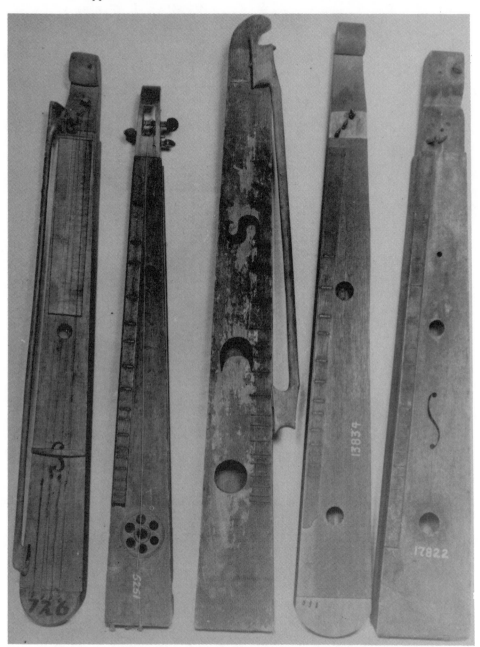

Pl. 4. Pennsylvania bowed *zitters*. Photograph by Maddox Photo Studio.
Courtesy of Bucks County Historical Society.

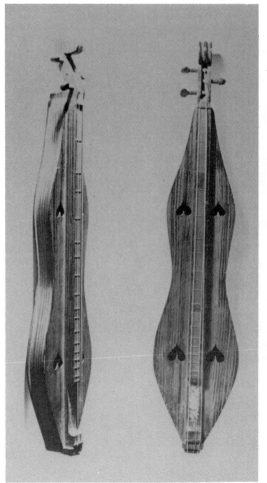

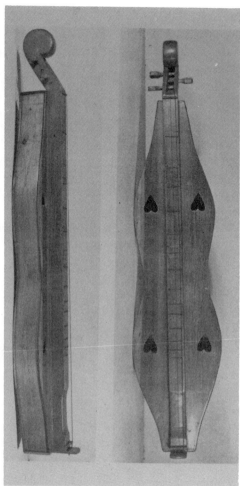

Pl. 5

Zither or dulcimer. Crosby Brown Collection. No. 988. Courtesy of the Metropolitan Museum of Art.

Dulcimer. Made by Nathan Hicks of Rominger, North Carolina, in possession of the author.

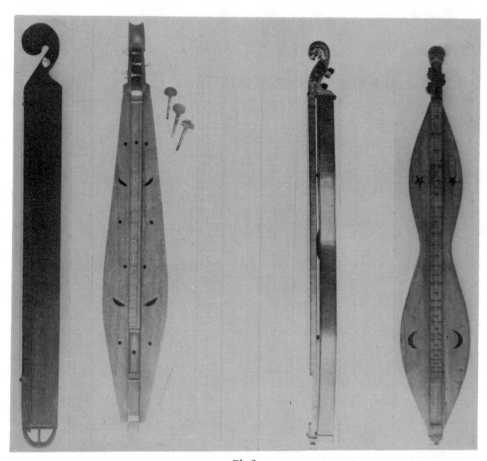

Pl. 6

The Campbell Dulcimer (see note 11. Three original hand wrought pegs have been replaced by geared banjo keys. The fretboard is hollowed out at least in part.

The Gamble Dulcimer. Presented by its maker to Wm. C. Gamble when Secretary of Berea College, Kentucky, 1901-11. The fretboard is solid and rests upon three bridges. There are three series of frets—one for each string.

claim to German provenience for the whole American variant, if such it is, the strongest of the several advanced. Collections of local history and popular antiquities in Pennsylvania[17] remain to be explored as do also travel books and memories of living makers and players and libraries and institutional records of Highland settlement schools.

The question of what are the distinguishing characteristics of the Appalachian dulcimer can best be answered by comparing the plates presented herewith and the excellent reproductions at the end of Walin's monograph. I would say they could be expressed as "slender symmetry." None of Walin's instruments—excepting, of course, his reproduction of CBC 988—exhibit this particular variant of the basic functional conception of the Griffbrettzither. Further search in European museums may uncover a tradition of such a variant. For the present, the American design, especially the one with the hollowed-out fretboard, would seem to stand as a well-defined folk tradition still current among the people who carry the older and more archaic folk traditions generally. There is no telling, of course, what effect the present mild popularity of the instrument in the cities will have upon its overall currency among the people at large.

How the dulcimer got its name is perhaps the most baffling, though certainly not the most important, question that can be asked about it. Obviously, the word *Scheitholt* or *Scheidholz* cannot with propriety be used by or even in close proximity to an English-speaking community. With even less propriety can it be formally anglicized. The word *zitter* might have passed into American English as *zither*. The fact that it did not is no challenge to the claim of German provenience. For the word *zither* probably did not exist in the limited and archaic vocabulary of eighteenth- and nineteenth-century Highland speech. The fact that a rechristening took place is perhaps some support for Cumming's suggestion. And what more attractive name could have been found for the delicate, wasted instrument by a hard-bitten, bible-reading lot of pioneers who found in music almost the sole recreation of their secluded life? Is it not sanctified by Holy Writ (Dan. 3:10)?

Not least among the difficulties of tracing the history of the dulcimer in the United States is the employment of the same name for two distinct members of the string family, the fretted zither and the hammered dulcimer. The earliest reference that has come to my notice (this, through the kindness of Sidney Robertson Cowell) is in Samuel Sewall's diary, in which the entry for 23 May 1717 mentions the dulcimer.[18] In estimating such references it is only too often impossible to know from internal evidence which type of instrument is meant. For rarely do general authors give any detailed information of the object or the manner of playing it.

Apparently, there is no ground for belief that the Appalachian dulcimer was known north of Pennsylvania, though of course, an individual specimen could have wandered up there.[19] The hammer dulcimer, to the contrary, has long been widely known in the Northeast, North Central, and Lake states. It is known in the Southeast, though not as well known as the Appalachian dulcimer. I have seen a pretty parlor model that stood upon four delicate legs, the whole painted in fine, aged, ivory enamel with colored festoons of flowers, probably of eighteenth-century workmanship, and said to have been long held in Vermont. At least one craftsman, Thomas Mann of Ortonville, Iowa, was still making them to order in the late 1930s.[20] The probability is that this is the sort of instrument mentioned by Sewall.

No transcriptions of dulcimer playing have come to my notice. Below, I give two skeleton notations of field recordings of simple playing of the instrument. Transcription of the more elaborate playing must await recording with sound camera, so fleeting or submerged in the overall twanging and buzzing are the sounds of the individual strokes of the plectrum and of the gliding from one fret to another.

Notations of Dulcimer Playing, transcribed from tape dubbings of aluminum discs in the Archive of American Folk Song in the Library of Congress, Washington, D.C., which were themselves dubbings of original field recordings on aluminum. No checks are known to have been made either of the electrical currents used or of the accuracy of the recording equipment. Keys and tempos indicated are therefore only approximate. The symbol ↓ indicates probable downstroke of plectrum—away from player; ↑ indicates probable upstroke of plectrum—toward the player. Barring and metrical signature is a problem in this idiom. It could be determined in any one of three ways: by downstrokes of the plectrum; by foot beat; by metrical pattern. Using the note values in the two examples, the first would double the number of bars and require a signature of 1/4; the second, which is followed here, marks the foot beat at the beginning of each measure and a signature of 1/2; the third would use one-quarter as many bars and a signature of 4/2. On the whole, the idiom is characterized by a general adherence to *ritmo di una battuta*. The third way is, therefore, improper. I would use the first if the players' foot beats marked the quarters—a technique often met with, in which the foot taps lightly (or even pounds quite strongly) as often as 200 or more times a minute. In the present examples, the downstrokes are of equal strength throughout. Occurrence of the foot beat with every other one recommends the barring and meters used.

GROUND HOG

Played and sung by Curtis Dartey. Recorded by Walter Garwick and Jean Thomas, Ashland, Kentucky, 1934, LC No. 302A1. The drones sound continuously but it is not possible to perceive the strokes of the plectrum upon them.

FIGURE 4

SOURWOOD MOUNTAIN

Played by Theodore Blevins. Recorded by Alan and Elizabeth Lomax, Smithsboro, Kentucky, 1937, LC No. 154B2. The drones are usually weak, sometimes inaudible, but occasionally so strong as to give an effect of syncopation.

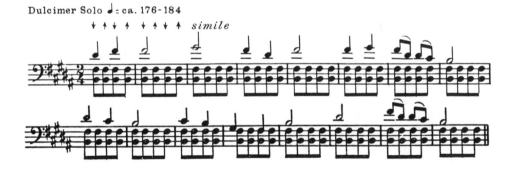

FIGURE 5

NOTES

1. References are meager. No investigation with even a pretense of musicological character has, to present knowledge, been made. The best account I have found is: Charles F. Bryan, "American Folk Instruments, I—The Appalachian Dulcimer," *Tennessee Folklore Society Bulletin*, XVIII, 1 (March 1952), 1-5; 3 (September 1952), plate opposite p. 66. Other references are: Allen W. Eaton, *Handicrafts of the Southern Highlands* (New York: Russell Sage Foundation, 1937), p. 199 ff.; John C. Campbell, *The Southern Highlander and His Homeland* (New York: Russell Sage Foundation, 1921), pp. 143-144; John Fetterman, "Tennessee Hill Country Dulcimer Builder," Nashville *Tennessean Magazine* (30 May 1954), pp. 8-9; Josephine McGill, "The Kentucky Dulcimer," *The Musician*, XXII (January 1917), 21; Henry C. Mercer, "The Zither of the Pennsylvania Germans," *A Collection of Papers Read Before the Bucks County Historical Society*, V (1926), 482-497; John J. Niles, "Deft Hands Carve the Dulcimer," Louisville *Courier-Journal Magazine* (20 January 1952), p. 26; Jean Ritchie, *Singing Family of the Cumberlands* (New York: Oxford University Press, 1954), p. 276; Jean Thomas, *The Singin' Gatherin'* (New York, 1939); Dorothy Scarborough, *A Song Catcher in Southern Mountains* (New York: Columbia University Press, 1937), pp. 70-72; Cecil J. Sharp, *English Folksongs from the Southern Appalachians* (London, 1953), pp. xviii-xix, xxvii; Henry W. Shoemaker, *The Music and Musical Instruments of the Pennsylvania Mountaineers* (Altoona, Pa.: Mountain City Press, 1923); *Mountain Life and Work*, I, 21; XII, 19.

2. I have seen about forty specimens, some half of them in the Appalachian area during the summer of 1936, in the hands of men and boys who played them in an apparently traditional manner.

3. This is a report, not upon completed investigations in American organography but upon some preliminary observations occasioned by neglect of two bits of evidence that might have engaged the closer attention of students at any time during the last fifty years, and that should be taken into account in the fieldwork with sound camera, which alone can report adequately upon the music rendered by the skilled player of the instrument concerned. See *Ethno-musicology—Newsletter*, no. 5 (September 1955), p. 17.

4. Jean Thomas describes a type of construction in which a piece of sassafras wood 38" long and 3" wide is (split? and) bent to make the sides of a soundbox 30½" long and a neck 7¼" long.

5. In the anthropomorphic presentation, the instrument is regarded as facing the viewer and having its own right and left, front and back, top and bottom. See Curt Sachs, *Handbuch der Musikinstrumentenkunde* (Leipzig: Breitkopf und Härtel, 1920), p. 155.

6. I have not seen a left-handed player. A double dulcimer, for two right-handed players sitting opposite each other was exhibited at a National Folk Festival in Washington, D.C., around 1940. It was said to have been owned in Iowa.

7. Michael Praetorius, *Syntagmatis Musici*, II, *De Organographia* (Wolffenbüttel, 1619), 57; *Theatrum Instrumentorum* (1620), pl. XXI, no. 8.

8. Stig Walin, *Die Schwedische Hummel* (Stockholm: Nordiska Museet, 1952).

9. The following items are rendered by the more reliable informants and listed in the *Check List of Recorded Songs in the English Language in the Archive of American Folk Song to July 1940* (Washington, 1942). Sung and played with dulcimer accompaniment: 291 A, "Run, Nigger, Run"; 302 A1, "Ground Hog"; 302 A2, "Turnip Greens"; 302 B, "Barbara Allen"; 1342 B2, "Little Brown Jug"; 1540 A2, "Henry of Knoxville"; 1540 B, "Barbara Allen"; 1541 A, "The Knoxville Girl"; 2854 A1, "George Collins"; 2855 A1, "Ground Hog"; 3161 A1, "Over the River, Charlie"; 3161 A3, "Sally Brown." Played on the

dulcimer, without singing: 1340 B1, "Liza Jane"; 1342 A3, "Sourwood Mountain"; 1342 B1, "Turkey in the Straw"; 1343 A5, "Water Bound"; 1343 B2, "Arkansas Traveller"; 1343 B3, "Brown Eyes"; 1343 B4, "Liza Jane"; 1347 A1, "Turkey Buzzard"; 1347 A2, "Going Down the Road Feeling Bad"; 1541 B2, "Sourwood Mountain"; 1541 B3, "Old Granny Hare"; 1553 A1, "Buck Creek Girls"; 1553 B1, "Redwing"; 1553 B3, "The Wreck of the Old 97"; 3160 B1-3, "Water Bound"; 3160 B4, "Turkey in the Straw"; 3160 B5, "Bonaparte's Retreat."

10. Accompaniment by guitar has become almost the rule in recent years.

11. The British rebec and crwth adduced by Niles, and the cruit or cruet (in nineteenth-century Pennsylvania) by Shoemaker would seem to be too far removed in kinship to have bearing upon the present inquiry. It is worth noting that Walin reports no specimens of the fretted zither from the British Isles. Thurston Dart (Cambridge, England) has told me that he knew of no such instrument in the organography of England. Perhaps I should report that in January 1957, Ed Cray (Los Angeles, California) acquired from the estate of Stella Campbell, deceased, of Pasadena, a handsome dulcimer of the Appalachian type, with tapered noter and quill (pl. 6). The label has not yet been deciphered. A handwritten slip of paper accompanying it designates it as Scotch and of the kind "made by the Clan Campbell for five generations." Inquiry addressed to John Lorne Campbell brings the reply: "I know nothing about the kind of dulcimer you illustrate being made in Scotland," though he does remember a hammer dulcimer being played on MacBrayne's Loch Fyne boats to entertain tourists. Reference of the inquiry to Francis Collinson, of the School of Scottish Studies, University of Edinburgh, elicits the reply: "I have never heard of the 'Scotch Dulcimer' myself . . . it is perhaps not without significance that the name Campbell is not unknown in Scandinavian countries, notably Sweden." Passed on to Robert Stevenson of the National Museum of Antiquities, the inquiry brings further reply from Lyndesay G. Langwill, C.A., Honorary Treasurer of the Galpin Society: "I feel sure that Miss Campbell's 'Scotch Dulcimer' has no connection with Scotland. The fretted zither is not known here. . . ." For the present, therefore, I am inclined to discount the claim of Scottish provenience.

12. Without more detailed study of the French épinette, it might be difficult, in some cases, to distinguish an instrument fashioned in accordance with a tradition known as such by its maker and one that is a mere sport or fantasy of an individual experimenter entirely ignorant of that tradition or a counterpart. For in many collections there are to be seen miscellaneous rectangular boxes, large and small, with strings stretched over them.

13. The first Mennonites came to Pennsylvania in 1720.

14. The description of CBC 988 given in the section "Europe" of the *Metropolitan Museum of Art Handbook No. 13—Catalogue of the Crosby Brown Collection of Musical Instruments of All Nations*, I (New York, 1902), 51, runs as follows: "Zither. Shallow body. Sound-board with long pointed ends and incurved sides, and having four heart-shaped sound holes. The peg-box with 3 wooden pegs inserted at the side and terminating in a moulded scroll. Three metal strings, 2 in unison sounding D, passing over 17 brass frets, the other string sounding a fifth below, G. Germany, 18th century. Length 2 feet 1 inch. Width 7½ inches." Perhaps I should add: (1) the length is 35¼, not 25, inches; (2) it is painted, in black, in what seems to be imitation of pine grain, concealing the natural wood, which may be poplar; (3) the tuning is indicated in black painted capital letters D DG on the fretboard just below the lower nut; (4) fret squares are numbered in black painted figures from the top down: 6, 7, 1, 2, 3, 4, 5, 6, 7, 1, 2, 3, 4, 5, 6, 7, 1 in the order

of the conventional major scale with the tonics at the third, tenth, and seventeenth frets; (5) the fret squares of the tonics show a faded black paint; (6) the fretboard is hollowed out at least in part; (7) a cluster of flowers in faded painted colors can be seen in the plucking well—an indentation on the fretboard under the place where the plectrum in the right hand plucks or sweeps the strings. Incidentally, the Crosby Brown Collection comprises a number of fine specimens of the Scheitholt, hummel, épinette family. One, no. 2475, has a scroll turned sideways like the Pennsylvania zitters pictured in plate 3, but stubby, rather than elongated.

15. The description of CBC 988 fits closely the Hicks instrument, except (1) the wood (poplar) was left unfinished by the maker, (2) no tuning is indicated, (3) there are only fourteen frets, (4) they are not numbered, and (5) the length is 35½ inches and the greatest width, 7-9/16 inches. Probably, comparative study of the cents values of the interval ratios produced by the string lengths at the various frets will yield results of the greatest interest of any measurements of the instrument. Individual instruments vary so astonishingly, however, that only statistical averages can render conclusions of musico-logical significance. For example, on CBC 988, the cents value of the interval produced by frets 12-13, a half step in the scale, is 168 instead of 100 (my measurements). The two succeeding intervals, frets 13-14 and 14-15, whole steps in the scale, are 149 and 163 instead of 200 each.

16. Niles lists as "truly great" dulcimer makers: Bristol Taylor, Berea, Kentucky; W. C. Singleton, Viper, Kentucky; Nathan Hicks, Rominger, North Carolina; (S.F.) Russel, Marion, Virginia. Theodore Blevins, of Marion, Virginia, made very good pear-shaped instruments in the 1930s. Jethro Amburgey (pl. 2) learned his craft from J. E. Thomas. Eaton names Lewis Hinkle of Volga, Upshur County, West Virginia. Homer Ledford has been making dulcimers at Berea College, Berea, Kentucky. J. J. Niles and Jean Ritchie (Pickow) (pl. 2) are largely responsible for the present urban interest in the dulcimer. Niles has made some fine instruments elaborated according to his own fertile imagina-tion. Jean Ritchie's husband, George Pickow, a pupil of Amburgey, has made a number of fine traditional dulcimers.

17. A list of museums can be found in Earl F. Robacker, *Pennsylvania Dutch Stuff* (Philadelphia: University of Pennsylvania Press, 1944), p. 155.

18. "23.5. To Salem, Meadford, Lodge at Cousin Porter's: See and Hear the Dulcimer." In "Diary of Samuel Sewall, Vol. 3," *Collections of the Massachusetts Historical Society,* 5th series, VII (Boston, 1882), 131. The editors offer the following footnote to the quotation: "A musical instrument played by striking the brass wires with sticks—Eds."

19. Wesley B. Reed, of North Woodstock, Conn., who has the largest local collection of musical instruments I know of in New England, states that he has never run across a Kentucky or Appalachian dulcimer, though he has never gone very far afield yet. He has three hammer dulcimers in his collection, two of about 1875, one probably before 1850.

20. The Library of Congress, Washington, D.C., has made available to the public some recordings of Mann's playing (Record No. AAFS 41).

XV
Versions and Variants of the Tunes of "Barbara Allen"*[68]

Probably it is safe to say that most English-speaking people in the United States know at least one ballad tune or a derivative of one. If it is not "The Two Sisters," it will surely be "When Johnny Comes Marching Home"; or if not "The Derby Ram," then the old Broadway hit "Oh Didn't He Ramble." If the title is given or the song sung to them, they will say "Oh yes, I know *that* tune." And probably that tune, more or less as they know it, is to them *the* tune of the song. If they hear it sung differently, as may be the case, they are as likely to protest as to ignore or even not notice the difference. Afterward, in their recognition or singing of it, they are as likely as not to incorporate some of the differences. If they do, they are as likely to be aware as to be entirely unconscious of having done so. But if they admit the difference yet grant that both singings are of *that* tune, they have taken the first step toward the study of the ballad tune. They have acknowledged that there are enough resemblances between the two to allow both to be called by the same name. Observe, however, that this sameness refers not to any one thing but to a notion regarding two separate things—A's singing and B's singing. This notion is a third thing, namely, a class of things to which both belong, which is to say, *what* is sung as distinguishable from the singing of it.

Suppose, then, one hears three, four, or more separate singings of *that* tune, sometimes with different titles or words or both by as many different singers. The name finally adopted for the lot will be found to cover an increasing number of differences. Probably each singer has sung the tune in his individual way; most, perhaps, slightly differently with each singing. The more separate singings one has heard, the more

*As sung in traditional singing styles in the United States and recorded by field collectors who deposited their discs and tapes in the Archive of American Folk Song in the Library of Congress, Washington, D.C. before July 1940. (To accompany AAFS L54 transcription)

differences may be noted among both words and tunes. These may be so marked that one may discover that more than one tune has been used to deliver almost identical texts and that almost identical tunes have been used to deliver the words of entirely different songs—children's songs, political songs, and even hymns.

Folklorists agree that printing has tended to stabilize variation of the words of folk songs, although at the same time it tends to vary them by elimination or addition of detail and by correction and improvement to suit the tastes of various classes of buyers of printed materials. Thus, new variants become current and in turn become varied by faulty or capricious memory and by fresh invention. But the printing of tunes has been, by comparison, rare. Few people can read notes.

It is much easier to identify a set of words than a set of notes as "belonging to" a certain ballad. Incidents and plot, names of persons, places, and events can be collated accurately enough to permit a consensus among both students and laymen that two separate sets of words are enough alike to be grouped together along with others sufficiently similar to them as a unit. It is then easy to select a name for the lot. And the name is a word or group of words, often as not selected from the words of the song. We name things in the art of speech. We do not, indeed, cannot distinguish, designate, much less *name* in the art of music. Consequently, there is, at present, no consensus among students of tunes such as that among students of words of ballads. There is no recognized musical or musicological way of naming a tune except by the title of whatever text or group of texts with which one thinks it is most commonly associated. The question whether any of these associations of words, tunes, and titles has any other validity than mere convenience becomes, therefore, a prime consideration of their study.

The works of Bayard[1] and Bronson[2] point to a negative answer to the question. Both, though working separately and independently, have classified hundreds of ballad tunes, regardless of their associations with particular texts, in enormous "tune families," of which there would seem to be comparatively few in the total repertory of British-American folk song.

The aggregate tunes of any one of the more widely sung ballads seems to give a positive answer to the question. Granted that we accept, as do Bayard and Bronson, the concept of "what is the tune"—that is, a skeleton notation—the resemblances among the majority of the singings of any one ballad are impressive. See, for examples, "Lady Isabel and the Elf Knight" (Child No. 4), "The Two Sisters" (No. 10), "Lord Randal" (No. 12), "Edward" (No. 13), "Young Beichan" (No. 53), "Lord Thomas and Fair Eleanor" (No. 73), "Fair Margaret and Sweet William" (No. 74),

"Lord Lovel" (No. 75), "Little Musgrave and Lady Barnard" (No. 81), "Bonny Barbara Allan" (No. 84). Bronson groups the tunes of each of these ten ballads under the letters, A, B, and C, with occasional recourse to D and E, breaking them down into subgroups Aa, Bb, and so on.[3] The average is two to three versions per ballad. "Sports," or unique instances of marked difference from any group are found, but the number is, usually, very low.

The tune-family approach, on one hand, leaves us with the impression that tunes and words are utterly promiscuous in their relationships and that marriages of any permanence between them are illusory. The majority-usage approach, on the other hand, leaves us with the impression that although both spouses are frequently unfaithful to their common-law kind of union, yet it has a permanence of a sort not lightly to be regarded.

Of course, small and even large variations among performances of concert and operatic music occur. But anchored, as all usually are, to a single written text, any variation can be referred to this text for purposes of identification. Thus, the consensus among adepts of the written tradition respecting the identity of individual items can be almost absolute, as is shown in such ensemble performances as symphonic and chamber music or in opera. It is the comparative invariance of the usually single printed or written text that one can see and hold in one's hand which defines the identity of the item.

But with the folk song that is sung in English in the United States the situation is opposite. The lack of any printed or written anchor not only encourages but enforces variance of performance. Thus, it is in the relationships of the resemblances and differences in the singings that the identity attributed to what is sung must be sought. In a nutshell the question is: how much can two singings differ and still be singings of the same tune? Or, conversely, how little can they vary and still be singings of different tunes?

Now, identity is a word—a construct on the art of speech in general, in the English language, in particular. On the one hand, it may refer to an abstract concept on a high, universal level. Its relevance can be sought in many connections other than music. When sought as a tune family, as by Bayard and Bronson, the identity of the ballad tune is a generalization dependent upon the resemblances among skeleton notations of separate singings in terms of a nest of descriptive concepts in accord with which hundreds—even thousands—of tunes are ordered, their relationships defined, their history investigated, and so on. On the other hand, the word may refer to the perception of a very concrete sensory phenomenon, for example, Dock Bogg's singing of "Pretty Polly" as recorded on a Brunswick ten-inch record. Almost any musical ear can identify it on the basis of other Pretty Pollies previously heard, or, for lack of such, distinguish it from Harry Belafonte's singing of "Water Boy." There are enough differences and similarities in the considerable area between singings to invite extensive study.

Ideally, musicologists should be able to step in here and show that short melodies such as ballad tunes could be classified by purely musicological methods and designated by purely formal names quite as arbitrary as Symphony no. 5 or Opus 30, no. 6. Elsewhere,[4] I have shown one possible base upon which such a classificatory and naming procedure might operate. It would, I believe, have to pay equal attention to the twin concepts of tune family and majority usage. The former might provide a counterpart to the Arne-Thompson index of motifs in the words;[5] the latter, a counterpart of the Child canon.[6] Since the preliminary investigation of the tune family has already been competently made and that of majority usage still waits, I shall essay here the latter only, leaving to another occasion outline of a melodic motif index.

To investigate this presentation of the problem of the identity of the ballad tune, it is necessary to select a ballad for which there is available for examination a large number of specimens that are representative of the mainstream of oral transmission as well in the British Isles as in North America. For as far as this kind of material is concerned, the two areas have formed one singing community for more than three centuries, maintained since 1620 by constant westward migration and now, by the eastward migration of the folk music revival movement. The ballad of "Barbara Allen," as it is known in the United States, seems to fulfill the conditions set forth above. Folklorists have frequently attested to the fact of its being the best and most widely known of all the Child ballads on both sides of the Atlantic.

The holdings of the Archive of American Folk Song (AAFS) in the Library of Congress are eminently suited to use for such a purpose. Of the total of seventy-six dubbings made available for the present study, most were recorded at or near the residences of the informants during the years 1933 to 1940 with what must be considered, at this writing, primitive equipment. For the most part, recording was made on aluminum blanks. Collectors were rarely experienced in field collection and few had had special training. Few could make the adjustments and repairs of the machines incident to wear and tear, rough handling, variation of electrical current, and obsolescence. Some of the original discs show blemishes of such basic character that subsequent sound engineering could not modify them without loss of essential features of the singing. In spite of these hazards, some of the soundtracks still

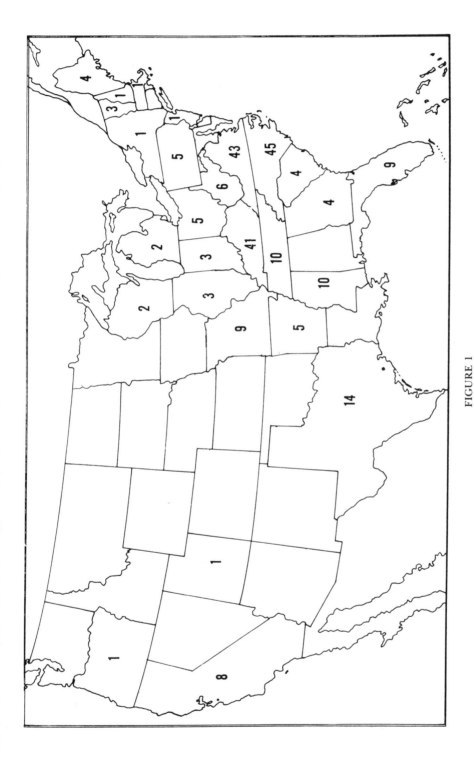

FIGURE 1

Distribution of the "field collection" of published variants of the ballad "Barbara Allen" in the United States as of December 1962: 243 notations, about one-third transcribed from sound recordings. (Commercial and revivalist sources are not included in this roster nor are those of British and Canadian field collection amounting to 93 items as of the same date.)

project a luminous quality through the veil of imperfections. Recordings not only of exceptionally talented but even of ordinary carriers of tradition often possess this quality, though to varying degrees.

It cannot be too strongly emphasized that what is sung and the singing of it are not, musically speaking, two things, but one. Abstraction of the song from its singing is a necessary procedure in talking about music which makes two things out of the original one. This is espcially evident when the song is envisaged as printed words and notes. A singing of the song in a singing style other than that of its own tradition is likely to be a distortion comparable to the translation of the words into a foreign language.

Two sets of complete notations of the whole AAFS collection were made by two transcribers, working separately and independently. Of these, thirty were chosen for (1) pressing on a twelve-inch LP disc (AAFS L54) and (2) publication in skeletal notations in present study (tables 1 and 2). For lack of space and uniformity, no complete notations—that is, of all stanzas of a singing—are included here. Of those selected for pressing, nine (nos. A1, 6, 7, 8, 11 and B1, 13, 17, 19) are given in their entirety as on the original recordings. For the rest, there is space for one or two stanzas only, as illustrative of the pattern or style already presented in the complete singings. Selection was made with reference to musical and musicological criteria alone.

The states represented by place of collection and/or location of the home of the informant (so far as known) are:

Virginia	3	Mississippi	2
North Carolina	4	Florida	2
Kentucky	3 (1 recorded in New York)	Missouri	2
Tennessee	3 (1 recorded in Washington, D.C.)	Arkansas	1
		Texas	4

Indiana	2	
Michigan	1	
Wisconsin	1	(migrant from Kentucky)
California	2	(1 migrant from Oklahoma)

Fifteen of the singers were men; fifteen, women. One recording (B1) was of "a family." This is less representative of the archive's holdings, in which by rough count women outnumber men about four to three.

It is not possible to speak with certainty of the ages of more than about half the total number of singers. For the rest, documentation other than that appearing in the *Checklist of Recorded Songs in the English Language in the Archive of American Folk Song to July, 1940*[7] is lacking. We can be reasonably sure that most, if not all, of the first twenty strips on the disc were recorded from the singing of informants of middle or advanced age and represent variants of what seems to be the older, more archaic singing style, without instrumental accompaniment or noticeably influenced by such accompaniment. The last ten strips were, for the most part, recorded from the singing of younger men and women, some with guitar accompaniment. No banjo-accompanied performance of the ballad was available for dubbing. There are entries for two singings with dulcimer in the *Checklist.* It is not known how widely ballads have been sung with fiddle as on strips A4 and B6. The last two items (B18 and 19) are not, strictly speaking, typical of traditional country singing. Miss Tarwater learned the ballad from an elderly relative who carried the traditional singing style; but being an educated young woman, she reproduced it to a large extent by deliberate cultivation of its excellencies. The result is probably the nearest to what the average urban concertgoer would consider "good singing."

Study of these materials was made in the frame of a roster of more than 200 additional variants of the ballad assembled from printed sources, recordings, and microfilms of hand notations, both British and American, publicly available to students in the United States. No attempt was made to cover private collections. For convenience, a set of transcriptions of all recordings was made in skeletal form to match the notations in printed sources. The whole 300-odd were then transposed so that their stanza finals fell upon G above middle C and the phrases were lined to match the lines of the words. The fact that the recorded tunes revealed far more notes and more tonal and rhythmic subtleties than were found in published skeletal transcriptions will not be considered here in detail.

The material from the southern United States shows, on the whole, more homogeneity than does that from Great Britain or New England, where, among a smaller number of variants, individual variation seems to have been more extensive. The number of defective items from any area is negligible. Some resulted from two successive singings of one half of the tune without rendition of the other. Momentary failure of memory sometimes resulted in isolated successions such as these. A few singers sang the words of the ballad to well-known tunes such as "Won't be Home Till Morning," "Auld Lang Syne," and "Polly Wolly Doodle," or to a tune more commonly associated with another ballad.

The task of putting such a large number of diverse materials into such order that their study can be pursued most conveniently and economically is primarily one of classification. Its first requirement is a set of

TABLE 1

Skeletal Notation Variants A1-B4

TABLE 2

SKELETAL NOTATION VARIANTS B5-B19

criteria in terms of which the materials may be described in the simplest but most precise and comprehensive manner possible; its second, a uniform taxonomy or series of categories or boxes, into which each individual variant may be grouped with others sufficiently like it in a class of variants in a box to be placed, along with other boxes containing classes of variants less resembling it, in a box of versions, boxes of versions in a larger box of classes of versions, eventually, in the boxes of families, families in the context of the repertory of the tradition as a whole, the tradition in its musicological, social, and cultural context, and so on. If this is done shrewdly and with common sense, comparative studies may be engaged in conveniently at any point along the way, not only within the confines of one particular idiom but cross-culturally, in accord with the aims of modern ethnomusicology.

The great majority of American ballads in the English language are cast in a single basic or gross form. It is strophic (stanzaic) in contrast with the older verse of line form still found, among other places, in the epics of southeastern Europe and among the Spanish *romances* (ballads). The words of many, including those of "Barbara Allen," usually written as four lines, the second and fourth rhyming, are twinned in the singing with four melodic phrases, the ends of the second and fourth often, but by no means always, comprising melodic patterns that might be called "musical rhymes," that is, identical or closely resembling tonal or rhythmic devices or both. Sometimes the last couplet or just the last line is repeated. This is less common in southeastern than in northeastern United States and in Nova Scotia, England, Scotland, and Ireland. The words of the ballad are invariably arranged in iambic ($\cup -$, short long; or $\cup$ / weak strong) poetic feet. The number of syllables in the lines conforms to the general pattern 8-7-8-7. As in other forms of English poetry, additional syllables may be crowded into the two-syllable foot. Two or more shorts often fill the place of one long; several shorts may occur in the place of one short. The accented syllable may not be long in duration but short, sometimes very short. Long syllables are not always accented. The normal accent pattern is 4-3-4-3. In reading the stanza, there is usually a pause after the end of the second line and a longer one after the fourth, separating the stanza from its successor. This combination of rhyme and short lines plus pauses tends to give the feeling of a basic couplet 8-8.

Normally, each syllable in the singing is accommodated by a note. We may refer to the union of the two arts upon this level as the "sung syllable."[8] The sung syllable must be regarded as an elastic concept. Its implications now become our immediate concern.

The actual sound of the sung syllable can be described most economically and conveniently in terms of the variance and nonvariance of the six essential functions or resources of the singing voice. These are essential because without any one of them there can be no tune, while with them all, there can be, namely:

tonal functions	*rhythmic functions*
pitch	tempo
loudness	proportion
tonal density	rhythmic density
(tone quality)	

Pitch, loudness, tempo, and proportion are simple functions; they may vary in only two ways or not vary. By varying (variance) is meant that a melody may rise or fall in pitch, may become louder or softer, its tempo (speed of beat) may become faster or slower, and the beats may be grouped in patterns, regular or irregular, of long, short, and so on. By not varying (nonvariance) is meant that the function, once it is set at the beginning, is maintained fairly steadily. The set and the variance of the simple functions can be measured in cycles per second, decibels, seconds, and relative durations in terms of some given unit.

Tonal density (timbre, quality, hardness or softness of sound) and rhythmic density (thickness or thinness of music events) are each compounds of two simple functions. The sound that we call a "note" is actually a complex of many simultaneously sounding pitches—most of them higher than the pitch we hear as the note—of varying degrees of loudness, the loudest among them being perceived by us as the note. Keen and practiced ears can hear some, but not all of them. The total effect is referred to as tone quality or timbre. Viewed in these terms, this function is one of each single note or fundamental pitch that we perceive in a song. There is a slightly different tone quality to each of the notes, and the singer has only limited control of the variance of the function as far as separate notes are concerned. The singer trained in the *bel canto* of Italian opera or in the tradition of the German *Lied* tries to produce a particular desired quality in the stream of sound rather than in each separate note (barring, of course, exceptional notes to which they wish to give special effect). The British-American folksinger, however, seems to give no special thought to quality of sound, but sings in as "natural" a voice as that in which he talks. Consequently, the singing voice varies greatly according to sex, age, and an infinite number of psychological and physiological factors. The lack of any preconception of what it ought to be gives to the quality of the traditional singer's singing a clearly recognizable character that can be instantly recognized by other carriers and connoisseurs of the tradition.

The case of accentuation in this tradition of ballad singing is similar, except that what matters is not the number of simultaneous pitches and loudnesses that are heard at once but the number of consecutive pitches and loudnesses that are heard in the course of a tune. It has been again and again demonstrated that a succession of exactly even or equally strong, loud, stressed, emphasized (or whatever) beats can neither be delivered nor felt. Thus, just as we hear a predominant fundamental or note, in the complex of simultaneous sounds in a tune, so it is that we hear a rhythmic pattern. This pattern depends to varying extents upon the relative pitch and loudness of the "notes" but even more upon the varying rates, of tempo beat and durations of the pitches—the rhythmic densities.

No scales of measurement of the compound functions have as yet been proposed. Their set and variance can be estimated upon the basis of the simple functions of which they are compounded, but their variance in kind is infinite.

In every tradition of song, each of the six functions or resources is exploited in a manner characteristic of that tradition. The carriers of the tradition, as well as knowledgeable students, can perceive immediately whether a song is or is not sung in the traditional singing style. In the music of the Occident, the tonal functions are organized quite independently of one another. That of pitch is the most highly organized. Continual variance is the rule. But singers and instrumentalists are conscious that they employ a limited number of principal pitches in a melody such as a ballad tune and that there is a hierarchy among these in which one serves as the "key note," known to students as the "final," "tonic," or "tonal center," around which the others move in diverse relationships that are fixed in the tradition and with respect to which their relationships among themselves are defined. Thus, the continual variance upon a lower level is ordered with respect to a nonvariance upon a higher. A singer "keeps the pitch" or "sings in the key."

Loudness is comparatively unorganized. It is customarily regarded as a characteristic of the way a whole piece or substantial part of it is performed. The sounding of a certain individual note slightly louder than its neighbors is usually referred to as accent. Even by the elite, the professional or fine art musician, loudness is not articulated beyond the somewhat vague steps of *pp, p, mp, mf, f, ff,* and so on. None of these has any significance in traditional ballad singing. Thus, while continual variance in loudness is the rule in twentieth-century concert music (and in the singing of folk songs by professional or professionally influenced performers), in the folk art the tendency is to invariance.

Although there is no musical measurement of tone quality and no notation for it, certain standards and rough classifications are in use in the fine and popular idioms, where, in addition, wide variance—some of it controlled, some random—is the rule. In folk song, there seems to be no particular attention paid to tone quality. To the extent that hymn singing, concert, and the more elaborate forms of popular music have influenced folk singers, there is often an intent to produce a "pleasing," "refined," or "good" tone quality. But for the most part, the singer sings with his "natural" voice and does not give special attention to platform exhibitionism.

While the tonal functions operate more or less independently of one another, the rhythmic functions, although susceptible to analysis as separate items, are so mutually interdependent that the tendency in all idioms is to regard them simply as one thing—"the rhythm." As in the tonal, so in the rhythmic functions there is a hierarchy. Both singers and instrumentalists tend to present them in "one package," to which all three contribute. The role of axis or center lies, then, partly in the tempo beat, partly in the proportional pattern, and partly in the accent. Change in any of them tends to change "the rhythm."

The tempo beat, often referred to as "pulse," tends to center in the range of the heartbeat, step, foot, or hand movement, roughly 40-200 per minute. In British-American folk song, the range may perhaps be set more narrowly—60-180. In this tradition, proportion is usually in two's and three's; that is, two or three tempo beats are likely to be grouped together by an accent either of the words, the tune, or both. When the tempo beat dominates, the rate of movement tends to be in the 120-180 range; when proportion dominates, half those values—60-100. Domination is by accentuation. We have, thus, three kinds or levels of accent: (1) of tempo beat, where each sung syllable is rendered in approximately equal strength; (2) proportional or metrical, where the first beats of groups of two's and three's are stronger; (3) "agogic" or rhythmic. Any one may dominate the others; but in theory, at least, the first gives way to the second and the second to the third. Accent, then, is not only a rather complicated function in a strictly music-technical sense, but is also largely a matter of individual psychological disposition, molded by the sociocultural context in which the singer is brought up and lives. Loudness of attack is only one way in which accent can be produced and is not by any means necessary. Tempo accent, or pulse, can be felt on a rest. Long notes, especially if integral parts of a proportional pattern, tend to receive, or to give, accentuation. Anticipation and delay of attack and a change of tone quality can produce accent. Ornamentation of a pitch level by a slide, by overshooting or undershooting of a skip, or by quick little accessory notes, and especially the prosodic accent, felt through the musical fabric, can produce it.

The potentials of the singing voice are about equal with respect to three different attitudes toward the song and the singing of it in the sociocultural context in which the tradition is current. They can best be understood in reference to the management of the six melodic functions or resources throughout the procession of sound from the beginning to the end. They are:

1. A firm initial broaching of the essential stuff of the tune, tapering off toward the end—a thetic, trochaic, strong-weak, tense-detense kind of delivery. It is typical of much Amerindian singing.
2. A gradual picking up of the tune, as if directing it toward a pre-conceived end—an anacrustic, iambic, weak-strong, detense-tense kind of delivery. It is typical of European-style concert music.
3. Establishment of an initial level and maintenance of it through-out—spondaic, firm between the alternatives of weak and strong, balanced between the alternatives of tension and detension, typical of plainsong.

Among the most admired carriers of the tradition of British-American ballad singing, the configuration of the basic melodic functions is effected as in 3 above, that is, the level of each is set at the beginning and none is varied intentionally, excepting only that of pitch (but pitch within the higher level of mode and key conforms to the rule). The degree of loudness and the characteristic tone quality with which the singing begins is maintained throughout except when incidentally or involuntarily compelled by high or low notes; and the less variance, the better. The rhythmic level is set at the beginning by a steady beat and a clear proportional pattern that are adhered to, within the freedom characteristic of the tradition, throughout the rendition. Some singers adhere to a uniform proportional and accentual pattern; others, to an irregular one. The loudness and tone quality remain steady, then, except under compulsion of physiological factors in the vocal mechanism, and are never varied on account of any word or detail of content or to produce a special effect upon listeners.

It is difficult for urban Occidentals to recognize the fact that although variance may be the spice of life, invariance may be the meat. Tough meat, sometimes, to be sure. But the spice is not worth much without the meat. Rather, it is through the teaming together of the variances of some and nonvariances of others of the six basic melodic functions that the diverse balances characteristic of each tradition are achieved. Indeed, the prediction might be ventured that if only its characteristic balances be maintained,[9] the tradition of British-American folk song might, in spite of more pessimistic views, successfully survive not only the assaults upon it by social and cultural change, technology, and commercialism, but also the defenses of it by the mass folk music revival movement.

The attitude, then, typical of the most admired traditional singer toward the song, tends to the serene and detached, however much force or gentleness may impel the line from its beginning to its end. Singing seems to be a natural thing for one to occupy himself with if he wishes. It requires of him no special preparation, effort, or pretense of an organized sort. Difficulty or ease in execution seems not to be a factor. It is not a vehicle for pathos but seems to meet accepted requirements of an ethos. In spite of the often romantic words, an almost classic reserve is maintained. There is no assumption by the singer of a position above or apart from the tune or text, but, rather, an implicit recognition that "life is that way." He keeps a straight face and unchanging posture, without attempting to win an audience by smiles or gestures. Yet there is nothing "deadpan" about the singing. There is usually a difference between singing to oneself and to another person or persons. Comparatively few singers, I understand, are unaffected by the presence of a microphone.

Within the single gross form in which the singing of the ballad "Barbara Allen" is cast, it is convenient and economical to distinguish two principal tune types or, as further studies may show, two among a number of versions of what may be regarded as a single tune family, and to divide each of these tune types or versions into classes of variants a, b, c, and x upon the basis of resemblances and differences in tonal and rhythmic configuration (see table 3).

In the use of conventional notation to illustrate these resemblances and differences, we must remember that this notation was developed for the purposes of composition and performance in the tradition of the professional, "high," elegant, elite, or fine art of Occidental music, not for performance of the folk art. There are, of course, enough resemblances between the two idioms to render the notation useful in the study of folk song; but it is deceptive because it can represent only these, not the differences between the idioms. And there are substantial differences. Furthermore, singers vary with respect to the degrees of contact they have had with the idioms of popular and fine art, and this shows in their employment of each of the six melodic functions.

Rhythmic modality, though long abandoned in the theory and practice of the fine and popular arts, is still significant in the analysis of folk song. This is not the place to resume the transformation of the tight medieval

TABLE 3

theory of six rhythmic modes based upon the theory of Greek prosody, in which relative length in "perfect" (triple) meter was the sole criterion. Suffice it to say that in the more highly diversified and experimental idioms of both poetry and music of the Western world, duration (quantity) and accent (quality) function together, with tempo beat, in such complicated interweaving that no one has yet been able to set up any general theory comprehending the rhythmic practice of either art—much less, their association in song—which has been able to achieve a wide consensus of experts.[10] Fortunately, the singing of the American ballad in the English language is simple enough to warrant classification of the rhythmic norms of both proportion and accent with some plausibility, granted, of course, that the steady tempo beat can be determined.

In terms of proportion, variant classes Ia, Ib, and Ic can be seen to be distinguished, among other ways, by even duration; classes IIa, IIb, and IIc, by uneven, but in a patterned unevenness. (The random, un-patterned, long notes in strips A1, A11, and B4, for examples, are not considered to alter the basic even pattern.) Class Ix shows the tonal con-figuration of Version I with the uneven proportion of Version II; class IIx the tonal configuration of Version II with the even proportion of Version I. Curiously enough, neither of these two common music-proportional patterns approximates the spoken patterns. A reading of a stanza in the manner of either (a) or (b) in example 1 would be in poor taste. Pattern (c), a variant of Version I, is rarely found in the United States, though more often in England, and resembles much more closely the rhythm of speech. And the latter would never show strict regularity, but would vary the pattern with doublets, both even (♩ ♩) and uneven (♩. ♪ and ♪ ♩.). A competent reader of the words alone would never conceive these divisions of these divisions of the foot as countable in terms of an arithmetic unit as musicians count the beats and divisions of beats in measures. Some singers approximate the spoken patterns of delivery, but sporadically. Observe, especially, the more detailed nota-tion of the first stanza of Mrs. McCord's singing (A6) where the orna-mentation of the sung syllables appears as a doublet, triplet, or quadrup-let, but rarely with much more than near accuracy. (see table 1).

The singer may take a breath after each phrase, or if the tempo is lively or the lungs capacious, only after the second and fourth phrases, as in variant B10 (Ford), in which case the quatrain verges still more closely upon the couplet. Incidentally, the word "Barbara" is invariably short-ened to "Barbra," "Barbry," "Bobby," or some such.

The three most common musical proportions associated with the poetic meter of our ballad are shown in example 1. The two former,

EXAMPLE 1

(a) and (b), were not among the six accepted by medieval rhythmic theory. The last, (c), conforms to rhythmic mode II. Neither of the former has been recognized as forming a poetic meter by classic prosodic theory.[11] Both the even (phrrhic, ᴗᴗ, or spondee, --, depending upon the speed of delivery when sung) and the uneven (fourth paeon, ᴗ ᴗ ᴗ-) were, however, recognized as prosodic feet that could be introduced occasionally in any accepted poetic metrical sequence as a variation of the overall poetic rhythm. In the singing of this and other ballads of similar gross form, the undeniably iambic rhythm of the words is, then, customarily sung, in the great majority of cases, to two very different musical meters, the prosodic counterparts of which are considered illegitimate for poetic use. The result is a rhythmic counterpoint between text and tune. The musical rhythm dominates most of the singings. But the poetical is always evident and serves a basic function in the inner organization of tonal and formal resources.

In the conventional theory, notation, and practice of the elite and popular idioms of European music for the last three centuries or so, musical meter has not been reckoned in terms of long and short (quantity) but as the grouping of even tempo beats in measures, that is, between bars. Among these beats a hierarchy of accents, strong and weak, had inevitably to be found, simply because a chain of equally accented or equally unaccented notes could be sustained only for a short time and with special effort. Random or chance accentuation was considered bad taste, unworthy of the professionally trained musician. But in spite of the dominance of relative accentuation (strong, weak) over relative duration (long, short), the latter has remained an important factor both in English poetic practice and in European music in general, and often dominates the former. Musical meter, then, as primarily a mere measurement of the number of tempo beats in a measure, came to imply an accentual hierarchy within it, strictly bound to the counts in the measure, the first being given precedence over the others regardless whether there was a sound to deliver it, subordinate beats, if any, being given secondary or less emphasis according to the theoretical or affective disposition of the performer.

This conception of musical meter seems not to be a necessary feature of the most admired ballad singing. It often intrudes and is evident, as in variant B3 (Harmon) and others on table 1. Hymn-singing encourages and instrumental accompaniment compels it. But judgment of its presence or absence—like that of "in tune-ness"— is largely subjective and may be "read into" the notation of a singing where it does not belong, as for example, wherever the tempo beat is very strongly marked. Variant B13 (Beeker) is a case in point. Each syllable is "punched out" with such nearly equal emphasis that some students might claim it should be notated with a metrical signature of $\frac{1}{4}$. This can easily be disproved by counting it in a triple meter. If in any—as surely it seems to be—it must be in a duple meter; but whether a simple $\frac{2}{4}$ or compound $\frac{4}{4}$ still remains a question.

Barring, then, likely to be a problem in the notation of any music idiom, poses an especially serious one in that of British-American folk song because conventions such as rule in the fine and popular arts are, more often than not, lacking. Many professional musicians and, probably, most amateurs seem to understand that the first beat of every measure should receive a strong accent, which is to say: it should be sung louder than other beats. In some written music, this is intended by the writer. But competent musicians and musicologists seem to be generally agreed that in any correctly written notation of measured music the metrical accent, like the tempo pulse (of which it is an elaboration), though always felt, must be surpassed in strength by phrase (agogic) accent. There are no grounds of adducing such considerations in the notation (least of all, in the skeletal notation) of British-American folk song. Prepared for, and for the most part read by, people of modest music literacy, no such hierarchy of accentual complexity as that briefly outlined above can be expected to be heeded, even if a resort to it could be justified. This is the more nearly true because it has become increasingly conventional to bar music by melodic pattern rather than by either relative duration or relative accentuation, both of which, together with the pitch function, are factors in the formation of conceptions of melodic pattern. These conceptions, the formation of which is sometimes more subjective than objective, are less atomic, more extended in nature and have led to choices of compound metrical signatures such as $\frac{4}{4}, \frac{5}{4}, \frac{6}{4}, \frac{6}{8}, \frac{9}{8}, \frac{12}{8}, \frac{3}{2}$, and so on. Thus, such singings as A2 and A4 (Graham, Bryant, Gevedon) could be written in accord with conventional usage in several different ways, three of which are shown in example 2.

EXAMPLE 2

But if, as seems likely, most readers are going to place strong accents on first beats, distortion of the singing style and, consequently, of the song will result.

Version II and Version I—when in the uneven proportion of Version II (class Ix)—permit several different fittings of the notes given to sung syllables within the various metrical signatures chosen by transcribers. Most often, these are $\frac{3}{2}$ or $\frac{3}{4}$. Sharp sometimes used the one; sometimes the other. It is not clear why he did so. Howard Brockway,[12] a trained professional musician, used $\frac{2}{4}$ (see example 3), which might have been

EXAMPLE 3

the most accurate (as it might also be for example A11). But many people have difficulty reading an apparently triple-metered tune in a duple meter, especially if many ties cross bar lines. Transcribers (Sharp, among them) have sometimes begun their notation as at (a) in example 4 and

EXAMPLE 4

sometimes as at (b). Perhaps, though one cannot be sure, an accentual difference is indicated. In the first of these cases, the triple meter can usually be maintained without change. But in the second, it is usually necessary to provide a duple signature for each of two measures, one in the second, the other in the fourth phrase, as shown in example 5.

EXAMPLE 5

It is on account of difficulties such as these that ethnomusicologists— and many editors of pre-1600 European composed music—often dispense entirely with the bar and the modern metrical signature. Some students compromise by dotting some or all bar lines; others may use the

Mensurstrich, or a portion only of a bar. At the bottom of this unsettled state of affairs is a real confusion of the pulse, step, or beat of tempo, and the accent of metered measures, with the accent required by melodic pattern, phrasing, and by unusual features such as high notes, long notes, dissonant notes, notes rendering certain words, and many other such exceptional and often irregular items. But the main confusion is, as said above, between the sound and the procession of that sound marked by the tempo beat which, once the sound as established it, is understood to "be there" whether or not there is a sound to mark it, as, for example, upon a rest. One can test this by holding an electric metronome in one hand and setting the dial with the other to the initial tempo beat. After running through a stanza of even such flexible renderings as those of Mr. Marlor (A1) and Mrs. Jackson (A11), one should be able to keep the instrument in time with the singer, even through the rests and in the occasional rubato passages. (This is most easily done at half-speed.)

A sung syllable may be divided—stuffed, as it were—with interpolated syllables. Thus, the usual "for love of" often becomes—"For the love of." The pitch rendering the interpolated "the" may be the same as that of the preceding or succeeding syllable, a passing note (if a skip is being made), or other. Its duration may be halved or quartered or run in uneven division as in A6.

A sung syllable may be prolonged randomly without alterations of the basic modal pattern and is almost invariably effected in strict accord with the tempo beat. Often, the prolonged syllable is not a prosodically long, strong, or stressed one, as in the first stanza of variant A1 (Marlor) where the last syllables of "remember" and "William" (in the repetition of the last line) are so treated. The rests (pauses) after the second and fourth lines of the quatrain are also often prolonged. Naturally, both of these practices result in distortion of the poetic meter and complicate any preconceptions of musical meter "read into" the singing of the ballad by concert-music bias. Thus, three beats are often given where the academic mind expects two, or four, where it expects three.

Several sung syllables, however, may be diminished so as to pack them into a single, even a weak beat. This is often done in the anacrusis (up-beat) of lines, as in the first stanza of B17 (Carr), where in place of the normal

$$\overset{\smile}{\text{It}}\ \overset{\prime}{\text{was}}\ \overset{\smile}{\text{all}}\ \overset{\smile}{\text{in}}\ \overset{\smile}{\text{the}}\ \overset{\prime}{\text{month}}\ \overset{\smile}{\text{of}}\ \overset{\prime}{\text{May}}$$

the singing is

$$\overset{\smile}{\text{'Twas}}\ \overset{\smile}{\text{a-}}\overset{\smile}{\text{bout}}\ \overset{\smile}{\text{in}}\ \overset{\smile}{\text{the}}\ \overset{\prime}{\text{mid'}}\overset{\smile}{\text{dle}}\ \overset{\smile}{\text{of}}\overset{\smile}{\text{the}}\ \overset{\smile}{\text{month}}\ \overset{\smile}{\text{of}}\ \overset{\prime}{\text{May}}$$

The stresses that should have fallen upon the second syllable of "about" and upon "month" are all but lost. Similarly, the pauses after the second and fourth lines and the long notes characteristic of Version II may be shortened, often running counter to preconceived notions of meter by taking two beats where three are expected, or three, where four are expected.

The accenting of prosodically short syllables is as common in the sung as in the spoken language. But the prolongation of them, impossible in many cases without phonetic and phonemic changes in the latter, is common in the former. See again, in variant B17, the singing of the first syllable of "middle" as "mere-" or "mear-."

In variant A11 (Jackson), the singer employs all these practices, with a resulting distortion of the poetic meter that is extreme even in her branch of the tradition. With a fairly normal text-syllable layout of 8-8-9-8, the stress pattern of her first stanza comes close to 2-2-4-2, instead of the normal 4-3-4-3, as

> ᵕ   ᵕ   ᵕ ∕ ᵕ   ᵕ   ᵕ   ∕
> It was all in the month of May
>
> ᵕ   ᵕ   ᵕ   ᵕ   ∕ ᵕ ⌐ᵕ˙ ᵕ⌐
> And the buds they was a-swel-ling
>
> ᵕ   ᵕ ᵕ   ∕ ∕ ᵕ ᵕ ᵕ   ∕
> Sweet Wil-lie died with a bro-ken heart
>
> ᵕ   ᵕ   ᵕ   ᵕ   ∕   ᵕ ⌐ᵕ ᵕ⌐
> For the love of Bar-bra Al-len

In some of the best singing (i.e., in what is recognized by carriers of the tradition and by connoisseurs as most representaive of the main stream of the tradition), the sung syllable is not always articulated as a proper note in as definitive a manner as is traditional in the fine and popular arts. Attacks are often—in some instances, usually—made by an ascending slide, even in a descending passage. Descending slides are not so common. Detection of articulated (passing) notes in slides is often possible. Even skeletal transcriptions must show some of them. It must be borne in mind, however, that such notations serve limited ends: (1) for quick scansion; (2) for classificatory and lexicographical convenience; (3) for typological study. For in these, only the generalities of the singer appear. As Fox-Strangeways put it, only the "substantive notes" are shown. To the extent to which we wish to probe more deeply into the particular musical event and to represent more thoroughly the nature of the music-communicatory substance, more notes and symbols must be added and pitches and proportional values more accurately measured. The more detailed such a notation is made, the less readily legible it becomes, even to the expert. Recourse may be had to modern electronic music-writing devices. Sometimes these support subjective judgments, but sometimes they run surprisingly counter to them. Such is the case with the first strong accent in the line quoted above from Mrs. Jackson's singing (A11). The fourth syllable, "in," of the initial line "It was all in the month of May," may be seen to be sung more softly than either the preceding or succeeding sung syllable. (A full graph of this extra-ordinarily free and admirably traditional singing is shown in table 4. It was made by the Model B "melograph" in the Institute of Ethno-musicology of the University of California, Los Angeles. The upper tracing shows the pitch line of the melody; the lower, the loudness. The dots on the bottom line of each frame show the lapse of time in seconds to be 25 mm. on the chart. The heavy vertical lines indicate possible metrical divisions enabling note readers to keep their place, but not with any implication that the singer necessarily made such divisions. To permit least reduction in print, the rests at the ends of phrases have been cut. These are indicated in the transcription in table 1).

If we are to believe that the tempos of the recordings are not very far from the tempos taken by the informants, they vary by nearly 350 percent. Mrs. Griffin (B9), an elderly singer with a large repertory, but obviously very nervous for she slowed down considerably in the course of her singing, ran through the first stanza in 11 seconds; Mrs. McCord (A6), in 38. Mr. Carr (B17) increased the speed of his delivery from nineteen to fouteen seconds for the stanza.

Perception of the speed of the tempo beat of these singings should not be difficult for one even slightly familiar with the tradition; and he should be able to mark it with foot or hand in a musically satisfactory manner corresponding to the flow of sung syllables of the ballad. For the changes of pitch and the duration of notes and rests conform, with rare exceptions, to a steady, undifferentiated, recurrent pulse or beat. It is not a clock beat. There is, as in most good concert singing, an ever-present rubato. There is therefore a continual interplay between the tempo beat and the flow of sung syllables. Sometimes the syllables seem to be compelled by the beat and sometimes the beat seems to yield to their exigencies.

There are three principal ways of expressing the speed of beat in written form. First, and least accurate, is the commercial metronome: the pendulum type (Maelzel) and the electric. The former operates only upon a set scale. The latter is more versatile and can be set at any number of beats per minute from forty to two hundred or so. But its calibration is usually not dependable and the amount of trial and error required to arrive at a result satisfactory at more than one session is sometimes frustrating. The second method is to time the stanza with a stopwatch and divide it by the number of beats—in this case, 69, as indicated in the notation in table 1 by quarter-notes and quarter-rests. By dividing the number of seconds in a minute by this product one obtains a more accurate metronome figure. The third method consists of recourse to a laboratory machine, or to a prototype of one such as the Model B melograph mentioned above. On a complete chart of the four frames shown in table 4, the length of the tune line is 668 mm., or 26.72 seconds marked in 25ths of a second. Division of the former by the number of beats gives a length of 9.681 mm. to a beat; of the latter, .3872 seconds. These, divided into 1500 and 60, respectively yield 154.54 and 154.95 for the metronomic speed of beat, which, for practical purposes can be regarded as 155, and accepted as supporting or correcting results obtained by the first two methods of expressing musical time in terms of general time. The musical validity of this figure can be tested in two ways: (1) it may be set as a medial point on the electric metronome and raised or lowered to follow the rubato quite closely and to form some notion of the extent above and below this point; or (2) it may be held unchanged throughout and the flexibility of the melodic line noted. In a thorough study, both should be used for each stanza and for the whole song.

The variance in number of beats for first stanzas of strips on the record is 32-45 for Version I and class IIx; 44-70, for Version II and class Ibx. Variants A11 and B4 are highest, with 69 and 68, respectively. The beats are unevenly distributed among the phrases. In only half the thirty are first and third phrases longer than second and fourth, reflecting, thus, the prosodic layout. Not one of the thirty could be given a metrical signature other than $\frac{1}{4}$ without suppression or addition of rests, if not during the singing of stanzas at least between them. Only two pairs of variants agree in the number of beats for the four phrases shown in the notations in tables 1-2: A7 and A9 (12-11-12-10) and B12 and B13 (8-8-8-7). Besides these four, there are seven others with only two different phrase lengths, while there are fifteen with three, and six in which all four are of different lengths, among these being A11, with 18-17-19-15 (=69). In table 4, I have marked bar lines for possible division into metrically countable measures; and it will be observed that no two successive measures carry the same metrical signature. The beat of nearly $\quad$ =155, or 9.7 mm., appears as a row of small dots under the words. It may be observed that Mrs. Jackson had a tendency to anticipate the beginnings of phrases and important words.

The absence of eighth syllables at the ends of the second and fourth lines is dealt with in two different ways. On the one hand, the spoken

TABLE 4

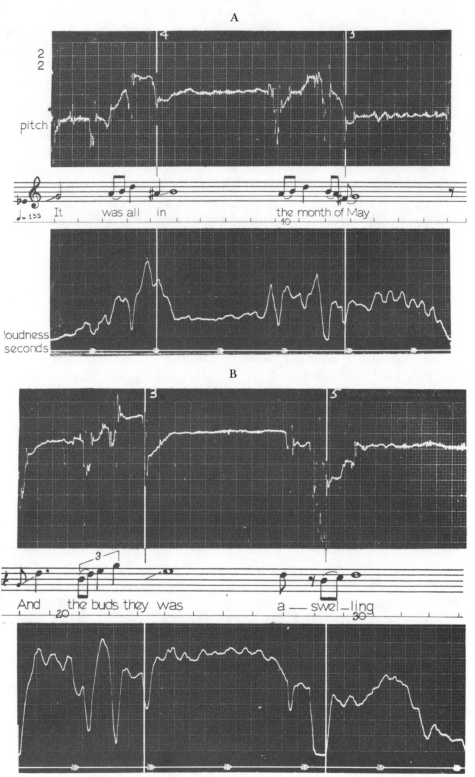

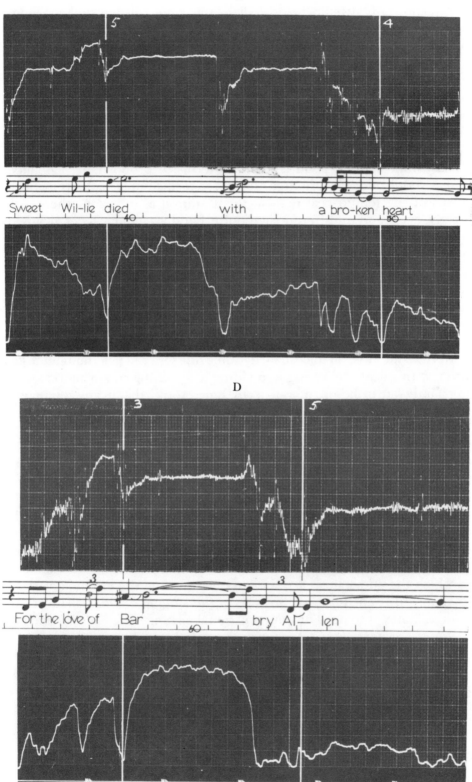

C

D

contractions of "dwelling" and "Allen" into one crowded spoken "long" are disregarded, as at (a) in example 1, and are spread over two or more beats, each of the two constituting separate sung syllables: long-long or long-short. This is typical of our Version I, in which the second note of each pair tends to be on the same pitch as the first. On the other hand, the spoken contraction is accepted, as at (b) in example 1, and is given what is sometimes called a "Scotch snap" on two different pitches, short-short or short-long. This is typical of Version II.

Classification of the versions and variants of tunes for "Barbara Allen" by rhythmic configuration is, then, in terms of proportional modality. But it should not be forgotten that these terms imply measurement in terms of the tempo beat that, in this tradition as in many others, is a steady, even, and undifferentiated pulse, hand, or foot beat, not grouped in uniform metrical patterns, but monometric. Each beat is heavily and uniformly accented by some singers; by others, scarcely at all. But it is always present. As in good concert singing, slight rubato is the rule, medial often met with and maximal, though common with some singers, not common with most. The axis or centricity of the mode, therefore, is on the lowest level the tempo beat, with whatever degree of accentuation the singer customarily gives it; on a higher level, it is its own recurring pattern. And thus, all the tonal-rhythmic units we call *notes* (and all rests) refer to this beat, delivering it, dividing it, spanning two or more, arriving a little late or before it, as to a rhythmic "tonic" that in any competent singing of a melody is alternately affirmed, moved away from and back toward as a center.

Classification by tonal configuration must be entirely in terms of pitch, regardless of loudness and tone quality. The subtle interplay among the three rhythmic functions has a counterpart, however, in an interplay among the pitch factors themselves and upon a far more highly elaborated series of four levels: the smallest melodic unit (usually only three or four notes), the phrase, the double phrases, the single tune setting a quatrain. Development beyond this point, by refrains, repetitions of lines or fragments of them, and alternate stanza combinations in which the odd stanzas are sung to one tune and the even to a variant or quite different tune, are so rare in the singing of this ballad in the United States as to need only an occasional passing notice here. Principal diagnostic criteria are: (1) intonation, including vibrato; (2) total contour; (3) phrase contour; (4) phrase levels; (5) tonal axis or center; (6) tonal mode; (7) prosodically and/or music-metrically accented notes; (8) phrase patterns; (9) phrase endings; (10) "trademark" formulas, such as the above mentioned Scotch snap; (11) cadential or beginning formulas.

Most of these require too much technical analysis for use here. Suffice it to say:

1. Intonation, in the tradition of British-American folk song, differs in some respects from that of the concert stage. No precise or comprehensive tono-metrical measurements have, to my knowledge, been made. Such as are at hand, although they encourage us to expect that this criterion could be of first-rate classificatory value, do not warrant use to that end at present. The same is true of vibrato studies. In my experience and in that of such students as I have been able to question, singing in or out of tune is not, ordinarily, mentioned among carriers of the traditional singing style. (One may observe, however, that in the four frames of table 4, Mrs. Jackson maintains her pitch very closely in all long notes except G. This is set at the very beginning and returned to at the end, but is raised more than a quarter-tone at the end of Phrase I and lowered by as much at the end of Phrase III. Whether there is artistic significance in this I cannot say.)

A similar unevenness is found in the vibrato. The word "May," for example, shows clear twinning of frequency (pitch) and amplitude (loudness) vibratos of about 6½ per second, considered a good rate in nineteenth-century "good" singing. But there is a heavy secondary frequency vibrato of about 45 per second, outlawed by every canon of concert usage simply as bad tone quality but typical of at least one strand of the American tradition of ballad-singing. The variance of pitch of the vibrato is slight, however, and not more than a quarter-tone above or below the perceived fundamental, narrow by concert standards of the past century. But the words "was," "died," and "with," all accented, long and high for this singer, are sung with no apparent primary vibrato and a very narrow secondary. On the words "heart," "For the love of," and "Barbry Allen," there is no apparent primary pitch vibrato and almost no loudness vibrato, but heavy secondary vibrato.

If we are to believe that the frequencies of the recordings are not far from those set by the informants, tessituras or average "lie" of the voices (as the *Harvard Dictionary of Music* puts it) on disc L54 are for the women low. Finals are usually between E-flat above and A-flat below middle C, with the highest notes an octave or less above and the lowest a tone or a fourth below. For the men, finals range somewhat more widely, but with a medial clustering a fouth or a fifth below middle C. The musical ear that is more highly trained to pitch than to rhythm can often place the intonation very accurately; but many people, though no less musically talented or trained, may have to determine it by recourse to pitch pipe, tuning fork, or instrument with fixed tuning. In the notating of pitches below or above the degrees of the equal tempered, twelve-tone, octave scale, based upon $A=440$ c.p.s., a small arrow pointing up or down is coming to be used in preference to plus and minus signs, or other symbols. By placing the record on a dependable variable speed turntable and choosing a rate of revolution that will set the final on some convenient, predetermined pitch, one can check by ear all variances from the standard scale. The small, stemless noteheads to the left of clefs in tables 1 and 2 represent the notes of the standard scale nearest the actual number of cycles per second as measured by a stroboconn—a device widely used for tuning student band and orchestral instruments.

2, 3. Version I shows a tonal overall pitch contour that emphasizes the couplet qualities of the ballad stanza, namely, a high first half and a high to low second. The individual phrases tend to be cast in bow or arc form; an initial ascent is followed by a descent to, or below, the starting point. Version II shows varieties of this form not only in the individual phrases but in the overall contour as well.

4. Typical of Version I is a pattern of phrasal pitch levels: high-high-high to low-low. Typical of Version II is the pattern: medial-high-high to low-low. One peculiar variety is found in the third phrases of both versions: the descent of the arc to the bottom of the ambit or range of the tune. Poladian, following Herzog, describes this as "an ascent by the interval of a second, then a descent with a bend in the opposite direction in the middle of the phrase of many."[13] It may be worth mentioning that in Sharp's Appalachian collection[14] the pattern HHH_{LL} is found often up to No. 45, which ends the Child ballad section, but rarely after that; whereas the pattern $\text{M}^{\text{HH}}_{\text{LL}}$ is common through both volumes. Classification by pitch levels of phrases, is, however, less significant in Version I than in Version II, where it provides the main criterion for distinction between variant classes IIa (variants A7-A11) and IIb (variants B1-B19).

5. Conventionally, tonal centricity is considered to be a factor of mode. Recognition of the tonal axis or center of any variant of Version II can be arrived at easily and correctly on this basis by any twentieth-century amateur. In tables 1 and 2, they all end on *G* above middle *C*. It is felt to be the "Key note." A major triad (chord), with *G* as its root or bass can be found among the components of every variant. Indeed, whole tunes can be—and traditionally often are—harmonized (chorded) with this chord alone, for the melody almost persistently outlines it. The mode is *G*-major.

There is no point in quarreling, here, with such self-evident reasoning in connection with our Version II, except to point out that in some cases it is an oversimplification and therefore obscures the facts (1) that there are in all these tunes other tonal axes or centers; (2) that it is upon the interrelationships of the lot that any one of them depends, in part, for its primacy; (3) but that equally important are the locations, durations, frequencies of occurrence, and accentuation—all four of which are rhythmic functions; and, finally, (4) that although conventional major-minor musical ears will not go far wrong in this matter as far as our Version II is concerned, presupposition of self-evidence cannot be trusted with the variants of Version I. They do not all end on the same component. No triad either major or minor can be formed of their components upon a final *G*. Secondary tonal axes are, in some cases, final. In a few instances, they have more weight and so suggest that the tune is "circular," that is, its last note lacks finality, seeming to lead back into the beginning.

Assuming that we are working only with accepted notations and not with the sound of singing, which interposes preliminary problems touched upon briefly here on other pages, the first step toward use of the factor of tonal centricity in a classification of ballad tunes is to arrange the notes found in each tune in ascending or descending order of pitch. This gives us the scale of the tonal aggregate. The second is to observe which, if any, of the parts of the tune are confined to any particular part of the scale; for if they are so confined, they are likely to define separate tonal centers whose interplay is basic to the art of voice leading and the determination of centers upon higher levels. Such a treatment of our notations of variants A1 to A5 appears in example 6, in which it is clear that the first half of the tunes are confined to the five highest notes and the second, to the six lowest. This is typical of the majority in the roster.

The third step in this analytical process is to measure the durations of the individual notes in the aggregate of tonal materials. This is most

EXAMPLE 6

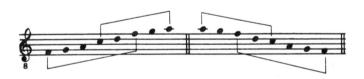

easily done on the base of the shortest note value in the notations. In example 7, using variant A3 (Bryant) as the paradigm, the eighth note is the unit of measure. (This step is undependable in all published notations in our roster, for they are given metrical signatures that do not change or are only seldom changed, so that the individual notes and rests must often have been shortened or lengthened or, in the case of rests, even ignored; we cannot be sure when this has been and has not been done.)

EXAMPLE 7

Several interesting facts are shown here: in the first half *D*s exceed high *G*s, but in the second are exceeded by low *G*s. (On account of the repetition of its last half, the duration of A1 are all higher than those of the other examples of Version Ia.) The high *G* is, nevertheless important because it is high and in both first and second phrases is sounded twice with only an *A* in between. The low *G* is important because it is the last note although it is heard only fleetingly until then. But *D* is clearly the axis of the ambit. It is strongly accented in both the first and second phrases and forms the semi- or mid-cadence.

The conclusion must be: in view of whatever the final significance of the factor of duration may be, Version I is heavily bicentric. There would seem to be some objective support for a subjective notion that there is an impulsive movement upward from the final low *G*, not only to the *D* but to the high *G* and, consequently, a tendency toward circularity. Other criteria may be cited in support of a view that the version as a whole is not to be regarded as out-and-out circular, as may be example 11*f*. Examples 11*g* and *h* can be cited as having completely given way to the circular tendency, with radical transformation of the tune. The low *G* and *F* have been eliminated, the low *A* is merely touched upon and *D* is clearly the tonal axis.

Customarily, the tonal axis is regarded as having two distinct kinds of relationship to the aggregate tonal components of a tune. On the one hand, it may be located in about the middle of the ambit when the tune is referred to as "plagal." Examples are variants A6, B1-B13 and B15-B19. On the other, it may be located at or very near either end, in which case it is referred to as "authentic." Examples are variants A1-A5. Variants A7-A11 are "mixed." These terms are, however, usually used in connection with tonal mode.

6. Tonal mode is usually conceived as a hierarchy of pitches based upon a grouping of the components of the tonal aggregate within an

octave and arranged in ascending order from a tonal center called the "final" or "tonic." The sameness but difference of two pitches an octave apart has perplexed musicologists and confused musicology throughout historical times. Any singer of a variant of our Version I would know that the sounds represented by the high and low *G*s, *F*s and *A*s are different. Probably few, unless especially adept in shape-note hymn-singing, would think of them as "the same" notes. But in the tradition of British-American ballad-singing, two singers can sing the "same" tune an octave apart and believe it is the same tune, which—unlike traditional singers, say, in the Caucasus or the Balkans—they would not do and could not, even as a stunt, a second, fourth, or fifth apart. There is nothing mystical in the matter but simply the fact that in music, as in many other things, a single object of attention can have more than one function in a particular process, as, for example, in the present instance when they are the same but different. The study of melody has viewed melody—especially, sung melody—mainly in terms of modal octave-scales in which every constituent is primarily bound to the final or tonic. This context requires that any sound outside a particular octave must be considered the same as some sound within it. But any singer or student of any song that exceeds an octave knows that *in the context of the singing* the sound outside the octave is not substitutable by a sound within the octave. The conflict—and to some minds, the paradox—lies in the verbalization of the musical event, not in the musical event itself.

The conventional modal scaling of our two versions is shown in example 8. In the gross outlines of skeletal transcriptions, most of the

EXAMPLE 8

variants of "Barbara Allen" in the holdings of the AAFS—as, indeed, in our whole roster—are, like the scales shown in example 8, in pentatonic modes (which is to say, in scales of five degrees in the octave). Where comparison with the actual sound of the singing is possible, as in sound recordings, additional degrees are often disclosed, as are also significant variations among the skeletal or more substantive sounds. The ascription of pentatonism is often, then, of the gross features only.

The number of pentatonic modes in the total musics of the world is probably uncountable. British-American folk song makes use of only one type, namely, that which can be sounded with approximate accuracy by the black keys of the pianoforte, organ, or accordion, without what are semitones in the twelve-tone, equal tempered octave scale. Five different modes can be formed within this aggregate, for any one of the five components can serve as final. Various nomenclatures have been suggested and used, but none has been universally accepted by students.

Two of the most logical and useful have been proposed by Bronson[15] and Kolinski,[16] and are shown above the staff in example 9. The concern of both scholars has been the derivation and the order of the naming of these modes. Both sets of names are based upon the "circle of fifths," in the terms of which many other fundamental musical relationships and processes are customarily explained. The circle of fifths is usually plotted by music theorists upward from *F*, as *F-C-G-D-A-E-B*. Downward from *F*, it runs into flats; above *B*, into sharps, to extents unlimited in either direction except by the practicability of musical or musicological use. The advantage of thinking in terms of the circle of fifths is that any five successive steps in it comprise the components of a traditionally used pentatonic scale in the British-American folk idiom; any six, a hexatonic; and any seven, a heptatonic.

A more precise nomenclature is placed below the staves of example 9, to designate progressions of degrees in a scale in conventional twelve-tone, equal tempered semitones. This provides a universal nomenclature for designation of scales of whatever number of components in whatever system of tuning, in terms of the equal tempered twelve-tone octave scale, now for some seventy years the standard among physicists and musicologists throughout the world. By reading the digits "2" and "3" (and "4" or more, if necessary) as "200," "300" (or more) the designation can be refined to the limits of the Ellis cent system, which is a division of the octave into 1200 equal parts and accommodates the optimal discrimination of the ear to 1/100 of a semitone. In these terms any particular British-American pentatonic scale can be compared with any other scale of whatever tuning of whatever number of degrees per octave.

Students of this particular tradition have found it convenient to remember pentatonic scales by the absence in them of the two additional degrees in diatonic seven-tone major or minor scales plotted upward from the same tonic or final. The numbers of these absent degrees, preceded by minus signs ($-$), are also given in example 9, below the staves. The labeling of modal scales as "gapped" merely because they comprise fewer than seven degrees is, however, to be discouraged. Some of them may already have filled in gaps in prototypes of a lesser number. Some may have had no ancestry of heptatonic relatives. And the

EXAMPLE 9

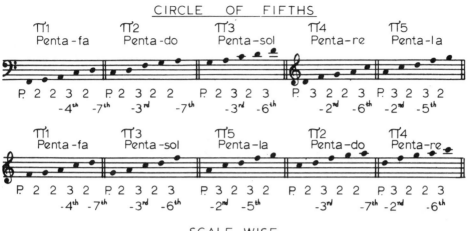

heptatonic scale itself could be as inappropriately called "gapped" with respect to those of more than seven degrees, as, for example, of the twelve of the equal-tempered keyboard. According to Kolinski, the only scales of whatever number of degrees that might legitimately be dubbed gapped would be those that (a) comprise the first and last of any series of successive fifths but (b) do not comprise one or more of the intervening fifths. For example, a tonal aggregate of *F-G-A-C* would be tetratonic; but its mode would be pentatonic because the *D* between *G* and the *A* in the successive series of fifths is omitted; therefore, it is gapped.

The pentatonic mode typical, then, of our Version I is $P_2 2^3$ (Bronson, π 3; Kolinski, Penta-sol; -3-6): of Version II, $P_2 2^2$ (Bronson, π 1: Kolinski, Penta-fa; -4-7). But we should not forget that most variants of Version I break into two somewhat opposed halves: the first giving us an aggregate of *C-D-F-G-A* and a pentatonic mode *D-F-G-A-C*, $P_3 2^3$; the second, except where there is no opposition, as in Ic, a variable aggregate (*F*)-*G-A-C-D*-(*F*) and a pentatonic mode *G-A-C-D-F*, $P_2 3^3$. In Version II, however, we have no such situation. The heavy durational weight of *D*, though sometimes greater than that of *G* in the modal condensation, is actually divided, part above and part below, thus offsetting each other's pull, whereas in Version I, the weights of both *D* and the *G* an octave above are in only one, unopposed direction-upward.

7. Prosodically accented beats, though often, as already pointed out, covered over by stronger random musical accents, do spell out, in more detail, the tonal phrase contour of criterion 3. Classification in these terms has been admirably developed by Bronson with the aid of statistical techniques too elaborate for use here.[17] Suffice it to say: the

iambic beat of the words remains evident, accentwise, never entirely obscured by the distinctly nonverbal tempo, proportion, and additional overlaying accents of the music. For example, the tonal pattern of the prosodically accented beats of variant A2 (Graham) is *D-G-G-D, D-G-G-D*; *F-F-C-F, G-C-G-G*. In arabic numerals, it would read: 5-8-8-5, 5-8-8-5; 7-7-4-7, 1-4-1-1.

8. Classification by phrase pattern is one of the most used but most abused resorts of ballad tune study. The pattern of the first phrase is designated A. If the second is the same, or virtually the same, as in the above accent pattern, some students will call it A or A^1, others B, and so on. If it is repeated in this or any other phrase exactly but upon a higher or lower pitch level, some will call it B, others, A^3, A^5, or A_3, A_5 according to whether it is a third or a fifth higher or lower, A', A'', even A^a, and so on, or by an entirely different numeral. The method cannot express tonal identity with rhythmic diversity, or vice versa. I would be inclined to label Version I as AA'BC and Version II as ABCD, though D is often a mixture of A and B.

9. Classification by phrase endings is one of the most useful and generally agreed upon of all criteria, also the quickest and easiest to handle, once the octave scale and final of the mode have been established. Thus the phrase ending pattern of variant A2 conforms to that of the majority of our variant classes Ia and Ix, namely, $45\bar{7}1$. Table 5 shows the distribution in the AAFS holdings and in the total United States roster.

TABLE 5

Variant	Class	Majority	Minority	AAFS	Total roster (U.S.)
A1-4	Ia	$45\bar{7}1$	$55\bar{7}1$	6	27
5	b	4511	5511	1	7
6	c	1111		2	3
5	x	$45\bar{7}1$ (ax)			16
			4511 (bx)	1	4
	misc.				6
7-11, 14	IIa	1511		15	30
B1-6, 15-19	b	1511		27	56
7-11	c	1551	$\bar{5}\bar{5}51$	11	29
12-13	x	misc.	$\bar{5}\bar{5}51$	3	13
	misc.				6

10-11. The two criteria, "trademark" and cadential formulas, have already been mentioned in other contexts—the characteristic third-phrase pattern of both versions and the "Scotch snap" skip of Version II. It may be worth noting that the United States variants show 80 percent skips *up* for ends of second and fouth phrases but a total of only 20 percent of the other six possibilities, whereas the British show 60 percent twin skips *down* as over against 40 percent of the others.

Variants of both our versions carry the words of other ballads and songs; but Version I does this far more commonly than does Version II. Participants in the current folk music revival movement in the United States will have found variants of the former most often in "Come All Ye Fair and Tender Ladies"; of the latter, in "Lord Bateman" ("Young Beichan," Child 53), "Geordie" (Child 209), and others. It appears with a religious text under the title "Heavenly Dove."[18]

The chronological and geographical provenance of the tunes must, therefore, be studied independently of any particular text as well as in connection with each with which it is associated. Although my search for British sources has hardly more than begun, I can cite here as example 10*a*, through the courtesy of S. P. Bayard, what seems to be the earliest printing of Version I, by D'Urfey in 1719,[19] but titled only "A song," with the first line "There Was A Knight and He Was Young" ("The Baffled Knight," Child 112). An introduction of four measures, which

EXAMPLE 10

seems not to have been sung, is omitted here. In the 1750s a variant of
the version, also with a section not shown here, was printed by Oswald
with the words of "Andro and His Cutty Gun" (later a favorite of Robert
Burns and with a stanza of words for an expanded introduction).[20] I give
this, also through the kindness of Mr. Bayard, as example 10*b*. The tune
appears as "The Dowie Dens of Yarrow,"[21] shown as example 10*c*, but
was found by Sharp only three times in his monumental collection of
nearly 3,300 English tunes, as "Boyne Water,"[22] "Navigation,"[23] and
"London Pride,"[24] a Morris tune. To the best of my knowledge, no
collector has reported it with the words of "Barbara Allen" in England.
But in the United States, we have it with these words in the sixty-three
variants of our Version I, fourteen of them notated by Sharp himself in
the Appalachians.[25] Variants were reported from various states, among
them Virginia, Maine, and Kentucky, from soon after 1900. Two
informants testified they had learned it from elders in the family during
the 1860s. It has been recorded recently as current in Scotland with the
words of "Barbara Allen" (see example 10*d*).[26]

Ewan MacColl kindly gave me the notation, 10*e*, or "Andro" as he
heard his father sing it. The identity of its first three phrases with those
of Mrs. McDowell's singing of "Barbara Allen," 10*f*, is as striking as the
differences in their final cadences. The latter, with examples 10*g*[27] and
10*h*—all three representative of the mutations in the American roster—
show the progressive weakening of the lower tonal center and strength-
ening of the higher, with consequent loss of the bimodality of the
majority of the roster.

Through the kindness of D. K. Wilgus, I am able to show a variant that
takes the opposite tack from that of examples 10*f-h*. This was notated
from a dubbing of the singing of Professor Patrick W. Gainer of the
University of West Virginia who tells me that this variant has been
traditional in his family, which came to the United States in the
eighteenth century and which had for generations been a fiddling and
singing family, both of secular music and of the shape-note hymns
introduced after the Civil War.[28] As can be seen in example 11, there is
an addition of two notes, *G* and *A* at the beginning, compensation being
made by deletion of one or two at the end of the phrase. I can find no
parallel for the addition of these or any notes at the beginning of the
tune. But the same notes, one or both, sometimes begin later stanzas in
the singing of Miss Stewart and Mrs. McDowell. The net result of the
Gainer variant is transference of the factor of bimodality inherent in the
version from an axis *D*-to-*G* to one of *C*-to-*F*. It is done by (1) increasing
the notes outlining an *F*-major chord with an accented *A* on the beat of
the first phrase, (2) accenting components of the chord in subsequent

EXAMPLE 11

In Scar-let Town where I was born There was a fair maid dwell – ing

phrases, and (3) harmonizing the final *G* with a *C*-major triad to serve as a dominant of a new tonic sounded at the opening of the next stanza, as in example 3. Thus, although it still preserves the circularity also inherent in the version, it weakens the original bimodality. For *F* is not one of the principal components in the majority of variants. One might expect from this modal instability that a further mutation would abandon the circularity as well, by substituting a final *F* in a clear-cut major-mode cadence. And this is just what is reported, by a notation in the University of Virginia archives, to have been the singing of Mr. Ed Davis of Shipman (see example 12).[29]

EXAMPLE 12

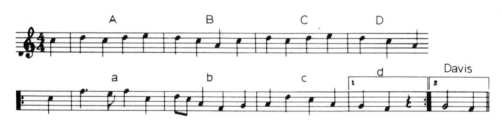

The modal instability of Version I is, then, one of its most interesting features, but at the same time one that makes investigation of its chronological provenance unusually difficult. One might suppose that the reappearances of D'Ufrey's final *D* in some twentieth-century American recordings (10*h*, 14) were evidence of the marginal survival in the colonies of an older tradition that had otherwise been lost. But D'Urfey's notation is itself open to suspicion. The Introduction, omitted in our notation here, is unashamedly minor-modal, even to a raised leading tone, *C* sharp. We cannot be sure that he did not "correct" or "improve" an existent final *G* and any other notes standing in the way of a fashionable *D*-minor ending. For until long after him, the "common people," though they did have some quaint tunes that everyone liked, did not know how to sing them—a complaint still heard even today.

Speculation upon the relative chronological provenance of our two versions is also interesting. The somewhat somber, non-major-minor archaism of Version I may seem to many necessarily older than the sweetly familiar major ring of Version II with its shorter history in print (having first appeared, and with the words of "Barbara Allen," in 1839[30] as in example 13*a*). Perhaps it is. But in this connection it is wise to keep

EXAMPLE 13

three facts in mind: (1) the identity of a folk tune is very difficult to pinpoint, so that the very notion "when it began to be itself" is metaphysical; (2) there were tunes in various modes in the thirteenth century which would pass today as major ("Summer is ioumen in" is an example); (3) Phillips Barry, the first and one of the most profound students of British-American folk song, wrote:

> It is no longer safe to say of any ballad tune, that, because it is cast in an ecclesiastical mode, it is *necessarily* ancient. On the contrary, it *may* not be older than the singer from whom it was recorded. Nothing in folk music is more evanescent than modality: instances are demonstrable of the origin of modal tunes, built up from variation of a phrase of a major air.[31]

The chronological provenance of our two versions, of course, intimately fuses with the geographical, so that historical changes in the tradition must be plotted with both in mind. With respect to the latter, there seems to be a general but untested agreement. Chappell wrote, "Under this name the English and the Scotch have each a ballad, with their respective tunes and a comparison will show that there is no similarity between the tunes."[32] Rimbault[33] and Graham,[34] writing not long afterward, concurred, as have others.

A second English tune is given in example 13*b*.[35] These two seem most widespread in England and have been reprinted with little or no alteration in many British publications, both scholarly and for popular use. Although often reprinted in the United States in cheap songbooks and school textbooks, neither 13*a* nor 13*b* is found in the AAFS. In each case, when, rarely, a folklore collector has published either, there has been strong suspicion of copying from British sources by literary-minded urbanites. The resemblance of these to the norms of our Version II and the recordings on disc L54 is not very close. A few British variants do show a close resemblance, as, for example, the one sung for R. Vaughan Williams in 1905, shown as example 13*c*.[36] The closest so far which has come to my notice is a recent recording from Ireland shown as example 13*d*.[37] The collector reports "this ballad seems to be the most widely known of the 'Child' ballads found in Ireland." Is it possible that the two versions making up over 95 percent of the United States repertory stem from Scotland and Ireland, respectively, and least, or indirectly, from England?

The Scottish tune most widely printed in England and Scotland as the Scotch (Scottish) version is shown as example 13*e*. It appeared first with the words of "Barbara Allen" in Oswald's *Pocket Companion*[38] already cited. There are no recordings of it in the AAFS. It has not been found in print in the United States. For completeness, I give it here as sung by Ewan MacColl.[39]

The influence of print, so strong upon the words of the ballad, seems to be nonexistent in the case of the tunes. Of the more than two hundred songsters examined by Ed Cray in connection with the present study or cited by folklorists, only four have been found with notations for "Barbara Allen,"[40] although many contained the words. And these tunes have not been members of the classes of variants found in oral transmission by folklorist collectors. They are not found in the AAFS roster. Fiddlers have often filled blank books with notations of the tunes they play or wish to learn. But although singers have as often written out compilations of the words of their repertory, notations are so rare as to be negligible as factors in the study of the tunes of our ballad.

More difficult to trace is the influence of commercial records upon country singing. From 1923 on, these inexpensive articles, often sold in five-and-ten-cent stores, flooded the country from coast to coast for a full ten to twenty years before the folkloristic field recordings deposited in the AAFS were made. They formed the staple repertory of rural radio stations. Indeed, D. K. Wilgus assures me that country singers were heard over the radio even before their singing was released on commercial records. It is inconceivable that many of the informants of the folklorist collectors were not accustomed to hearing their own songs sung both from recordings and over the radio. In some cases, we are assured by the singers themselves that they learned a song by hearing it from such sources or had actually sung it for broadcasting. Some folklorist collectors feared "contamination" by radio and record and avoided collection of songs said to have been learned or sung in connection with them. Others, we know, thought so little of the matter that they did not even question informants about it.

Probably, before 1930, most of the singing that was commercially recorded or broadcast was not very different from what was normally current in rural areas. Considering the admittedly wide popularity of "Barbara Allen," it seems strange that more country singing of it is not found on commercial records. With the generous help of such specialists in the field of hillbilly music discography as Edward Cray, Joe Drochetz, Will Roy Hearne, Ed Kahn, Guthrie T. Meade, Jr., and D. K. Wilgus, this writer has been able to make a list of fifty commercial records of the ballad by ten different singers under thirty different labels. Often, a single matrix appeared under a number of different labels. Sometimes the original singer's name or the title was changed. With such hurdles to surmount, it may not be surprising that the discography of country and hillbilly music has grown slowly.

From such as it is, however, we may suppose that the most widely distributed releases were those of Marion Try Slaughter, a small-part grand and light opera singer in New York in the 1920s. He was born in Jefferson, Texas, in 1883, and sang under at least thirty known pseudonyms, the most used being Vernon Dalhart.[41] He was responsible for the sale of millions of discs from 1927 to 1930, one of which—"The Wreck of the Old 97"—is said to have netted him over $100,000 royalties. With his collaborator, guitarist, and "idea man," Carson J. Robison, he sang for commercial recording (under at least nineteen different labels) or published in cheap, wood-pulp songbooks (for purposes of copyright claim) at least four different variants of our Version II. Two of them are found in the AAFS holdings. One is the widely known Class IIb, which was collected, notated, and printed in both England and America, long before Dalhart or Robison began their country music careers. The other is unique. It is in the "odd-and-even" stanza or two-part form. In this there are two slightly different but related tunes of four phrases each, one for the odd- and the other for the even-numbered stanzas (as in the Jacobite song "Wae's Me for Prince Charlie";[42] a tune, by the way, occasionally found carrying the words of other ballads, as well as those of "Barbara Allen").[43] Two closely associated singers in Florida sang identical, note perfect renditions of the even stanza tune alone of the Dalhart and Robison "copyrighted" tune (see AAFS 987B1 and 988B1). A Mississippi singer sang the whole tune, but in $\frac{6}{8}$ instead of $\frac{2}{4}$ (see AAFS 3111B1). To the best of present knowledge, the only other report of this variant is from North Carolina,[44] where it was sung with considerable variance, including a confusion of odd- and even-stanza tunes similar to that mentioned above with respect to first and second halves of single-stanza tunes. The other two Dalhart and Robison variants are note-for-note copies of printed British tunes that have not taken root in oral tradition in the United States.

Before we conclude that the influence of the commercial record and printed songbook upon oral tradition in music in the United States is as slight as the above account would seem to indicate, a far more extensive survey of surviving discs and a sufficient number of similar studies of other ballads would have to be made. The basic difficulty involved would be to show that the singer recorded on the record did not himself learn the tune from oral tradition or that it was not already current before the recording.

No serious study of the ballad tune and its singing style in the twentieth century can afford to omit consideration of the factor of instrumental accompaniment. Although widely regarded by conservative students as an innovation—and disapproved of by them—we cannot be sure that it was never traditional in the British Isles and is not in America. It seems not unlikely that in the early days of its development the ballad was accompanied by the harp, fretted zither, or the bowed lute. There are many reasons to suppose that ballads were sung where those instruments were played—and competently played.[45] For ballad singing may not always have been, as it came to be in the nineteenth century, mainly a rural, even peasant art. However that may be, folklorists have assured us that during the nineteenth and twentieth centuries the unaccompanied singing of ballads has been the unexceptionable rule among the most highly esteemed carriers of the tradition in England. Therefore, when Sharp made his famous field collection trips in the Appalachian mountains, 1916-1918, his schedule (we may suppose) was prepared in such a way as to have him hear chiefly unaccompanied singing. As a consequence, a belief that such singing was the only traditional one in the United States became accepted by many students. It is clear that singing style is influenced by accompaniment and that singers who sometimes use accompaniment and sometimes do not, may have, virtually, two distinct singing styles. We may prefer one to the other or find both acceptable when competently done and preserving the basic essentials of the tradition. But when commercial recording was begun, banjo and guitar accompaniment was customary. Judging from the skill with which this was done, it must have been a common practice long before Sharp's visit. It may be significant, however, that among the holdings of the AAFS we have no accompanied renditions of our Version I from a country singer. Among commercial, or semi-commercial, recordings, I know of only the one shown as example 11. Accompaniment of Version II, however, is common both in field recordings of country singers and on commercial discs.

By way of summary, it may be stated that in the light of present knowledge and in view of present techniques of study, no such entity as "*the* 'Barbara Allen' tune" can be set up other than for temporary convenience. The fact that with a few intermediate steps we can easily change one version into the other must be regarded in the light of the fact that we can change either version into any other tune of like length with a little, less, or more ease. Melodies are, by their very nature, infinitely changeable or interchangeable. Shown in melodic contour, there is considerable resemblance between the two versions, certainly enough to make possible, through precisely such variation as is shown by the notations in this article, transformation of a variant of one into a variant of the other. Effected little by little, as would be such ordinary variation in oral tradition, only three principal steps are required: (1) to lower the level of the first phrase of I or raise that of II; (2) to twist the simple arcs of I ("B" type, in my table of basic contours of tonal variance[46] or smooth out the zigzag courses of the four phrases of II (all "N" or "F" types, in the table cited); (3) to blur or make ambiguous the modal functions during the process of change, leaving to the final appearance of the variant changed into its clear modality. With such a transformation in view, the objective can be reached almost unnoticed in the singing of five or six consecutive stanzas of the ballad. Of course, no such objective might occur to a carrier of the tradition. But we have, in a recent publication,[47] a variant of Version I with "Scotch snap" of Version II at mid and final cadences. In another,[48] the whole fourth phrase is a variant of the typical form of Version II. And about 25 percent of the total American roster of Version I show the last two short-short or short-long sung syllables of second and fourth lines, typical of Version II. Of the opposite transformation—long-short or long-long mid and final

EXAMPLE 14

cadences typical of Version I—less than 3 percent of a total roster over twice as large are found in Version II, and some of these are suspect of notational ineptness. Poladian has perceptively provided an "intermediary class" of "Barbara Allen" tunes.[49] While not accepted here on account of its small size and heterogeneous content, such a class might very well be found convenient by more mature research. In the present study, it will have been noticed, two groups of six items each—"leftovers" of the classificatory process—have been listed in table 5 as "miscellaneous." But they could not be thrown into one class of twelve items.

As they stand, the two versions have such distinct characters that it is very easy to determine when one takes on a feature of the other. That one and the same ballad should be sung to two such different kinds of tunes—and, with rare exceptions, only these two—should certainly serve as a restraint upon the reckless positing of one-to-one correspondence between texts and tunes. Still, the question "why these two and only these two?" cannot fail to pique our curiosity.

NOTATIONS

Most of the transcriptions of the thirty variants in tables 1 and 2 were made from first stanzas of singings only. In some cases, the recordings were partially defective and a later stanza was chosen for pressing on disc L54. In others, first stanzas were not typical of majority usage in the respective singings of the complete ballad. The singer was not, as it were, in his stride. Sometimes, too, there has been a slip in an otherwise acceptable first stanza. Except for excessive cost of publication, complete notations of whole singings must remain the scholarly ideal.

Not all notations are equally "skeletalized" by sung syllable. Some, by this technique—for example, variants A11 (Jackson), B3 (Parks), B17 (Carr), and B18 (Tarwater)—would have so misrepresented what actually occurred at the recording session that a more inclusive treatment seemed indicated. The nature of a still fuller transcription can be seen in table 4 between the upper graph of the pitch line and the lower, of the loudness.

It would be a pleasure to be able to mention the names of the many people whose advice and counsel I have sought in this excursion, not outside but by the side of my main interest. But the list would be too long for inclusion here. Of course, the guidelines for study were laid down by the early comparative musicologists in Europe. For the United States, Philips Barry, Helen H. Roberts, George Herzog, S. P. Bayard, and B. H. Bronson have been my main reliance. The Institute of Ethnomusicology of the University of California, Los Angeles, under the direction of Mantle Hood, provided facilities unequaled for the work. Edward Cray checked the transcriptions of the words. Sam Chianis made parallel notations of the thirty strips as a check against mine; and I have often taken his alternative.

NOTES

1. Samuel P. Bayard, "Aspects of Melodic Kinship and Variation in British-American Folk Tunes," *Papers Read at the International Congress of Musicology* (New York, 1939) (New York: American Musicological Society, 1944), pp. 122-129; "Prolegommena to a Study of the Principal Melodic Families of British-American Folk Song," *Journal of American Folklore*, 63 (1950), 1-44.

2. Bertrand H. Bronson, "Some Observations about Melodic Variation in British-American Folk Tunes," *Journal of the American Musicological Society*, 3, 3 (1950), 120-134; "Toward the Comparative Analysis of British-American Folk Tunes," *Journal of American Folklore*, 72, 284 (1959), 165-191.

3. Bertrand H. Bronson, *The Traditional Tunes of the Child Ballads*, vols. 1 and 2 (Princeton: Princeton University Press, 1950 and 1962).

4. Charles Seeger, "On the Moods of a Music Logic," *Journal of the American Musicological Society*, 13 (1960), 248-249.

5. Stith Thompson, *Motif-Index of Folk Literature*, 6 vols. (Bloomington: Indiana University Press, 1932-1936; revised and enlarged, 1955-1958).

6. Francis J. Child. *The English and Scottish Popular Ballads*, 5 vols. (Boston: Houghton Mifflin Co., 1882-1898; New York: The Folklore Press, 1956).

7. *Checklist of Recorded Songs in the English Language in the Archive of American Folk Song to July, 1940*, 3 vols. (Washington: Library of Congress, 1942).

8. Charles Seeger, "Singing Style," *Western Folklore*, 17, 1 (1958), 3-11.

9. Bertrand H. Bronson, "The Morphology of Ballad Tunes," *Journal of American Folklore*, 67 (1954), 1-13.

10. Edward A. Sonnenschein, *What is Rhythm?* (Oxford: B. Blackwell, 1952).

11. David S. Raven, *Greek Meter* (London: Faber and Faber, 1962); Paul Maas, *Greek Metre* (Oxford: Clarenden Press, 1962).

12. Loraine Wyman. *Lonesome Tunes* (New York: G. Schirmer, 1916), p. 1.

13. Sirvart Poladian, *A Study in Variants*, published by the University of California,

Department of Music, as a Report on Unit A-25 of Official Project No. 65-1-08-62, conducted under the auspices of the Works Projects Administration; Edward B. Lawton, Jr., Faculty Adviser; Sidney H. Robertson, Supervisor (Berkeley, January 1940). Typescript, viii + 91 + 117 positive photostats of music notations, 26 pages. P. 46.

14. Cecil J. Sharp, *English Folk Songs from the Southern Appalachians* (London: Oxford University Press, 1932, 2d edition, 1952).

15. Bertrand H. Bronson, "Folk Music and the Modes," *The Musical Quarterly*, 32 (1946), 37-49.

16. Mieczyslaw Kolinski, "Musicological Analysis," in Melville J. and Frances S. Herskovits, *Surinam Folklore* (New York: Columbia University Press, 1936), pp. 489-740; "Classification of Tonal Structures," in *Studies in Ethnomusicology*, 1 (1961), 38-76.

17. Bertrand H. Bronson, "Toward the Comparative Analysis of British-American Folk Tunes."

18. John G. McCurry, *The Social Harp* (Philadelphia: S. C. Collins, 1868), p. 23.

19. Thomas D'Urfey, *Wit and Mirth: or Pills to Purge Melancholy* (London: W. Pearson. 1719-1720), 5:112.

20. James Oswald, *The Caledonian Pocket Companion* (London: James Oswald, 175-?), bk. 6. p. 4.

21. Frank Kidson, *Traditional Tunes* (Oxford: Chas. Taphouse and Son, 1891), p. 22.

22. Cecil J. Sharp, *Collection of English Folk Songs in the Clare College Library*, microfilm 9547 in Music Library at the University of California, Berkeley, notations numbers 2419 and 2420.

23. Ibid., notation 1757.

24. Ibid., notation 2597.

25. Cecil J. Sharp, *English Folk Songs from the Southern Appalachians*.

26. Lucy Stewart, *Traditional Singer from Aberdeenshie, Scotland*, collected, edited, and annotated by Kenneth S. Goldstein, Folkways Records FG 3519 (New York, 1961), vol. 1: *Child Ballads*, Side 2, band 4; *Jimmy Stewart*, collected and edited by Jean Ritchie, Collector Ltd. Ed., LP 1201, side A, band 7.

27. Jan P. Schinhan, *Frank C. Brown Collection of North Carolina Folklore*, vol. 4, *The Music of the Ballads* (Durham: Duke University Press, 1957), p. 62, no. 17G.

28. Patrick Gainer, *Folk Songs of the Allegheny Mountains*, Folk Heritage Record, DB 2122.

29. Arthur K. Davis, Jr., *Traditional Ballads of Virginia* (Cambridge, Mass.: Harvard University Press, 1929), p. 578 (V).

30. William Chappell, *A Collection of National English Airs* (London: Chappell, 1839), 2:114, no. 242.

31. Phillips Barry. "American Folk Music," *Southern Folklore Quarterly*, 1, 2 (1957), 29-47.

32. Chappell, op. cit. (1840). 1:183.

33. Edward F. Rimbault, *Musical Illustrations of Bishop Percy's Reliques . . .* (London: Cramer, Beale, 1859), p. 35.

34. George F. Graham, *The Popular Songs of Scotland* (Glasgow: J. M. Wood, 1887), p. 81n.

35. Kidson, op. cit., p. 37.

36. *Journal of the Folk-Song Society*, no. 7 (1905), II, second part, p. 80 (second version), sung by Mrs. Bennefer.

37. *The Lark in the Morning*, collected by Diane Hamilton, Tradition Records, T LP, 1004, sung by Thomas Baynes.

38. Oswald, op. cit., bk. 2, p. 37.

39. Ewan MacColl, in *The English and Scottish Popular Ballads,* sung by Ewan MacColl and A. L. Lloyd, edited and produced by Kenneth S. Goldstein.

40. *The Amateur's Songbook* (Boston: E. Howe, Jr., ca. 1843), p. 36; *Heart Songs Dear to the American People* (Boston: Chapple Publishing Co., 1909), p. 247; Philips Barry, *British Ballads from Maine* (New Haven: Yale University Press, 1929), bibliography cites *Charlie Fox's Minstrel Companion* (Philadelphia: Turner and Fisher, 1860) and *Trifet's Monthly Budget of Music,* no. 15, n.p. (March 1892).

41. Jim Walsh, "Favorite Pioneer Recording Artists, *"Hobbies, the Magazine for Collectors,* 65, 3-10 (May-December 1960).

42. George P. Jackson, *Spiritual Folk-Songs of Early America* (New York: J. J. Augustin, 1937), p. 58.

43. Reed Smith, *South Carolina Ballads* (Cambridge, Mass.: Harvard University Press, 1928), p. 130.

44. Schinhan, op. cit., p. 61, no. 27B.

45. Chappell, op. cit., "An Essay on the Ancient Ministrelsy of England," pp. 2 ff.

46. Charles Seeger, "On the Moods of a Music Logic."

47. Archur K. Davies, Jr., *More Traditional Ballads from Virginia* (Chapel Hill: University of North Carolina Press, 1960), p. 191.

48. George W. Boswell, "Kentucky Folksongs in the Tennessee Archives," *Kentucky Folklore Record,* 4, 3 (1958), 118.

49. Poladian, op. cit., p. 85.

XVI
Professionalism and Amateurism in the Study of Folk Music[39]

Distinction between the professional and the amateur is commonly drawn, I believe, upon an economic basis. The professional cultivates a field as a vocation, a means of livelihood; the amateur, as an avocation, a hobby. Perhaps it is equally common to view the professional as a disciplined and the amateur as a comparatively undisciplined worker.

The distinction is a useful one but does not always stand upon either count to even upon both. We all know persons who do not earn a cent from their activity in a field of study but are well disciplined either by training or experience or both. There are also persons without any discipline to speak of who make a living at a study. And some of the best disciplined obviously pursue scholarly work more with the air of a hobby than do some comparatively untrained workers.

There is a third, not so commonly held, but important, basis for the distinction between the professional and the amateur. This, too, has merit but does not always stand. It involves both etymological and methodological considerations. Derivation of the word *amateur* from the Latin *amare*, to love, has resulted in the curious situation in which cultivation of a field as a pastime presupposes love of it, whereas cultivation of it as a task may imply that love of it is irrelevant, if not dangerous. We all know of amateurs who are so enthralled by the object of their devotion that their activity is sometimes not quite rational. Conversely, we know professional workers who are themselves dry as dust and make everything they touch dry as dust. It is sometimes found that the discipline of study may shackle love of the field studied. Even though he begins with a warm love of a field and the objects in it, the worker who submits to the discipline of study must control his emotional attachment simply because it imperils maintenance of the detachment necessary for objective analysis. In short, he must discipline his love. This does not necessarily mean that the love be diminished, but rather that it be raised to a higher level. Part of the love of the field can be

321

transferred to the study. But love of the study and love of the field studied are two quite different things. Of course, one may enter the situation the other way around and transfer some of the love of study to the field studied. In either case, the ideal might be said to constitute a balance between the two. And some rare people achieve it, especially in the better established studies where agreement upon viewpoints, methods, and aims is very general. Clearly, however, there is a difference between the natural and the social sciences in this respect. The emotional reaction of the student of the former group is of an order quite other than that of a student of the latter, especially in those branches of the social sciences that deal with the arts, where aesthetic factors are more highly developed. The love of the physical or natural scientist for the data he deals with would seem to be of a more abstract nature, be these spiral nebulas, electrons, snakes, or nerve ganglia. It may be integrated with the precision, comprehensiveness, and orderliness of his methods of work in a mystical love of a cosmic whole. The social scientist or humanist may find the same generalized experience in his study but has in addition the love of particular things such as works of art, where personalized expression and reaction is highly emphasized. It is upon these grounds that I would withhold the designation "scientific" from the studies of the arts, although many objects of them may be.

That there is some merit in this contention we must admit. And the situation in which we find ourselves with respect to the study of folk music gives evidence that the problem is a serious one, though it has not yet, so far as I know, been succinctly stated. I shall, therefore, try to do so here.

I

During the eighteenth and nineteenth centuries, the great scholarly disciplines were being established in the forms in which we know them today. Students were busy, among other things, with definition of fields, their viewpoints, data, methods, and aims. Inevitably, a number of gaps were left uncultivated. One of these gaps comprised, as a subfield, what we now refer to as the field of folk music. Two opposite approaches were made toward the filling of this gap. I shall label one the amateur and the other the professional.

The amateur approach had this in common with the physical and natural sciences: it began in the here and now of the student. This involved a logical progress from the most familiar to the least familiar.

The word *folklore*, coined by Thoms in 1846, was intended to designate a modest study of "popular antiquities," not, perhaps, to fill one of these gaps but to squat, as it were, upon a part of it, a vague area left untouched by the study of European history and various other studies, among them music, which were concerned, supposedly, with more important things.

Not being a professional folklorist, I am not going to attempt to deal with that study as a whole but only with the part of it which concerns music. Suffice it to say, the study of folk music has grown to some extent within the larger study of folklore, though only too often not very closely related to or governed by it. For it has involved or overlapped another study, music, in which most folklorists have not even been amateurs. On top of this mischance, the musicians who were called upon for help by the folklorists, or who wandered in of their own accord, were almost without exception not even amateurs in folklore. What a field for the tyro folk music has been—and still is!

The century of development that folklore has undergone has resulted, as we all know, in the raising of the level of this amateur or less than amateur approach. But it remains a fact that most of the work in folk music in the United States—perhaps more than nine-tenths of it—is either plain tyro or amateur, a meeting of popular but not of scholarly interest or need. The few jobs that have been out of this category are not so much the result of the improvement of the amateur approach as, rather, of the professional approach to the field by two other studies.

This second, or professional, approach perceives that the gap in which the music branch of folklore was active was originally created by the fences already erected by more solidly organized contiguous studies. The situation of the student of folk music has been very much like the situation one would find oneself in upon taking up residence in a walled town where all the houses were occupied but with some vacant lots in between. One would have to build upon a vacant lot whose boundaries were already defined by the fences of the built-up lots. The fences that enclosed the gap called "folk music" have been, mainly, those of anthropology (including ethnology, study of culture, etc.) and of musicology. These studies, belonging to the humanities or studies of man, adopted the methods of the physical and natural sciences, but did not (in their modern form) begin with the here and now of the student, as did the amateur approach. To the contrary, anthropology established itself by studying the earliest available evidences of human life and society, and those most distant from the great cities and universities where most of the students lived. Musicology began by studying the music of the most ancient times and only in the twentieth century approached that of the most distant peoples. Thus, the gap above mentioned was left to form.

Little by little, the fences of both anthropology and musicology have been pushed forward in time and nearer in space to the here and now of the student. In so doing, the fence of anthropology has completely enclosed the vacant lot occupied by the "squatter," folklore, and the musical member of his family. At the same time, a sizable portion of the lot has also been enclosed by the fences of musicology. This double fencing-in of the area that we call folk music has involved some conflict between anthropology and musicology. It also involves both in conflict with those musical members of the squatter's family who do not realize or who choose not to admit the possible change in the situation. The real situation now is that a good case can be made for the view that the professional study of folk music has set, as requirements for entry, major competence in anthropology or musicology and minor in the other.

I must hasten to say that there are some things to be said on the side of the musical members of the squatter's family. In the first place, the number of scholars in the United States who can meet the dual requirements of anthropology and musicology today can be counted on less than the fingers of one hand.* They have produced little work. And little attention is paid to it. In the second place, the wave of popular and learned enthusiasm for folk music demands a wide cultivation of the field. In the third place, the squatters have developed, during the last ten years some surprising new views that quite transform not only the traditional amateur but also the traditional professional approach to the study. And above all, they have provided us with perhaps nine-tenths of the data we have today. Without this, there might be no study.

II

Up to this point, I have considered the professional and the amateur as functioning only in the *study* of folk music. But how about the *field*? Is there not a distinction homologous to the distinction we have made in the *study* of the field? I believe we must admit there is. We may find no large economic considerations nor spectacular skills. But folksingers and players are not uncommon who have earned portions of their living through their art. Their training has not been as highly organized, but has been in many instances we know of deliberately sought and cultivated. There is a difference between the outstanding performers of a

*Things have changed in the twenty-eight years to 1976.

local community and the rank-and-file of the population. And it is generally recognized in the community. We should not ignore this even though the music performed by the outstanding performers is virtually the same as that performed by the rank-and-file. We must admit, as urban professionals, that the outstanding performers have about them the essential qualities we have customarily found in "the professional" in scholarly life and upon levels of concert music activity. In this context, the rank-and-file of the community where a folk culture can be said to thrive have similarly the essential qualities of those we have called *amateurs. But we cannot class folk music, as a whole, as an amateur idiom.*

What makes the study of folk music an unusual problem for scholarship is a situation in which the amateur and professional students of folk music study the amateur and professional performers in the field of folk music. But how about the students of folk music themselves? Are they amateurs or professionals in folk music? Frankly, the very large majority of them are amateurs or not even that—mere tyros. The question naturally presents itself: are students of folk music—even if they have higher degrees in both anthropology and musicology—to be considered competent in the study of folk music if they are mere tyros or at best amateurs in folk music itself?

The point I raise here is a delicate one. I do not suggest that to be a competent student of folk music one must be a competent performer of folk music. I do suggest that a certain minimum of competence in performance *of* folk music is necessary for the evaluation of the knowledge *about* the idiom that is the essential stuff of the study. To possess the qualifications in musicology above referred to means that the student must have a minimum competence in fine-art (concert) music necessary for the evaluation of the knowledge about that idiom, in terms of which modern musicology is organized. The crux of the dilemma—and it is a dilemma—may be stated more or less as follows.

The fine art of music, upon a moderate technical competence in which modern musicology, as I have said, is formally organized, is one of four main classes of music idiom: primitive art (better, tribal art), fine art, folk art, and popular art. The modern fine art of music is a predominantly written tradition, cultivated *by* a special class of professionals *for* sections of a community that either make no music themselves or make very little, and that in an idiom other than fine art, which is, by its nature, beyond their technical competence. Fine-art music is, in the Occidental world, cosmopolitan in character.

Folk music, however, is a class of music idiom without formal or informal integration with musicology. Indeed, in the cultivation of the

fine-art music, the embryo musicologist, along with others of the more
highly educated classes in the Occidental world, is expressly steered away
from folk music both technically and with respect to content. For the
idiom of folk music is in many ways technically opposite the fine art of
music though in others complimentary. Folk music is primarily an oral
tradition, cultivated by people who make it for themselves. It is technically within reach of the vast majority of a community, though, as I
have said, exceptionally talented individuals can give more and better
presentations of the repertoire than can the average member of the
community. Folk music, in the Occidental world, is regional and even
local in character.

The functioning of the written tradition of the fine art of music in a
culture differs radically from the functioning of the oral tradition of folk
music in the same culture. Cultivation of the fine art is an activity of from
2 to 5 percent of our population; folk music of the vast majority. The
factor of the composer, so important in the fine art, is practically
negligible in folk music. The inviolability of the composer's text, so
important in the fine art is a nonexistent consideration in the folk art.
The individuality of the composer's expression in the fine art contrasts
with the character of the most typical expression of the folk art where,
after sufficient passage from ear to mouth (or hand), the marks or even
traces of individual composition have worn off, even as a jagged piece of
stone is smoothed down to a rounded pebble by sufficient grinding in the
bed of a running stream.

In the United States, as in other areas, the character of voice used in
singing folk music and the type of instruments and the manner of
playing them differ radically from the character of voice and the types of
instruments and the manners of playing them employed in fine-art
music. The handling of tonal and rhythmic functions differs radically in
the two idioms. There are different conceptions of tempo, beat or pulse,
accent, inflections, and nuances of many kinds. There are radically
different attitudes toward dynamics and their change—gradual or
sudden—as there are also of changes in tempo.

For a person trained in the fine art of music from an early age for
twenty or thirty years as are practically all musicologists, it is practically
impossible to turn the music-making apparatus sufficiently upside down
to handle folk music in any but an amateur way. And even to do that
involves a Copernican twist as well in the head as in the heart of the
music-making apparatus. One need not unduly censure the student for
ineptness here, but one cannot help surmising that an inability to observe
certain data, or an actual hostility toward them, may be a result of an

ineptness on the part of the student in the idiom studied, of which he is unaware.

III

Perhaps I have said enough to indicate my conviction that though our fine and folk arts of music are not exactly two languages foreign to each other, they are not interchangeable in technical or critical detail, nor can the student trip from one to the other on one passport. Although either one can and does borrow incessantly from the other and although hybrids of the two and of both of them with popular music are freely and easily made, they exist side-by-side in our culture as more or less autonomous domains, each with its technical and critical integrity. From the point of view of style, our folk art was, until the advent of phonographic and electronic duplication, quite as well established as our fine art. Its values steadily underwent change, as have the values of the fine art, but not so rapidly nor so extensively. It is a question whether even upon the most abstract level could their values be compared. There are two distinct sets of criteria and the values that can be asserted upon their evidence are not interchangeable. Although Bartok ventured the categorical equating of the two, there is no precise way of comparing a folk song with a symphony. One may be preferred to the other, but at least for the present it would appear they are critically incommensurable. Their social functions are utterly diverse and as is their very nature. There is, for example, only one authentic version of most symphonies. But no well-distributed folk song is known in any one authentic version to which another equally authentic version might not, for all we know, exist.

With the prejudices and resistances bred into a professional musicologist by years of training in and association with the fine art of music, it is not to be wondered at if some comparatively untrained amateur can get at the insides of a folk-music situation better than he. I am thinking especially of the jolt received by all of our musical idioms by the advent of the phonograph disc, the radio, and the sound film. The fine art certainly, is reaching an audience never contemplated by a master before 1900. Folk music is recapturing an audience—that of the city—which it lost in the decades before 1900. Professional students with the qualifications required by anthropology and musicology will perhaps hesitate to mix in or to speculate upon what the future will bring. But the amateurs are taking to wings. Starting with their here and now, with a minimum of historical knowledge, they are doing some prediction and attaining at least a momentary success. Although they may call it folk song, they are not making the classic music known before the phono-electronic revolution, but an acculturated variant that may be expected to settle eventually into the form of invariance in time accepted even by conservative students as a criterion for recognition of folk art. The situation is not unlike that in a number of other studies, some of them of more venerable academic standing. I ran into the following passage the other day in a textbook on astronomy by Russell, Dugan, and Stewart: "For the advanced student there is no field in which it is possible sooner to get out to the front line of scientific advance and to learn how territory is being won in a very active sector. Indeed, the number of objects that will repay observation is so great, and the opportunities for elementary calculation are so considerable, that undergraduate students, and amateurs without university training, have made and are making genuine contributions to the advance of astronomical knowledge." This can, in substance, be said as well for the study of folk music today.

As I see the immediate future, the study of folk music in the United States, as perhaps throughout the world, is entering a lusty teenage. It will not be, because it cannot be, a well-integrated or organized phase. There will be a diversity of standards. There will be some awfully sweet prettifying for city people, a lot of slicking down of good folk stuff in radio stations and some terrible "folk symphonies." Out of it, will come, I feel sure, a more unified continental music culture for North America and perhaps, for the world as a whole. The professional must unceasingly lash the amateur for sloppy fieldwork, sloppier transcription, lack of documentation, secrecy, preoccupation with the quaint, and failure to deposit collectanea in permanent archives. But the amateur has a task also—to goad the professional out of too great preoccupation with the archaic and into a willingness to face the present and future.

And some Fate or Fury should fill all, professional and amateur alike, who have asserted or try to assert property rights over the genuine folk stuff they may have collected, with a decent sense of shame. Assertion of property rights in folk music must somehow be stopped. There should be a maximum charge of a dollar or so for republication of collected material, or better still, complete freedom to republish providing only credit is given. Genuine folk music belongs to the whole people, and no one, not even if he has paid fifty cents or five dollars to an informant for the privilege of recording or notating it, has any right whatever to stand between that singer and the people to which he and his music belong. Of course, if the material is not clearly of the oral tradition, this exhortation would be out of order. But then, the material should not be either held or presented by the collector as folk music.

IV

I have offered the foregoing analysis of the situation in the study of folk music in the United States today with the sole purpose of outlining some norms in the relationship between the amateur and professional approaches to the study. I hope I have given the impression that while both have their drawbacks, both are essential to the well-being and present progress of the study, though it is the latter that I expect will and should be increasingly emphasized in the coming years. Before I close, however, I should touch upon one prime factor that has been mentioned only in passing. That is the factor of personality of the individual student. Here again, I am not an expert and cannot venture any definite integration of this factor with those of whose normal adjustment I have been speaking. Nevertheless, I must state very clearly that every one of these adjustments must be reconsidered in each case where the factor of personality enters. The science of personality being a very young study, most of us—rank amateurs—are faced with the necessity of making these adjustments with little or no expert guidance, mostly with only the common sense of our personal experience. For example: suppose one is faced with decision which of two applicants for a folk-music job to support—one a comparative amateur, the other, a professionally trained student. One might cast one's vote in either direction depending upon the nature of the job and the nature of the personalities involved—and this, in clear view of a conviction definitely weighted in favor of more professionalism in the study. Some professionals are absolutely unfit for a field collection project. They would turn informants into stony-eyed statues. No amateur, however, should normally have precedence over a trained worker in respect to a transcription, editing, or archive project. But economic considerations, adaptability to organizational procedures, freedom from predatory attitude toward the materials—in short, integrity of character—might weigh heavily even in those situations.

Any one, two, or more of a number of personality factors might, then, upset any of the norms I have proposed. But only in a particular case. In general, I support them as stated.

XVII
Folk Music in the Schools of a Highly Industrialized Society[46]

We may, I believe, assume that any substantial change in the organization of a society will eventually be reflected in the inheritance, cultivation, and transmission of such traditions as those of folk music. For a folk music is, above all else, a summary of the way of life of a culture community, the attitudes and feelings of those who comprise it toward life and death, work and play, love, courtship, and marriage, heath and hearth, children and animals, prosperity and adversity—a veritable code of individual and social behavior. Industrialization of a modern country is, for us, the example par excellence of substantial social change. Especially in its early and middle phases, it has uprooted not only individuals but whole communities from well-known, well-tried ways of living, often moving them bodily into novel improvisations of crowded slums and noisy mills and mines, whose products in turn have eaten at the roots of the way of life of those who were left behind. Under such conditions, the survival of songs of a way of life increasingly different from that actually lived by the singers is hardly to be expected.

We may concede that where industrialization has been limited, slow and gradual, there may have been minimal disturbance of traditions of folk music. But where it has been extensive, rapid, and uneven, the disturbance has been maximal. Gradual loss of the oldest songs in a repertory, while new materials are being added, is a normal course of a vigorous tradition. But where the loss of the older materials is almost total and the new has little of the nature of oral tradition, and so is hard to digest, even the middle-aged materials may have gone by the board and the very process of oral transmission thwarted for lack of occasion for its cultivation.

The history of the last hundred years or so has shown, however, that the process of oral transmission has far greater vitality than the repertory it has built. Though it may not have incorporated new materials as fast as the old were lost, we cannot claim that it has failed to preserve its integrity and continued, against unusual odds, its age-old digestive, formative function even though manifestly crippled by the changed social conditions under which it must operate.

The vast majorities of the populations of even the most highly industrialized societies are still musically illiterate. Music can be *made for* these majorities through written techniques. But it still can be *made by* them only through oral techniques. That a majority will long remain content exclusively with music *made for it* is now to be doubted. Present indications, at least in the United States, are that it has not. The resurgence of orally learned singing and instrument playing here has even been implemented with industrial products that originally were considered to be militating against this practice. The steps leading to this reversal are interesting. They have been taken mainly by city dwellers. The culture and social organization of all the American nations is, after all, neo-European. That a similar trend may be observable in Europe and colonies of European countries is not surprising. For in spite of many variations of detail, they have a common history with respect to reactions to industrialization.

After a predominantly rural folk has for some time shown signs of weakening its hold upon its peculiar traditions of music, its contemporary urban elite has reacted in two distinct directions. One branch, spearheaded by educators, has joined the forces of destruction and by condemnation and ridicule sought to substitute, throughout the areas it can influence, not only the products but even the process of the written tradition for those of the oral. Another smaller branch of this elite, composed of folk-lorists, professional and amateur, and surrounding circles (who had themselves been among the first to lose what they shared of the ancient traditions) has "discovered" and presently set about "reviving" them. Both of these opposed courses of action can be traced in England from around 1800, on the continent during the nineteenth century, and in the United States from about the 1830s when the minstrel show, on the one hand, and Lowell Mason's drive to have music education included in the public school system, on the other, both adopted the former course.

While the urban elite was thus working in these two opposite directions, both the rural and urban masses led an increasingly depressed musical life. In the United States the lowest point must have been reached during the decades just before and after 1900. Shortly after that time, younger generations, far removed from both elite groups, deprived of an uninterrupted cultural tradition, set about, as best they could, to create for themselves some kind of substitute for the inheritance their ancestors had denied them. These substitutes can easily be identified as products of the changed way of life brought about by industrialization. Compared with the best of the oldest traditions that were brought to new light by folklorists, they are obviously mongrel and, many people think, fugitive. Folklorists, intent upon reviving most ancient traditions, have looked upon them with distaste and have rarely recognized these popular movements as typical of the procedures by which their most admired ancient traditions themselves may have operated. Revivalistic fervor has, therefore, only too often opposed popular movements. (In the United States, I think of such genres as jazz, hillbilly, swing, bebop, etc.)

As in doctoring, so here, success in reviving depends partly upon how dead the corpus is and partly upon how skillful the revivers are, first in diagnosis, second in treatment. I believe it is not incorrect to say that the elite groups that have deliberately tried to either destroy or revive folk music traditions have invariably embarked upon such treatment without much, if any, attempt at diagnosis. Treatment, ranging from publication of written texts that are mere skeletons, simplified to a point of misrepresentation, to unabashed commercial exploitation, has exhibited a conception of folk music as solely a corpus, and a very dead one at that—a repertory already virtually out of currency and closed irrevocably to further additions. In other words the view has been structural and static. The program has been authoritarian. In failing to recognize the true character of the substitutes for established tradition evolved by the masses of the people themselves, they have snubbed the best ally they could have hoped for.

We have to thank folklorists for the work of preservation which they have done. But it must be admitted that until the revivalists began, somewhat tardily to be sure, to be conscious of the value of the use of folklore in public life, neither correct diagnosis nor practical treatment of the dislocation caused by intensive industrialization has been possible. For the revivalist sees the situation not in the structural and static terms of repertory but in those of social function and dynamic policies of growth for ordinary individuals in an ever-changing world. Where the folklorist has looked primarily to the *past of the song*, the revivalist has looked toward the *future of the singer*.

Clearly, the situation indicates cooperation between folklorists and revivalists. This is not impossible. But it is not easy. For the folklorist inclines to the belief that unless there are high standards, activity is useless or worse than useless; whereas the revivalist believes that unless there is activity, there can be no standards at all. Perhaps a *modus operandi* can be found if we leave to the folklorists all matters pertaining to the *survival* of the traditional materials and to the revivalists all those having to do with their *revival* among living people. If we accept this division of labor, the point of beginning for the revival will be not where the folklorist or revivalist is, but where the child is. If the folklorist can identify some old traditions as in a state of survival—well and good. The revivalist may use them as the base and add to them. But if, as is so often the case, the hybrid substitutes hold sway, these must be the bases of the operation of revival.

If, as I take it, the common ultimate goal is maximum continuity between the best known of the past and the best conceivable for the future, what we have to deal with here is an equation between what people will accept from their ancestors (either directly as survival or indirectly as revival) and what they will create for themselves and their children. No matter what the reviver thinks of the present state of affairs, therefore, he must accept it as his given quantity and use it as the base that it inevitably is for whatever accretion it may accept. This base will in all probability be a conglomeration of opera arias, salon music, popular songs of various vintages, some folk and near-folk materials (such as hillbilly, makwaya, mambo, jazz, bebop, and their successors) with more and more exotic music and—not to be forgotten—the commercial exploitation of the whole lot. Indigestible? By no means. Oral tradition can digest anything, give it but enough time.

Preservation and development of oral tradition and giving it enough time in which to do its work is, therefore, the key to the situation and is just what is happening. From this viewpoint, the error of folklorists and revivalists has been one and the same—overemphasis upon written tradition. The folklorist has stressed the importance of the "authentic text," ignoring the paradoxical situation he thus produces, in which the people are supposed to keep alive by reading what writing tends to destroy— the oral tradition of transmission. The revivalist, too, has stressed written tradition almost to the exclusion of oral tradition for years and needs a grave reorientation before the revival of folk music will be more than an illusion in our schools. We shall have an ally in this undertaking in the fact that music literacy, the only weapon that can deal oral tradition a mortal blow, is still and for a long time to come will be rare among the populations of even the most highly industrialized countries. And long before it may become a general trait of the masses of populations, we may confidently expect that written traditions themselves will surely recapture their own peculiar techniques of oral tradition which, logically enough, were lost when the art of improvisation went out of fashion in that same heyday of the industrial revolution when oral traditions of folk music, too, weakened and urban elite circles first became aware that a cultural good of inestimable value was in danger of loss.

When we speak of the revival of folk music, therefore, we must view it not alone as a dead repertory but perhaps even more importantly as a living process. The focus of attention should always be upon singing and playing "by ear," not from books, but using the natural, untrained voice, and, when necessary, the simpler, portable instruments or, at the worst, the playing by ear of any others.

Platform performance and its graces should be anathema to the sincere reviver of folk music. The guiding principle should be that of variation as over against repetition of the single, authentic text.

Introduction of materials more nearly authentic from the folklorists' viewpoint should be gradual and carefully planned. Local traditions should first be consolidated; later, and progressively, those more distant. The teacher should watch *acceptance* as the main guide for the direction of a program of development. He must remember that the descendant of the tradition which made and preserved the great folk music of the past is still working over the new materials that industrialization has heaped upon it. It is not in the best of health. But it has been given, by the very process that has weakened it, some new tools with which it may enable it not only to regain its old powers but possibly also to surpass them. I refer to the mass media of communication. The disc and tape, for example, at last puts in the hands of folklorists and revivalists alike a means of bypassing the bottleneck of the notation of the folk song. Millions are now learning to sing from hearing the voices of authentic singers. We do not have to give the increasing fashion of "fake-singing" any other treatment. Time and popular taste will eventually take care of it.

A word in closing must be to watch the concept labeled "the folk." It is a question to what extent the majority of the population that is now coming to carry the oral tradition of an idiom that can be called folk music will ever resemble any that in the past carried the tradition of the great ballads. Rather, however, than say "the folk is dead" and attempt to keep folk song alive as something quaint, antique, and precious, let us say "the folk is changing—and its songs with it," and then help what it is changing into—which may be the whole people welded into one by the new media of communication—not to be ashamed of its ancestors, but to select the makings of a new, more universal idiom for the more established society that we may hope may eventually come into being, from the best materials available, whether old or new. Better than to lament the loss of ancient gold will be to try to understand its permutation into another metal that, though it might be baser, may still surprise us in the end by being nobler.

XVIII
The Folkness of the Nonfolk and the Nonfolkness of the Folk[70]

In a prescient paper "The Folkness of the Folk" (*The English Journal, College Edition,* XXVI, 6 [June 1933]), B. A. Botkin wrote, "The tendency has been to treat folklore from the evolutionary and historical rather than from the functional approach, from the point of view of the lore rather than of the folk, from the outside rather than from within." In the study of the music of folklore, the tendency has been similarly restricted and even less comprehensive. Attention has tended to be directed mainly to material artifacts—structures, particular "pieces" of speech, and music (instrumental music played a role in study secondary to song)—their collection, their classification in repertorial canons, their sequestration in bodies of collectanea often as not regarded as private property by collectors and sometimes even copyrighted in the collectors' names. True believers in the excellence of these materials have tended to take for granted that by the time any particular student began to study it, the stream of oral transmission had mostly dried up under pressure of the ubiquity of the printing press and the contempt of urban elites. It seemed as if a point had been reached at which evolution stopped, leaving only frozen artifacts no longer free to take on new forms but to lie still enough in the symbols of written and printed transcriptions for leisurely dissection into themes, motifs, skeletal outlines, and other such devices.

The structural approach—music as an object—has also dominated musicology ever since the days of its earliest recorded history in the sixth and fifth centuries of ancient Greece. Thus, students of the music of folklore have agreed in their approach to their study regardless of whether their preparation has been in literary or in musical studies. They concurred in the supposition that the stream of orally transmitted music had been dried up by "outside" events and collaborated in the building, out of essays, books, and archives, of a kind of dam to retain the "few remaining traces" of archaic tradition. It made a pretty lake.

For about a century the structuralists had the lake all to themselves. They fenced it round about, built academic dachas on its shores, and came to think of it—if not as their own private preserve—as held in trust by them. But they made one fatal mistake. They let it be known, through the publication of collectanea, that the fishing was good. Soon after 1900 poaching became a hobby, then a more or less organized sport, then a business. Both urbanity and rurality liked the resulting black-marketing. Everyone but the folklorists seemed to be delighted when Tin Pan Alley moved to tin pan valley (Nashville, Tennessee) where it could pursue more conveniently its refresher course in folklore or, as some unkindly put it, "fakelore." It turned out, in fact, that the waters, their flora and fauna, possessed extraordinary properties. Even a small amount could encourage propagation of an almost unlimited number of fish. That most of them were mutations, sometimes taking fantastic shapes and colors, dismayed the structuralists but delighted a new breed of operator—a Janusfaced, Jekyll-Hyde class of beings who became known as "functionalists," which was composed on the one hand of the poachers, sportsmen, and businessmen, who did not know that they were functionalists, and on the other, of a younger generation of folklorists and musicologists, who knew very well that they were. But the higher the dam was built, the richer became its content and the more copious its overflow. More seeped through the books that had helped to build it, was siphoned off or punctured with high-power drills, not, necessarily, for sheer love of the fish or their mutations but for the money that could be made in their marketing. By the 1940s, there was a "folk music revival." In the 1960s each of the members of one three-man combo of self-styled folk-music performers was reliably said to have grossed a million dollars a year for several years by shrewd artificial insemination of their hauls with nonfolkness. Structuralists chorused anew the old song that folklore was dying, but nobody paid them attention except their students who had to, and for the most part cultivated on the sly inordinate hunger for the new fish fertilized by the utterly promiscuous unions of the gracious waters of ancient tradition and the heady distilled liquors of industrially revolutionized cities.

By the 1960s the functionalists, having come rather late onto the scene, had put up such a strong battle that they felt they had won their argument with the purists. They forgot the placid lake upon which they had caught their Ph.D.s, for the functional approach had disclosed to them many other waters, lakes, and fish, with dams in all states of repair and disrepair in other parts of the world. They became more anthropologists than folklorists and came to look upon the situation with scientific detachment, carefully subduing at least some of the valuative propensities of the purists. Obviously, the strange new fish procreated by these almost countless streams, their poachers and dam-puncturers, did not taste quite like the ones they had been brought up with. But the taste was no longer a criterion for the functionalists—that is, their own tastes. The tastes of others were. In terms of quantity, as in rating polls, the tastes of others could be regarded as statistics, be fed into computers, and be considered authentic scientific data. So, the urbanites came to the conclusion that the building of the dam had been ill advised. Folkness was discovered to be "a funded treasury of attitudes, beliefs, and feelings toward life and death, work and play, love, courtship, and marriage, heath and hearth, children and animals, prosperity and adversity—a veritable code of individual and collective behavior belonging to the people as a whole." In spite of the genteel tradition, which had tampered with it in the cities, the old code had kept on functioning, though crippled by the attempt to subdue or to translate the essence of its old myths, legends, proverbs, riddles, tales, and songs into censored formulas blended with new myths of conspicuous consumption, honorific distinction, and pecuniary emulation (and copyrighted). Anyway, it was not the code that the genteel tradition had fought but only its expression in visual and auditory artifacts whose production people could "come by natural." Thus, the revivalists set up a new code one could "come by it *un*natural," by interposition of formal instruction, the printed books, attendance at concerts, even invention. It was not necessary to make music one's self. It could be made for one, by specialists. Sufficiently edited, such materials could be handled in schools by ladylike teachers. But "Lamkin," "The Two Sisters," "Gypsy Davy," "The Brown Girl," "Little Musgrove," not to speak of "Pretty Polly," "Pearl Bryan," "Careless Love," "The House of the Rising Sun," "Harry Sims," "Pie in the Sky," could not be so handled. Least of all at the proper age—the cradle, preschool, and earliest grades.

It was a two-way drive based upon a very general realization of the widened and widening gulf between a rapidly changing urban variant of the culture and a slowly stabilizing rural variant of that culture. For at least a century, individual carriers of each variant had been groping for what they felt they had lost and were losing. The *gesunkenes Kulturgut* sought at Walden Pond, at the Shaker and other colonies, was paralleled in thousands of villages and small towns by "literary societies" dedicated to inspiration of the "higher things of life"—the *gehobenes Kulturgut* attained by the wealth and fashion of the cities. Chatauquas followed and, finally, mass-produced national magazines, comic books, movies, radio, and television. The folk music revival movement was a deliberate urban putsch that happened to mesh neatly with a trend among rural musicians carrying viable traditions of folk and folk-popular music. The folk music revival was an American shotgun wedding of oral (folk) and written (fine and popular art) idioms. It brought about no such deep integration as that which had grown over the centuries in some of the geographically long-settled cultures of man, that of the German-speaking peoples being the outstanding example. No such comprehensive and thorough integration of music idioms such as Bartók achieved has even been attempted in the United States. We can hardly credit the occasional introduction of a popular or folk tune into the thoroughly European texture of a conventional concert piece or a set of variations upon such tunes for concert instruments as more than a gesture toward a dreamed-of end. The spectacular naissance of composition in the fine art of music in the United States during the twentieth century was fathered quite epigonically by contemporary European composers and mothered by American money. As yet, it has no roots in American Life. The "American music" that has spread all over the world and is hailed by millions—even emulated by them—is folk, folk-popular, and the hybrids of them from old-timey music, hillbilly, country and western, jazz in its myriad forms, and rock in possibly more myriad forms. The historical significance of what is actually being done by the nonfolkness of the nonfolk in the United States is still far from clear. For the moment it seems a viable counterpart of the metalanguage of speech, a metamusic. At one time, the objective of its developers seemed outspokenly to destroy the "grand tradition," first by eliminating key and tonality, next, the regular beat, fixed pitch, and finally all traditional forms. But tonic-dominant-subdominant feeling is still widespread; $\frac{4}{4}$ meter and thematic development likewise. If history is to guide our thinking, we can be sure that it will be many years, probably centuries, before they change gradually into what may be called by other names.

The lesson, of course, is that you cannot kill a culture unless you kill most or all of its carriers. If a sufficient number of them live together socially, even in bondage, you can suppress it, cripple it, acculturate it and its principal traditions. But its continuity and creativity are built into the very bodies of its carriers. Sooner or later it will burst its bonds. We can see the operation of both these processes in full swing in our own day. It is not only scholarship and business enterprise that launched the folklore revival movement in the United States.

Meanwhile, what had the folk been doing with its folkness? It had been doing what it has always done, when it could, and strictly "according to folk-Hoyle": appropriating all the nonfolkness it could digest. What was novel in the first half of the twentieth century was the increased speed with which this could be done with the help of radio, phonograph, and "personal appearances" of musicians—all of them devices provided by the supposedly nonfolk. Put any good "authentic," traditional singer before a microphone or on a platform before an audience not of its own kind, and soon the peculiar requirements of the situation produce the typical traits of exhibitionism. To my personal observation, it took Molly Jackson only a few months after her expulsion from Harlan County, Kentucky, to convert herself, when expedient, from a traditional singer, who seemed never to have given any particular thought to whether anyone liked or disliked her singing, into a shrewd observer of audience reaction, fixing individual listeners one after another with her gaze, smiling ingratiatingly, gesturing, dramatizing "by" words in her songs. Leadbelly was already an astute handler of the nonfolk by the time I met him (about the time he left John Lomax). Woody Guthrie was another case, almost swamping his native talent in Greenwich Villagese. The avidity of the hillbilly most remote from the city for the city's nonfolkness is quite as self-propelled as that of the city-billy most remote from the country for the country's folkness. Since each has now exploited the other for a couple of decades in the large frame of the United States, there must exist few, if any, persons left ratable as 100 percent either folk or nonfolk. The vast population lies between these limits, each individual made up of varying proportions of inhibited or released folkness or nonfolkness. Perhaps we could venture some definitions now, as, for example, "nonfolkness is that which tries not to be folkness"; "folkness is that which knows of no more nonfolkness that it can try to be." The possibility cannot but occur to one that perhaps the two are not mutually exclusive opposites but overlapping complements or, perhaps, two aspects of one unbroken continuum.

Folkness is a concept referent to a property of cultural structures and functions whose weight increases in direct proportion to the decrease in logic and increase in pure, mystical belief, which is close to saying: the less something is pinned down to the factual and to objective reality and the more to the valual and to subjective reality, the more it partakes of the nature of folkness. If one leans toward a hierarchy of values, the higher the value, the more the exposition partakes of folkness. If one prefers the canonized values—love, beauty, goodness—ah! there is pure folkness. Mathematics, logic, phenomenologies, objective observation cannot touch it. Only we do not call it "folkness" or even "myth," unless it is someone else's. Subjective reality—for that is what it is—is close to God. And are not all gods myths (except one's own, of course), or, on a less prestigious level, folkness?

With such a field for study, it is saddening to hear, as one does at meetings of folklorists, the gentle, oft-repeated complaints that so little support is given to folklore by universities and foundations (so little *money*)—so few courses in the subject, no departments, rarely a higher degree. May this state of affairs not be traceable, at least in part, to excessive structuralizing, getting bogged down in artifacts, especially artifacts of the more archaic kind; to placing a higher value upon the values of the past than upon those that are being created in the present and that we may hope will be, in the future? And too little thinking of what is within the without? Surely, if the inner eye could see it, the modern university, like the nation itself, is founded on folklore. There is not a discipline in the whole catalog that is not based upon the simple value-judgment that it is *worthwhile*. We have no proof, except a consensus of 99+ percent, that life is worthwhile. But the consensus that physics or chemistry is worthwhile is not in the same class. If we kill off the whole human race by misuse of nuclear fission or novel chemical production, were physics and chemistry worthwhile? Granted: the development of both could not have been avoided. But it is well to remember that their unavoidance is predicated on folklore and an all-pervading folkness consisting in a willingness to believe it. The same can be said of law, politics, medicine, government, diplomacy, education—every activity of social man. There is not one that is not founded upon and shot through and through with folklore. And folklorists do not, as a group, though some of them know this only too well and from Andrew Lang to van Gennep have pointed it out, do anything whatever about it.

This lack of enterprise seems to be intimately associated with the structuralist view of folkness and nonfolkness as two mutually exclusive opposites rather than as each other's complements or as potentially two segments of a single strand in the general social-cultural continuum that become marked off only by the datedness of the intruding student as observer. It is in keeping with the fashion in humanistic studies for the past several centuries to emphasize the historical (structural) orientation as over against the systematic, or, in Botkin's vocabulary, the functional. It is high time we relax the tyranny of this fashion. Precision in study does indeed require their separate pursuit; but comprehensiveness requires equal cultivation of both, and credibility, their integration. Alone or separate, neither makes sense, either for theory or for practice.

In the melee of contemporary life—for that is the way it must appear to the candid student—the facts (data) of history, which are, principally, structures, serve as the bases of our belief in what were the values of their makers, our ancestors. The values (dicta) we hold to, which are principally functions of our appetite to take part in the life of our day, serve as the bases for our belief in what will be the facts made by their makers, our descendants. What is *now* to us is at once the culmination of history, whose materials are facts, and the point of departure of system, whose materials are values. History tries to tell us how things came to be as they are: system, how things are coming to be what they will be. *What* they are, as of now, may be viewed variously according to the unique structural-historical-factual and functional-systematic-valual imbalance that characterizes the behavior of each one of us. As individuals, we may seem not to weigh much in the melee. When allied in a group of a sufficient number of similar imbalances, the gross weight may be thrown around and can exert pressure. And it is in terms of pressure groups, that all "without-thinking" must be done, if it is to amount to anything. But all thinking, whether outer- or inner-directed, is done by individuals. Pressure groups define trends. But all pressure groups have leaders who are individuals. The stronger the pressure, the stronger the trend. Whether the social-cultural unit is large or small, a trend is usually an intimate mixture of fact-thinking and value-feeling, of nonfolkness and folkness. If folklorists could only soft-pedal the inlooking and infighting and get busy with the outlooking and outfighting, the discipline and the folklore revival, too, would profit. It would be a blessing to the country at large. It would mean, however, the building of an applied folklore, a wedding of folkness and nonfolkness. I do not suggest, here, any handing out of learned largesse to an ignorant world. Quite the contrary. There is a lot of folkness being very skillfully applied throughout the world today. And often as not on a scale that professional folklorists have never operated on. If the complaints regarding the lack of support for the study of folklore are sincere—and there is no reason to doubt that they are—the complainers should study this already applied folkness just as carefully as they have studied the unapplied artifacts of orthodox study. For it is an integral element in folkness. It is the oral tradition of the managerial and administrative level, as distinguished from the oral tradition of the technical level and the academic man. This application of old home-learning to the new techniques of public life is one of the least understood features of our day. It is the imagination—even the fantasy (Beckwith was on the right track)—that has always served the highest (and lowest) values and aspirations of every man, but in a new guise. To the extent that pressure groups have expressed formulations of these features, they have served the policies of nations and the destinies of man—usually with what is, essentially, folklore.

If students of folklore would agree upon the organization of an applied branch of their discipline in the big world—there has already been talk of such enterprise—they would have as much to learn as to teach. They would have to take fully into account the choice between pitting book-learning against home-learning. The structuralist and purist could be expected to lean to the former. He would want to dictate, which would not help matters. The functionalist would be the one to handle an operating, functioning pressure group. Collection would be equally for use and study. Applied folklorists might even be folklore attachés of embassies to keep ugly Americans from riding roughshod over the sensibilities of peoples they are accredited to, perhaps, occasionally, even preventing an ambassador from passing the salt in Java with a left hand, offering indiscriminately to shake hands in Moslem countries and *not* belching at dinners in (where is that, now?). An applied folklore study could be designated like any other applied discipline— engineering or medicine—to serve, not to dictate. As to the danger of "watering down" the discipline, the purists' abiding fear, the timid could be comforted by the assurance that no academic study, in the long run, has suffered from a development of an applied branch. To the contrary, the pure learning has often learned from the applied. As in the cases of all dichotomies when viewed as two separate structures, so in the case of the pure and applied learning: we must first talk about them in terms of their many parts. Then, the literary job is to turn them back into a one. Perhaps, therefore, the first task of an applied study of folklore would be an investigation (more rigorous than is attemped in the present rather jaunty little piece of home learning) of the folkness of the nonfolk and the nonfolkness of the folk: first as two structures, second as one function, third as the best we can make of what seems to be one thing in one context and at the same time two things in another. The soul-searching question would be a name for it. Perhaps folkness would do. Ideally, though of course impracticably, it should be a tune.

As I read over this paper now, ten years after its publication, and make a few revisions, I think back to those days when there was such a hullabaloo about the definition of the word *folk*. The trouble stemmed, I believe, from its understanding as exclusively referent to people as users of language and to the subsequent social grading of people in accord with ability to read and write, to their failure to use the vocabulary, grammar, and syntax of those who can read and write, and to pronounce the words as the best readers and writers pronounce them. Since a language is the chief tool in the building and maintaining of a society, those expert in its use—and the physically powerful who can engage the services of the experts—inevitably become members of a ruling class that is comparatively small in relation to the vast majority of the people, who become the vulgar, the common people, the folk.

With the democratization of twentieth-century Western society, the ruling class has become less conspicuously distinguished by royal, noble, and priestly panoply. It has become much larger, more homogeneous in its variety of wealth, political power, professional and linguistic expertness. Viewed in terms of communicatory systems other than language, the distinction between language-expert rulers and less language-expert ruled presents altogether different classifications.

From the viewpoint of the study of these various social, economic, political, and linguistic classifications, a number of difficulties that arise in the study of folklore can be clarified. I shall mention here only those that bear upon the study of music.

The musically vulgar common people or folk is a vast majority of the population of the United States. It comprises first everybody whose ability to make music is limited to the singing or, if there is demonstrable vocal evidence of physical impediment, the playing with one finger on a pianoforte of an ordinary hymn tune, popular melody, or childrens' song. Second, a stage higher, those who can improvise a short melody that is something of a complete unit. A few children do this readily but are usually taught not to or in some way discouraged. Third would be those who could read or write such a tune.

The musically expert who carry a repertory composed of music in their head, who can sing or play with rank and file musicianly competence and improvise new tunes with more or less elaborate accompaniments, comprises a miniscule percentage of the population. One percent, 5 percent? We do not know.

To the large majority belong, with rare exceptions, presidents and cabinet officers, senators, congressmen, corporation executives, their wives, most professional people and scholars. They are for the most part, along with most of the linguistically-rated common people, the musically nonliterate and dumb. What they listen to in the way of music is accessory to this classification, though devoted listening is a first step out of the musical lower class. Interestingly enough, the linguistic lower class probably makes a lot more of what music it can than does the linguistic upper class.

Thus, musically speaking, the people of the United States are divided into two classes: a majority that does not know it is a folk; a minority, that thinks it isn't.

Bibliography

PUBLISHED PAPERS

1. *Outline of a Course in Harmonic Structure and Musical Invention.* With E. G. Stricklen. Berkeley: Privately printed, 1913. 48 pp.
2. "On Style and Manner in Modern Composition," *Musical Quarterly,* IX, 3 (July 1923), 423-431.
3. "Music in the American University," *Educational Review,* LXVI, 2 (Sept. 1923), 95-99.
4. "On the Principles of Musicology," *Musical Quarterly,* X, 2 (April 1924), 244-250.
5. "Prolegomena to Musicology: The Problem of the Musical Point of View and the Bias of Linguistic Presentation," *Eolus,* IV, 2 (May 1925), 12-24.
6. "Reviewing a Review," second part of "The Revolt of the Angels," the first being "Carl Ruggles and the Future of Dissonant Counterpoint," by D. Rudhyar, *Eolian Review,* III, 1;16-23.
7. "A Fragment of Greek Music," *The Baton* (Institute of Musical Art, New York), VIII, 7 (May 1929), 5-6.
8. "Dissonance and the Devil: An Interesting Passage in a Bach Cantata," *The Baton* (Institute of Musical Art, New York), IX, 7 (May 1930), 7-8.
9. "On Dissonant Counterpoint," *Modern Music,* VII, 4, (June-July 1930), 25-31.
10. "Lines on the Grace Note," *The Baton* (Institute of Musical Art, New York), X, 4 (Feb. 1931), 6-7.
11. "Music and Musicology," In *Encyclopedia of the Social Sciences.* New York: MacMillan, 1933. XI:143-150; "Music, Occidental," 155-164.
12. "Carl Ruggles," *Musical Quarterly,* XVIII, 4 (Oct. 1932), 578-592. Reprinted in *American Composers on American Music.* Ed. Henry Cowell. Stanford: Stanford University Press, 1933. Pp. 14-35.
13. "Ruth Crawford." In *American Composers on American Music.* Ed. Henry Cowell. Stanford: Stanford University Press, 1933. Pp. 110-118.
14. "On Proletarian Music," *Modern Music,* XI, 3 (March 1934), 121-127.
15. "Preface to All Linguistic Treatment of Music," *Music Vanguard,* I, 1 (March-April 1935), 17-31.
16. "Music in America," *Magazine of Art,* XXXI, 7 (July 1938), 411-413, 435-436.
17. "Grass Roots for American Music," *Modern Music,* XVI, 3 (March-April 1939), 143-149.
18. "Charles Ives and Carl Ruggles," *Magazine of Art,* XXXII, 7 (July 1939), 396-399, 435-437.
19. "Systematic and Historical Orientations in Musicology," *Acta Musicologica,* XI (1939), 121-128.
20. "The Importance to Cultural Understanding of Folk and Popular Music." In *Conference on Inter-American Relations in the Field of Music, Digest of Proceedings.* Washington: Department of State, 1940. 10 pp.

21. "Henry Cowell," *Magazine of Art*, XXXIII, 5 (May 1940), 288-289, 322-325, 327.

22. *Music as Recreation.* Works Projects Administration, Technical Series, Community Service Circular no. 1, Washington, May 20, 1940, 27 pp.

23. "Contrapuntal Style in the Three-Voice Shape-Note Hymns," *Musical Quarterly*, XXVI, 4 (Oct. 1940), 483-493.

24. "Folk Music as a Source of Social History." In *The Cultural Approach to History*, Ed. Carolyn F. Ware. New York: Columbia University Press, 1940. Pp. 316-323.

25. "Inter-American Relations in the Field of Music: Some Basic Considerations," *Music Educators Journal*, XXVII, 5 (March-April 1941), 17-18, 64-65.

26. "Music and Culture," *Proceedings of the Music Teachers National Association*, 35th ser. (1941), pp. 112-122.

27. "American Music for American Children," *Music Educators Journal*, XXIX, 2 (Nov.-Dec. 1942), 11-12.

28. "Inter-American Relations in the Field of Music," *Proceedings of the Music Proceedings of the Music Teachers National Association*, 36th ser. (1942), pp. 41-44.

29. "Wartime and Peacetime Programs in Music Education," *Music Educators Journal*, XXIX, 3 (Jan. 1943), 12-14.

30. "Music and Government: Field for an Applied Musicology." In *Papers Read at the International Congress of Musicology Held at New York, September 11-18, 1939*. New York: Music Educators National Conference for the American Musicological Society, 1944. Pp. 12-20.

31. "Musicology and the Music Industry," *National Music Council Bulletin*, V, 3 (May 1945), 8-10.

32. "Music Education and Musicology" (with Curt Sachs), *Music Educators Journal*, XXXI, 6 (May-June 1945), 78-79.

33. "Music in the Americas: Oral and Written Traditions in the Americas," *Bulletin of the Pan American Union*, LXXIX, 5 (May 1945), 290-293; 6 (June 1945), 341-344.

34. "Music and Musicology in the New World," *Proceedings of the Music Teachers National Association*, 40th ser. (1946), pp. 35-47. Reprinted in Spanish translation: "Música y musicología en el Nuevo Mundo," *Revista Musical Chilena*, II, 14 (Sept. 1946), 7-18. Reprinted, with extensive revision, in *Hinrichsen's Musical Yearbook*, VI (1949-1950). London: Hinrichsen Ed. Ltd., 1949. Pp. 36-56.

35. "Toward a Unitary Field Theory for Musicology" (abstract), *Bulletin of the American Musicological Society*, nos. 9-10 (June 1947), p. 16.

36. "Music Education and Musicology." In *Music Education Source Book I*. Ed. H. N. Morgan. Chicago: Music Educators National Conference, 1947. Chap. 36, pp. 195-198.

37. "UNESCO, February 1948," *Music Library Association Notes*, 2d ser., V, 2 (March 1948), 165-168.

38. "The Arts in International Relations," *Journal of the American Musicological Society*, II, 1 (Spring 1949), 36-43.

39. "Professionalism and Amateurism in the Study of Folk Music," *Journal of American Folklore*, LXII, 244 (April-June 1949), 107-113. Reprinted in Spanish translation: "El Professional y el aficionado en el estudio de la musica folklórica," *Revista Musical Chilena*, XIII, 68 (Nov.-Dec. 1959), 70-79. Reprinted in original English in McEdward Leach and T. P. Coffin, eds. *The Critics and the Ballad*. Carbondale: Southern Illinois University Press, 1961. Pp. 151-160.

40. "Oral Tradition in Music." In *Standard Dictionary of Folklore, Mythology and Legend*. New York: Funk and Wagnalls, 1949. Pp. 825-829.

41. "Systematic Musicology: Viewpoints, Orientations and Methods," *Journal of the American Musicological Society*, IV, 3 (Fall 1951), 240-248.

42. "An Instantaneous Music Notator," *Journal of the International Folk Music Council*, III (1951), 103-106.

43. "Music and Society: Some New World Evidence of their Relationship." In *Proceedings of the Conference on Latin-American Fine Arts, June 14-17, 1951.* Austin: University of Texas Press, 1952. Pp. 84-97. Reprinted with substantial revisions: Washington: Pan American Union, 1953. 9 pp.

44. Foreword to G. P. Jackson, *Another Sheaf of White Spirituals.* Gainesville: University of Florida Press, 1952. Pp. vii-viii.

45. "The Musician: Man Serves Art. The Educator: Art Serves Man," *UNESCO Courier*, VI, 2 (Feb. 1953), 12.

46. "Folk Music in the Schools of a Highly Industrialized Society," *Journal of the International Folk Music Council*, V (1953), 40-44. Reprinted in David A. De Turk and A. Poulin, Jr., *The American Folk Scene.* New York: Dell Publishing Co., 1967. Pp. 88-94.

47. "Preface to the Description of a Music." In *Kongressbericht, Internationale Gesellschaft für Musikwissenschaft, Utrecht 1952.* Amsterdam: Vereneging voor Nederlandse Muziekgeschiedenis, 1953. Pp. 360-370.

48. "A Proposal to Found an International Society for Music Education." In *Music in Education.* Paris: UNESCO, 1955. Pp. 325-331.

49. "Folk Music: USA." In *Grove's Dictionary of Music and Musicians*, 5th ed. New York: St. Martin's Press, 1955. III:387-398.

50. "Music and Class Structure in the United States," *American Quarterly*, IX 3 (Fall 1957), 281-294.

51. "Toward a Universal Music Sound-Writing for Musicology," *Journal of the International Folk Music Council*, IX (1957), 63-66.

52. "Singing Style," *Western Folklore*, XVII, 1 (Jan. 1958), 3-11.

53. "The Appalachian Dulcimer," *Journal of American Folklore*, 71 (Jan.-March 1958), 40-51.

54. "Prescriptive and Descriptive Music Writing," *Musical Quarterly*, XLIV, 2 (April 1958), 184-195.

55. "Musicology." Representing the American Musicological Society. No. 23, in the series *The World of the Mind*, 25 radio broadcasts by Broadcast Music Incorporated in association with the American Council of Learned Societies and the American Association for the Advancement of Science, New York: Broadcast Music Inc., 1958. 5 pp.

56. "Otto Kinkeldey," *Acta Musicologica*, XXXI, fasc. I (1959), 7-8.

57. "On the Moods of a Music Logic," *Journal of the American Musicological Society*, XIII (1960), 224-261.

58. "Semantic, Logical and Political Considerations Bearing Upon Research in Ethnomusicology," *Ethnomusicology*, V, 2 (May 1961), 77-80.

59. "The Cultivation of Various European Traditions in the Americas." In *Report of of the Eighth Congress of the International Musicological Society, New York, 1961.* Kassel, Basel, London, New York, 1961. Pp. 364-375.

60. "Who Owns Folklore?—A Rejoinder," *Western Folklore*, XXI, 2 (April 1962), 93-101.

61. "Music As a Tradition of Communication, Discipline and Play," *Ethnomusicology*, VI, 3 (Sept. 1962), 156-163.

62. "On the Tasks of Musicology," *Ethnomusicology*, VII, 3 (Sept. 1963), 214-215.

63. "Symposium on Transcription and Analysis: A Hukwe Song With Musical Bow . . . Report of the Chairman-Moderator." *Ethnomusicology*, VIII, 3 (Sept. 1964), 272-277.

64. Introduction. In *Primera conferencia interamericana de etnomusicología, Trabajos presentados, Cartagena de Indias, Colombia, 24 a 28 de febrero de 1963:* Washington, D.C.: Union Panamericana, 1965. Pp. 9-11.

65. "La Realdad sobre la Educación Musical y el Profesorado de la Música Culta," *Revista Musical Chilena*, XVIII, 87-88 (Jan.-June 1964), 14-19.

66. "Preface to a Critique of Music." In *Primera Conferencia interamericana de etnomusicología: Trabajos presentados*, Cartagena de Indias, Colombia, 24 a 28 de febrero de 1963. Washington: Union Panamericana, 1963. Pp. 39-63. Reprinted, as "Preface to the Critique of Music," with corrections and revisions, in *Boletin interamericano de música*, 49 (Sept. 1965), 2-24.

67. "Folk Music," *Colliers Encyclopedia* (1965), X:132-140.

68. "Versions and Variants of 'Barbara Allen' in the Archive of American Folk Song in the Library of Congress." In *Selected Reports*, vol. 1, no. 1, Institute of Ethnomusicology, University of California, Los Angeles, 1966. Pp. 120-167. Reprinted as brochure for Album L54 (phono disc). Washington: Library of Congress, 1966.

69. "The Music Process as a Function in a Context of Functions." In *Yearbook, Inter-American Institute for Musical Research*. New Orleans: Tulane University, 1966. II:1-36.

70. "The Folkness of the Nonfolk vs. the Nonfolkness of the Folk." In *Folklore and Society*. Essays in Honor of Benj. A. Botkin. Ed. Bruce Jackson. Hatboro, Pa.: Folklore Associates, 1966. Pp. 1-9.

71. "Tradition and the (North) American Composer." In *Music in the Americas, Inter-American Music Monograph Series*, I. Indiana University Research Center in Anthropology, Folklore, and Linguistics, Bloomington, 1967. Pp. 195-212.

72. "Factorial Analysis of the Song as an Approach to the Formation of a Unitary Field Theory" (for Musicology). *Journal of the International Folk Music Council*, XX (1968), 272-277.

73. Foreword to *Studies in Musicology*, Essays in the History, Style and Bibliography of Music in Memory of Glen Haydon. Ed. James W. Pruett. Chapel Hill: University of North Carolina Press, 1969. Pp. vii-xiii.

74. "On the Formational Apparatus of the Music Compositional Process." *Ethnomusicology*, XII, I, 2 (May 1969). Pp. 230-247.

75. "Toward a Unitary Field Theory for Musicology," *Selected Reports*, vol. 1, no. 3, Institute of Ethnomusicology, University of California, Los Angeles, 1970. Pp. 171-210.

76. "Reflections Upon a Given Topic: Music in the Universal Perspective," *Ethnomusicology*, XIII, 3 (Sept. 1971), 385-398.

77. "Foreword" to Mantle Hood, *The Ethnomusicologist*. New York: McGraw-Hill, 1971. Pp. v-vii.

78. *An American Musicologist*. Oral History Program, University of California at Los Angles. Typescript. 1972. 513 pp.

79. "Ethnomusicological Materials in Music Education in the United States." *Music Educators Journal* (Oct. 1972), pp. 107-111.

80. "In Memoriam: Carl Ruggles." *Perspectives of New Music*, 10, 2 (1972), 171-174.

81. "Tractatus Esthetico-Semioticus." *In Current Thought in Musicology*. Austin: University of Texas Press, 1976.

82. "Folk Music USA." *Groves Dictionary of Music and Musicians.* 6th edition. London, in press.

83. "Sources of Evidence and Criteria for Judgment in the Critique of Music," revision of Part 3 of "Preface to the Critique of Music," (1965), awaiting publication in Festschrift for Klaus Wachsmann.

REVIEWS

"Reviewing a Review," in *Eolian Review,* III, 1 (Nov. 1923), 16-23.

"New Yorks at the Coolidge Festival." Reviewed in *Modern Music,* XVII, 4 (May-June 1940), 250-254.

Bosquejo del proceso de la música en el Peru, by Abraham Viscarra Rozas (Cuzco: Universidad Nacional del Cuzco, 1940); *Los orígines del arte musical en Chile,* by Eugenio Pereira Salas (Santiago: Imprenta Universitaria, 1941); *Panorama de la música mexicana desde la independencia hasta la actualidad,* by Otto Mayer-Serra. Reviewed in *Hispanic American Historical Review,* XXII, 1 (Feb. 1942), 171-173.

Mission Music of California . . . , by Owen Francis da Silva. Los Angeles: Warren F. Lewis, 1941. Reviewed in *Hispanic American Historical Review.*

Harvard Dictionary of Music. By Willi Apel. Cambridge: Harvard University Press, 1944. Reviewed in *Music Educators Journal* (April 1945), p. 38.

Papers Read at the International Congress of Musicology Held at New York, September 11-18, 1939. New York: Music Educators National Conference for American Musicological Society, 1944. Reviewed in *Music Library Association Notes,* 2d. ser., II, 1 (Dec. 1944), 62-66.

"Latin American Music," in *The Americana Annual* (New York: Americana Corporation, 1944), pp. 393-394; 1945, pp. 409-410; 1946, 423-424; 1947, pp. 399-400; 1948, pp. 375-376; 1949, pp. 378-379.

"Sonata da Chiesa," by Virgil Thomson, in *New Music,* XVIII, 1 (Oct., 1944). Reviewed in *Music-Library Association Notes,* 2d. ser., II, 3 (June 1945), 180-181.

A Guide to Latin American Music. By Gilbert Chase. Washington, D.C.: U.S. Government Printing Office, 1945. Reviewed in *Music Library Association Notes,* 2d ser., II, 3 (June 1945), 170-171.

The Schillinger System of Musical Composition. By Joseph Schillinger. Ed. Arnold Shaw. New York: Carl Fischer, Inc., 1945. Reviewed in *Music Library Association Notes,* 2d ser., II, 4 (Sept. 1945), 299; IV, 2 (March 1947), 183-184.

Music of Latin America. By Nicholas Slonimsky. New York: Thomas Y. Crowell Co., 1945.

12 American Preludes for Piano. By Alberto Ginastera. New York: Carl Fischer, Inc., 1946. Reviewed in *Music Library Association Notes,* 2d ser., IV, 1 (Dec. 1946), 102-103.

Ozark Folksongs. Collected and ed. Vance Randolph. 4 vols. Columbia: State Historical Society of Missouri, 1946-1950. Reviewed in *Music Library Association Notes,* 2d ser., IV, 3 (June 1947), 330-332; V, 4 (Sept. 1948), 576; VI, 3 (June 1949), 469; VII, 3 (June 1950), 469-470.

A Dictionary of Musical Themes. Comp. Harold Barlow and Sam Morgenstern. Introduction by John Erskine. New York: Crown Publishers, 1948. Reviewed with Richard S. Hill in *Music Library Association Notes,* 2d. ser. V, 3 (June 1948), 375-376.

Music and Society: England and the European Tradition. By Wilfrid Mellers. London: Dennis Dobson, Ltd., 1946. Reviewed in *Journal of the American Musicological Society,* II, 1 (Spring 1949), 56-58.

Living Music of the Americas. By Lazare Saminsky. New York: Howell, Soskin and Crown Publishers, 1949. Reviewed in *Music Library Association Notes*, 2d ser., VII, 1 (Dec. 1949), 110-111.

A Collection of Ballads and Folk Songs, by Burl Ives, New York: Decca Records, 1945, Personality Series, Album no. A-407, four 10-inch discs; *Ballads and Folk Songs*, Vol. II, by Burl Ives. New York: Decca Records, 1947, Personality Series, Album no. A431, four 10-inch discs; *Ballads and Blues,* by Josh White, New York: Decca Records, 1946, Personality Series, Album no. A-447, four 10-inch discs; *American Folk Music Series,* by Richard Dyer-Bennet, New York: Decca Records, 1947, Personality Series, Album no. A-573, four 10-inch discs. Reviewed in *Journal of the American Folklore Society*, LXII, 243 (Jan.-March 1949), 68-70.

Tone Roads No. 1 for Chamber Orchestra. By Charles E. Ives. New York: Peer International Corporation, 1949. Reviewed in *Music Library Association Notes*, 2d ser., VII, 3 (June, 1950), 432-433.

Joseph Schillinger. By his wife, Frances Schillinger. New York: Greenberg Publisher, 1949. Reviewed in *Music Library Association Notes*, 2d ser., VII, 3 (June 1950), 476.

Sinfonía India. By Carlos Chávez. New York: G. Schirmer, Inc., 1950. Reviewed in *Music Library Association Notes*, 2d ser., VII, 4 (Sept. 1950), 627-628.

Terzetto for Two Violins and Viola. By Richard Donovan. South Hadley and Northampton, Mass.: Valley Music Press, 1950. Reviewed in *Music Library Association Notes*, 2d ser., VIII, 3 (June 1951), 568.

Folksongs of Florida, collected and ed. Alton C. Morris. Gainesville: University of Florida Press, 1950; *Texas Folksongs,* by William A. Owens, Publications of the Texas Folklore Society, XXIII. Austin: Texas Folklore Society, 1950; *Folksongs of Alabama,* collected by Byron Arnold. University: University of Alabama Press, 1950. Reviewed in *Music Library Association Notes*, 2d ser., VIII, 3 (June 1951), 523-525.

Journal of the International Folk Music Council. Ed. Maud Karpeles. 5 vols. Cambridge: W. Heffer and Sons, 1949-1953. Reviewed in *Music Library Association Notes*, 2d ser., VIII, 3 (June 1951), 525-526; IX, 1 (Dec. 1951), 129; X, 2 (March 1953), 282-283; X, 4 (Sept. 1953), 642-643.

Manual for Folk Music Collectors. Prepared by Maud Karpeles and Arnold Baké. London: International Folk Music Council, 1951. Reviewed in *Music Library Association Notes*, 2d ser., IX, 2 (March 1952), 294.

Serbo-Croatian Folk Songs . . . By Béla Bartók and Albert Lord. Columbia University Studies in Musicology, no. 7. New York: Columbia University Press, 1951. Reviewed in *Journal of the American Musicological Society*, V, 2 (Summer 1952), 132-135.

Music in Mexico: A Historical Survey. By Robert Stevenson. New York: Thomas Y. Crowell Co., 1952. Reviewed in *Music Library Association Notes*, 2d ser., X, 2 (March 1953), 269-270.

Collection Musée de l-Homme. Catalogue établi par . . . (C.I.A.P.). Archives de la musique enregistrée, Sér. C: Musique ethnographique et folklorique, vol. 2. Paris: UNESCO, 1952. Reviewed in *Music Library Association Notes*, 2d ser., X, 2 (March 1953), 283-284.

Cancionero Popular de la Provincia de Madrid. Collected by Manuel Garcia Matos. Vol. 1. Barcelona and Madrid, 1951. Reviewed in *Musical Quarterly*, 39, 2 (April 1953), 289-293.

Rhythm and Tempo: A Study in Music History. By Curt Sachs. New York: W. W. Norton and Co., 1953. Reviewed in *Music Library Association Notes*, 2d ser., X, 3 (June 1953), 435-438.

Collection Phonothèque Nationale. Catalogue établi par . . . (C.I.A.P.). Archives de la musique enregistrée. Sér. G: Musique ethnographique et folklorique, vol. 1. Paris: UNESCO, 1952. Reviewed in *Music Library Association Notes,* 2d ser. X, 4 (Sept. 1953), 628-629.

Harmony. By Heinrich Schenker. Chicago: University of Chicago Press, 1954. Reviewed in *Music Library Association Notes,* 2d ser., XIII, 1 (Dec. 1953), 53-55.

Bibliografia musical brasileira (1820-1950). Por Luís [sic] Heitor Corrêia de Azevedo, Cleofe Person de Matos, and Mercedes de Moura Reis. Ministério da Educacão e Saúde, Instituto Nacional do Livro, Col. Bl, Bibliografia 9. Rio de Janeiro, 1952. Reviewed in *Music Library Association Notes,* 2d ser., XI, 4 (Sept. 1954), 551-552.

Die Schwedische Hummel; eine instrumentkundliche Untersuchung. Von Stig Walin. Nordiska museets handlingar, 43. Stockholm: Nordiska Museet, 1952. Reviewed in *Music Library Association Notes,* 2d ser., XI, 4 (Sept. 1954), 567-568.

America's Music: From the Pilgrims to the Present. By Gilbert Chase. New York: McGraw-Hill, 1955. Reviewed in *Music Library Association Notes,* 2d ser., XII, 3 (June 1955), 431-434.

Columbia World Library of Folk and Primitive Music. Alan Lomax, ed. New York: Columbia Records, 1955. Vols. I-XIV (SL-204-SL-217), 14 Phono discs, 12-inch LP, with bound brochures. Reviewed in *Journal of the International Folk Music Council,* VIII (1956), 113-114.

Les Colloques de Wégimont: Cercle Internationale d'Études Ethno-Musicologiques. Ed. Paul Collaer. Bruxelles: Elsevier, 1956. Reviewed in *Ethnomusicology,* II, 1 (Jan. 1958), 38-41.

Music in Primitive Cultures. By Bruno Nettl. Cambridge, Mass.: Harvard University Press, 1956. Reviewed in *Journal of American Folklore,* 71 (Jan.-March 1958), 90-91.

The Music of the Ballads. Ed. Jan Philip Schinhan. Frank C. Brown Collection of North Carolina Folklore, vol. 4. Durham, N.C.: Duke University Press, 1957. Reviewed in *Music Library Association Notes,* 2d ser., XV, 3 (June 1958), 399-401.

The New Oxford History of Music. Vol. I: *Ancient and Oriental Music.* Egon Wellesz. London: Oxford University Press, 1957. Reviewed in *Ethnomusicology,* III, 2 (May 1959), 96-97.

The Traditional Tunes of the Child Ballads . . . By Bertrand Harris Bronson. Princeton, N.J.: Princeton University Press, 1959. Vol. I. Reviewed in Music Library Association Notes, 2d ser., XVI, 3 (June 1959), 384-385.

An Introduction to Research in Music. By Allen M. Garrett. Washington: Catholic University of America, 1958. Reviewed in *Journal of Research in Music Education,* VII, 2 (Fall, 1959), 221-222.

Norwegian Folk Music. Ser. I: *Slåttar for Hardin fiddle,* Vol. I. Olav Gurvin, ed. Oslo: Oslo University Press, 1958. Reviewed in *Journal of the American Folklore Society,* LXXIII, 287 (Jan.-Mar., 1960), 73-74.

New Methods in Vocal Folk Music Research. By Karl Dahlback. Publication of the Norwegian Folk Music Institute, no. 2. Oslo: Oslo University Press, 1958. Reviewed in *Ethnomusicology,* IV, 1 (Jan., 1960), 41-42.

EDITOR

Bulletin of the New York Musicological Society, nos. 1-3 (1930-1934).

American Library of Musicology, 1931-1933: Joseph Yasser, *A Theory of Evolving Tonality.* New York, 1932; Helen H. Roberts, *Form in Primitive Music.* New York, 1933.

A Series of American Songs Rarely Found in Popular Collections, nos. 1-8, 10. With original pen-and-ink drawings by Charles Pollock. Washington: Special Skills Division, Resettlement Administration, 1936-1937.

Boletin latinoamericano de música, Tomo V, Primera Parte: Estudios estadounidenses, pp. 25-434; *Suplemento musical,* pp. 12-161. Montevideo: Instituto interamericano de musicología, 1941.

Army Song Book. Comp. by the Adjutant General's Office in collaboration with the Library of Congress, Washington, 1941. 96 pp.

Check-list of Recorded Music in the English Language in the Archive of American Folk Song to July, 1940. 3 vols. Washington: Music Division, Library of Congress, 1942.

Music Series, Pan American Union, nos. 1-16 (1942-1949).

National Anthems of the American Republics. Facs. ed. Official versions. Washington: Pan American Union, 1949. Unpaged.

Handbook of Latin American Studies. 1943-1953. Music Section.

Folk Song, U.S.A. By John A. Lomax and Alan Lomax. Music ed., Charles Seeger and Ruth Crawford Seeger. New York: Duell, Sloan, and Pearce, 1947. Pp. xvi, 407. Reprinted as *Best Loved American Folk Songs,* New York: Grosset and Dunlap, n.d.

Bulletin of the Pan American Union, 79 (1945), "Four Christmas Songs," pp. 700-703; 81 (1947), "Four Christmas Songs," pp. 691-694.

Folk Music of the Americas. Album 15: *Venezuelan Folk Music.* From the Archive of American Folk Song. Ed. with Juan Liscano. Washington: Library of Congress, ca. 1948. 26 pp.

Cancionero popular americano: 75 Canciones de las republicas americanas. Washington: Union panamericana, 1950. 128 pp.

American Folk Songs: Sung by the Seegers. Ed. with Peggy Seeger. New York: Folkways Records and Service Corp., 1957. Phonodisc, 10-inch LP, no. FA 2005. Brochure.

American Folk Songs for Christmas. Ed. with Peggy Seeger. New York: Folkways Records and Service Corp., 1957. Phonodisc, 10-inch LP, no. FC 7053. Brochure "Christmas Old and New." 12 pp.

Journal of the American Musicological Society, Vol. XIII (1960).

MUSIC

Overture to an unfinished opera, "The Shadowy Waters" (Yeats), 1908 (manuscript). For orchestra, 51 pp. Performed by the Boston Symphony Orchestra at a "Pop" concert, June 1908; Munich, 1908; Bohemian Grove, Sonoma County, Calif., 1912.

"Sonata, for Violin and Pianoforte," 1908, rev. 1915 (manuscript): 1. Moderato con moto; 2. Dialogue—Grave; Academic Rondo—Allegro. 37 pp.

Seven Songs for High Voice and Pianoforte. New York: G. Schirmer, 1911. "Asleep," Keats; "Endymion," Wilde; "The Pride of Youth," Scott; "Till I Wake," Hope; "Song to—," Wheelock; "When Soft Winds and Sunny Skies," Shelley. (Separata)

Twelve Songs for high voice and pianoforte, 1907-1912 (manuscript): "On a Faded Violet," Shelley; "Sampan Song," Hope; "To Helen," Poe; "The Lady of the South," Shelley; "From the Arabic," Shelley; "Song," Hartley Coleridge; "Ach, die Quälen," Adam Mieckiewicz; "Wie ein Schiff," Anon; "Think not of it," Keats; "When as in Silks my Julia goes" and "My Love in her attire doth shew her wit," Herrick; "Alguna vez," De Castillejo; "Encouragement to a Lover," Suckling.

"Two Parthenias" (manuscript). Pageants presented by the women students of the University of California, Berkeley, California, in the Faculty Club Glade: 1. "Derdra," April 14, 1914, orchestral score, 180 pp., utilizing some work of student, Ruth Cornell Cook; 2. "The Queen's Masque," April 9, 1915, and August 19, 1915, orchestral score, including harpsichord, voices offstage, 164 pp., utilizing some work of student, Ruth Cornell Cook.

"A Baker's Dozen Rounds for the Undepressed," 1933-1935 (manuscript).

Scena, "The Middleman" (Nicholas Ray), 1936 (manuscript): Three recitatives and three arias, for one or four voices, with guitar accompaniment.

"Three Songs for Mezzo-soprano, Microphone and Orchestra" (manuscript): "John Riley"; "Wayfaring Stranger"; "John Henry." Composed for the celebration of the 75th anniversary of the founding of the U.S. Department of Agriculture, Nov. 17, 1937. 47 pp.

"Danza Lenta." In *Boletin latinoamericano de música, Suplemento musical, Instituto interamericano de musicología.* Montevideo, 1941. P. 89.

"John Hardy" (manuscript). For small orchestra. Commissioned by the Columbia School of the Air [1940].

"The Letter," song for solo voice (1931): "Psalm 137," declamation for solo voice (1923). In *New Music,* XXVI, 3 (April 1953), 10-15.

N.B. The scores and parts of the two masques, an unfinished string quartet (1910), and other compositions were burned in the Berkeley fire, 1923.

Index